Praise for *Bicycling & the Law*

"This book should be read, digested, and practiced by cyclists and motorists alike. It should be a part of driver education and bicycle safety programs. *Bicycling & the Law* has one further, rare quality: it is eminently—and delightfully—readable."

—*Rep. James L. Oberstar (MN)*
Chairman, House Committee on Transportation and Infrastructure

"Cycling can be a tough job, whether you're riding to work or training for a race. Bob Mionske sets the record straight on cyclists' rights. If you love to ride, you should know what's in this book."

—*George Hincapie*
Discovery Channel Cycling Team

"Bob Mionske's superb *Bicycling & the Law* has filled a critical gap on our bookshelf, synthesizing essential information on the legal rights and responsibilities of cyclists into a coherent, comprehensive, and engaging volume. Anyone who rides a bicycle in the United States, whether commuter, roadie, tourist, messenger, or joy rider, should have a copy of this book at hand. It works beautifully as both a reference and a very readable narrative—pick it up anytime for fascinating tales of bicycle code and culture, and zoom in on the specifics and particulars as you need them."

—*Andy Thornley*
Program Director, San Francisco Bicycle Coalition

"Knowing the rules is a key to safe bicycling. Bob Mionske sheds light on our complex legal system and arms bicyclists with the knowledge to make smart decisions to protect their rights."

—*Dan Grunig*
Executive Director, Bicycle Colorado

"Big gains require real effort, and Bob Mionske has done the heavy lifting for all cyclists. *Bicycling & the Law* is a huge step forward for our rights on the road. In fact, everyone who rides should have a copy of this book."

—*Chris Carmichael*
Carmichael Training Systems

"Bob Mionske's book should be a must read for all cyclists to educate and inform them on their rights and responsibilities. We all hope that accidents won't happen to us, but common sense, common courtesy, and safe riding procedures are things we should all understand and follow. Cyclists should never leave the house without a rain jacket, a frame pump, a spare tire, and basic knowledge of this book."

—*Bobby Julich*
Olympic medalist, Team CSC cycling team

"*Bicycling & the Law* will promote cycling as a fun and affordable means of transportation and help create healthier, more livable cities. Mionske sets a positive example for both cyclists and drivers on how to share the road."

—*Dorcas Adkins*
Director of Education Programs, Washington Area Bicyclist Association

"What an exciting book to read for all cyclists. The information here will only enhance your riding as you will be aware of your rights as a legal road user. It is a must read."

—*Bill Lazenby*
Co-President, Coalition of Arizona Bicyclists

"Anyone who has ever spent much time riding on the road knows how vulnerable it can feel to be a cyclist sharing the roads with cars, SUV's and trucks. This book is a fantastic resource to arm cyclists with basic information that will both educate and empower them."

—*Brad Tucker*
ColoBikeLaw.com

"A comprehensive and up-to-date guide to virtually all aspects of the legal system as they affect bicycling. Although directed at cyclists, this volume is also an important reference for law enforcement officers, attorneys, and judges."

—*Bicycle Transportation Institute*

"Everyone from the serious cyclist to the person thinking about dusting off the long-neglected bike in the garage will benefit from reading this book. Cycling instructors, avid riders, beginning cyclists, bike messengers, parents concerned about the perceived dangers of cycling for their children, those who are charged with providing suitable accommodations for cyclists, those charged with protecting the rights of cyclists, should at least scan Mionske's book."

—*Bob Chauncey, PhD*
National Center for Bicycling & Walking

BICYCLING & THE LAW

YOUR RIGHTS AS A CYCLIST

Bob Mionske, JD
with Steven M. Magas, JD
and Rick Bernardi, JD

BOULDER, COLORADO

1830 North 55th Street • Boulder, Colorado 80301-2700 USA
(303) 440-0601 • Fax (303) 444-6788
E-mail velopress@insideinc.com

Library of Congress Cataloging-in-Publication Data

Mionski, Bob.
  Bicycling & the law / Bob Mionski.
    p. cm.
Includes index.
ISBN-13: 978-1-931382-99-1 (pbk. : alk. paper)
ISBN-10: 1-931382-99-9 (pbk. : alk. paper)
1. Bicycles—Law and legislation—United States. 2. Cycling—Law and legislation—
United States. I. Title. II. Title: Bicycling and the Law.
KF2220.B5M56 2007
343.7309'44—dc22
                           2007009955

Cover design by Stephanie Goralnick
Interior design by Andy Clymer
Typeset in Mercury Text by Hoefler & Frere-Jones and Legato by Evert Bloemsma

Printed on acid-free paper

Distributed in the United States and Canada by Publishers Group West

For information on purchasing VeloPress books,
please call (800) 234-8356 or visit www.velopress.com.

07 08 09 10 / 10 9 8 7 6 5 4 3 2 1

Contents

Foreword

I first met Bob Mionske when we were racing in Europe. Shortly thereafter, at the 1992 Olympic trials, Bob was winding down his cycling career while I was just getting started, but for a few hot and humid days in Altoona, Pennsylvania, we were both amateur cyclists trying to make the three-man road team, our ticket to the Olympic Games in Barcelona, Spain.

The Olympic trials consisted of two long road races. On day one, my childhood friend and training partner Chann McRae soloed in to become national champion. I chose not to chase down Chann, and because they were teammates on Saturn, neither did Bob. I won the sprint for second, and Bob was third. Day two would decide the team for Barcelona.

Bob and I, along with his teammate Kevin Livingston, rode in a small group all day. The course had a steep climb that was maybe two miles long. Bob was getting dropped on each lap, but Kevin would hang back with Bob and then tow him back to the group on the long, gradual descent. And so it went, lap after lap.

Of course, Bob was intent on making the Olympic team again (he first competed in the 1988 Olympic Games in Seoul)—so intent that he was using everything in his arsenal, including his powers of persuasion, to make it to the line with the group. As he began to fall off the back he would yell out, "I don't see why you guys are going so hard. . . . I'll just catch you later," and "You're wasting your time trying to drop me!" The image of Bob trying to argue his way to the finish line still brings a smile to my face, and I guess we all should have known that Bob would later pursue a law career. Bob did make it to the line that day, and onto his second Olympic team, thanks to Kevin.

When I entered my first Tour de France the following year, Bob retired from his pro career to become director of Team Saturn for a season before heading off to law school. It's often said that my seven Tour de France victories raised the profile of cycling in the U.S., and I would suggest that Bob Mionske has raised the profile of the cyclist as he defends everyday cyclists against the countless situations where their rights can be derailed.

I know firsthand what it's like to face harassment as a cyclist. Prior to my Tour de France comeback, I was on a training ride with some friends in my home state of Texas and we were "buzzed" by a motorist. Words were exchanged and we thought that was the end of it, but then this guy did something crazy—he turned around and drove straight at us. My friends rode out of the driver's path by going up a driveway, but I was forced to ride into a ditch to escape, which caused me to flip over my handlebars. Fortunately, I was only bruised from the encounter. The driver was arrested later that day. He turned out to be a real charmer—he had punched his six-year-old daughter in the face in 1996, and when he decided to assault us he was out on bail for beating and raping his wife. I decided that I wanted this guy prosecuted; I testified at his trial, and he was eventually convicted of aggravated assault and sentenced to ten years in prison.

I was lucky because I survived a dangerous encounter, and lucky too that we were able to put this guy behind bars, where he belongs. Now cyclists everywhere can use *Bicycling & the Law* as a resource for protecting their own right to the road. Bob explains the history of cyclists' rights, beginning with the bike boom of the 1890s and continuing on to your rights today. You can find practical advice for any problem you face as a cyclist, from protecting your bike against theft, to fighting a traffic ticket, to prosecuting harassers like the one who tried to run me over.

Bob's aggressive and garrulous fighting style may not have won him many friends on race day, but his irrepressible technique perfectly suits his efforts to defend the rights of cyclists. Bob has successfully argued his way to the finish line with this book—it's a winner!

Lance Armstrong
AUSTIN, TEXAS
JUNE 2007

Preface

Fifty-seven million Americans ride a bicycle; while that number undoubtedly represents a wide spectrum of cyclists, ranging from the avid enthusiast to the occasional rider, it is clear that cycling is an activity that is enjoyed by a large segment of the American population. In fact, the League of American Bicyclists enjoys a membership of some 300,000 cyclists, which undoubtedly represents only a portion of the cyclists on the "avid enthusiast" end of the spectrum. In short, there are a large number of cyclists in the United States who are more than occasional riders. If you ride a bike—which is practically a given, or you wouldn't be reading this now—this book was written for you.

But why a book on bicycle law? Isn't bicycling about getting out on your favorite ride and *riding*? What does bicycling have to do with the law? In a word, everything. The law permeates every aspect of cycling, from the traffic laws to problems with shippers, to assaults on cyclists, and to the question of a constitutional right to the roads. Furthermore, cyclists are *hungry* for information about their rights. As a group, serious cyclists tend to be better informed about traffic law than other users of the road. Paradoxically, misinformation about bicycle law is also widespread among cyclists; it's not uncommon for some cyclists to put forth legal arguments, for example, that undercut their own right to the road.

This book is intended both to educate cyclists about their rights and to serve as a preliminary resource for bicyclists to consult when faced with a legal question. That doesn't mean that this book can take the place of legal counsel—in fact, if you have a serious legal problem, obtaining competent counsel is an absolute necessity. However, this book will explain legal issues that cyclists commonly face and will inform you about what your rights are as a cyclist and what steps to take if you do encounter a legal problem. Most importantly, whether you commute to school or work on your bike, ride on weekends just for fun or train on the road at a competitive level, this book will provide you with the knowledge you need to avoid many legal problems in the first place.

One of the difficulties of writing a book on cycling law is that there are so many laws governing matters related to cycling. Not only are there fifty different states, each with its own statutes affecting bicycles, there are also fifty different state court systems, each with its own interpretations of what the law is. Furthermore, the law changes over time—new statutes are written, old statutes are repealed, courts issue decisions on new legal questions. The challenge posed to the author of a treatise on bicycle law is to make the law easily understood for the nonlawyer, while still endeavoring to present an accurate and thorough explanation of the relevant points of law, and all while avoiding an exhaustive discussion of the specific laws of fifty states.

Fortunately, the law provides a solution to this challenge. Despite the fact that there are fifty separate vehicle codes and fifty separate state court systems, there are themes that run throughout the law. Thus, the laws of one state will often be virtually identical to the laws of another state, which allows us to discuss the themes presented by these similar statutes and to contrast those themes with the themes presented in dissimilar statutes from other states. In a similar vein, the courts in one state will often decide a case according to principles established in a similar case in another state. Where courts disagree, an opportunity is provided to contrast the themes of those decisions. This discussion of themes and principles within the law will assist cyclists in understanding the laws in their state.

Finally, a word about the structure of this book: It can be used as a front-to-back primer on bicycle law as well as a guide to specific legal issues. If you take the approach of reading it from cover to cover, it progresses from an explanation of general legal theories about cyclists' rights and corresponding duties to a more detailed examination of those rights and duties in each succeeding chapter. Thus, I begin with a discussion of the rights and duties of cyclists: why and how cyclists gained legal rights, including the right to the road; the legal sources of cyclists' rights and duties; and what those rights and duties are. From there, we progress to a more specific discussion of rights and duties, as expressed in the traffic code, followed by a chapter on negligence and accidents, which are usually the result of somebody's failure to observe his duty, and usually result in the subsequent violation of another person's rights. As a complement to the chapter on negligence and accidents, Ohio bicycle law attorney Steve Magas contributes a chapter explaining what every cyclist needs to know about insurance. We then proceed to a chapter on cyclist harassment—intentional acts committed against cyclists. A chapter on bike theft—another type of intentional act against cyclists—follows. So far, we've progressed from a general discussion of rights and duties to a more specific discussion of rights and duties, and then to discussions of what happens when those rights and duties are violated, whether as the result of somebody's negligence or because of somebody's intentional acts. From there, we shift gears a bit; Steve Magas contributes another chapter, this time on product liability for cyclists. The final chapter explores whether you can be forced to "waive" somebody else's liability for negligence.

So that's one way to read this book; there's another way, however. If you have a specific legal issue you want answers to, you can turn directly to the chapter covering that issue—although each chapter builds on information from previous chapters, each chapter also generally functions as a stand-alone chapter. At the beginning of each chapter you will find an index of the issues addressed. Thus, whether you want a quick answer to a question or you are searching for a more in-depth understanding of bicycle law, this book will get you there.

That said, there are two things this book can't do for you. First, it can't possibly cover every legal situation you might encounter in every state. Instead, I've tried to give you a sense of what the law is, how it works, and why it works that way. Within that context, I've endeavored to cover the main legal issues most cyclists encounter.

Second, it can't take the place of an attorney. If you are facing a legal problem with serious consequences—if you've been injured in an accident, for example, or are facing criminal charges—you need a competent attorney to represent you. Usually, in bicycle-related legal issues, that will mean an attorney who has some expertise in bicycle law. There is simply no way you can competently represent yourself in serious cases. Many people are reluctant to hire attorneys because they believe that they cannot afford one. The reality is that many attorneys offer a free initial consultation, and even when charges for an initial consultation apply, those charges are usually reasonable and within reach of most people needing advice. And, depending on the case, attorneys will typically be willing to take your personal injury case on a contingency basis, which means your attorney only gets paid if you do. In short, if you're facing a serious legal problem, there's no reason for you to fear consulting with an attorney.

On the other hand, if you're facing a relatively minor legal problem, such as defending a noncriminal traffic ticket, there's no reason you can't represent yourself. This book shows you how. Finally, and most importantly, many legal problems can be circumvented altogether with just a few preventative measures; this book will show you how to protect yourself from legal problems before they occur.

That's it: a guide to your legal rights, written just for you. It is my sincere hope that it will help you to protect yourself and defend your rights, should the need arise. Last but not least, it is my sincere hope that you will simply enjoy reading this book as you begin the first steps on your journey of discovery about your legal rights. And now, I'm going for a ride—maybe I'll see you on the road.

Bob Mionske, JD
PORTLAND, OREGON
JUNE, 2007

Acknowledgments

My special thanks to everyone who helped with the book directly or through their personal support, from

- ☀ those who helped develop the bike/law book concept:

  Charles Pelkey, Bruce Epperson, Steve Magas, Ray Thomas, and everyone at VeloPress

- ☀ those in the bike industry:

  SRAM, B.I.K.E., River City Bicycles, Cronometro, Veloshop, and least but not last, Yellow Jersey Bicycles

- ☀ and those who, whether they know it or not, have been integral to my efforts to complete this work:

  Scott Kuenzi, Colin Obrien, Michael and Dede Barry, Tom Danielson, Lance Armstrong, Bobby Julich, John Benate, Mark Onteveros, Dave Guettler, Andy Muzi, Greg Mecker, Governor Jim Doyle, Tom Schuler, Grant Gehrmann, and Rich Walton

Last, for his tireless efforts, keen legal insight, and brilliant legal research and writing efforts in this book, I thank Rick Bernardi.

BICYCLING
& THE LAW

1

An Introduction to Your Legal Rights

INTRODUCTION

If you were a New Yorker who had the good fortune to be young—or at least young-minded—and wealthy in the spring of 1896, you were likely to be swept up in the bicycle craze that had taken hold of the nation, and indeed, the entire industrialized world. To be sure, most New Yorkers did not have the good fortune to find themselves young and wealthy that spring; two-thirds of Manhattan's nearly 2 million residents found themselves, instead, living in the squalid tenements that were the focus of muckraking journalist Jacob Riis's 1890 exposé, *How the Other Half Lives*.[1] That grinding poverty was only exacerbated by the economic depression that had begun in 1893, and was still in effect in the spring of 1896.

Nevertheless, despite the continuing depression, there were enough people of means, and those who aspired to acquire the means, to fuel the bicycle craze that was sweeping the city and the nation. And you had to have the means in the spring of 1896, because a bicycle would set you back dearly: In a city where the average working person's monthly income was $30, Albert Pope's Columbia bicycles sold for the firm price of $100. Still, if you really wanted a bicycle—and everybody who fancied themselves anybody really wanted a bicycle—you could always scrape together a $5 down payment, and if you could manage the monthly payments of $10, you'd have yourself a bicycle, even if it wasn't a Columbia.

Even if one could afford one of the better bicycles, in that gilded age of conspicuous consumption the very wealthy found ways to set themselves apart from those who had the means to pay $100 for a bicycle. One nouveau riche New Yorker paid $500 for a silver-plated bicycle as an anniversary gift to his wife; another New Yorker paid $1,000 for a silver-plated bicycle with pearl handlebar grips. These New Yorkers were mere pikers, though, in comparison with New York financier "Diamond Jim" Brady, who built his own plating plant and gold-plated a dozen Columbia bicycles for himself, with silver-plated spokes, and then demolished the plant after the plating job had been completed. The cost of this undertaking is unknown, but the price of the Columbia bicycle he had made for Lillian Russell—gold-plated, with mother-of-pearl handlebars monogrammed in diamonds and emeralds and jewel-encrusted spokes— was rumored to be $10,000. Together, they could be seen cycling on Sundays on their custom bicycles. Despite these nouveau riche displays of conspicuous consumption, New York's old money seemed satisfied with stock bicycles of the best quality.

---

1 The term "muckraker" was coined by Riis's friend Theodore Roosevelt.

And that's what Miss Evylyn Thomas was riding in the spring of 1896: a bicycle of the best quality—a Columbia. It's not entirely clear that Miss Thomas was new money; it's not even entirely clear where she lived. Although she was reported as living way out on the Upper West Side, at 459 W. 90th Street—she certainly wasn't old money, if that was indeed her address—there's one little problem: There is no "459 W. 90th" in New York City. There is, however, a 459 W. 19th. Wherever it was that she actually lived, riding that Columbia, it seems unlikely that she was living in one of the shanties or subsistence farms that could still be found on the Upper West Side. If she was living on the Upper West Side, it seems far more likely that Miss Thomas was living in one of the new apartment houses, or the new "American basement" houses of the newly rich, who, unable yet to afford a prestigious address farther south, were flooding into the area as the city advanced north into the shanties. By that spring, the bicycle craze was at its peak, and on the Upper West Side, both Broadway and Riverside Drive had become popular cycling boulevards, day and night. On one Sunday alone in June 1896, it was estimated that 100,000 cyclists rode out of the city to enjoy a day of riding on Long Island, while another 50,000 cyclists remained behind to enjoy riding the boulevards of Manhattan Island.

And so it was that, about noon on one particularly beautiful spring day in New York City, Miss Evylyn Thomas was riding her Columbia bicycle south on Broadway, on the Upper West Side, as was the fashion

PHOTO 1.1 Women with Bicycles

PHOTO 1.2 Broadway in 1896

for fashionable New Yorkers on beautiful spring days. It was Memorial Day—a Saturday—May 30, 1896, and as would be expected, Miss Thomas wasn't alone in riding her bicycle on this weekend holiday; the streets were filled that morning with cyclists riding to cycling resorts outside the city, although by noon, there were fewer cyclists about.

Driving north on Broadway was one of those new horseless carriages that people had heard about, but were seeing for the first time only now.[2] At the wheel of the Duryea Motor Wagon—that's what the Duryea brothers, Charles and Frank, called their new horseless carriage—was Mr. Henry Wells of Springfield, Massachusetts. The vehicle Wells was piloting was one of four Duryeas making their first appearance in the city that day; they were there, along with a Booth-Rogers and an import from Paris—an Armstrong—to take part in the "Cosmopolitan Race," the second American automobile race, sponsored by *Cosmopolitan* magazine. Yes, that *Cosmopolitan*. The automobiles had first assembled at the post office in City Hall Park at 9 A.M., and after parading about in the vicinity for most of the morning, they left just before noon for the race's checkpoint at King's Bridge.[3]

2 In addition to his bicycle fleet, Diamond Jim Brady was the first in the city to acquire an electric-powered horseless carriage, which he drove about even before this Memorial Day. What people were seeing for the first time on this Memorial Day was a horseless carriage powered by an internal combustion engine.

3 "Horseless Carriage Contests," *New York Times*, May 31, 1896. The *New York Times* account of the race refers to Kingsbridge as the starting point, while a modern source on the Italian Wikipedia describes Kingsbridge as as the checkpoint.

PHOTO 1.3 1896 Duryea Cosmopolitan Race winner

As Mr. Wells was driving north near Broadway's intersection with West 74th Street, Miss Thomas was approaching the intersection from the opposite direction. Shortly after noon, near this intersection, something went wrong with Wells's vehicle, and their paths fatefully crossed. Wells lost control of the Duryea, and it began to zigzag up the street toward Miss Thomas. The sight of a horseless carriage erratically bearing down on her in a zigzagging path appears to have confused Miss Thomas; Wells's vehicle collided with her, and Thomas was knocked from her bicycle into the street. As a crowd gathered at the scene of the collision, Miss Thomas was picked up, unconscious, and taken by ambulance to Manhattan Hospital with a fractured leg. Wells was arrested and taken to the police station at West 125th Street, where he was held while the police awaited word of Miss Thomas's condition; the Duryea continued on to the race's checkpoint with another driver at the wheel. It was reported later that night that Miss Thomas would soon recover.

It's unclear what the final resolution of the collision between Mr. Wells's Duryea and Miss Thomas's Columbia was, but the events of that long-ago Memorial Day are significant for being the first reported automobile accident resulting in an injury, as well as the first reported automobile accident resulting in an arrest. From our twenty-first-century vantage point, we cyclists can note with some irony that the first reported automobile accident involved a collision with a bicycle. However, from a nineteenth-century perspective, this did not seem ironic at all—at least not in the same sense. The streets were filled with traffic of all sorts—pedestrians, horses and horse-drawn vehicles, trolleys, and bicycles. A horseless carriage was just one more vehicle in the mix, although it was certainly considered an odd-looking vehicle with no horse pulling it. This nineteenth-century diversity of street traffic survives in the law to this day; many states have a provision in their vehicle codes that defines traffic to include "pedestrians, ridden or herded animals, vehicles, street cars, and other conveyances."[4]

If New Yorkers saw any irony in a collision between a bicycle and a horseless carriage, it was that one of the more hazardous vehicles on the streets of New York had just been laid low by the comical newcomer. Although cycling was enormously popular, cyclists were widely scorned as scofflaws who had no regard for others. Pedestrians were frequently endangered, and occasionally knocked down, by speeding cyclists; horses were routinely frightened, and the newspapers regularly reported cyclist-on-cyclist collisions. Speeding cyclists, known as "scorchers," were such a problem that Theodore Roosevelt, the chair of the New York Police Commission, organized a special squad of bicycle-mounted police officers for the express purpose of apprehending scorchers.

The day of the Wells/Thomas accident, a number of other bicycling-related incidents were reported. Across the river in Jersey City, three cyclists were injured on Hudson Boulevard. In one accident, Miss Ida Sweezey was knocked down by an ice wagon driven "at reckless speed." Miss Sweezey's bicycle was wrecked, and Miss Sweezey was severely injured when one of the wagon wheels rode over her. On the same boulevard, two cyclists collided while scorching. Both bicycles were wrecked, and both cyclists were taken to City Hospital; one of the cyclists, Robert Taylor of New York, was treated for a broken nose. Tessie McNally, a six-year-old, was also injured in Jersey City that day when she was knocked down by a bicyclist while running across the street; a doctor treated her at home for a severe cut to her cheek. In Brooklyn, there were two cycling accidents. In the first, Milton S. Bibby was struck by a runaway horse while cycling and treated for a fractured left leg at St. John's Hospital. In the second, brothers John and William Foell fell from their tandem; John suffered a severe scalp wound, and William's upper jaw was fractured. Finally, five cyclists were arrested for scorching that day in New York City; before fining the miscreants, the magistrate remarked: "Some of you people think that no one has a right in the streets but

---

4   Uniform Vehicle Code Section 1-207.

yourselves. I know I have had to run for my life to get out of the way of reckless bicycle riders."[5]

The problem facing New York and other cities and towns across America was complex: What to do about the traffic havoc in the streets? Although we tend to think of the traffic laws as statutes that were enacted for the benefit of automobiles, with laws specific to bicycles added as an afterthought, it's a mistaken notion. Instead, traffic laws were enacted to regulate traffic, which already included pedestrians, horses, horse-drawn vehicles, and trolleys. New York City's first traffic regulation—a prohibition against driving wagons too fast on Broadway—was enacted by Peter Stuyvesant, the director general of New Amsterdam in 1647; it would be another seventeen years before the English captured the city and named it for the Duke of York. By 1896, the once-small Dutch village at the southern tip of Manhattan Island was the largest American city, and the streets were bustling with traffic. By the time the bicycle entered the traffic stream, the traffic conditions had become chaotic. The basic traffic problem—figuring out a way for pedestrians, horses, horse-drawn vehicles, trolleys, and bicycles to coexist in the streets—could not be addressed by speed limits alone. There were in fact two related problems to contend with once bicycles entered the traffic stream.

One problem was that bicycles were an undefined entity under the law, and so it was unclear which, if any, regulations applied to them. The solution to this problem was first adopted by the New York state legislature in 1887 when it passed a statute declaring that bicycles were carriages, and therefore that cyclists were entitled to the same rights and subject to the same restrictions as drivers of horse drawn carriages. The other, related problem was that because the rights of bicyclists had not been defined under the law, their corresponding responsibilities were also undefined. The solution adopted by the courts was to bring bicycles into the legal system by granting them the same common-law legal rights to the streets that other vehicles enjoyed, and thereby subjecting them to the same legal duties.

As bicycles were brought into the legal system, cyclists began to lobby for paving improvements to the dirt roads; two influential proponents of paving were Albert Pope, of Columbia Bicycles, and the League of American Wheelmen.[6] When the automobile began to appear on the streets of American cities, the roads were already beginning to be paved for bicycles, and the traffic principles that had previously been adopted in the statutes for bicycles were subsequently adopted for automobiles.

---

5 "Many Bicyclists Came to Grief," *New York Times*, May 31, 1896.

6 The League of American Wheelmen is now known as the League of American Bicyclists.

The Right to Ride

1-1 THE STATUTORY RIGHT TO RIDE

NEW YORK LAW 1887, CHAPTER 704. AN ACT IN RELATION
TO THE USE OF BICYCLES AND TRICYCLES

**Bicycles, tricycles, etc. declared to be "carriages" within this
title of R.S. Section 1.** Bicycles, tricycles and all other vehicles propelled by manumotive or pedomotive power, are hereby declared
to be carriages . . . and all persons by whom bicycles, tricycles
and said other vehicles are used, ridden or propelled upon the
public highways of this state, shall be entitled to the same rights
and subject to the same restrictions in the use thereof as are pre-
scribed in said Revised Statutes in the cases of persons using carriages drawn by horses.

Entitled to free use of roads, etc. Section 2. The commissioners,
trustees or other authorities having charge or control of any public street, public highway, public parkway, driveway or public place
in this state, shall have no power or authority to pass, enforce or
maintain any ordinance, rule or regulation by which any person
using a bicycle or tricycle, shall be excluded or prohibited from the
free use of any public highway, street, avenue, roadway, driveway,
parkway or public place, at any time when the same is open to the
free use of persons having and using other pleasure carriages.

Limitation of this act. Section 3. Nothing in this act shall be so
construed as to prevent the passage, enforcement or maintenance
of any regulation, ordinance or rule, regulating the use of bicycles
or tricycles in public highways, streets, driveways, parkways and
public places in such manner as to limit and determine the proper
rate of speed with which such vehicles may be propelled, nor in
such manner as to require, direct or prohibit the use of bells, lamps
and other appurtenances, nor to prohibit the use of any vehicle
upon that part of the street, highway or parkway, commonly known
as the foot-path or sidewalk.

As bicycles began to appear on the roads in ever larger numbers, conflicts between cyclists and other users of the road—horses, horse-drawn
carriages, and pedestrians—also began to appear in ever larger numbers.
The conflict was as equally attributable to cyclists, who often rode as if
they had no responsibilities to other users of the road, as it was to the

AN INTRODUCTION TO YOUR LEGAL RIGHTS

more traditional users of the road, who often behaved as if cyclists had no right to use the roads. The problem, of course, was that nobody was sure of what, if any, laws were applicable to cyclists. Bicycles, after all, were a new phenomenon, and therefore unaddressed by the law.

The New York state legislature paved the way with its groundbreaking 1887 statute clearly establishing that bicycles were vehicles and that cyclists had all of the rights as well as all of the duties as drivers of horse-drawn carriages. Additionally, the 1887 statute prohibited the passage of any law that excluded bicycles from the public roads and sidewalks, or that required or prohibited the use of either bells or lamps, while allowing for the passage of laws regulating the speed of bicycles.

And with that, the legal status of bicycles—at least in New York—had been decided. The rights of cyclists, as well as their duties, had been established in law. Of course, as we see to this day, conflicts would still arise, but the difference is that once bicycles were brought into the legal system, the rights of cyclists as well as their corresponding duties were now enforceable by the courts. Other states passed their own bicycle statutes, and as automobiles began to appear on the roads, they were brought into the legal system in the same manner.

Today, the New York legislature's basic statutory scheme establishing the rights and duties of cyclists is in effect in most states. For example, let's compare the 1887 law with the Uniform Vehicle Code and the comparable section of the West Virginia code:

> **New York Law 1887, Chapter 704. Bicycles, tricycles, etc. declared to be "carriages" within this title of R.S. Section 1.** Bicycles, tricycles and all other vehicles propelled by manumotive or pedomotive power, are hereby declared to be carriages . . . and all persons by whom bicycles, tricycles and said other vehicles are used, ridden or propelled upon the public highways of this state, shall be entitled to the same rights and subject to the same restrictions in the use thereof as are prescribed in said Revised Statutes in the cases of persons using carriages drawn by horses.
>
> **Uniform Vehicle Code Section 11-1202. Traffic laws apply to persons on bicycles and other human powered vehicles.** Every person propelling a vehicle by human power or riding a bicycle shall have all of the rights and all of the duties applicable to the driver of any other vehicle.
>
> **West Virginia Code Annotated 17C-11-2. Traffic laws apply to persons riding bicycles.** Every person riding a bicycle upon a roadway

> shall be granted all of the rights and shall be subject to all of the
> duties applicable to the driver of a vehicle.

Most states have versions—often word-for-word—of this statute on their books. Many—but not all—of those states also have a statutory provision defining bicycles as vehicles. Typically, the statute will grant the cyclist all of the rights applicable to the driver of a vehicle, but will qualify the duties applicable to the cyclist to exclude those duties "which by their nature can have no application." Generally, the distinction between laws that are applicable to cyclists and laws that are not applicable to cyclists is made by a distinction in the traffic code between "vehicles" and "motor vehicles." If the traffic code makes this distinction, and if a law specifies that it applies to "motor vehicles" rather than to "vehicles," then it is usually not applicable to bicycles. Another approach that states take is to specify which sections of the vehicle code are not applicable to bicycles. Regardless of the approach a state takes, the meaning of the law is that bicycles must obey the general laws regulating traffic, and must also obey any laws that specifically apply to bicycles. If a law specifically applying to bicycles is in conflict with a general traffic law—for example, if the traffic code generally allows vehicles to occupy any lane, but specifies that bicycles must ride in the bicycle lane—then the bicycle-specific law applies.

1-2 THE COMMON-LAW RIGHT TO RIDE

> "The Question raised . . . is whether a bicycle is a carriage or vehicle. . . . We are of the opinion that it is a carriage or vehicle which carries a person mounted upon it, and which is propelled or driven by him. The word 'vehicle' is certainly broad enough to include any machine which is driven on the traveled part of the highway for the purpose of conveyance upon the highway."
> *State v. Collins*, Supreme Court of Rhode Island (1888)
>
> "We think, however, that a bicycle must be regarded as a vehicle within the meaning of the law. Webster defines a bicycle as a 'two-wheeled velocipede,' and a velocipede is defined to be a 'light carriage.' Substantially the same definition is given by a law writer. 2 Amer. & Eng. Cyclop. Law, 191. Under these definitions it must be regarded as a sort of vehicle, and so the courts have regarded it."
> *Mercer v. Corbin*, Supreme Court of Indiana (1889)
>
> "Although but few courts have passed upon and defined the rights of persons riding on and propelling or driving bicycles, yet such as

> have, have unanimously placed them upon an equality and gov-
> erned by the same rule as persons riding or driving any other vehicle
> or carriage; and we think this is the proper rule to adopt."
>
> *Holland v. Bartch*, Supreme Court of Indiana (1889)

As bicycles began to appear on roads across America, conflicts inevitably arose between cyclists and horses, horse-drawn carriages, and pedestrians, which, cumulatively, were the traditional elements of traffic. Some of these conflicts stemmed from a belief that bicycles had no right to use the roads—or sidewalks, for that matter—and some stemmed from cyclists' disregard for the rights of other users of the road.

Whatever the cause, these conflicts were brought before the courts, and the courts were faced with the task of deciding the rights and duties of cyclists. The courts rose to the challenge through the common law—the body of centuries of judicial decisions that, cumulatively, provide precedential direction for both trial and appellate courts. In applying the common law, the courts merely looked at legal precedents in historical cases with similar facts and applied those principles to bicycles. Although bicycles were clearly something new—they weren't horses, and they weren't horse-drawn carriages—the courts nevertheless recognized that bicycles fit into the category of vehicles, along with horses and carriages. By the time automobiles began to appear on the roads, it was a well-settled principle of law that bicycles were vehicles, and that cyclists had the same rights and responsibilities as drivers of other vehicles.

Today, over a century after automobiles first began appearing on the roads, that common-law principle remains in effect. However, in most states the principle has been supplanted by identical statutory provisions. The practical effect is that the courts follow the statute in those states that have codified the principle into statutory law, while the common law would direct the courts in those states that do not have a statutory provision addressing the rights and duties of cyclists.

1-3 THE CONSTITUTIONAL RIGHT TO RIDE

> "The rights of locomotion, freedom of movement, to go where one
> pleases, and to use the public streets in a way that does not inter-
> fere with the personal liberty of others are basic values 'implicit in
> the concept of ordered liberty' protected by the due process clause
> of the fourteenth amendment."
>
> *Bykofsky v. Borough of Middletown*, United States
> District Court, M.D. Pennsylvania (1976)

"The constitutional right to travel from one State to another, and necessarily to use the highways and other instrumentalities of interstate commerce in doing so, occupies a position fundamental to the concept of our Federal Union. It is a right that has been firmly established and repeatedly recognized."

United States v. Guest, Supreme Court of the United States (1966)

"It would be meaningless to describe the right to travel between the states as a fundamental precept of personal liberty and not to acknowledge a correlative constitutional right to travel within a state."

King v. New Rochelle Municipal Housing Authority,
United States Court of Appeals, Second Circuit (1971)

"Each citizen has the absolute right to choose for himself the mode of conveyance he desires, whether it be by wagon or carriage, by horse, motor or electric car, or by bicycle, or astride of a horse, subject to the sole condition that he will observe all those requirements that are known as the 'law of the road.' This right of the people to the use of the public streets of a city is so well established and so universally recognized in this country that it has become a part of the alphabet of fundamental rights of the citizen."

Swift v. City of Topeka, Supreme Court of Kansas (1890)

"There is no constitutional right to a particular mode of travel."

State v. Scheffel, Supreme Court of Washington (1973)

In addition to the statutory and common-law rights accorded to cyclists, the courts—including the Supreme Court—have consistently held that there is a constitutional right to travel. This constitutional right has been held to be a fundamental right—a right that is so essential to liberty that any attempt by government to curtail it will be strictly scrutinized by the courts. Although courts across the country have uniformly agreed that there is a constitutional right to travel—a right that is fundamental to liberty—courts have not been in uniform agreement on the source of that right. This is because there's nothing in the Constitution that *explicitly* says you have a right to travel. Nevertheless, courts have found an *implicit* right to travel, although different courts have found it under different theories of law. Thus, the right to travel has been found by various courts to be derived from the Privileges and Immunities clause of the Constitution, the Privileges and Immunities clause of the Fourteenth Amendment, the Due Process clause of the Fifth Amendment, as well as from general constitutional principles, or from the "penumbra of rights"—fundamental rights implied by the Bill of Rights. The important thing to remember is that, regardless of which theory a particular court is following, all courts agree that there is an implicit, fundamental constitutional right to travel.

That fundamental right is much broader than the *act* of locomotion; for example, it includes the right to move from one state to another. Nevertheless, the right to travel does include the right to locomotion. The right to travel, however, has not been uniformly held to be so broad as to cover *all* travel; rather, courts have uniformly agreed that the constitutional right to travel is a right to *interstate* travel—travel *between* states. When governmental action infringes upon that right to interstate travel, it will be strictly scrutinized for constitutionality by the courts. There is less uniform agreement among the courts on a constitutional right to *intrastate* travel—travel *within* a state. Nevertheless, many courts and most constitutional scholars have agreed that there is a fundamental right of intrastate travel, and some state constitutions have explicitly established a right to intrastate travel. Although the source for the constitutional right to intrastate travel has been found by various courts to derive from the Privileges and Immunities clause of the Constitution, the Privileges and Immunities clause of the Fourteenth Amendment, and the Equal Protection clause of the Fourteenth Amendment, it has been argued that the Due Process clause of the Fourteenth Amendment is the best source for that right.[7]

CONCLUSION

Before the advent of the motor vehicle, the right to travel was held to include the right to choose a particular mode of travel. However, that right to choose the mode of travel has been curtailed with the advent of licensing and DUI laws for motor vehicles. When driver's licenses have been revoked under DUI laws, those revocations have been challenged as an unconstitutional infringement of the right to travel. However, courts have uniformly upheld the licensing laws, holding that laws allowing for the revocation of driver's licenses do not interfere with the constitutional right to travel because it is the mode of travel, rather than the right to travel, that is restricted.

At first glance, this might seem to be an erosion of the right of cyclists to choose their mode of conveyance, a principle the Supreme Court of

7 Andrew C. Porter, Toward a Constitutional Analysis of the Right to Intrastate Travel, 86 N.W. U. L. Rev. 820 (1992).

Kansas upheld in 1890 when it affirmed a citizen's right "to choose for himself the mode of conveyance he desires" in *Swift v. City of Topeka*. However, a closer reading of the DUI cases doesn't indicate that the right to choose one's mode of travel has been curtailed outside of the DUI context. There are two related reasons for this interpretation. First, the state may revoke driving privileges because driving is an activity that is licensed by the state and therefore subject to the state's permission. Because cycling isn't licensed by the state, the state has no power to "revoke" an individual cyclist's choice to cycle. This doesn't mean that the state can't place restrictions, such as a requirement to obey traffic laws, on cycling, but it does mean that the state has no power to prohibit you from cycling. Thus, the right to choose a bicycle as your means of exercising your constitutional right to travel hasn't been limited by the rulings upholding the constitutionality of the state licensing and DUI laws.

Second, the Bicycle Civil Liberties Union has advanced the argument that preserving the right to other forms of transportation, such as cycling, is a necessary adjunct of the state's right to restrict driving privileges. In other words, because you have a constitutional right to travel, preserving nonlicensed forms of transportation, such as cycling, is essential to maintaining the constitutionality of the state's power of revocation for licensed forms of transportation.

In the 1880s, the central legal problem facing cyclists was the right to the road—whether cyclists even *had* a right to the road was contested by government and private individuals across America. Cyclists fought for their rights to the highest courts, and they won their right to the road. The more things change, the more they stay the same. Today, the central legal problem facing cyclists is the violation of cyclists' rights, whether by government or private individuals.

Today we have legal tools to defend our rights; the law was no stranger to our 1880s cycling forebears, however. We have the right to the road today precisely because the early cyclists used the law to advance their rights. Thus, in addition to merely defending our rights, we can learn from our cycling forebears and *advance* our rights. Gaining the right to the road was the cycling cause of the late nineteenth century; *securing* that right will be the cycling cause of the early twenty-first century.

2

Your Rights and Duties
under the Law

INTRODUCTION

When the cyclists of the 1880s gained the right to the road, they were recognized to have all of the rights and all of the duties applicable to drivers of any other vehicle. Those rights and duties are derived from both the common law and the statutes. That was partly the point of bringing cyclists into the law in the first place—although cyclists had always owed a duty of care to others, on or off the bike, there was no clarity in the law as to whether the traffic statutes applied to cyclists. Bringing cyclists into the law made it clear that the traffic statutes *did* apply to them. In return, cyclists were recognized as having a right to the road.

That's certainly one way of thinking about rights and duties—that duties are the flip side of rights; with rights come duties. Unfortunately, that's not a very adequate way of understanding what is in fact a complex web of social relationships. Imagine that you have a right—the right to the road, for example. Every other person owes you a corresponding duty not to infringe upon your right to the road. Now imagine that every other person also has a right to the road. Your right to the road is not absolute, nor is theirs—you owe a corresponding duty to every other person not to infringe upon their right to the road, just as every person owes you the same duty. Now let's expand that a bit: You don't have one right; you in fact have several rights, for which every other person owes you a corresponding duty. In turn, every other person has a similar bundle of rights, for which you owe them a corresponding duty. Thus, each right encompasses elements of both a right and a duty: Where one person has a right, other persons owe a duty. Similarly, each duty encompasses elements of both a duty and a right: Where one person owes a duty, other persons have a right. It is because rights and duties are so inextricably bound together that we say "with rights come duties."

Know the Law

Okay, so you have both rights and duties. How do you know what those rights and duties are? Put simply, the law defines your rights and duties as follows:

- *Your common-law rights and duties* are found in case law;
- *Your statutory rights and duties* are found in the state and federal codes and in municipal ordinances; and

- *Your constitutional rights and duties* are found in the state and federal constitutions, as interpreted by case law.[1]

Traffic statutes are typically the easiest place to start, and ironically enough, the traffic statutes applicable to bicycles can be found in the same place as the statutes applicable to automobiles—the state vehicle codes.

Uniform Vehicle Code Section 11-1202. Traffic laws apply to persons on bicycles and other human powered vehicles. Every person propelling a vehicle by human power or riding a bicycle shall have all of the rights and all of the duties applicable to the driver of any other vehicle under chapters 10 and 11, except as to those special regulations in this article and except as to those provisions which by their nature can have no application.

Uniform Vehicle Code Section 11-1201. Effect of regulations. (a) It is a misdemeanor for any person to do any act forbidden or fail to perform any act required in this article. (b) The parent of any child and the guardian of any ward shall not authorize or knowingly permit any such child or ward to violate any of the provisions of this article.

Wyoming Statutes Annotated 31-5-701. Prohibited acts. (a) It is a misdemeanor for any person to do any act forbidden or fail to perform any act required in W.S. 31-5-701 through 31-5-706. (b) The parent of any child and the guardian of any ward shall not authorize or knowingly permit the child or ward to violate any provision of this act.

Minnesota Vehicle Code Section 169.96. Interpretation and effect. (b) In all civil actions, a violation of any of the provisions of this chapter, by either or any of the parties to such action or actions shall not be negligence per se but shall be prima facie evidence of negligence only.

Vermont Statutes Annotated 23 Section 1143. Not evidence of negligence. A violation of any provision of sections 1136 through 1141 of this title by any person under sixteen years of age is not negligence or evidence of negligence.

---

1 You even have contractual rights and duties, which are specified in contracts you are a party to, and which are interpreted by case law. However, contracts between private parties do not affect the rights and duties of travelers on the public highways.

2-1 STATE VEHICLE CODES

Under our federal system of government, those powers that are not specifically delegated by the national Constitution to the federal government are reserved either to the states or to the people. The state vehicle codes are one example of this principle of federalism: Each state has its own separate vehicle code, adopted by the legislature of that state. One would think, with fifty separate state legislatures creating fifty separate state vehicle codes, that the laws would be hopelessly contradictory from state to state. And yet, the reality is that the vehicle codes are remarkably similar, sometimes with provisions that are virtually identical from one state to another. There is a reason for this similarity: All of the states have the same guidelines, called the Uniform Traffic Laws.

In 1923, the National Conference of Commissioners on Uniform State Laws decided that there was a need for uniform traffic laws in the states. Meanwhile, in 1924, Herbert Hoover, then secretary of commerce of the United States, organized a meeting of a National Conference on Street and Highway Safety to "devise and recommend measures which would reduce the traffic accidents in the country." Out of these beginnings, a Uniform Traffic Law was developed for adoption by the various states. The work of developing uniform traffic laws continues today through the National Committee on Uniform Traffic Laws and Ordinances. This private, nonprofit organization drafts uniform traffic laws that all of the states are encouraged, but not required, to adopt. States are free to adopt all of a proposed traffic law, to adopt just some of the law, or to reject the proposed law. Typically, because the uniform traffic laws are vetted thoroughly by experts before they are released to the states, they tend to be adopted by the states.

Nevertheless, there are fifty state vehicle codes, sometimes called transportation codes or traffic rules, and in order to know what your statutory rights and responsibilities are, you'll need to know which statutes apply to you, where to find them, and how to interpret them. *Statutes* are state laws that are enacted by the state legislature and usually applicable statewide (the exceptions would be statutes that specify that they are applicable to a limited area—for example, within a state park).[2]

2-2 LOCAL ORDINANCES

In addition to statutes, which apply throughout a state, municipalities are empowered by the state legislatures to adopt their own local ordinances

---

2 Federal laws are also statutes.

regulating traffic. *Ordinances* are applicable only within the jurisdiction of that municipality and must not be in conflict with state law. For example, a municipality may prohibit riding a bike on the sidewalk in its business district, even though there is no state law prohibiting riding on the sidewalk. However, if state law specifies that riding on the sidewalk is legal, a municipality could not adopt an ordinance prohibiting riding on the sidewalk without state authority to do so. As you can see, in order to ride in compliance with the law, you will need to know both your state and local laws. This can easily become quite complex if your ride takes you through several towns, each with its own set of ordinances.

2-3 FEDERAL AND STATE REGULATIONS

Finally, both federal and state regulations may affect cyclists. *Regulations* are rules made by government agencies rather than by a legislative body; these rules fulfill mandates from the legislative body to clarify how the law will be applied. For example, the Consumer Products Safety Commission, under the authority of the U.S. Congress, adopts regulations specifying what equipment new bicycles must have. The underlying statute may direct the agency to adopt regulations that accomplish certain legislative goals, but leave it up to the agency to determine specifically how those legislative goals will be met. For the cyclist, the difference between laws and regulations is this: You are required to obey state and local laws, but you are not required to obey equipment regulations (that responsibility will instead fall on the manufacturers and retailers). However, some regulations do have the force of law—specifically, regulations adopted by agencies such as parks. These types of regulations apply to areas within the jurisdiction of the promulgating agency and will tell you, for example, whether you may ride on trails, or whether you *must* ride on bicycle paths, and under what conditions the regulations apply.

There are several places to find the laws and regulations that apply to you as a cyclist:

1. Your public library should have a copy of both state statutes and local ordinances.

2. Law libraries will also have copies of state laws, as will courthouse libraries.

3. Websites for your state legislature and local government may archive this information.

4. Your local bicycle advocacy organization is often an excellent resource. To find out if there is a local bicycle advocacy organization in
your area, check with local bike shops or with a national organization
such as the League of American Bicyclists.

5. The Department of Motor Vehicles may also be able to provide information on state bicycling statutes.

2-4 INTERPRETING THE LAW

Sometimes a statute will be relatively straightforward; for example, it
may state that a bicycle is a vehicle and is subject to the traffic laws.
That's not very ambiguous. However, it can also be the case that a statute seems straightforward but actually contains ambiguous terms or
statements. For example, suppose a statute says you may not enter into
the path of another vehicle that is "so close as to constitute an immediate hazard." What did the legislature mean by "immediate hazard"?
How do you figure out what the legislature meant? One easy way is to
look in the definitions section of the code book[3] to see if the legislature
defined what it meant by the term. Another way is to get a copy of your
state's annotated statutes; these are code books that have the statutes as
well as annotations on legal articles and judicial opinions interpreting
the provisions of the statute. Annotated legal articles will tend to discuss
legal principles rather than specific provisions of the law, whereas annotated cases will often interpret specific provisions in the law.

For example, suppose a statute states that "a person commits the offense of improper use of lanes by a bicycle if the person is operating a
bicycle on a roadway at less than the normal speed of traffic using the
roadway at that time and place under the existing conditions and the
person does not ride as close as practicable to the right curb or edge of
the roadway." Cases annotating this statute may interpret what "normal
speed" means or what "practicable" means. Looking up these annotations is an extremely useful tool for interpretation. There's no need for
you to try to figure out what a statute means if a court has already made
that interpretation for you.

That's how the *common law* works: An appellate court interprets the
law, and that interpretation provides guidance for future courts under
that appellate court's jurisdiction. In fact, appellate decisions may be persuasive to other courts outside their jurisdiction when an issue has not
yet been interpreted by those courts. Of course, some statutes have
not yet been interpreted by a court, either because they are new or because

3   A code book is a book of related statutes, such as the state vehicle code.

they have not yet been at issue in a case that was appealed. Although courts have a number of rules of interpretation for such instances, the rules of statutory interpretation are complex and beyond the scope of this book. As a general rule of thumb, if you follow a commonsense interpretation of a statute that hasn't yet been interpreted, you will probably be in compliance with the law.

The Duty of Care

Uniform Vehicle Code Section 11-504. Notwithstanding any other provisions of this chapter or the provisions of any local ordinance, every driver of a vehicle shall exercise due care to avoid colliding with any pedestrian or any person propelling a human powered vehicle and shall give an audible signal when necessary, and shall exercise proper precaution upon observing any child or any obviously confused, incapacitated or intoxicated person.

"The rule that a person traveling upon a highway has a right to assume that all other persons using the highway will obey the law and that one is not bound to keep a lookout for others who may violate the law applies only to those cases where the automobile is being driven in conformity with the law and not in violation thereof."
Cushing Refining & Gasoline Co. v. Deshan, 300 P. 312 (Okla. 1931)

Under the common law, all persons owe all other persons a "duty of care." When that duty of care is breached and an injury results, the person breaching the duty is held liable for the *tort* of *negligence*.[4] However, when the injury is the intended consequence of the act, the tort is intentional and therefore more serious than mere negligence. In between negligence and an intentional act is gross negligence, in which, even though the injury was unintended, the act was so careless that the tortfeasor, or person committing the act, knew or should have known that injury was a likely consequence, but acted in disregard of that likely consequence.

---

4 A tort is a civil "wrong," rather than a criminal act, committed against another person. Nevertheless, even though a tort is a civil wrong, it may be so extreme that it is also a criminal act. In general, the difference between a tort and a crime is that in a tort, the person wronged files a civil lawsuit against the tortfeasor–the perpetrator of the wrong. When a crime has been committed, in contrast, the "people"– that is, the district attorney locally, or the Department of Justice at the state or federal level–conduct the prosecution. In a civil suit, if the defendant loses he is held "liable," whereas if he loses in a criminal trial, he is found "guilty." In a civil trial, the penalty will usually be money damages, payable to the plaintiff (the person filing the lawsuit); in a criminal trial, the penalty will be a fine, imprisonment, or both.

One of the duties that all vehicle operators owe to cyclists and pedestrians is to "exercise due care." This duty is set forth in the Uniform Vehicle Code (UVC), Section 11-504, and obviously applies to motorists. Because cyclists have all of the rights and all of the duties applicable to the drivers of any other vehicle, it also applies to cyclists. Thus, motorists and cyclists both have a statutory duty to exercise due care to avoid colliding with any pedestrian or cyclist.

Although the statute doesn't explicitly state that motorists and cyclists must exercise due care to avoid colliding with motorists, it cannot be concluded that motorists aren't owed a similar duty. The duty to avoid colliding with a motorist would simply be a common-law duty rather than a statutory duty. When negligence is alleged, the evidence will be considered differently based on whether there was a breach of statutory duty or of common law. A violation of the statute would be either *prima facie* evidence of negligence or negligence *per se*, depending on the state. In states that follow the prima facie evidence rule, a violation of the statute is presumed to be evidence of negligence, unless contradictory evidence is introduced to rebut that presumption. In states that follow the negligence per se rule, upon proof that the statute has been violated, negligence has been proved. In contrast, a breach of the common-law duty of due care would be a question for a jury to decide.

The common-law duty to exercise due care applies to all travelers using the public highways—motorists, cyclists, pedestrians, equestrians, and others. Under the common law, all travelers have a duty to exercise due care, and all travelers have a corresponding right to assume that all other travelers will exercise due care. This means that all travelers must exercise reasonable care and caution to avoid a collision, and that all travelers have a corresponding right to expect that all other travelers will exercise reasonable care and caution to avoid a collision; what constitutes "reasonable care" will depend upon what is prudent in a particular set of factual circumstances. Because of this common-law right and its corresponding duty, all travelers have a duty to obey the applicable traffic laws, and all travelers have a corresponding right to assume that all other travelers will obey the applicable traffic laws.

That's the explicit rule in the common law; what the common law is implicitly telling us is that a traveler who is a victim of negligence cannot be held liable for failing to anticipate another traveler's negligence. In fact, the common law also states this explicitly, although this explicit rule is qualified with the caveat that the other traveler's negligence must not be apparent. In other words, you can assume that somebody else is exercising reasonable care, and that he is obeying the traffic laws, as long as there is no indication apparent to you that the other person is not exercising reasonable care, or is not obeying the traffic laws. As long as the other person appears to be exercising due care and appears to be obeying the traffic laws, you can't be held liable for failing to anticipate that person's negligence.

So now you know that you have a right to assume that others will exercise due care; you also know that you have a corresponding duty to exercise due care. But how do you know if you're "exercising due care"? How do you protect yourself from liability for negligence? The simplest way is to ride in compliance with the statutes.[5] This is the simplest way for two reasons. First, in comparison with the common law, the statutes are easily accessible and generally easy to understand; you know what your duties are because the statutes tell you what your duties are. Second, if you're riding in compliance with the statutes, you are shielded from a rebuttable presumption of negligence in the event of an accident. Although negligence might still be proved, it isn't *presumed* as long as you are in compliance with the statutes. Shielding yourself from this presumption of negligence is by far the preferred legal position to be in if you are involved in an accident; therefore, you should always ride in compliance with the statutes.

But what about the common law: Can you ride within the statutory law but still be found liable for negligence? Possibly, although the risk is greatly reduced. Let's go back to that duty of care that every person owes to every other person. The simplest way to protect yourself from liability for common-law negligence is to follow the "reasonable person" standard. This is the standard of behavior that juries use to determine negligence under the common law. It's an objective rather than subjective standard, and thus is not based on what you personally believe to be prudent. If it were a subjective standard, nobody could ever behave negligently, because different people have different subjective thresholds for what they believe to be prudent. For that reason, the *reasonable person standard* is neither the standard of behavior of the person who takes no precautions nor the standard of behavior of the person who takes excessive precautions; instead, it is the standard of behavior of the ordinary, prudent person who takes "reasonable" precautions. What is deemed reasonable will depend upon what precautions a particular jury believes are prudent in a particular set of factual circumstances.

Now let's look at some specific situations cyclists may encounter that involve the duty of care.

5 In the context of this discussion, the term "statutes" includes statutes, ordinances, and regulations.

2-5 ASSUMPTION OF RISK

> "The law does not require a person to surrender the lawful exercise
> of a valuable right [use of a public street] or assume the risk of in-
> jury merely because someone else's conduct or failure to exercise
> due care threatens harm."
>
> *Bell v. Chawkins*, 460 S.W.2d 850 (Tenn. 1970)

Suppose somebody who owes you a duty of care breaches that duty, and you're injured as a result of that person's negligence. Now that person needs a good defense. "Assumption of risk" is one such defense—it's the negligent person's way of saying, "Whether I was negligent or not, *you knew the risk, and you took it anyway*, so I shouldn't be held liable for your injuries."

Assumption of risk is a powerful defense in negligence cases. Even if the person who injured you is held liable for your injuries, your "assumption of the risk" may reduce the amount of compensation that you would otherwise be entitled to.

Think for a moment about how problematic this defense would be, however, if it were applied to negligence in an auto accident: You get into your car, you drive to work, somebody negligently causes an accident, and then blames *you* for being on the road in the first place.

Would this argument make any sense to you? Hopefully not, and yet that is exactly what is being claimed when the assumption-of-risk defense is used in the context of auto/bike collisions. That said, assumption of risk is a legitimate defense in some contexts, such as injuries incurred in sporting events, which I discuss in more detail in Chapter 8. However, barring a few exceptions, courts have universally agreed that it is not a legitimate defense outside of the sporting context.[6]

2-6 PROPER LOOKOUT

> "It is the obligation of an operator of a motor vehicle to keep proper
> lookout. The whole theory of motor vehicle law is based on the re-
> quirement that the operator keep his vehicle under control at all
> times, considering actual and potential hazards, which of necessity
> contemplates proper lookout by the operator. It is not only the duty
> of the operator to look, but it is his duty to see and be cognizant

---

6 Assumption of risk was allowed as a defense in one case where a cyclist rode for a quarter of a mile over loose gravel before falling, and in another case where a cyclist broke his wheel and fell on a rough railroad crossing because he had been riding over the crossing for two years and was therefore familiar with the danger.

> of that which is plainly visible or obviously apparent, and a failure
> on his part in this regard, without proper justification or reason,
> makes him chargeable for failure to see what he should have seen
> had he been in the exercise of reasonable care."
>
> *Drury v. Palmer*, Supreme Court of Idaho (1962)

One common-law duty that applies to all operators of vehicles—motorists and cyclists alike—is the duty to maintain a proper lookout. This duty means that you must maintain a proper lookout for the movement of your bicycle as well as for the movement of other vehicles, persons, and hazards on the highway. In turn, motorists owe the same duty to you. And as you might have guessed, the legal standard for maintaining a proper lookout is that of the reasonable person.

If you're maintaining a proper lookout, and you're riding in compliance with the statutes, the common law allows you to assume that others on the road are also obeying the law. This relieves you of any legal burden to anticipate somebody else's illegal behavior. This legal principle cuts both ways. If a motorist is both keeping a proper lookout and obeying the statutes, the motorist is entitled to assume that you are also obeying the law; if you are actually riding in violation of the law, the motorist cannot be held liable for not anticipating your illegal behavior. Once again, you can see how riding in compliance with the statutes confers significant legal benefits, whereas riding in violation of the statutes imposes significant legal liabilities.

2-7 PASSING DISTANCE

> **Uniform Vehicle Code Section 11-303. Overtaking a vehicle on the left.** (a) The driver of a vehicle overtaking another vehicle proceeding in the same direction shall pass at a safe distance to the left of the vehicle being overtaken and shall not drive again to the right side of the roadway until safely clear of the overtaken vehicle.
>
> **Uniform Vehicle Code Section 11-504. Drivers to exercise due care.** Notwithstanding any other provisions of this chapter or the provisions of any local ordinance, every driver of a vehicle shall exercise due care to avoid colliding with any pedestrian or any person propelling a human powered vehicle and shall give an audible signal when necessary, and shall exercise proper precaution upon observing any child or any obviously confused, incapacitated or intoxicated person.

Arizona Revised Statutes Section 28-735. Overtaking bicycles.

(a) When overtaking and passing a bicycle proceeding in the same direction, a person driving a motor vehicle shall exercise due care by leaving a safe distance between the motor vehicle and the bicycle of not less than three feet until the motor vehicle is safely past the overtaken bicycle.

"'Safe distance' is not measured by cold inches, but by circumstances and the variations from perfectly straight driving or riding which may be anticipated from ordinarily careful persons."

Stockfisch v. Fox, Supreme Court of Michigan (1936)

An increasingly common phenomenon with which many cyclists are unfortunately all too familiar is the unsafe pass, commonly referred to as "buzzing." This occurs when a motorist passes a cyclist at an unsafe distance, often mere inches away, and often at relatively high speeds. Undoubtedly, many of these unsafe passes are unintentionally unsafe, reflecting the motorist's lack of awareness. And we can be equally sure that many of these unsafe passes are intentionally unsafe, reflecting the motorist's hostility toward cyclists. Regardless of whether the unsafe pass is intentional, it's clear that the cyclist's life is placed in danger when it happens, and cyclists are understandably angered when it happens. What's less clear to many cyclists is that *both the safe-passing-distance statute and the due-care statute apply equally to motorists and cyclists:* A cyclist must pass other cyclists (and automobiles, for that matter) at a safe distance, and a cyclist must exercise due care to avoid colliding with pedestrians and other cyclists.

If an unintentionally unsafe pass results in an injury, the violation of the statutory requirement will be prima facie evidence of negligence. If the unsafe pass is intentional, the motorist has committed the tort of assault; and if the unsafe pass results in injury to the cyclist, the motorist has committed the tort of battery.[7] In torts, "injury" is a legal rather than a medical term. This means that there is no need to prove a particular level of physical injury: For assault, it is enough that there has been a *successful* attempt to frighten the person assaulted; for battery, it is enough that there has been *offensive* physical contact. This is true even if the physical contact was unintended and if the person committing the battery intended only to frighten the person suffering the injury.

Tortious acts can also be criminal; if the cyclist has physical injury as a result of an intentional attempt to injure the cyclist, the crime of

7 Note that a cyclist intentionally making an unsafe pass could also be liable for assault and/or battery.

assault and battery has been committed. Even negligent acts, such as involuntary manslaughter, may be criminal when the act is the result of extreme carelessness.

So how do you know whether a pass is unsafe? As a cyclist, you know when it "feels" unsafe, of course, but that isn't necessarily the legal standard for an unsafe pass. Many states specify that the passing distance must be "safe." This is the distance that a "reasonable person"—remember him, the person of "ordinary prudence"?—would consider prudent when passing, and it is determined by a jury. A small but increasing number of states are improving upon the safe distance rule by specifying a minimum safe passing distance—usually two to three feet. The advantage to this approach is that there's a minimum safe passing distance that is easy to gauge: If the statute says the minimum is three feet, and a motorist passes within one foot, the motorist is clearly in violation of the statute and could not argue in court that one foot was a safe distance. At the same time, it's a *minimum* safe passing distance, so a motorist would be legally required to pass with even more distance when safety requires it. The question of whether safety requires even more than the minimum safe passing distance would be a question for a jury to decide.

In *Stockfisch v. Fox,* the Supreme Court of Michigan held: "It cannot be said as a matter of law that four or six feet from the right edge of an eighteen-foot pavement is a 'safe distance' to pass a bicycle when the truck speeds up without warning at a speed of 25 or more miles per hour, although the bicycle occupies only eighteen inches or two feet of the space and is traveling close to the edge. The distance allows for too little margin for possible change of position of the bicycle, from ordinary operation or because the bicyclist may be startled by the unheralded appearance of the truck, to be held legally sufficient."

The question before the court in *Stockfisch* was whether the passing distance between a truck and the bicycle it passed was a "safe distance." But in a case from Kentucky, the issue instead involved the duty to be "safely clear" of the bicycle before completing a pass. On May 29, 1999, Nollaig Previs was riding on a two-lane road in Bourbon County. She was riding uphill at a speed of approximately one or two miles per hour when she was approached from behind by Pete Dailey, who was driving a pickup truck that was pulling two flatbed wagons. The total length of Dailey's vehicle was approximately 48 feet. At the crest of the hill, Dailey crossed into the left lane to pass Previs, and assuming that he had passed her, crossed back into the right lane. However, he had not actually completely passed her, and as he merged back into the lane, her handlebars became wedged under the second wagon he was towing. Her bike was pulled under the wagon, and she was thrown into a ditch on the side of the road. Previs filed a personal injury lawsuit against Dailey; however, the jury returned a verdict in favor of Dailey.

And that would have been the end of *Previs v. Dailey*, except that after the trial, the jury foreman called the judge and said that he was troubled because the jury had discussed an issue that was not presented at trial. Under oath, the foreman testified that the jury discussed whether a reasonable bicyclist would have pulled off of the side of the road to allow a large vehicle to pass. The jury had not discussed whether Dailey had violated his duties as a passing motorist. Based on this testimony, Previs made several motions to change the verdict or to have a new trial. All her motions were denied, and she appealed. Eventually, her case was heard by the Supreme Court of Kentucky.[8]

In its analysis of the issues at trial, the court first addressed Dailey's duties as a passing motorist. Although the jury had not discussed Dailey's duties, the lower court had in fact instructed the jury on Dailey's duties. The jury instruction, based on both common-law and statutory duties,[9] provided:

> *It was the duty of the defendant, Pete Dailey, upon the occasion about which you have just heard evidence, in driving his automobile to exercise ordinary care for his own safety and for the safety of other persons using the roadway, and this general duty included the following specific duties:*
>
> 1. *To keep said automobile under reasonable control;*
>
> 2. *To drive and keep his automobile to the right-hand side of the roadway, and not to pass the Plaintiff on her bicycle moving in the same direction ahead of him unless the overtaking and passing could be completed without interfering with the safe operation of the bicycle ridden by the Plaintiff;*
>
> 3. *After passing the Plaintiff to not drive to the right until reasonably clear of her;*
>
> 4. *To maintain a lookout both to the front and to the rear for other vehicles near enough to be affected by the intended movement of his automobile;*

---

8 *Previs v. Dailey*, 180 S.W.3d 435 (Ky 2000).

9 Kentucky Revised Statutes Section 189.340(1) provides that "vehicles overtaking other vehicles proceeding in the same direction shall pass to the left of them and shall not again drive to the right until reasonably clear of those vehicles."

5. *To exercise ordinary care to avoid collision with other automobiles on the roadway.*[10]

According to the testimony presented at trial, Dailey had admitted that he violated his legal duties to Previs when he stated, "If I had looked in my rearview mirror . . . I wouldn't have probably seen Nollaig anyhow." Notice that he said, *"If* I had looked in my rearview mirror." In other words, using the language of the statute, what Dailey was saying was that when he passed Previs, he "again drove to the right" without looking in his mirror to see if he was "reasonably clear" of Previs's bicycle.

But Dailey had more to say: "My thought is, when I pass a grown person, whether it be a lady or a man—I have no thought of trying to protect her. . . . I mean, once I started passing her, I felt it would be her obligation to allow me around her." So Dailey passed Previs, and without looking in his mirror to see if he was "reasonably clear" of her, "again drove to the right," because, as the Kentucky Supreme Court observed, he "believed that it was solely Previs's obligation to make sure he safely passed her." Referring to the Kentucky statute on which the jury instruction had been based, the Kentucky Supreme Court concluded, "Clearly that is not the law. . . . The evidence presented at trial was uncontroverted that Dailey had not fully passed Previs at the time he maneuvered his truck back into the right lane. Such is a clear violation of Dailey's statutory duties and constitutes negligence per se."

"Negligence per se" is negligence based on proof that a statute was violated. When Dailey admitted at trial that he broke the law, his act became negligent as a matter of law, and therefore, according to the Kentucky Supreme Court, "the trial court erred in submitting the question of Dailey's negligence to the jury, and we must conclude that the jury's verdict absolving him of liability was so flagrantly and palpably against the weight of evidence as to indicate that it was reached as a result of passion or prejudice."

On that basis, the Kentucky Supreme Court sent the case back to the trial court with instructions to grant Previs a "Directed Verdict"—that is, the trial court would enter a judgment finding Dailey negligent, because no other verdict is possible with the evidence presented. However, the Kentucky Supreme Court observed that "a jury is still entitled to consider Previs's duties in operating her bicycle, and apportion fault should it find that Previs was negligent as well."

10 The jury instructions are the law that the court instructs the jury to consider when it decides, based on the facts, whether the defendant (in this case, Dailey) violated his legal duties to the plaintiff (in this case, Previs).

Now, *Previs v. Dailey* is precedential in Kentucky, which means that all Kentucky courts must follow this holding. In other states, *Previs v. Dailey* is persuasive authority, but not binding precedent. Even though it isn't binding, however, courts in other states would be likely to agree with it, because, as the Kentucky Supreme Court observed, requiring cyclists to be responsible for their own safety when a motorist passes is clearly "not the law."

2-8 FOLLOWING TOO CLOSELY AND MOTORPACING

Uniform Vehicle Code Section 11-310. Following too closely.
(a) The driver of a vehicle shall not follow another vehicle more closely than is reasonable and prudent, having due regard for the speed of vehicles and the traffic upon and condition of the highway.

Oregon Revised Statutes Section 811.135. Careless driving. (1) A person commits the offense of careless driving if the person drives any vehicle upon a highway . . . in a manner that endangers or would be likely to endanger any person or property.

Oregon Revised Statutes Section 811.140. Reckless driving. (1) A person commits the offense of reckless driving if the person recklessly drives a vehicle upon a highway or other premises described in this section in a manner that endangers the safety of persons or property.

Oregon Revised Statutes Section 811.060. Vehicular assault of bicyclist or pedestrian. (2) A person commits the offense of vehicular assault of a bicyclist or pedestrian if: (a) The person recklessly operates a vehicle upon a highway in a manner that results in contact between the person's vehicle and a bicycle operated by a person, a person operating a bicycle or a pedestrian; and (b) The contact causes physical injury to the person operating a bicycle or the pedestrian.

Uniform Vehicle Code Section 11-809. Racing on highways.
(a) No person shall drive any vehicle in any race, speed competition, drag race or acceleration contest, test of physical endurance, exhibition of speed or acceleration, or for the purpose of making a speed record; and no person shall in any manner participate in any such race, competition, contest, test, or exhibition.

One of the duties that all operators of vehicles owe to others is not to follow another vehicle too closely. The reason should be obvious: If the vehicle being followed must stop suddenly, the vehicle behind it may not be able to make a safe stop if it is following too closely. Sometimes, the tailgating is merely negligent; at other times, it's intended to harass. (Find more on harassment by motorists in Chapter 5, §5-9–§5-11.) And sometimes, cyclists follow too closely because they're "motorpacing." I do not recommend that you motorpace in your training rides.

This, of course, is the classic "do as I say, not as I do" lecture. With that in mind, before you decide whether to include motorpacing in your training, you should be aware of the legal ramifications, as well as some basic good advice, which will be more than I knew when I was racing and training. In fact, I was not even smart enough to limit my motorpacing to willing and complicit drivers.

Take, for instance, the time I was riding a borrowed cyclocross bike with limited gearing and was spun out going downhill with my head down, when the woman I was drafting hit her brakes for no reason (or maybe she *did* have a reason!). We had made eye contact through her rearview mirror, and I remember thinking that she had a strange resemblance to the woman in the movie *Misery*.

Anyway, this was a two-lane, one-way street, and after I ran into her bumper, I flew upside down between the lanes for a long time before I landed on my back still strapped into the toe-clips. The driver didn't stop, and for a while, neither did the other traffic, which continued to pass me on both sides. After I managed to drag my carcass off the street, an ambulance arrived, as well as the police. I was on my way to convincing the cop that I was lawfully riding in traffic and "changing lanes" when this driver "unexpectedly braked," when up walked an off-duty police officer. He presented his version of the story. Apparently, he had been traveling too slowly for me, and I had passed between him and other vehicles before settling in behind the Kathy Bates look-alike. I was injured, but not badly, and the officer ticketed me for following too closely.

One of the only times I organized a motorpacing session was almost equally disastrous. A friend of a friend kept offering to take me out motorpacing, and I finally agreed. We made our way to a quiet country road and began our session. I got up to speed, but he simply followed *behind* me. I kept waving for him to pass me, and he took my waving as a command to get even closer to my rear wheel and rev his engine louder, Johan Bruyneel–style. Eventually, I pulled over and asked him what he was doing. He thought motorpacing this way was an effective method of speed training because the cyclist would force himself to go faster and faster to avoid being run over by the motor vehicle. I opted for an easy ride by myself, and I still laugh out loud every time I reflect on this innovative "ride-for-your-life" training method.

There is an oft-repeated saying about lawyers: "We'd do it, but the lawyers won't let us." It reflects the widespread general impression that lawyers tend to be overly restrictive. But when it comes to motorpacing, the lawyers are right. If you motorpace, both you and your friend can get into trouble—in fact, you would be amazed at all the different ways you can get into hot water.

Let's start with the obvious violation, using the laws in Oregon as an example, because its traffic laws are fairly standard. Oregon Revised Statutes, Section 811.485, makes it a Class B traffic offense to "follow another vehicle more closely than is reasonable and prudent." This section of the Oregon Vehicle Code is comparable to UVC Section 11-310, which prohibits following too closely. So, at a minimum, law enforcement can cite you for a traffic violation.

That's not the only potential charge, however. Under Oregon Revised Statutes, Section 811.125, both you and your driver could be cited for "speed racing on a highway," which would be applicable "if, on a highway in this state, the person drives a vehicle or participates in any manner in any of the following in which a vehicle is involved: (a) A speed competition or contest (b) An acceleration contest. (c) A test of physical endurance. (d) An exhibition of speed or acceleration. (e) The making of a speed record. (f) A race."

Although it is absolutely certain that the racing statute would not be applied against a cyclist who is merely riding or training—despite that "test of physical endurance" language—it is less certain that you would not be cited for racing if you are caught motorpacing. In Oregon, this is a Class A traffic violation and carries a maximum penalty of a suspended license and a $600 fine, and the license-suspension penalty could apply to both the cyclist and the motorist. This is not the case in every state, however, so you should check your state laws if you are considering motorpacing.

But wait, there's more. Oregon Revised Statutes, Section 811.140, makes reckless driving a Class A *misdemeanor*. This means that it's not just an offense that goes on your driving record; if you're convicted of reckless driving, it's also going on your criminal record. Under Oregon's reckless driving statute, "A person commits the offense of reckless driving if the person recklessly drives a vehicle upon a highway or other premises described in this section in a manner that endangers the safety of persons or property." By "reckless," the statute means that "a person is aware of and consciously disregards a substantial and unjustifiable risk that the result will occur or that the circumstance exists. The risk must be of such nature and degree that disregard thereof constitutes a gross deviation from the standard of care that a reasonable person would observe in a situation."

This criminal standard seems comparable to the civil standard for gross negligence—the person knew, or should have known, that the harm would be a likely result, and acted in disregard of that knowledge. However, this is a criminal charge rather than a civil one, and the potential penalty is stiff. Because reckless driving is a misdemeanor, one could face up to a year in jail for this violation. Although it's highly unlikely that you would receive the maximum penalty for this violation in your state, you would very likely end up with some sort of penalty if you were caught. This might be a particularly attractive offense for a law-enforcement officer to cite you for, because *both* you and your friend could get busted for the same act. Not every state will necessarily have a reckless driving statute, however, and the penalties will vary from state to state.

Of course, you and your friend could both get lucky and merely draw tickets for careless driving. Under Oregon Revised Statutes, Section 811.135, "A person commits the offense of careless driving if the person drives any vehicle upon a highway . . . in a manner that endangers or would be likely to endanger any person or property." That's a Class B traffic offense like following too closely, unless you crash, in which case you could both be cited for a Class A traffic offense—which, again, results in a maximum penalty of a suspended license and a $600 fine. And again, in Oregon and possibly other states, both of your licenses will be subject to suspension.

Suppose you're motorpacing, despite my warnings, and you crash. If a law-enforcement officer just felt like ruining your day—not to mention your friend's day—he could cite your friend for vehicular assault of a bicyclist. Does that sound like a stretch to you? Consider this: Oregon Revised Statutes, Section 811.060(2)(a), includes the following clause within the definition of that offense: "A person [who] recklessly operates a vehicle in a manner that results in contact between the person's vehicle and a bicycle operated by a person or a person operating a bicycle." Because "recklessly" is defined the same way as in reckless driving, if you are motorpacing, bump into the back of your friend's car, and crash, your friend could be cited for a Class A misdemeanor and face a possible year in jail, even though he or she never *intended* to harm you.

Of course, this is all worst-case-scenario stuff, and in all the years my teammates and I motorpaced, I don't remember anyone ever having any problems with the police. If you are stopped by a police officer for motorpacing, I recommend calmly discussing the competitive reasons for motorpacing and your *vast experience* in doing so, all the time using a voice of contrition. The officer may let you continue, with a caveat "to be careful," or he may command you to cease pacing altogether, both of which are better than being ticketed.

There's one more thing to think about: insurance coverage for injuries sustained while motorpacing. Most automobile insurance policies exclude coverage if the car is used in a "race or other contest of speed." In a 1966 Alabama case, *Alabama Farm Bureau Mutual Casual Insurance v. Goodman*,[11] two friends, one on a bicycle and the other in a car, raced each other down the block. The bicyclist was drafting the car when they collided, and the cyclist was injured. Because the "speed of their respective vehicles was of the essence" in their contest, the judge determined that they were involved in a "competitive speed test" and that the motorist's insurance carrier did not have to pay the bicyclist's claim.

Let's assume that, rather than looking to your friend's automobile insurance carrier, you try to get your medical insurance or homeowner's insurance policy to pay. In *State Farm Insurance Companies v. Seefeld*,[12] a 1992 Minnesota case, the court concluded that when an accident results from an incident involving a motorized vehicle and a nonmotorized vehicle, insurance carriers (either homeowner's or medical) can be forced to cover the expenses of their customers. However, most homeowner's and medical insurance carriers contain what is called an "extraordinary risk" exception. If the customer engages in an unusual activity that is extraordinarily dangerous and gets hurt, the insurance company is off the hook. Although normal bicycle riding has frequently been held *not* to be an "extraordinarily dangerous activity," motorpacing a foot behind a car at 30 mph is going to be problematic.

Although my personal experience and belief lead me to conclude that motorpacing has proven value for serious cyclists, I do not recommend using this form of training, as it is both dangerous and clearly illegal. If you are going to motorpace despite this advice, you should take steps to minimize the potential pitfalls. I suggest using a motorcycle instead of a car to set the pace, as it is easier to avoid collisions, simulates race conditions better than an auto, and makes it less likely that you will get pulled over by the police. If you are going to motorpace behind an automobile, use only someone who has hours of experience driving with a cyclist on his or her bumper. Make sure you can see through the windows of the vehicle (don't look at the bumper), and motorpace only on lightly traveled roads. Before drafting behind either a motorcycle or an automobile, make sure you and the driver have gone over all commands and contingencies, including how to handle sudden stops, intersections, potholes, police,

11 *Alabama Farm Bureau Mut. Cas. Ins. Co. v. Goodman*, 188 So.2d 268 (Ala.1966).

12 *State Farm Ins. Cos. v. Seefeld*, 481 N.W.2d 62 (Minn. 1992).

variations of speed, and the like. Regardless of how careful you are, however, motorpacing is both illegal and a breach of your duty of care. If you are caught motorpacing, or involved in an accident while motorpacing, you will be held liable despite any precautions you may have taken.

2-9 TRAFFIC SIGNALS

UVC Section 11-201. Obedience to and required traffic-control devices. (a) The driver of any vehicle shall obey the instructions of any official traffic-control device applicable thereto placed or held in accordance with the provisions of this code, unless otherwise directed by a police officer, subject to the exceptions granted the driver of an authorized emergency vehicle in this code.

Idaho Code 49.720. Stopping—turn and stop signals. (1) A person operating a bicycle or human-powered vehicle approaching a stop sign shall slow down and, if required for safety, stop before entering the intersection. After slowing to a reasonable speed or stopping, the person shall yield the right-of-way to any vehicle in the intersection or approaching on another highway so closely as to constitute an immediate hazard during the time the person is moving across or within the intersection or junction of highways, except that a person after slowing to a reasonable speed and yielding the right-of-way if required, may cautiously make a turn or proceed through the intersection without stopping.

(2) A person operating a bicycle or human-powered vehicle approaching a steady red traffic control signal shall stop before entering the intersection, and shall yield to all other traffic. Once the person has yielded, he may proceed through the steady red light with caution. Provided, however, that a person after slowing to a reasonable speed and yielding the right-of-way if required, may cautiously make a right-hand turn. A left-hand turn onto a one-way traffic highway may be made on a red light after stopping and yielding to other traffic.

Some of the most common questions cyclists have are related to traffic signals. I'm asked about them all the time, in large part because there's so much jurisdictional variation on what cyclists must do to obey the law. The three most common issues are:

1. Observing the traffic signals

2. What constitutes a proper stop

3. What a cyclist can do if the traffic signal doesn't trigger

OBSERVING THE TRAFFIC SIGNALS AND STOP SIGNS

Cyclists are generally required to observe all applicable traffic laws, including the laws requiring vehicles to obey all traffic signals. There really isn't any question about this point; however, while some cyclists studiously observe this requirement, others just as studiously violate it, believing that the statute was designed with automobiles, rather than bicycles, in mind. Cyclists with this view of the law argue that because cars are massive vehicles capable of causing injury or even death to others if they violate the law, it is necessary for them to observe the traffic signals. However, the argument goes, cyclists will injure themselves only if they violate the law, and therefore should be free to choose their own level of risk.

Unfortunately, this line of reasoning is absolutely wrong on the law, because it completely disregards the fact that all persons owe all other persons a duty of care. Thus, a cyclist proceeding through an intersection owes all others on the road—drivers, cyclists, and pedestrians—a duty of care not to injure them or to damage their property. Now, while the possibility that a cyclist could injure a motorist in a collision is remote, the possibility still remains. A more likely consequence of a collision would be property damage to the motor vehicle. The possibility that a cyclist could injure another cyclist or pedestrian is less remote; although these types of collisions happen less frequently than collisions involving automobiles, they do happen, and people are injured. Thus, the argument that the cyclist is risking injuring only himself is a false one.

Some cyclists argue that bicycles are not cars and therefore shouldn't be subject to laws regulating cars. There are two variations of this argument. The first variation in effect confuses "vehicles" with "cars" and disregards the fact that all vehicles—including bicycles—are subject to the law. In fact, as we've seen, cyclists gained legal rights when bicycles were classified as vehicles; they were given all of the rights that operators of other vehicles enjoy. Thus, the argument that cyclists shouldn't be subject to the law because they're "not cars" actually undermines the cyclist's right to the road. The second variation of the argument is that bicycles are vehicles but they are not cars, and that there's no reason the laws should not reflect the differences between these classes of vehicles in ways that actually meet the needs of cyclists. This argument is more sophisticated and is legally defensible. There is some risk that creating separate laws for bicycles and automobiles could lead to a second-class legal status for bicycles. However, some would argue that in some respects bicycles already have second-class legal status, and therefore that fear of second-class status should not deter cyclists from pursuing legislation that meets the needs of cyclists.

One example of specialized legislation for cyclists is Idaho's "stop as yield" statute. Under this statute, a cyclist approaching an intersection regulated by a stop sign may treat it as a yield sign, proceeding through the intersection without stopping if there is no traffic with a superior right-of-way, and yielding if another vehicle or pedestrian is present and has the right-of-way. This section of the law benefits cyclists by allowing them to conserve momentum when the intersection is clear. The law also addresses red lights, requiring cyclists to stop at them, but allows them to proceed through if no cross-traffic is approaching. This section of the statute is intended to allow cyclists to avoid waiting at the intersection and reflects a technological reality: The magnetic plates that detect waiting vehicles and trigger the lights to change are often designed to detect the larger mass of automobiles and are not sensitive enough to detect a bicycle.

Many cyclists who dislike traffic signals believe that Idaho's statute should be widely adopted to govern the actions of cyclists at intersections. But there are two points cyclists must keep in mind. First, and most obviously, the Idaho statute is *not* the law in most states. Thus, cyclists are still required to observe traffic signals according to the laws of their state. Second, and perhaps most importantly, proponents of the Idaho law often fail to understand that it still requires cyclists to stop at red lights. Thus, even if the "stop as yield" law were adopted by every state, cyclists would still be required to stop at red lights, and they would still be subject to traffic citations for failure to stop. Cyclists who run red lights would still be in violation of the law if they ran red lights following passage of a "stop as yield" law. This is not to say that such laws *shouldn't* be adopted; rather, it is simply to point out that cyclists must stop at red lights whether their state adopts the law or not.

Now, although the law in every state requires vehicles to obey traffic signals, at least one motorist has argued that motorists have no duty to yield to cyclists at intersections. In *People v. Marr* (2001), a New York trial court heard a case in which a motorist, Irene Marr, struck cyclist Joseph Bunke at an intersection in which the motorist had a stop sign and the cyclist didn't. The trial court noted that after the prosecution had presented its case, "the defense then made a motion to dismiss, not by disputing the fact that the intersection was controlled by a stop sign, not by disputing the fact that [Ms. Marr] failed to yield to Mr. Bunke, but on the basis that [state law] did not require [Ms. Marr] to yield to Mr. Bunke because [the cyclist] was not operating a vehicle as that term is defined in the [traffic code]. It is not disputed that Mr. Bunke was operating a bicycle, which is a device operated by human power, and is therefore not a vehicle as defined in the [traffic code]."[13] However, the court further noted that in New York, bicyclists have all the rights and duties of those operating vehicles. The court reasoned that had the tables been turned, Bunke would have been required to yield to Marr, and that he therefore had the same "right to proceed through the intersection without being struck."

WHAT CONSTITUTES A PROPER STOP?

This is one of the most perplexing legal questions cyclists face. Let's assume that a cyclist comes to an intersection and must stop. What must the cyclist do to be in compliance with the law? If you're driving a car, it's a simple question to answer: Your car must come to a complete stop to be in compliance with the law, and you must look for and yield to traffic with a superior right-of-way. But what if you're on your bike? The law requires you to observe the traffic signals, which means you must stop at a stop sign or red light, but what exactly does "stop" mean? Clearly, it should mean "complete stop," but that doesn't really tell us enough. What if a cyclist comes to a "complete stop"—that is, the cessation of all forward momentum—but is making a trackstand? Does that count as a complete stop? Or must the cyclist stop and set a foot down? And if the cyclist must put a foot down, for how long?

There's a legal answer to this question, but there are also the practical considerations of the interpretation of the statute in a given jurisdiction. However, even taking these practical considerations into account, the standards in a given jurisdiction may not be consistent. For example, the Traffic Division of the Police Bureau in Portland, Oregon, is on record as saying that a complete stop is all that is necessary—there is no requirement to put a foot down. Nevertheless, at least one Portland cyclist has been cited for not putting a foot down.

The legal requirements for a stop depend, however, on case law. For roadway vehicles, "stopping" at a traffic control device has two components: coming to a halt and looking for, and yielding to, vehicles with a superior right-of-way. In a 1951 Minnesota case, *Bohnen v. Gorr,* in which a cyclist and a motor vehicle collided after both ran through stop signs, the court put it this way: "One of the main purposes of the statute requiring a vehicle to stop before entering a through highway is to afford the driver a reasonable opportunity to observe approaching traffic on the highway to be crossed or entered. . . . It was not enough to stop at the 'Stop' sign.

13 *People v. Marr,* 721 N.Y.S.2d 737 (N.Y. Just. Ct. 2001).

It was their duty to stop and to observe where stopping and observing would be efficient and meet the purpose of the 'Stop' warning."[14]

Thus, merely meeting the technical formality of stopping is legally inadequate. The stop must be sufficient to allow the cyclist to appraise the right-of-way conditions and make a safe judgment. This argument cuts both ways, however. Even a brief trackstand is adequate if it gives the cyclist enough opportunity to observe and make a decision. If you want to fight an unfair "stop means dismount" argument, this is the logic to use: *I did stop, and the stop was of sufficient duration under the circumstances that any reasonable cyclist of my level of experience could safely and courteously observe and appraise the need to yield or proceed.*

Many municipal officials believe that to "stop," a cyclist is required to put at least one foot on the ground. I have tracked model traffic codes back to their origins and can find no such provision. However, it is possible that this belief came out of a judge's decision in the 1897 case *Robertson v. Pennsylvania Railroad Company*. He wrote: "The facts in regard to the decedent's negligence are not disputed. He was riding a bicycle, and when he came to the railroad, which at that point had four tracks, a freight train was passing, for which he had to wait. He did not dismount, but made what is called a 'bicycler's stop,' by circling on his wheel round and round. When the freight train passed, he started across, without dismounting, and was struck by the train coming in the opposite direction."[15]

Marion Robertson sued the railroad for negligently causing her husband's death; the railroad claimed that the cyclist was to blame for his own death. The family countered that Robertson had followed the *spirit* of the law; however, the court wasn't buying this argument: "The real contention of the [family] is embodied in the proposition that the circling round and round constituted a legal as well as a bicycler's stop. No such proposition can be entertained for a moment. . . . The law requires a full stop, not only for the sake of time, and opportunity for observation, but to secure undivided attention, and the substantial, and not merely perfunctory, performance of the duty to look and listen. Riding round and round in large or small circles, waiting for a chance to shoot across, is not a stop at all, either in form or substance."

By the time a remarkably similar case, *Cullen v. New York, Philadelphia, and Norfolk Railroad Company* (1916), was tried in New York nearly twenty years later, the "Robertson Rule" had become the standard; quoting Robertson, the Cullen court declared: "It was the duty of the de-

14 *Bohnen v. Gorr*, 47 N.W.2d 459 (Minn. 1951).

15 *Robertson v. Pennsylvania R. Co.*, 36A. 403 (Pa. 1897).

ceased [cyclist] to stop there and to dismount in order to make a stop effective for the purpose of looking and listening. The general rule requires that a bicyclist must dismount, or, at least bring his wheel to such a stop as will enable him to look up and down the tracks and listen in the manner required of a pedestrian."[16]

The common law duty to stop has been superseded by formal legislative laws, which are typically based on the Uniform Vehicle Code. However, although the law requires cyclists to stop at uncontrolled intersections, stop signs, and red lights, the UVC is silent on the definition of "stopping" as specifically applied to cyclists. Therefore, the "Robertson Rule" may have both historical interest as well as precedential value in determining what cyclists must do to comply with the law. First, *Robertson* instructs as to where the rule that you must "dismount"—or at least put a foot down—comes from. Second, because *Robertson* is the seminal case that defines what it means for a cyclist to stop, it may be persuasive evidence in a traffic case to show that the law does not require a dismount as long as the stop is a full stop and as long as it is effective in meeting the duty to look and listen.

TRIGGERING A TRAFFIC SIGNAL

Many times, when a cyclist arrives at an intersection controlled by a traffic light, the cyclist is unable to trigger the light to change because the sensor placed under the road surface to detect the presence of automobiles is incapable of detecting an object as small as a bicycle. The result is that the cyclist will wait for the light to change.

And wait. And wait. And wait. And nothing will happen, because the traffic signal doesn't "know" that the cyclist is there. Increasingly, some cities are installing sensors that are capable of detecting a bicycle, but despite this progress, many signals are still incapable of detecting the presence of a cyclist.

So what happens when you come to an intersection and your bicycle does not "trigger" the light? What are your options under the law? Do you have the right to break the law by running the light, or do you have to get off the bike and hit the pedestrian walk button?

First, let's talk about how traffic signals work. The technology used at most intersections is called an "inductive loop sensor." The sensor functions as a type of metal detector for cars, trucks, and even bicycles. An electrical field is created around the wire under the ground, which detects the metal material of the vehicle to cause a change in the electrical

16 *Cullen v. New York, Philadelphia, and Norfolk R. Co.* (1916).

field. Once the change is sensed, a message is sent to the traffic signal controller, and soon after this the light changes to green. Of course, the system is not foolproof, as you no doubt have experienced. So, to return to our initial question, what does a cyclist do when faced with the problem of a sensor not recognizing a bicycle?

As you already know from the discussion above, bicyclists are required by law to stop at red lights and must follow the same rules as cars about remaining stopped until the light changes to green. If you come to a red light on your bicycle and run into this problem, you have several options. First and foremost, stop at the red light and wait for the light to turn green. If your bicycle does not seem to have enough metal to trigger the sensor, look on the ground for a square or octagonal pattern of thin lines in the pavement. These lines represent slots that were cut for the sensors. The cut line in the road is the ideal spot to ride your bike over because of the placement of the wires within these lines.

Once you have located the cut lines in the road and positioned your bicycle above the lines, what if the light has still not triggered? Should you run the red? Should you wait for a car to come up behind you? Should you get off your bike and push the pedestrian walk button (if one exists)? It turns out that in every state, this is one instance where you can legally run a red light. The sensor is considered defective in this case, and it is not considered against the law to go through a defective red light. However, in order to be sure that the signal is defective (and to be able to demonstrate in court that you had sufficient reason to be sure), you should sit through the equivalent of one complete light cycle—about three minutes—without the light being triggered. If you still don't get the green, the light is defective, and you can then proceed through the intersection, yielding the right-of-way to any approaching vehicles. If you were to receive a ticket for running the red light, fault should be placed on the person who installed the sensor. If you were to become involved in an accident as a result, fault would be apportioned among the person who installed the sensor, you, and the motorist, according to your comparative liabilities.

2-10 CARRYING LIMITS

Uniform Vehicle Code Section 11-1203. Riding on bicycles. No bicycle shall be used to carry more persons at one time than the number for which it is designed or equipped, except that an adult rider may carry a child securely attached to adult rider in a back pack or sling.

Uniform Vehicle Code Section 11-1205. Clinging to vehicles. (a) No person riding upon any bicycle, coaster, roller skates, sled or toy vehicle shall attach the same or himself to any (streetcar or) vehicle upon a roadway. (b) This section shall not prohibit attaching a bicycle trailer or bicycle semitrailer to a bicycle if that trailer or semitrailer has been designed for such attachment.
Uniform Vehicle Code Section 11-1207. Carrying articles. No person operating a bicycle shall carry any package, bundle, or article which prevents the use of both hands in the control and operation of the bicycle. A person operating a bicycle shall keep at least one hand on the handlebars at all times.

In some parts of the world, bicycles are true workhorses, carrying people and loads to the limits of the bicycle's capacity and rider's ability. Not so in our part of the world. There are three separate provisions in the UVC relating to the carrying limits of bicycles. First, a bicycle may carry only as many riders as it is designed to carry. Thus, unless a bicycle is a tandem, triple, or greater—or unless it is equipped with more than one seat—it is illegal to carry more than one rider on the bike. There are exceptions for additional seats—especially for parents carrying children. The law recognizes standard methods of taking a child along, whether in a special seat on the parent's bike, on a trail-a-bike or in a trailer, or in a backpack or sling.

A separate section of the UVC in fact specifies that trailers may be attached to bicycles. Bicycles with more riders than seats are usually the forté of kids and of the Dutch, who ride bicycles far more frequently than Americans do and seem completely comfortable piling on as many riders as can fit. Nevertheless, in this country having a passenger sitting on your handlebars or sitting on the saddle, while you stand, is a statutory violation of the duty cyclists owe to others to safely operate their vehicle. However, that duty applies to the cyclist only; generally, a passenger riding in violation of the statute will not be held liable in the event of an accident, unless the passenger exercised some control of the bicycle.

In addition to these provisions, a third section prohibits carrying any "package, bundle, or article which prevents the use of both hands in the control and operation of the bicycle." This is a somewhat ambiguous provision; for example, it obviously means that you can't ride while carrying a package that would prevent you from operating your bicycle with both hands. But could it mean that you can't carry any item at any time—a water bottle, a banana, or a cell phone, for example? Possibly. However, this section also requires that one hand be kept on the handlebars at all times, which means that you're not required to use two hands to operate your bike. So perhaps drinking from your water bottle, eating that banana, or making that call isn't illegal?[17] The statute is certainly ambiguous enough to lend itself to more than one interpretation. Following the conservative interpretation—that you cannot carry any article that will prevent you from operating your bike with both hands, but you are not required to keep both hands on the bars at all times—should keep you free from any legal problems. Although it's unlikely that a law-enforcement officer would cite you for carrying a water bottle, for instance, there is a possibility that riding in violation of this statute would create a rebuttable presumption of negligence in the event of an accident.

2-11 DISTRACTED RIDING

As any bike commuter can tell you, distracted drivers are a major problem on the roads, leading to many close encounters, or worse. In fact, the Network of Employers for Traffic Safety estimates that distracted driving is at the root of anywhere from one-quarter to one-half of the 6 million traffic accidents that occur each year. Distracted driving is characterized by a "triggering event"—something external to the driver—that distracts the vehicle operator from the task of driving. This triggering event can be any external distraction, such as eating, adjusting the stereo, looking for an item, having an argument, disciplining the kids, shaving, applying makeup, reading, talking on the phone, or text messaging. Distracted driving can be distinguished from its close relative, inattentive driving, by the fact that it requires that external trigger; inattentive driving is instead characterized by daydreaming, or being distracted by your own thoughts. Although distracted driving encompasses many activities, what little legislative action there has been has generally focused exclusively on cell-phone use.

However, some states have "careless driving" or "inattentive driving" provisions that *might* be construed to cover earplug use while cycling, depending on the language of the statute. For example, consider the following statutes:

> **Oregon Revised Statutes 811.135. Careless driving.** A person commits the offense of careless driving if the person drives any vehicle upon a highway or other premises described in this section in a manner that endangers or would be likely to endanger any person or property.

17 But before you make that call, see the two following subsections in this section (§2-11), dealing with cell phones and earplugs.

Colorado Revised Statutes 42-4-1402. Careless driving. Any person who drives any motor vehicle, bicycle, or motorized bicycle in a careless and imprudent manner, without due regard for the width, grade, curves, corners, traffic, and use of the streets and highways and all other attendant circumstances, is guilty of careless driving.

Regardless of whether your state explicitly prohibits the use of cell phones or earplugs, it's *possible* that their use could be considered careless or inattentive cycling; however, not every state has a careless or inattentive driving prohibition. Keep in mind that this is a changing area of the law. As the use of iPods and cell phones on the road proliferates, you should count on other state legislatures addressing the issue. Keep current on the laws in your state to make sure you know what you're allowed to do on those long training rides. Now let's take a closer look at the laws on cell phones and earplugs.

CELL PHONES

Several studies have shown that cell phones are a significant distraction for drivers. For example, one study found that a driver who is using a cell phone has significantly slower reaction times, taking up to three times as long to brake as a driver who is not using a cell phone. In another study, drivers who were using cell phones performed at a more impaired level than drivers who were on the cusp of being legally drunk. An Australian study found that drivers who use cell phones—whether handheld or hands-free—were four times more likely to be involved in an accident. Finally, other studies have shown that drivers exhibit a type of "tunnel vision" while on the phone, failing to notice peripheral objects and events, and that the distraction from cell-phone use occurs regardless of whether the phone is handheld or used with headsets and speakerphones. The source of distraction isn't the task of manipulating the phone—it's the "cognitive overload" from engaging in a telephone conversation while operating a vehicle.

Nevertheless, where state legislatures have chosen to address the problem—and only a few have addressed it so far—they have focused exclusively on banning use of handheld phones while driving, despite strong public support for a ban on all cell-phone use while driving.[18] Some states do have specific restrictions on cell-phone use that stop

18 Sixty-nine percent of the general public support a ban on cell phones while driving. To date, the wireless communications industry has been extremely effective at derailing any legislation curbing the use of all cell phones while driving, despite overwhelming public support for the legislation.

FIGURE 2.1 Cyclist with Cell Phone

short of complete bans (such as bans on cell-phone use for new drivers or bans for drivers of school buses), and more states are now debating proposals to ban cell phones. The number of states banning cell phones while driving is likely to increase, so keep abreast of the laws in your state. However, even when cell-phone use while driving is not illegal, it can be used as evidence of negligence in the event of an accident.[19]

But what about using a phone while riding a bike? Can you be cited for that in a state that has banned cell-phone use while driving? Or even in one that has not? Possibly, although it seems unlikely. It would all depend on whether you're being cited for cell-phone use or for operating a bicycle while carrying an "article which prevents the use of both hands in the control and operation of the bicycle." If you are stopped for the first offense, using a cell phone while riding, it would have to be in a state that has banned the use of cell phones while driving. None of the states that have done so thus far have made a cell-phone ban explicitly applicable to cyclists, but that does not mean such a law would not apply to you.[20] Moreover, if your state has a statute on the books saying you cannot operate a bicycle while carrying any article that prevents you from using both hands, you could be cited under it for using your cell phone. I'm not

19 Proving cell-phone use is a simple matter of subpoenaing the cell-phone records of the driver and entering them into evidence. For more information on cell-phone laws in each state, see http://www.statehighwaysafety.org/html/stateinfo/laws/cellphone_laws.html.

20 The statutes prohibit the use of handheld cell phones by operators of "motor vehicles." Emergency calls are exempted from the prohibition.

aware of any cases like this, but that doesn't mean that cyclists haven't been, or couldn't be, cited.

Furthermore, as with automobiles, we have to consider negligence. If you are riding while using a phone, and you are involved in an accident, the question of your negligence will be raised. If riding while using a cell phone *is* a statutory violation, then your cell-phone use would be prima facie evidence of negligence.[21] If prima facie evidence of your negligence is introduced, you will be presumed negligent unless you can present contradictory evidence. And even if using a cell phone while riding is *not* a statutory violation in your state, your use of a cell phone while riding could still be introduced as evidence of negligence in the event of an accident. However, in the absence of a statutory violation, the introduction of the evidence would not lead to a presumption of negligence; rather, it would just be evidence of negligence for the jury to consider. Because distracted riding and liability for negligence have potentially serious consequences, you should consider protecting yourself by pulling over and stopping anytime you need to use your phone while riding.

EARBUDS AND HEADSETS

> **General Laws of Rhode Island Section 31-23-51. Earphones and headsets prohibited.** (a) A person shall not drive a bicycle or motor vehicle upon any highway while wearing earphones or a headset. **Annotated California Codes Section 27400. Wearing of headsets, earplugs, and hearing protectors.** No person operating any motor vehicle or bicycle shall wear any headset covering, or any earplugs in, both ears. The prohibition of this section does not apply to any of the following: . . . (d) Any person wearing personal hearing protectors in the form of custom earplugs or molds that are designed to attenuate injurious noise levels. The custom plugs or molds shall be designed in a manner so as not to inhibit the wearer's ability to hear a siren or horn from an emergency vehicle or a horn from another motor vehicle. (e) Any person using a prosthetic device which aids the hard of hearing.

There is some evidence that, like cell-phone use, listening to music also distracts drivers. In particular, the higher the volume of the music, the longer it will take for the driver to react. Additionally, there is some evidence that the type of music listened to affects mood, and therefore

21 In some states, it would be per se negligence, which means that, because you violated the law, you were negligent.

47

driving, with some types of music enhancing feelings of calm, and other types enhancing feelings of aggression. Despite this evidence, statutes limiting the use of earphones and headsets by cyclists and drivers are focused on the ability of the cyclist or driver to hear sirens and horns from other vehicles, rather than on distracted or aggressive riding.

The majority of states have no prohibition against wearing headsets or earphones while driving; about a quarter of the states do regulate their use. Most of these states prohibit the use of headsets by operators of vehicles, and because cyclists are subject to the same duties as operators of vehicles, the prohibition reaches cyclists as well as motorists. Of the states that do regulate the use of earphones, about half prohibit the use of any headsets, whether covering one ear or both; Rhode Island specifically includes cyclists in the prohibition. The other half of the states prohibit the use of headsets covering *both* ears but allow an earplug to be inserted in one ear. Delaware and Maryland specifically prohibit their use by cyclists; however, in Maryland the prohibition does not apply to cyclists riding on a bike path.

Generally, the codes make exceptions for hearing protection and hearing aid devices in specific circumstances, but nobody out there should be under the impression that all you have to do is claim that you're wearing iPod earplugs for "hearing protection" and you can avoid a ticket. It doesn't work like that; you'll need to meet one of the specific exceptions outlined in the code to avoid a ticket.

Now let's throw another layer of complexity into the mix: What about cell-phone headsets? Four states that prohibit the use of headsets make an explicit exception for cell-phone earplugs covering one ear only; those states are Florida, Illinois, Louisiana, and Pennsylvania. Six states do not prohibit the use of cell-phone earplugs in one ear; those states are California, Delaware, Maryland, Minnesota, Ohio, and Virginia. Even though Colorado prohibits the use of earphones while cycling, it does not prohibit their use for *cell phones* while cycling, because, as in Ohio, prohibited earphones must be a "device which provides the listener with radio programs, music, or other recorded information," a definition that does not include cell phones.[22] Georgia permits the "proper use" of cell phones, although earplugs are prohibited; similarly, Rhode Island does not prohibit the use of cell phones, but it does prohibit the use of earplugs. This list should not be considered definitive. For example, New York, New Jersey, Connecticut, and the District of Columbia all *require* the operator of a vehicle to use an earplug for cell phones. As you can see, the law regarding cell phones and earplugs varies widely from state

22   Newer cell phones with music technology would obviously fall under the prohibition, however.

to state, and with new technologies that offer telephone, camera, music, and more all in one device, new complications will be presented.

Ultimately, whether a state actually prohibits the use of earplugs or not, we should all keep in mind the purpose behind the statutes: to prohibit a use that would "inhibit the wearer's ability to hear a siren or horn from an emergency vehicle or a horn from another motor vehicle." Whether earplugs are prohibited or not, impaired hearing and cognitive overload are things we all need to consider when we're sharing the road with so many tons of fast-moving steel.

2-12 BICYCLING UNDER THE INFLUENCE

Oregon Revised Statutes, Section 813.010. Driving under the influence of intoxicants; penalties. (1) A person commits the offense of driving while under the influence of intoxicants if the person drives a vehicle while the person: (a) Has .08 percent or more by weight of alcohol in the blood . . . (b) Is under the influence of intoxicating liquor, a controlled substance or an inhalant; or (c) Is under the influence of any combination of intoxicating liquor, an inhalant and a controlled substance . . .

Utah Code Annotated, Section41-6a-1102. Bicycle and device propelled by human power and moped riders subject to chapter—exception. (1) Except as provided under subsection (2) or as specified under this part, a person operating a bicycle or device propelled by human power, or a moped has all the rights and is subject to all of the provisions of this chapter applicable to the operator of any other vehicle. (2) A person operating a nonmotorized bicycle or a vehicle or device propelled by human power is not subject to the penalties related to operator licenses under alcohol and drug-related traffic offenses.

Annotated California Codes, Section 21200.5 Riding under influence of alcohol and drugs; chemical tests; punishment. Notwithstanding section 21200, it is unlawful for any person to ride a bicycle upon a highway while under the influence of an alcoholic beverage or any drug, or under the combined influence of an alcoholic beverage and any drug. Any person arrested for a violation of this section may request to have a chemical test made of the alcoholic or drug content of that person's blood, breath, or urine for the purpose of determining the alcoholic or drug content of that person's blood . . . and if so requested, the arresting officer shall have the test performed. A conviction of a violation of this

section shall be punished by a fine of not more than two hundred fifty dollars ($250) . . .
Revised Code of Washington Section 46.61.790. Intoxicated bicyclists. (1) A law enforcement officer may offer to transport a bicycle rider who appears to be under the influence of alcohol or any drug and who is walking or moving along or within the right of way of a public roadway, unless the rider is to be taken into protective custody under RCW 70.96A.120 . . .
South Dakota Codified Laws Section 32-23-22. Chapter not applicable to person riding animal or foot-pedal conveyance. The provisions of this [driving under the influence] chapter do not apply to any person who is riding: (1) A horse or any other animal; and (2) A bicycle, tricycle, or other unpowered foot-pedal conveyance.

When a bicycle has the legal status of a vehicle, one of the questions raised is what duties are applicable to the operator of a bicycle? Generally, cyclists have all of the duties applicable to operators of other vehicles. Of course, this implies that cyclists have some sort of duty—whether common-law or statutory—not to ride while under the influence of intoxicants. And in fact, cyclists do have common-law and statutory duties not to ride while under the influence of intoxicants.

As we're beginning to discover, riding a bike while under the influence of intoxicants is hazardous. The Johns Hopkins Medical Institutions Office of Communications and Public Affairs reported the following in a press release:

> *Drinking alcohol and bicycling don't mix well, say Johns Hopkins researchers, whose study of 466 Maryland bicyclists found that a third of fatally injured riders had elevated blood alcohol levels at the time of their accident. In addition, a blood alcohol concentration of 0.08 grams per deciliter—the legal level of drunkenness in most states—was found to increase the rider's risk of fatal or serious injury by 2,000 percent. . . .*
>
> *Alcohol may play an even greater role than indicated by this study, the researchers said, since the group did not look at bicycle injuries occurring at night, when 56 percent of fatal bicycling injuries and 32 percent of serious bicycling injuries occur.*
>
> *"Riding a bike requires a higher level of psychomotor skills and physical coordination than driving a car, so alcohol has an even*

stronger effect on bicyclists than drivers," says Guohua Li, associate professor of emergency medicine and lead author of the study.[23]

The risks are clear: Though motorists driving under the influence account for most cycling fatalities, a significant number of cycling fatalities are caused by the cyclist's own impairment. Even if impaired cyclists escape the risks to their lives, there are legal risks involved as well. In every state, there is a common-law duty of care owed to all other persons. Any cyclist who is riding while impaired and is involved in an accident would be subject to the reasonable person standard: Would a reasonable person have ridden while impaired by alcohol?

There's a statutory legal hazard as well. When it comes to Bicycling Under the Influence (BUI), the states have enacted a range of approaches. Because the consequences can be quite severe in those states that do make it an offense, if you drink alcohol at all you should be familiar with the laws in your state. There are four basic approaches to BUI:

1. DUI law applies to cyclists.

2. DUI law (but not the penalties) applies to cyclists.

3. BUI is treated as a separate offense.

4. DUI law does not apply to cyclists.

Generally, depending on the state, BUI will fall into one of these four categories. Let's take a closer look at some specific state examples to see how these four approaches work.

DUI LAW APPLIES TO CYCLISTS

As you may recall from Chapter 1, most states have adopted some form of the statement that "every person riding a bicycle upon a public way shall have all of the rights and all of the duties applicable to the driver of any other vehicle." In some states, such as Oregon, this ubiquitous statement is interpreted, among other things, to mean that cyclists are subject to the provisions of Oregon's DUI statute, and cyclists can and will be prosecuted for DUI in Oregon. In Oregon, a first conviction for DUI is a Class A misdemeanor; it rises to a Class C felony if there have been three convictions within the previous ten years. Unlike many traffic offenses, a conviction for DUI is a criminal offense rather than a traffic offense, and will result in jail time and a criminal record. Under Oregon's Habitual Offender Program, three convictions for DUI within a

---

23 "One in Three Fatal Bicycle Accidents Linked to Alcohol," Johns Hopkins Medical Institutions Office of Communications and Public Affairs, February 20, 2001.

five-year period will result in a revocation of your driving privileges, and this is in addition to the criminal penalties imposed for DUI. Thus, in Oregon, bicycling under the influence is treated exactly the same as driving under the influence.

DUI LAW (BUT NOT THE PENALTIES) APPLIES TO CYCLISTS

In Utah, the DUI statute applies to bicycle riders, as it does in Oregon. However, Utah law specifies that the "penalties related to operator licenses under alcohol and drug-related traffic offenses" do not apply to cyclists. Thus, in Utah, cyclists can be prosecuted for criminal offenses ranging from a Class B misdemeanor to a third-degree felony, depending upon the circumstances, for bicycling under the influence, and will be subject to fines and jail time for the offense, but will not have their driving privileges restricted.

BUI IS TREATED AS A SEPARATE OFFENSE

In California, bicycling under the influence is a criminal offense rather than a traffic offense, as in Oregon. However, California treats bicycling under the influence and driving under the influence as two separate matters. BUI is punishable by a fine rather than by jail time. For underage drinkers, each conviction for bicycling under the influence will result in a one-year suspension of that person's driving privilege. If the person does not yet have a driver's license, each conviction will result in a one-year delay in receiving driving privileges. Otherwise, bicycling under the influence in California will not affect one's driving record as it would in Oregon.

There are a couple of other important differences between DUIs and BUIs in California. Under California's DUI statute, there's a rebuttable presumption that you are over the limit if your blood alcohol level is 0.08 or higher within three hours of operating a motor vehicle. This means that it's presumed that you were over the limit when you were operating the motor vehicle unless you produce evidence to rebut that presumption. However, there is no such presumption in the BUI statute; instead, the prosecution would have to prove that you were actually over the limit at the time you were operating your bicycle. Additionally, if you are stopped for suspicion of DUI, you are deemed to have consented to a blood alcohol test. There is no such consent if you are stopped for BUI. The statute does allow the cyclist to request a blood alcohol test, but the cyclist is not required to submit to a test.

DUI LAW DOES NOT APPLY TO CYCLISTS

Finally, in some states, BUI is not an offense. However, even when it is not an offense, BUI may be handled differently from state to state. For purposes of comparison, let's look at how two states, Washington and South Dakota, handle BUI.

The Washington Approach

In Washington, bicycling under the influence is not an offense at all. However, if a cyclist "appears to be under the influence of alcohol or any drug" and is either walking or riding "within the right of way of a public roadway," a law-enforcement officer "may offer" to transport the intoxicated rider to "a safe place" or to release the intoxicated rider "to a competent person." However, if the rider refuses the officer's help, the officer "shall not provide the assistance offered."

That doesn't mean the cyclist may continue to ride while intoxicated. If "the officer determines that impoundment is necessary to reduce a threat to public safety, and there are no reasonable alternatives to impoundment," the officer may impound the bicycle. Additionally, law-enforcement officers are authorized to take "a person who appears to be incapacitated or gravely disabled by alcohol or other drugs" into protective custody. However, the protective custody does not constitute an arrest, and the person taken into custody may not be charged with a crime.

The South Dakota Approach

In South Dakota, the state legislature has amended state law to specify that the DUI statute does not apply to any person who is riding "a bicycle, tricycle, or other unpowered foot-pedal conveyance." Before the statute was changed, the DUI laws applied to persons who were driving or "in actual physical control of any vehicle." Now, with the revision to the law, cyclists can no longer be prosecuted under the DUI statute for riding a bicycle while intoxicated, and there is no separate BUI statute under which they can be prosecuted; the legislature has determined that having people ride their bicycles and horses home after they've had one too many is preferable to having them drive home. Nevertheless, that doesn't mean you can't be prosecuted in South Dakota for riding while intoxicated. As state legislators noted when discussing the bill, you can still be prosecuted for disorderly conduct, which is a Class 2 misdemeanor punishable by thirty days' imprisonment, a $500 fine, or both. So while bicycling under the influence won't be treated as a DUI in South Dakota, there are still potential consequences.

TRAVELERS BEWARE

In addition to state penalties for bicycling under the influence, cyclists should be aware of potential restrictions placed upon travelers with DUI convictions. As an example, under Canadian law, cyclists convicted of a criminal offense—such as bicycling under the influence—will be deemed "criminally inadmissible" by Citizenship and Immigration Canada and will not be permitted to enter the country. Canada determines criminal inadmissibility by comparing the elements of Canadian law with those of the foreign jurisdiction. If you've been convicted of a BUI or DUI in your state, Canada will look at the elements of the crime in your state to determine whether they are comparable to the elements of DUI in Canada; if they are comparable, Canada will deny entry.

In order to gain entry to Canada after a criminal conviction, a cyclist would need to demonstrate "rehabilitation," which means that "you lead a stable life and that you are unlikely to be involved in any further criminal activity." In order to be considered rehabilitated, you must apply for rehabilitation at a visa office outside of Canada. You will usually need to supply proof that five years or more have elapsed since the end of your sentence and that further criminal activity is unlikely. An application for rehabilitation can take a year or more to process, so you will want to apply well in advance of your trip. You should also be prepared to pay a hefty fee with your application; all fees are at least $200 Canadian, while other, more serious crimes require a $1,000 Canadian fee. You would need to consult with Citizenship and Immigration Canada to determine the fee required. For those cyclists who would like to visit Canada but have a conviction in their past, you can learn more about the process through Citizenship and Immigration Canada.[24]

But Canada's rules and regulations are just an example of the obstacles you may encounter if you wish to travel abroad. A DUI or BUI conviction could affect your chances of participating in a cycling event overseas. So whatever the rules are in your state, be aware that bicycling under the influence can affect you in many ways. The bottom line, of course, is your safety and the safety of others with whom you share the road. If you have a conviction and wish to visit another country, check with the immigration department of country.

---

24 See Canada's immigration website at http://www.cic.gc.ca/english/visit/faq-inadmissibility.html.

Where to Ride

In addition to *how* you ride, your duties—as well as your rights—determine *where* you can ride. In fact, the question of where to ride was often central to the seminal cases that established the cyclist's right to the road—local governments began restricting where cyclists could ride almost as soon as they began appearing on the roads. In turn, cyclists defended their access to the roads, both in the courtroom and in the statehouses. Over a century later, the question of where to ride remains central to cyclist rights. Cyclists continue to resist government attempts (and, as we shall see in Chapter 5, private attempts) to restrict their constitutional rights. But before we examine the constitutional issues raised by government attempts to restrict where you can ride, let's consider how your duties, as well as your rights, determine where you can ride.

2-13 THE NORMAL AND REASONABLE FLOW OF TRAFFIC

> **Uniform Vehicle Code Section 11-801. Basic rule.** No person shall drive a vehicle at a speed greater than is reasonable and prudent under the conditions, including the actual and potential hazards then existing. Consistent with the foregoing, every person shall drive at a safe and appropriate speed when approaching and crossing an intersection or railroad grade crossing, when approaching and going around a curve, when approaching the crest of a hill, when traveling upon any narrow or winding roadway, and when any special hazards exist with respect to pedestrians or other traffic or by reason of weather or highway conditions.

"The normal and reasonable" flow of traffic is a term that appears in at least three statutes of the UVC, and it has the potential to impact where and how you can ride. The relevant statutes are:

- The statute requiring cyclists who are not riding at the "normal speed of traffic" to ride as close as practicable to the right

- The statute prohibiting vehicle operators from driving "at such a slow speed as to impede the normal and reasonable movement of traffic"

- The statute prohibiting cyclists who are riding two abreast from impeding "the normal and reasonable flow of traffic"

Unfortunately, the courts haven't really told us what "the normal and reasonable flow of traffic" means. Well, let's try to make some sense of it anyway. When states use the phrase "normal and reasonable flow of traffic," it's always within the context of a law that addresses where you may ride in relation to other traffic. In one case, *Satter v. Turner* (1957), the Minnesota Supreme Court held that these "slow speed" statutes were "intended to apply to vehicles traveling in the normal stream of traffic."[25] This implies that the "normal flow of traffic" is the mainstream flow of traffic on a roadway, rather than traffic at the margins of the roadway. And in fact, that interpretation is consistent with UVC Section 11-301 (b), which requires that slow-moving vehicles be driven either in the right-hand lane or as close as practicable to the right-hand curb.[26]

However, in Minnesota, as in many other states, *traffic* means "pedestrians, ridden or herded animals, vehicles, streetcars, and other conveyances, either singly or together, while using any highway for purposes of travel." Despite this all-inclusive definition of traffic, in *Satter v. Turner* the Minnesota court was referring specifically to the mainstream flow of traffic, rather than to the flow of all traffic, when discussing "the normal stream of traffic." Thus, the slow-speed statutes are applicable only to *vehicles traveling in the mainstream flow of traffic, rather than to vehicles outside the mainstream flow of traffic.*

Okay, so that's one part of the phrase "normal and reasonable." Now let's look at what "reasonable" means. In traffic laws, the word "reasonable" is also used in the "basic speed rule," which prohibits speeds that are greater than is "reasonable or prudent." What is reasonable or prudent will depend upon "conditions, including actual and potential hazards then existing."[27] In *People v. Banat* (1990), the California Supreme Court held that "reasonable" refers "to the speed at which a vehicle is driven."[28] Factors that courts have used to determine whether a speed is "reasonable" include the nature, width, and grade of the roadway; the locality; traffic conditions; the driver's familiarity with the road; and the condition of the car. Essentially, this means that a reasonable speed is one that is in compliance with the basic speed rule.

Now that we understand what the "normal and reasonable" flow of traffic is, let's take a closer look at some of the statutes that utilize the "normal and reasonable flow of traffic" concept to help determine where

---

25 *Satter v. Turner*, 86 N.W.2d 85 (Minn. 1957).

26 This requirement is nearly identical to UVC Section 11-1205, which requires that bicycles traveling at less than the normal speed of traffic ride as close as practicable to the right-hand curb.

27 UVC Section 11-801 states that "no person shall drive a vehicle at a speed that is greater than is reasonable and prudent under the conditions, including actual and potential hazards then existing. Consistent with the foregoing, every person shall drive at a safe and appropriate speed when approaching and crossing an intersection or railroad grade crossing, when approaching and going around a curve, when approaching the crest of a hill, when traveling upon any narrow or winding roadway, and when special hazards exist with respect to pedestrians or other traffic or by reason of weather or highway conditions."

28 *People v. Banat*, 100 P.2d 374 (Cal. Super. 1940).

you can ride, beginning with the statute requiring you to ride "as close as practicable" to the right.

2-14 A "PRACTICABLE" DISTANCE

Uniform Vehicle Code Section 11-1205. Position on roadway.
(a) Any person operating a bicycle or a moped upon a roadway at less than the normal speed of traffic at the time and place and under the conditions then existing shall ride as close as practicable to the right-hand curb or edge of the roadway except under any of the following situations:

1. When overtaking and passing another bicycle or vehicle proceeding in the same direction.

2. When preparing for a left turn at an intersection or into a private road or driveway.

3. When reasonably necessary to avoid conditions including but not limited to: fixed or moving objects; parked or moving vehicles; bicycles; pedestrians; animals; surface hazards; or substandard width lanes that make it unsafe to continue along the right-hand curb or edge. For purposes of this section, a "substandard width lane" is a lane that is too narrow for a bicycle and a motor vehicle to travel safely side by side within the lane.

4. When riding in the right-turn-only lane.

(b) Any person operating a bicycle or a moped upon a one-way highway with two or more marked traffic lanes may ride as near the left-hand curb or edge of such roadway as practicable.

A common mistake made by law-enforcement officers (and others) is to interpret the requirement to ride "as close as practicable to the right" to mean "as close as possible." So if "practicable" means "possible," why wouldn't the state legislatures just say "as close as possible"?

Because "practicable" doesn't mean "possible." In fact, "practicable" doesn't even mean "practical," and it certainly doesn't mean "X number of feet." Yet law-enforcement officers and prosecutors have often asserted that "practicable" means "possible," "practical," or "X number of feet from the curb." In a word, they're wrong. Okay, that's two words, but you get the idea.

When the law is telling you to *ride as close as practicable to the right, it means you are required to ride as close as can reasonably be accomplished under the circumstances to the right.* Quite a mouthful, isn't it? Perhaps you can see why the statute uses the word "practicable" instead.

As you can perhaps see, the statute allows for some degree of subjectivity on the rider's part. First, the rider makes the determination of what can be "reasonably accomplished under the circumstances." This doesn't mean the rider has carte blanche to ignore the requirement to ride to the right, but it does mean that to some degree, the rider has to determine how far to the right she can reasonably ride. For example, suppose there's debris near the right curb; the rider is under no legal obligation to ride through debris. Now suppose that cars are parked along the right curb; how close to the right can the cyclist reasonably accomplish riding? Certainly, it would be *possible* for the cyclist to ride very close to the line of parked cars. But would that be a safe practice? What if a driver suddenly flings open a car door that is directly in the cyclist's path? From the perspective of what can *reasonably* be accomplished under the circumstances, the cyclist must make a subjective determination of how close to the "door zone" of the parked cars she can safely ride. That would be the distance at which the cyclist can safely ride "as close as practicable to the right" in that circumstance. The exact distance that is "as close as practicable to the right" will vary from one situation to the next, and the determination of "practicable" involves some degree of subjectivity.

Suppose, however, that the road surface adjacent to the right curb is free of any obstructions, and riding close to the curb can reasonably be accomplished without risk of injury. In that circumstance, the rider is not free to disregard the requirement to ride to the right, based on some "subjective" determination that it cannot be "reasonably accomplished." This is because the determination of what can be accomplished is not entirely subjective; the determination must also be "reasonable," and reasonable is not a subjective standard. Instead, reasonable is what the "reasonable person of ordinary prudence would do in the same situation." This is an objective, rather than a subjective, standard. It doesn't have anything to do with what you personally believe to be prudent; instead, it is the standard of behavior of the person who uses reasonable prudence—usually determined by a jury, but in traffic court, often determined by the judge.

Notice that there are two different circumstances under which you are not required to ride as close as practicable to the right. In the first circumstance, if you are riding at "the normal speed of traffic at the time and place and under the conditions then existing," you are not required to ride "as close as practicable to the right." This is a somewhat different formulation from the one using "normal and reasonable" flow of traffic as the standard in the other slow-speed statutes. Basically, it means that as long as you are riding at least as fast as other traffic is traveling on the road, you can ride in any traffic lane, unless state law prohibits that—for example, by requiring you to ride in a bike lane. Obviously, the reference to "normal speed" means that you would not be required to ride as fast as vehicles that are traveling faster than the "normal speed." Of course, that raises a question: What is meant by "normal speed"? There's no definitive answer from either the legislatures or the courts, but based on the context of the statutory language and judicial interpretations of "normal" flow of traffic and "reasonable" speed, it seems clear that "normal speed" refers to a requirement to travel at the mainstream speed of traffic when in the mainstream flow of traffic, rather than to a requirement to match the speed of any scofflaw who happens to be on the road. Note, however, that not every state makes an exception for riding at the same speed as other vehicles; therefore, you will want to check the statute in your state.

In the second circumstance, the statute allows you to depart from the requirement to ride "as close as practicable" to the right under five defined situations. One of those situations is when it would be "reasonably necessary to avoid conditions *including but not limited to:* fixed or moving objects; parked or moving vehicles; bicycles; pedestrians; animals; surface hazards; or substandard width lanes that make it unsafe to continue along the right-hand curb or edge." This is an awkward formulation. The listed hazards are exactly the sort of circumstances that make a practicable distance a fluid concept in the first place, and yet they're listed as *exceptions* to the requirement to ride "as close as practicable" to the right.

Let's look at two possible explanations. The first explanation is that "practicable" doesn't really mean "practicable"; rather it means "possible." Although this construction would make logical sense, it doesn't fit with the rules of statutory interpretation, because if the statute's authors had meant "as close as possible," they would have used "as close as possible." And as we know, they used "as close as practicable." In fact, early versions of this statute used "possible" instead of "practicable," so we know from the statute's legislative history that the authors are aware of the difference between "possible" and "practicable." Therefore, the explanation that the authors meant "possible" is not the correct interpretation of this statute. The second explanation is that an exception to the requirement to ride "as close as practicable" to the right is when it is "not practicable," with some examples of what the statute means by "not practicable." Although this interpretation might lead to the erroneous inference that "practicable" means "possible," it's a better fit with the accepted definition of practicable, and is therefore the correct interpretation. As I said, it's an awkward formulation.

The other defined situations under which you are not required to ride "as close as practicable" to the right include:

- *"When overtaking and passing another bicycle or vehicle proceeding in the same direction."* Although you are not required to be riding at "the normal speed of traffic at the time and place and under the conditions then existing" when overtaking or passing, this exception should be understood to mean that you can overtake or pass only when it would be safe to do so. For example, if there is a statute that prohibits you from entering the path of another vehicle that is so close as to constitute an immediate hazard, you must wait until there is a safe opportunity before you pass. Approaching vehicles are governed by the state equivalent of UVC Section 11-504, which requires that "every driver shall exercise due care to avoid colliding with any pedestrian or any person propelling a human powered vehicle." This doesn't mean that you can disregard the law that applies to you, but it does mean that under all circumstances—even when you are in violation of the law—a motorist must exercise due care, and when you are passing legally, motorists must allow you to complete your pass. Keep in mind, however, that once you have overtaken the other bicycle or vehicle, you are once again required to ride as close as practicable to the right. Also keep in mind that your pass will also be governed by the state equivalent of UVC Section 11-303, which requires you to pass at a safe distance and not return to the right side of the road until clear of the overtaken vehicle.

- *"When preparing for a left turn at an intersection or into a private road or driveway."* Note that the statute says "when preparing to turn left." This means that you are permitted to leave the right side of the road at a reasonable distance necessary to position yourself to make the left turn. It also means you are not in violation of the statute when you are stopped at a traffic control signal while you are waiting to make your left turn. A 1984 Oregon case, *Taylor v. Bohemia, Inc.* (1984), affirmed that the requirement to ride "as close as practicable" to the right does not apply to cyclists making left turns.[29]

- *"When riding in the right-turn-only lane."* This should be self-explanatory; the law doesn't require you to ride in the right-turn lane when you are proceeding straight through the intersection.

Finally, the statute provides that "any person operating a bicycle or a moped upon a one-way highway with two or more marked traffic lanes may ride as near the left-hand curb or edge of such roadway as practicable." This means that if you are proceeding at "less than the normal speed of traffic at the time and place and under the conditions then existing" on

29 *Taylor v. Bohemia, Inc.*, 688 P.2d 1374 (Ore. App. 1984).

a one-way road, you have the choice of riding either as close to the right, or as close to the left, as practicable. Of course, if you're riding at the normal speed of traffic at the time and place and under the conditions then existing, you may ride in any lane you choose, unless state law specifies that you must ride in a bike lane.

Let's say you're riding in compliance with this statute, and you're nevertheless cited for violating the statute. It happens, because police officers often do not understand the statute. The officer may not understand that you are required to ride to the right only under certain circumstances; likewise, he or she may not understand that a practicable distance is fluid and depends upon the particular circumstances present at any given time and location. In any legal proceedings, pay close attention to the prosecutor's argument; law enforcement and/or the prosecution will often contend that the statute requires you to ride "as close as possible to the right." As you now know, this is *not* what the statute requires. If you are defending yourself, you must challenge attempts by the prosecution to change the wording or meaning of the statute to "as close as possible," "as close as practical," or "X number of feet."

In some jurisdictions, this may be difficult, because the local ordinance may actually deviate from state law, substituting the word "practical" for "practicable." If you are being prosecuted under a local ordinance that doesn't use the same language as the state statute, you must make this argument: *Either the language of the local ordinance has the same meaning as the "practicable" language in the state statute, or the state statute is controlling and the local ordinance is void because it is in conflict with state law.* That might sound like you can't make up your mind what your argument is, but don't worry about that. Courts accept—even expect—alternative arguments from attorneys, so there's no reason you shouldn't offer an alternative argument in this particular situation.

2-15 IMPEDING TRAFFIC

Uniform Vehicle Code Section 11-805. Minimum speed regulation. (a) No person shall drive a vehicle at such a slow speed as to impede the normal and reasonable movement of traffic except when reduced speed is necessary for safe operation or is in compliance with the law. (b) Whenever the (State highway commission) or local authorities within their respective jurisdictions determine on the basis of an engineering and traffic investigation that slow speeds on any highway or part of a highway impede the normal and reasonable movement of traffic, the (commission) or

such local authority may establish a minimum speed below which
no person shall drive except when necessary for safe operation or
in compliance with the law, and that limit shall be effective when
posted upon appropriate fixed or variable signs.

The requirement that vehicle operators not drive "at such a slow speed as to impede the normal and reasonable movement of traffic" seems straightforward enough at first glance: Slow-moving vehicles are prohibited from impeding traffic. Right? Wrong.

Although that's how law enforcement has sometimes interpreted the statute, slow-moving vehicles are not in fact prohibited from impeding traffic. Let's take a second look at what the statute prohibits: "No person shall drive a vehicle at such a slow speed as to impede the normal and reasonable movement of traffic." Based on what we know about "normal and reasonable," one might say, the statute surely must be prohibiting impeding traffic if you're not moving at a "reasonable" speed in the mainstream flow of traffic. Well, not quite. And it certainly isn't saying that slow-moving vehicles are prohibited from impeding traffic. To understand why, we need to look at *Trotwood v. Selz*, a case heard in 2000 by the Ohio Court of Appeals.[30]

On July 16, 1999, a cyclist named Steven Selz was stopped by a Trotwood, Ohio, police officer and cited for violating a Trotwood ordinance that prohibited the operation of a vehicle "at such a slow speed as to impede or block the normal and reasonable movement of traffic." According to the testimony of the officer who stopped Selz, he had been riding "in the middle of the traffic lane causing cars to stop and have to go over to the other lane to get around him." Although Selz was traveling in the middle of the lane, on a road that had a posted speed limit of 45 mph, the officer testified that Selz had been "traveling at no more than 15 mph." Doesn't that *sound* like he was impeding traffic?

Not to the Ohio Court of Appeals. The problem for the court was that, contrary to what the police officer believed, the statute does not prohibit slow-moving vehicles from impeding traffic. Relying on precedent from a Georgia case involving an accident between an automobile and a slow-moving corn combine, the Ohio court explained that if the statute did prohibit slow-moving vehicles from impeding traffic, it would "be tantamount to excluding operators of these vehicles from the public roadways, something that each legislative authority, respectively, has not clearly expressed an intention to do." For both the Georgia and Ohio courts, the key to what this statute really meant lay in the capability of

---

30 *Trotwood v. Selz*, 746 N.E.2d 235 (Ohio Ct. App. 2000).

the vehicle; in each case, the slow-moving vehicle was traveling at or very close to its highest possible speed. Agreeing with the Georgia court, the Ohio court concluded that "a bicyclist is not in violation of the ordinance when he is traveling as fast as he reasonably can."

However, the court added that if Selz had been charged instead with a violation of the Ohio statute requiring him to operate his bicycle as near as practicable to the right, his conviction would have been upheld. Here's the distinction the Ohio court is making: The statute prohibiting impeding traffic applies to vehicles that are capable of traveling faster, but which are being operated at such a slow speed as to impede the normal and reasonable movement of traffic. The statute does not apply to vehicles—including bicycles—that are traveling as fast as they reasonably can, even if they are otherwise impeding traffic. However, a cyclist who is traveling as fast as he reasonably can could still be cited for violating the statute requiring bicycles to be operated as near as practicable to the right.

Keep in mind that this ruling applies only in Ohio. However, it has persuasive authority in other states, which means that courts may, if they wish, consider the Ohio court's interpretation of this statute. Because it's clear that the Ohio court interpreted the impeding traffic statute correctly, it seems likely that other courts would agree with Ohio.

2-16 RIDING IN FORMATION

> **Uniform Vehicle Code Section 11-1206. Riding two abreast.**
> Persons riding bicycles upon a roadway shall not ride more than two abreast except on paths or parts of roadways set aside for the exclusive use of bicycles. Persons riding two abreast shall not impede the normal and reasonable movement of traffic and, on a laned roadway, shall ride within a single lane.

Most states follow the UVC provision allowing cyclists to ride two abreast. In a few states, however, there is no statute allowing cyclists to ride two abreast; in those states, cyclists must ride single file. In those states that do follow the UVC's two-abreast riding rule, the statute has established four provisions.

First, you are allowed to ride two abreast. The statute doesn't explicitly say this, but that's the meaning—"Persons riding bicycles upon a roadway shall not ride more than two abreast."

Second, you cannot ride more than two abreast, except "on paths or parts of roadways set aside for the exclusive use of bicycles." This means that echelons and double pacelines that spread across the lane are prohibited, unless you're riding on a bicycles-only trail, or if you're riding on a roadway that has been set aside for the exclusive operation of bicycles—which probably means you're riding in a bicycle race. Although riding in these formations is an essential part of race training, you can be cited; in the event of an accident, riding in violation of the prohibition could be prima facie evidence of negligence.[31]

The third provision is a little more complicated, so bear with me. On "a laned roadway," persons riding two abreast "shall ride within a single lane." In the UVC, a "laned roadway" is a roadway that is divided into at least two clearly marked lanes for vehicular travel. This provision means that although you are permitted to ride two abreast, you can't take up more than one traffic lane on a laned roadway; on roads that are not laned roadways, all vehicles must be driven upon the right half of the roadway, as required under UVC Section 11-301.

And fourth, regardless of whether you're on a laned or unlaned roadway, you are prohibited from impeding "the normal and reasonable movement of traffic" while riding two abreast. This is an interesting provision. As we've seen, the "normal flow of traffic" is the mainstream flow of traffic on a roadway, rather than the flow of traffic at the margins of the roadway. Thus, the statute is applicable only to bicycles traveling in the mainstream flow of traffic; it is not applicable to bicycles traveling outside the mainstream flow of traffic. Furthermore, that mainstream flow of traffic must be traveling at a "reasonable" speed, which means a speed that is not greater than is "reasonable or prudent." What constitutes a "reasonable" speed will be highly dependent upon the particular "conditions, including actual and potential hazards then existing."

Now that we have an idea of what "normal" and "reasonable" mean, let's put them together—literally—to see what the law is telling you. In the UVC, "persons riding two abreast may not impede the 'normal and reasonable' flow of traffic on the roadway." In order for this law to be applicable, the flow of traffic must be both normal and reasonable—it can't be just "normal flow" or "reasonable flow"; it must be "normal and reasonable flow." Furthermore, the law is applicable only if you are riding two abreast. What this means is that

- if you are riding two abreast, and
- if you are riding within the normal stream of traffic, and
- if the normal stream of traffic is moving at a reasonable speed,
- you may not impede the flow of that traffic.

31 *Prima facie* evidence of negligence is evidence of negligence that will be presumed unless contradictory evidence is introduced to rebut that presumption.

If each of these elements is present, it is possible that you could be convicted of violating this statute. However, if any one of these elements is missing, you cannot be convicted of violating it. Let's look at some examples. First, suppose you're riding two abreast, but you're not riding within the normal stream of traffic, which is moving at a reasonable speed. Because you're not within the normal stream of traffic, you can't be convicted of impeding the flow of traffic. Let's look at another example. Suppose you're riding two abreast, and you're riding within the normal stream of traffic, but traffic is not moving at a reasonable speed; again, you can't be convicted of impeding the flow of traffic. Finally, suppose that you're riding two abreast, within the normal stream of traffic, which is moving at a reasonable speed, but you are riding at that same speed. Again, you can't be convicted of violating the statute. As long as you're riding in compliance with each of these four elements, or alternatively, if any one of these four elements is not applicable, you can't be convicted of violating this section of the statute.

Now, the possibility of a conviction raises an interesting problem. As we saw in *Trotwood v. Selz*, a bicycle that is moving as fast as it reasonably can is not impeding traffic. We also saw that a bicycle is nevertheless subject to the statutory requirement to ride as close as practicable to the right. So what happens when you're riding two abreast? If riding two abreast is legal—as long as you're moving as fast as you reasonably can—and if you are permitted to take an entire lane in order to ride two abreast, do both of you still have to ride as close as practicable to the right?

Both the statutory duty to ride as close as practicable to the right and the statutory right to ride two abreast are applicable to cyclists, and neither statute indicates that the other statute doesn't apply. Therefore, the most reasonable interpretation of the requirement to ride as close as practicable to the right is that it still applies when you're riding two abreast—the outermost cyclist should ride as close as practicable to the right, while the innermost cyclist should ride as close as practicable to the outermost cyclist. Under most circumstances, this will likely mean that it simply wouldn't be practicable to ride two abreast and safely share the lane, so the two of you will simply take the lane. If the two of you are taking the lane, the practicable distance from each other and from the right-hand edge of the road is the distance necessary to take the lane.

Rarely, if ever, would the lane be wide enough for the two of you to safely share the lane with motor vehicles. In those rare situations where the lane *is* wide enough to safely share the lane with motor vehicles, you would ride two abreast and share the lane with motor vehicles. Remember, a practicable distance—whether between a rider and the curb or between the two of you—is one that can reasonably be accomplished under the existing conditions, and determining what that distance is in any given situation will involve some degree of subjectivity on your part as to what is safe. You're under no obligation to endanger your safety, but when safety allows for it, "reasonableness" requires you to accommodate other users of the road.

When you cannot safely share the lane with motorists—which likely is most of the time—common sense and common courtesy, as well as safe riding practices, should dictate when you ride two abreast and when you ride single file. On one hand, if you're on a relatively lightly traveled road with room for motorists to safely pass you, riding two abreast is an acceptable practice. On the other hand, if you're riding on a heavily traveled road with no room for motorists to safely pass you, common sense, common courtesy, and safe riding practices would all indicate that you should ride single file.

2-17 BICYCLE LANES AND PATHS

Oregon Revised Statutes Section 814.420. Failure to use bicycle lane or path; exceptions. (1) Except as provided in subsections (2) and (3) of this section, a person commits the offense of failure to use a bicycle lane or bicycle path when a bicycle lane or bicycle path is adjacent to or near the roadway. . . . (3) A person is not in violation of the offense under this section if the person is able to safely move out of the bicycle lane or path for the purpose of: (a) Overtaking and passing another bicycle, a vehicle or a pedestrian that is in the bicycle lane or path, and passage cannot be safely made in the lane or path. (b) Preparing to execute a left turn at an intersection or into a private road or driveway. (c) Avoiding debris or other hazardous conditions. (d) Preparing to execute a right turn where a right turn is authorized. (e) Continuing straight at an intersection where the bicycle lane or path is to the right of a lane from which a motor vehicle must turn right.

Bicycle lanes are a controversial topic among cyclists, with some cyclists swearing by them and others swearing at them. Regardless of which camp you fall into, in some states you are required to use a bicycle lane if one is available.

Oregon, for example, requires cyclists to ride "as close as practicable" to the right, as do other states. However, in addition to that requirement, in Oregon a cyclist must use a "bicycle lane or path when a bicycle lane or path is adjacent to or near the roadway." As in the statutes requiring cyclists to ride "as close as practicable" to the right, the requirement to ride in the bicycle lane has some exceptions.

There are five situations in which a cyclist is not required to ride in the bicycle lane:

1. when passing another vehicle or pedestrian in the lane;
2. when preparing to make a left turn;
3. when preparing to make a right turn;
4. when continuing straight at an intersection and the bike lane is to the right of the right-turn lane; and
5. when "avoiding hazardous debris or other conditions."

Compare the fifth situation with the "as close as practicable" statute, which makes an exception for situations when it is "reasonably necessary to avoid conditions" that are hazardous. They're really both saying the same thing. In the bicycle lane context, although you're required to ride in the lane, you have the discretion to avoid debris or other hazardous conditions.

Remember, in the "practicable" context, that discretion is the discretion of the "reasonable person." The reasonable person standard is not a subjective standard. Instead, if you'll recall, that which is "reasonable" is what the "reasonable person of ordinary prudence would do in the same situation." Although there's nothing in the wording of the bike-lane statute that would suggest the "reasonable person" standard, it's a safe assumption, because of the similarities between the two statutes, that following the reasonable person standard when using your discretion to leave the bike lane will keep you out of legal trouble.

2-18 SIDEWALKS AND CROSSWALKS

Uniform Vehicle Code Section 11-1210. Bicycles and human powered vehicles on sidewalks. (a) A person propelling a bicycle upon and along a sidewalk, or across a roadway upon and along a crosswalk, shall yield the right of way to any pedestrian and shall give audible signal before overtaking and passing such pedestrian. (b) A person shall not ride a bicycle upon and along a sidewalk, or across a roadway upon and along a crosswalk, where such use of bicycles is prohibited by official traffic-control devices. (c) A person propelling a vehicle by human power upon and along a sidewalk, or across a roadway upon and along a crosswalk, shall have all the rights and duties applicable to a pedestrian under the same circumstances.

In general, you may ride on the sidewalk unless you are specifically prohibited by statute or ordinance from doing so. Some states specifically say that riding on the sidewalk is permitted, while others remain silent on the matter. As a New Jersey court held in *Gibson v. Arrowhead Conditioning Company* (1991), if the law doesn't prohibit riding on the sidewalk, "then it is lawful to ride a bike on the sidewalk."[32] However, you will also need to be aware of local ordinances, because municipalities often restrict sidewalk riding in at least some areas under their jurisdiction. For example, sidewalks in a business district may be off-limits to cyclists.

So what about crosswalks? Let's take a look at some definitions from the Uniform Vehicle Code:

→ STREET or HIGHWAY *is the entire width between the boundary lines of every "way" if a part of the way is open to the use of the public for purposes of vehicular travel.*

→ THROUGH HIGHWAY *is a highway or portion of a highway at which vehicular traffic from intersecting highways is required to stop before entering or crossing and when stop signs are erected.*

→ INTERSECTION *is the area within the extension of the boundary lines of two highways that meet at any angle if vehicles traveling on those joining highways may come in conflict.*

→ SIDEWALK *is that portion of a street that is between the boundary lines of a roadway and the adjacent property lines and that is intended for the use of pedestrians.*

→ CROSSWALK *is the intangible extension of the sidewalk across the roadway at an intersection. A crosswalk can also be "any portion of a roadway at an intersection or elsewhere that is distinctly indicated for pedestrian crossing by lines or other markings on the surface."*

→ RIGHT-OF-WAY *is the right of one vehicle or pedestrian to proceed in a lawful manner in preference to another vehicle or pedestrian.*

What does all of this mean in a crosswalk, and what does it mean for cyclists in a crosswalk? Remember, a crosswalk is an extension—let's call it an imaginary extension—of the sidewalk across the roadway at an intersection (and remember, a crosswalk does not need to be at an intersection if it is marked as a crosswalk). And, as we saw, a sidewalk is intended for the use of pedestrians. In every state, a pedestrian has the right-of-way in a crosswalk: "The driver of a vehicle shall yield the right-of-way,

32 *Gibson v. Arrowhead Conditioning Co., Inc.*, 602 A.2d 800 (N.J. Super. C. 1991).

slowing down or stopping if need be in order to yield, to a pedestrian crossing the roadway within a crosswalk." Well, it's not actually quite that simple, because a pedestrian must obey any traffic-control signals present at intersections, but if the pedestrian is lawfully within the crosswalk, the pedestrian has the right-of-way. In fact, even if the pedestrian *doesn't* have the right-of-way, the driver of a vehicle still has a duty to exercise due care (of course, as you realize by now, "every driver of a vehicle" includes you, the cyclist):

> **Uniform Vehicle Code Section 11-504. Drivers to exercise due care.** Notwithstanding other provisions of this chapter or the provisions of any local ordinance, every driver of a vehicle shall exercise due care to avoid colliding with any pedestrian or any person propelling a human powered vehicle and shall give an audible signal when necessary and shall exercise proper precaution upon observing any child or any obviously confused, incapacitated or intoxicated person.

Although pedestrians have the right-of-way in crosswalks, there is generally no requirement for a pedestrian to cross at a crosswalk.[33] A pedestrian may cross outside of a crosswalk—unless the crossing point is "between adjacent intersections at which traffic control signals are in operation"—but must yield the right-of-way to all vehicles on the roadway.

And so, if you can ride your bicycle on the sidewalk, and if a crosswalk is an extension of the sidewalk, then, by logic, you can also ride your bike in the crosswalk. However, although you can ride your bike in the crosswalk, the question of right-of-way still remains, because a pedestrian has the right-of-way in a crosswalk, and a bicycle is not a pedestrian. If you think about it, though, you'll see that a pedestrian has the right-of-way while in a crosswalk and in observance of any traffic-control signals. It stands to reason, then, that if a cyclist is also in the crosswalk, and in observance of the traffic-control signals, the cyclist has the right-of-way in respect to vehicular traffic.

But what if there are no traffic-control signals? When a pedestrian is crossing at a crosswalk that is not controlled by traffic signals, the pedestrian still has the right-of-way, but "no pedestrian shall suddenly leave

---

33 But remember to check your state and local laws to be certain that there is no requirement to use a crosswalk.

a curb or other place of safety and walk or run into the path of a vehicle that is so close that it is impossible for the driver to yield."[34]

Now let's compare that with the situation when a vehicle approaches a "through highway":

> **The driver of a vehicle shall stop as required** . . . at the entrance to a through highway and shall yield the right-of-way to other vehicles that have entered the intersection from the through highway or that are approaching so closely on the through highway as to constitute an immediate hazard, but the driver having so yielded may proceed and the drivers of all other vehicles approaching the intersection on the through highway shall yield the right-of-way to the vehicle that is proceeding into or across the through highway."[35]

That sounds very similar to the requirement for pedestrians to yield to closely approaching vehicles, doesn't it? These requirements are so similar that, despite no explicit guidance from the law regarding cyclists, it's safe to say that when a cyclist is crossing at an intersection that is not regulated by a traffic-control signal, the cyclist has the right-of-way while in the crosswalk, but that before entering the crosswalk, the cyclist must yield the right-of-way to all other vehicles that are approaching so closely that they would be an immediate hazard (because it would be impossible for the driver to yield).

Now, what about those situations where a bike trail crosses a street? As we saw above, we know from the statutes that a "highway" is the entire width between the boundary lines of every "way," if a part of the way is open to the use of the public for purposes of vehicular travel. We also know that a "through highway" is "a highway or portion of a highway at which vehicular traffic from intersecting highways is required to stop before entering or crossing and when stop signs are erected." Generally, because a bicycle path is "for the exclusive use of bicycles," and because bicycles are usually vehicles, the trail will be treated as an intersection with a through highway. This means that before proceeding through the intersection, the cyclist must yield to all other vehicles that are approaching so closely that they would be an immediate hazard.

If a crosswalk is designated at the trail crossing, then the laws applicable at any crosswalk would also be applicable at the trail crossing. Therefore, because you can ride on the trail, you can ride in the crosswalk. If the crosswalk is governed by traffic-control signals, a cyclist would have

---

34 UVC Section 11-502 (b).

35 UVC Section 11-403 (c).

the right-of-way if the cyclist is within the crosswalk and in observance of the traffic-control signals. If the crosswalk is not governed by traffic-control signals, the cyclist has the right-of-way while in the crosswalk, but before entering the crosswalk must yield the right-of-way to all other vehicles that are approaching so closely that they would be an immediate hazard.

In order to be a crosswalk, must the trail be "distinctly indicated for pedestrian crossing by lines or other markings on the surface" where it crosses a roadway? The truth is, there's no clear answer to that question. Good arguments can be made either way. Nevertheless, I believe that the answer is no; the trail does not need to be painted where it crosses the roadway in order for it to be a crosswalk. Let's look at the arguments on each side to see why.

THE "LETTER OF THE LAW" ARGUMENT:
THE TRAIL CROSSING IS NOT A CROSSWALK

In most states, a bicycle is a vehicle, so a bicycle trail is considered a "highway." And because a bicycle trail is a highway, the place where the trail and the roadway cross is an intersection. As we have seen, a crosswalk is an extension of the sidewalk across the roadway at an intersection. Based on these facts, one could argue that

- because a bicycle trail is a type of highway "designed for exclusive or preferential use by persons using bicycles"; and

- because a sidewalk is that portion of a highway between the curb or shoulder and the adjacent property that is "intended for the use of pedestrians"; and

- because there is no portion of the bicycle trail between the trail roadway and the adjacent property "intended for the use of pedestrians," there is no sidewalk;

- therefore, the intersection of the trail and the roadway cannot be a crosswalk unless it is "distinctly indicated for pedestrian crossing by lines or other markings on the surface"; and

- because the intersection is not painted as a crosswalk, it is not a crosswalk.

The "letter of the law" argument relies on statutory definitions for its strength. So if the statutory definitions tell us that this isn't a crosswalk, isn't that the end of it? What's the argument that it is a crosswalk?

THE "SPIRIT OF THE LAW" ARGUMENT:
THE TRAIL CROSSING IS A CROSSWALK

The counter to that "letter of the law" argument is that, although technically, the definitions in the statute place sidewalks at the margins of the highway, there is no indication that the legislature intended so narrow a construction of the law. Instead, the statute should be interpreted to reflect the intent of the legislature; this is the "spirit of the law."

Because a sidewalk is that portion of the highway intended for pedestrians, and because the entire width of the trail is intended for pedestrians, even if the trail is "designed for preferential use by persons using bicycles," the entire trail should be considered the functional equivalent of a sidewalk for pedestrians. Therefore, because the entire trail is the functional equivalent of a sidewalk at the intersection, the crossing is legally a crosswalk, whether or not the crosswalk is indicated with paint. I believe that this argument best reflects the intent of the state legislatures and that therefore it is the correct interpretation of the statute.

In the end analysis, you don't want to be hit while crossing the street, even if you have the right-of-way. But if you are hit while crossing the street, having the right-of-way puts the liability for the collision on the vehicle that failed to yield, rather than on you. And really, we should remember that the point of observing the right-of-way is to avoid collisions in the first place. Observe the right-of-way, use your common sense even when you have the right-of-way, and pay attention to what those drivers are doing, because, well, somebody has to.

Equipment Laws

2-19 BELLS AND HORNS

Uniform Vehicle Code Section 12-707. Sirens, whistles prohibited. No bicycle may be equipped with a siren or whistle. No person may use a siren or whistle when operating a bicycle.

New Jersey Statutes Annotated Section 39:4-11. Audible signal. No person shall operate a bicycle unless it is equipped with a bell or other device capable of giving an audible signal for a distance of at least one hundred feet, except that a bicycle shall not be equipped with nor shall any person use upon a bicycle any siren or whistle.

Kentucky Revised Statutes Section 189.080. Horns and other sound devices. Every motor vehicle, when in use on a highway, shall be equipped with a horn or other device capable of making an abrupt sound sufficiently loud to be heard from a distance of at least two hundred (200) feet under all ordinary traffic conditions. Every person operating an automobile or bicycle shall sound the horn or device whenever necessary as a warning of the approach of such vehicle to pedestrians, or other vehicles, but shall not sound the horn unnecessarily. A bell may be used on a bicycle.

Bicycles have been required to be equipped with bells since their first appearance on the roads over a century ago, when the silence of the approaching machines, combined with their high speeds, made them some of the most dangerous vehicles in traffic. However, that requirement is no longer universal today. Some states still require bicycles to be equipped with a bell and to make an audible signal when approaching a pedestrian. Other states, however, have no requirement that a bicycle be equipped with a bell. Instead, they simply allow a bicycle to be equipped with a bell or a horn. No state, however, allows bicycles to be equipped with a siren.

Today, the needs of cyclists for an audible signal are somewhat different than they were a century ago, and the use of two distinct types of audible signals may be helpful. As it was a century ago, the first is a signal to alert pedestrians that the cyclist is approaching, and is best accomplished with a bell or horn; as noted above, in some states this is required equipment, and in those states you will be required to use your bell or horn to alert pedestrians of your approach. In other states, it is permitted equipment, and you are not required to alert pedestrians of your approach. Even in these states, you will nevertheless owe pedestrians a duty of due care not to collide with them. This means that if you are approaching a pedestrian from behind, and you don't alert the pedestrian of your approach, you could be held liable for negligence, even if the pedestrian inadvertently steps into your path as you pass. If you choose not to use a bell or horn, you should either take care to give pedestrians a wide berth as you pass or wait until it is safe to pass.

The second type of audible signal cyclists often have need of is a horn that is loud enough to alert motorists to their presence. This is not required in any state, but it is an important safety consideration for cyclists; whereas the first type of bell or horn is for the safety of pedestrians, this second type of horn is for the safety of the cyclist. This horn—typically an airhorn—is by necessity significantly louder than a horn to alert pedestrians. Although the equipment statutes typically prohibit the use of a siren, there is no definition of "siren" in the vehicle code. Nevertheless, it is safe to say that an airhorn is not a siren and thus is permitted equipment.

2-20 BRAKES

> **Code of Federal Regulations Section 1512.5. Requirements for braking system.** (a) Braking system. Bicycles shall be equipped with front- and rear-wheel brakes or rear-wheel brakes only.
> **Uniform Vehicle Code Section 12-706. Brake required.** Every bicycle shall be equipped with a brake or brakes which will enable its driver to stop the vehicle within 15 feet from a speed of 10 miles per hour on dry, level, clean pavement.
> **Oregon Vehicle Code Section 815.280(2)(a). Bicycle equipment requirements.** A bicycle must be equipped with a brake that enables the operator to make the braked wheels skid on dry, level, clean pavement.

Without exception, all bicycles operated on "highways" must be equipped with brakes. Seems pretty straightforward, right? Except there were those brakeless bicycle trials in Oregon. . . .

But let's start at the beginning. If your great-great-grandfather was riding a bicycle in 1896, chances are it wasn't equipped with brakes. It wasn't for lack of technology—earlier bicycles had been equipped with brakes—it was just that brakes were considered by some cyclists to be a superfluous and unsafe addition to the bicycle. However, by 1897, New York City horsemen were vociferously lobbying for brakes on bicycles. What had happened to draw the wrath of horsemen upon the bicyclists?

It was the attempt to bring bicycles into the legal system through the traffic laws. In 1887, the New York state legislature declared that cyclists had the same rights and duties as drivers of horse-drawn carriages; by 1889, the courts had begun to recognize these same rights and duties of cyclists in the common law. In 1897, the rights of cyclists were further developed when New York City enacted a traffic ordinance that brought bicycles even more into the legal system. The horsemen were outraged because the traffic ordinance set a speed limit of 5 mph for horses and 8 mph for bicycles. Horsemen not only were now required to share the road with bicycles and pedestrians, but they were actually subject to a lower speed limit than were bicyclists.

They knew they weren't going to get the speed limits altered, so instead they asked for something that they knew would annoy the cyclists, but would nevertheless seem reasonable to the rest of society: Require bicycles to be equipped with brakes. Although the first bicycles had fixed gears and no separate braking mechanisms, "spoon brakes" had become standard features on bicycles by the 1870s. Somewhat ironically, however, the new "safety bicycles" that were fueling the bicycle craze of the

1890s were not equipped with brakes. The horsemen were right: Bicyclists were not pleased with the proposed regulation, and they let City Hall know. As bicycle historian Robert Smith reports:

> *They answered that if brakes were required, the bicyclist would never really learn to control his steed but would rely abjectly on the mechanism, never learning the "flying dismount" that the cyclemaniacs thought was necessary. They ridiculed the language of the proposal, which called for brakes of a certain "power," hooting at the idea that the device had any power at all—it was manpower that set the brake! They contended that if a cycler felt he had to have brakes he would buy them and put them on his own bicycle, but that it was wrong to force a "useless adjunct" on people who did not need it and were better off without it. They argued that requiring brakes would mean "confiscation of the poorer classes whose wheels are mostly of the make of two or three years ago; the brakes to be offered for sale would not fit the older machines, and therefore, the poor would be legally deprived of the right to ride their bicycles.*[36]

When the bicycle manufacturers perfected better braking technology, brakes became standard equipment on new bikes, and the issue became moot. Well, sort of. Brakes still became mandatory, at first under state law, and later under federal law as well. Today, every state has a statute that requires bicycles operated on a "highway"[37] to be equipped with a brake, although the particular requirements vary from state to state. The majority of states require a brake that enables the operator to make the braked wheels skid on dry, level, clean pavement. However, several states require brakes that will stop a bicycle within 25 feet from a speed of 10 mph,[38] and a few states require bicycles to be equipped with the clear-as-mud standard of an "adequate" brake. Although every state requires bicycles to be equipped with brakes, the state braking standards have been rendered anachronistic in varying degrees by three separate phenomena.

The first of these phenomena was the development of federal regulations. Since 1978, the federal government has had its own bicycle brake

36 Robert A. Smith, *A Social History of the Bicycle* (New York: American Heritage Press, 1972).

37 Under the Uniform Vehicle Code, a highway is the "entire width between the boundary lines of every way publicly maintained when any part thereof is open to the use of the public for purposes of vehicular travel."

38 The Uniform Vehicle Code requires a brake that will stop the bicycle within 15 feet from a speed of 10 mph on dry, level, clean pavement. This suggested statutory standard is equivalent to the federal Consumer Product Safety Comission regulation that manufacturers are required to meet. Not one state requires bicycles to be equipped with brakes that meet this standard.

regulations, promulgated by the Consumer Product Safety Commission (CPSC). The CPSC regulations are far more comprehensive in their engineering and performance requirements than are the state laws. Although the regulations are directed at manufacturers rather than riders, they have broad application: *With the exception of track bicycles and "sidewalk bicycles," all bicycles introduced into the stream of commerce in the United States today must be equipped with brakes.* The stream of commerce is so broad that the federal regulations are at least applicable to any bicycle that is sold, and arguably may apply to any bicycle that is ridden. Despite this breadth, local and state law-enforcement agencies do not enforce the CPSC regulations; instead, law-enforcement agencies enforce the statutes of their jurisdiction. The task of enforcing the CPSC regulations is left to the CPSC.

Although the CPSC regulations are not traffic statutes that the states enforce, they have been adopted as the bicycle brake standard in the Uniform Vehicle Code, and thus could conceivably become state law. So far, no state has adopted the CPSC/UVC standard—brakes capable of stopping a bicycle within 15 feet from a speed of 10 mph—but as we saw above, several states have adopted the similar, but less stringent, standard of brakes capable of stopping a bicycle within 25 feet from a speed of 10 mph. If a state were to adopt the UVC standard, the CPSC standards would, in effect, become enforceable by local and state law-enforcement authorities.

The second phenomenon rendering the state braking standards anachronistic has been the advent of new disc brake technology, which provides superior stopping performance. Paradoxically, because disc brakes do not lock up, they also render bicycles incapable of meeting the dry-skid requirement employed by the majority of states. This is, of course, an absurdity in the law.

Which brings us to the Oregon cases—the third phenomenon affecting the current statutory requirements. On June 1, 2006, Ayla Holland, a Portland bike messenger, was cited while riding a fixed-gear bike that was not equipped with brakes. At her trial, she argued that her bicycle was not in violation of the Oregon traffic law requiring brakes because the fixed gear functions as a brake on a fixed-gear bike. Unfortunately for Holland, the judge wasn't buying her argument that the law doesn't require a brake to be a separate mechanism, and she was convicted of violating the Oregon traffic law requiring brakes. However, in September 2006, another Portland cyclist went to trial for the same violation and convinced a different judge, who happens to be a cyclist himself, that a fixed gear functions as a brake.

This set up an interesting tension in Oregon—one trial court had ruled that a fixed gear was not a brake, and another trial court had ruled that a fixed gear was a brake. In November 2006, another ten cyclists were convicted in Portland, by the same judge who had heard the Holland case. Now Portland's fixed-gear riders were really confused. How could the police still be writing tickets when a judge had said that a fixed gear was a brake? How could one judge say a fixed gear was a brake, and another judge say a fixed gear wasn't a brake? The answer was simple, but not readily understood by the average cyclist in the street. At the trial level, the judge decides whether the accused is innocent or guilty based on the facts of the case and whatever statutes and common law apply. The decision in one trial has no bearing on the decision in any other trial. Because no appellate court had ever ruled on the question, each trial court was left to decide for itself whether a fixed gear was a brake.

The confusion stems from the language of the statute itself, which is virtually identical to the language used in the majority of state statutes: It inadequately defines what is required of a cyclist. Let's take a closer look at the Oregon statute to see why: "A bicycle must be equipped with a brake that enables the operator to make the braked wheels skid on dry, level, clean pavement." Although the statute specifies what a brake must be capable of doing, it does not specify what a brake is. Although federal regulations do specify what a brake is, and thus could resolve the question, the state statutes are not based on the federal regulations. Because the statute is unclear, the question must eventually be decided by either the legislature or the courts.

Regardless of what may actually qualify as a brake, one thing is clear. By law, virtually all bicycles must be equipped with a brake. Many states also specify that a violation of the traffic laws is prima facie evidence of negligence, which means that in an accident, a violation of the traffic laws will be considered evidence of negligence unless contradictory evidence is introduced that rebuts that presumption of negligence.

Here's how that works. Suppose a cyclist riding a brakeless fixed-gear bike is involved in an accident. The other party raises the issue of the cyclist's negligence for riding without a brake in violation of the law. If there is no statute or common-law rule instructing the jury on whether a fixed gear is a brake, the jury would decide the issue. If a jury agreed that the fixed gear was a brake within the meaning of the law, then the jury would find that the cyclist was riding in compliance with that law and could not be found liable for negligence on *that* issue. However, if the jury agreed that a fixed gear was not a brake, then the jury would find the cyclist negligent for riding in violation of the law, unless the cyclist were to rebut the presumption of negligence with evidence that the violation of the law did not contribute to the accident.

This presumption of negligence is not limited to the individual cyclist. For bicycle-oriented businesses, such as messenger or delivery services, the prima facie presumption of negligence would also be applicable to the business itself under the doctrine of *respondeat superior*, which holds employers liable for the negligence of employees who are acting within the scope of their duties.

In any case, the twin developments of comprehensive federal brake standards and new braking technology, along with existing weak state standards and ambiguous statutory language, all point to the need for a resolution of these issues, both through the legislatures and in the courts.

At least in Oregon, the legal questions will be addressed in the courts. In August 2006, Ayla Holland filed an appeal of her conviction with the Oregon Court of Appeals; the court will be called upon to interpret what the legislature meant by the word "brake" when it enacted the statute. Ultimately, however, the statutes will need to be addressed by the state legislatures. On July 28, 2006—by sheer coincidence, the day after Ayla Holland was convicted—the Washington, D.C., city department of transportation became the first governmental body in the nation to address the issue, changing the language of its traffic regulations to make an explicit exception for fixed gears:

> **1204.1.** Each bicycle shall be equipped with a brake which enables the operator to cause the braked wheels to skid on dry, level, clean pavement; provided, that *a fixed gear bicycle is not required to have a separate brake*, but an operator of a fixed gear bicycle shall be able to stop the bicycle using the pedals. (Emphasis added)

Although the statutory language was given a quick fix, it still uses the outdated skid standard, which leaves bikes equipped with superior braking technology in the absurd legal position of being out of compliance with the law. Thus, the task of the state legislatures will be to bring the brake requirement up to date in its entirety.

2-21 LIGHTS AND REFLECTORS

> **Uniform Vehicle Code Section 12-702.** Headlight and taillight required at night. Every bicycle in use [during darkness] shall be equipped with a headlight on the front emitting a white light visible from a distance of at least 500 feet to the front, and a taillight

on the rear emitting a red light visible from a distance of at least 1,000 feet to the rear. **Uniform Vehicle Code Section 12-703.** Rear reflector required at night. Every bicycle shall be equipped with a red reflector of a type approved by the department which shall be visible for 600 feet to the rear when directly in front of lawful lower beams of headlights on a motor vehicle. **Uniform Vehicle Code Section 12-704.** Side reflector or light required at night. Every bicycle when in use [during darkness] shall be equipped with reflective material of sufficient size and reflectivity to be visible from both sides for 600 feet when directly in front of lawful lower beams of head lamps on a motor vehicle, or, in lieu of such reflective material, with a lighted lamp visible from both sides from a distance of at least 500 feet. **Uniform Vehicle Code Section 12-705.** Additional lights or reflectors authorized. A bicycle or its rider may be equipped with lights or reflectors in addition to those required by the foregoing sections. These lights and/or reflectors may be LED or regular, steady or flashing, as long as they comply with the requirements or limitations of the department.

Bicycle lights are not a new phenomenon—cyclists have been required to equip their bikes with lights since the 1890s. Pedestrians at that time needed some visual signal to alert them of the cyclist's approach. A bell alone, while sufficient to alert the pedestrian during daylight hours, would not be sufficient after dark, when the pedestrian would not be able to tell from the bell alone how fast the cyclist was bearing down upon them or exactly where he or she was coming from. The solution was to require bicycles to be equipped with lights. These lights—small kerosene lamps—were always running out of fuel, or being extinguished by the jarring inherent in riding on unimproved roads, so they were not particularly popular pieces of cycling equipment. Nevertheless, there were so many cyclists out riding at night in New York City that "after dark, Riverside Drive seemed alive with fireflies, so numerous were the varicolored bicycle lamps flashing under the trees."[39]

Today, the reason for lights has shifted. Whereas lights were once necessary to alert vulnerable pedestrians to the presence of a bicycle approaching in the darkness, today they are necessary to alert motorists to the presence of the vulnerable cyclist. Also new is the sheer effectiveness of the latest lighting technology, fueled by the need of mountain bikers

39 Lloyd Morris, *Incredible New York* (New York: Random House, 1951), p. 212.

for *effective* lighting after dark. Before the advent of mountain biking, bicycle lights tended to be feeble affairs, barely capable of lighting the road ahead, let alone of warning motorists that there was a cyclist on the road. Overriding one's bicycle light—riding fast enough that your bike arrived at a surface defect faster than your lights could alert you to its presence so that you could react—was both easy and common. While the contemporary cyclist can still find ineffective lights, the range—and effectiveness—of lighting available today, thanks to the lighting revolution driven by the needs of mountain bikers, is nothing short of phenomenal.

The requirement to equip your bike with lights only applies if you are operating your bike "during darkness," which is defined as "any time from one-half hour after sunset to one-half hour before sunrise and any other time when visibility is not sufficient to render clearly discernible any person or vehicle on the highway at a distance of 1,000 feet."[40] This is a much broader definition than "at night"; it includes any period of low visibility, even if that low visibility is occurring during daylight hours. If you are operating your bike without a light "during darkness," you may be cited; more importantly, in the event of an accident, riding without lights will be either per se negligence or prima facie evidence of negligence, depending on your jurisdiction. Consequently, if you intend to ride during darkness, you must equip your bike with a light.

The specific requirements for bicycle lights will vary from state to state. The UVC requires a headlight that is visible for 500 feet from the front, and a taillight that is visible for 1,000 feet from the rear. The UVC permits, but does not require, cyclists to equip their bikes with additional lights.[41] Many states have lighting statutes that require significantly less than the UVC does. For example, California requires a headlight that illuminates the highway ahead of the cyclist and is visible for a distance of 300 feet; no taillight is required.[42] Given the technology available to cyclists today, it is unfortunate that the states are unable to meet the rather modest requirements of the Uniform Vehicle Code in their own codes.

The truth is, while you are required to meet the legal standard for lighting, that legal standard is simply not sufficient for your nighttime riding safety. Even a lighted match, for example, is visible at the UVC's standard of 500 feet.[43] Thus, in addition to meeting the legal standard of equipping your bike with a light or lights, you should also consider

40 UVC Section 12-201.

41 UVC Section 12-705.

42 California Vehicle Code Section 21201 (d).

43 Jeffrey P. Broker and Paul F. Hill, *Bicycle Accidents: Biomechanical, Engineering, and Legal Aspects* (Tucson: Lawyers and Judges, 2006), p. 289.

what you need for your own safety, and that can be summed up in one word: brightness. At night, the main cue motorists use to judge the distance of a bicycle is the brightness of the bicycle's lights. The dimmer the light, the farther away the motorist judges the bike to be, while the brighter the light, the closer the motorist judges the bike to be. Even when two cyclists are on their bikes, side by side, if one cyclist has dim lights, while the other cyclist has bright lights, an approaching motorist will perceive the cyclist with the bright lights to be much closer. Therefore, the brighter the lights you're riding with, the closer the motorist will judge you to be, and the sooner the motorist will begin to react to your presence on the road.

While the cyclists of today, like the cyclists of the 1890s, are required to equip their bicycles with lights, contemporary cyclists have one additional requirement to fulfill: The lighting requirement has been expanded to include reflectors, which are required passive conspicuity equipment for new bicycles. "Passive conspicuity" means you don't have to do anything to activate the system—unlike lights, reflectors do not require batteries or some other means of power in order to work, nor does the cyclist need to turn them on; reflectors work whenever a light shines on them. They are a kind of "failsafe" conspicuity system. In order to be in compliance with UVC reflector requirements, a bike must be equipped with both a rear reflector and side reflectors or lights; the UVC allows the use of reflectorized tires in lieu of side reflectors. Again, state law may vary from the UVC requirements. Note, however, that the reflectors requirement only applies to new bicycles, and to all bicycles if they are ridden during darkness. If your bike is operated only at times other than "during darkness," you are not required to have lights or reflectors.

Reflector technology is regulated stringently by the federal government to ensure a minimum level of effectiveness, but there is no corresponding federal regulation for the effectiveness of lighting systems. The only requirement for lighting effectiveness is contained in state law, and meeting even that minimal requirement is left up to the individual cyclist. If a cyclist is in compliance with state-law requirements for reflectors and lights, the cyclist has met the reasonable person standard for lighting in the event of a collision and thus cannot be held liable for failing to have the most effective lighting available; however, because state-law requirements for lights lag significantly behind the state of technology, and because the better lighting technology confers significant safety benefits, the safety-conscious cyclist will likely choose to go beyond the reasonable-person standard and exceed minimum lighting requirements.[44]

2-22 CONSPICUITY

"A careful examination of the record in this case fails to disclose even a scintilla of evidence to support the charge that decedent rode his bicycle in a reckless, heedless, and dangerous manner without any care or caution. He had a lawful right to be on the highway; he was riding his bicycle on the right-hand side of the center line of the road; there is no evidence whatever that he was riding in any unusual way; and in so far as his clothing is concerned, there is no rule of the common law, nor is there any statutory provision, which requires a person before venturing upon the highway to dress in light, rather than dark clothing."

Spence v. Rasmussen, Supreme Court of Oregon (1951)

"There is ample evidence that the decedent himself was negligent. He was wearing dark clothing at night, traveling on a bicycle that had no lighting equipment and was in the south-bound lane of the traveled portion of an unlighted highway which had wide shoulders suitable for bike riding."

Weise v. Lazore, Supreme Court, Appellate Division, New York (1984)

"I didn't see him."

It's heard regularly when automobiles collide with bikes—the driver just didn't see the cyclist.[45] And remarkably, cyclists involved in these collisions regularly indicate that they believed they were visible to motorists when the accident occurred. Although cyclists can readily see motor vehicles, there is a 7 to 1 difference in size between an automobile and a bicyclist that cyclists must take into account; this size differential means that while the cyclist may see the automobile, it doesn't necessarily follow that the driver will see the cyclist. Furthermore, consistent with driver reports that they just didn't see the cyclist, most collisions between automobiles and bicycles occur at night, when visibility is reduced by low light conditions.[46]

---

44 In fact, in the unfortunate event of an accident, the fact that a cyclist exceeded the legal standards for lights and was injured anyway may be additional evidence of the motorist's negligence.

45 Bernard S. Abrams, Ph.D., and Leslie Weintraub, Ph.D., in *Bicycle Accidents: Biomechanical, Engineering, and Legal Aspects* (Lawyers & Judges Publishing Company, 2006).

46 Ibid.

Enhancing the cyclist's conspicuity—the ability to be seen—is essential to safe cycling in traffic, because conspicuity affects both perception and recognition distances. *"Perception distance"* is the distance at which a motorist perceives that there is "something" ahead of the vehicle, whereas *"recognition distance"* is the distance at which the motorist recognizes what that "something" is. In turn, both perception distance and recognition distance affect the motorist's reaction time; the more time the motorist has to perceive a cyclist "suddenly appearing" in the road ahead, the more likely the motorist will be able to react and avoid the cyclist.[47]

Because most accidents happen at night, one obvious strategy for increasing safety is to avoid night riding. For many cyclists, however, this strategy is either not possible or not desirable. Cyclists who ride at night should therefore develop a strategy for minimizing their risk by maximizing their conspicuity. The most effective strategies will assist the motorist in

- perceiving that something is out there;
- recognizing that what she is perceiving is a cyclist on a bicycle;
- determining whether the cyclist is on the same road as the motorist;
- determining the distance of the motorist to the cyclist; and
- determining the speed and direction of the cyclist's travel.

Some factors within the cyclist's control that affect conspicuity are:

→ LIGHTS. *Although state laws may require bicycle headlights to be visible for up to 500 feet, and taillights to be visible for up to 1,000 feet, actual lighting systems will vary, and some may not meet the standard required by state law. Perception and recognition distances will depend on the actual conspicuity of individual lighting systems.*

→ REFLECTORS. *State laws may require reflectors to be visible for up to 600 feet; the nighttime perception and recognition distances of reflectors will be at least equal to those of bicycle lights and may actually exceed them.*

→ REFLECTIVE MATERIAL. *The nighttime perception distance for reflective material will vary from 1,200 to 2,200 feet, depending on ambient light conditions; reflective material is more conspicuous against a darker background than it is against a brighter background. Reflective material is effective in aiding perception even in drivers with elevated blood alcohol levels. Nighttime recognition distances vary from 600 to*

47 Ibid.

700 feet, but with brighter background lighting decreases to a range of 260 to 325 feet. However, motorists have difficulty recognizing what it is they are perceiving unless the reflective material is used in conjunction with a lighting system. Motion is a particularly important factor in recognition; for this reason, it is more important to have reflective material on the arms and legs than on the torso.

→ COLOR. *Dark and drab colors tend to blend in with the background, rendering the cyclist virtually invisible. With dark colors, nighttime perception distance is only 75 feet, giving the driver less than 1 second of reaction time. With reaction times this short, it is virtually impossible for a motorist to avoid a cyclist "suddenly appearing" in the motorist's headlights.*[48]

Paradoxically, light colors also tend to blend into the background as a motorist approaches a cyclist, decreasing the cyclist's conspicuity as the approach distance closes. Nevertheless, light colors are more conspicuous. Fluorescent colors—particularly yellow-green, but also yellow, lime green, and orange—are the most conspicuous. In daylight, fluorescent colors may be up to four times brighter than their nonfluorescent counterparts, and these fluorescent colors are particularly effective during periods or conditions of low visibility, such as dawn, dusk, haze, and fog. The helmet is often the most visible part of the cyclist, and fluorescent helmet colors increase the perception distance to greater than 600 feet. Fluorescent paint colors on the bicycle also aid the motorist in recognition. With fluorescent clothing, the daytime perception distance can increase from 400 feet to 2,200 feet, and nighttime perception distance can increase from 150 feet to 560 feet.[49]

Although conspicuity has obvious safety advantages for the cyclist, beyond the statutory requirements for lights and reflectors (see §2-21) there is no statutory requirement to increase conspicuity. Now let's say you're riding in compliance with the reflector and lighting statutes of your state. Is that all that's required of you? Or could you be held liable for negligence if you're not as conspicuous as you *could be*?

It seems unlikely, although you should understand that the equipment statutes are the bare minimum required of you to protect both yourself and others. Think of compliance with the equipment laws as the floor below which you cannot legally go; there's nothing in the law that prohibits you from meeting a higher standard. Here's how that "floor" works: In every state, a violation of the traffic laws is prima facie evidence of negli-

48 Ibid.
49 Ibid.

YOUR RIGHTS AND DUTIES UNDER THE LAW

gence. This means that in the event of an accident in which the cyclist's conspicuity is an issue, a violation of the lighting and reflector requirements would be evidence of the cyclist's negligence *unless* contradictory evidence was produced. If a cyclist and a motorist were both found to be negligent, that could reduce the cyclist's damages award in many states, and it could completely bar the cyclist from recovery in a handful of states. As you can see, negligence has real-world consequences that can be quite severe.

But could you be found liable for not meeting a higher standard? Let's revisit the two court cases cited at the beginning of this section. In *Spence v. Rasmussen*, a 1951 case, the Supreme Court of Oregon concluded that the cyclist was by no means negligent because "there is no rule of the common law, nor is there any statutory provision, which requires a person before venturing upon the highway to dress in light, rather than dark clothing."[50]

In contrast, in 1984 the Supreme Court of New York observed, in *Weise v. Lazore*, that there was evidence of negligence because the cyclist "was wearing dark clothing at night, traveling on a bicycle that had no lighting equipment and was in the south bound lane of the traveled portion of an unlighted highway which had wide shoulders suitable for bike riding."[51]

Although these two cases address conspicuity, neither court definitively formulated a common-law rule that wearing dark clothing is or is not negligent. But wait a minute—didn't the Oregon court just say that wearing dark clothing is not negligent? And didn't the New York court just say that wearing dark clothing is negligent? Sort of, but not really. These aren't actually rulings on an issue of law; they're just the courts' commentary on the facts before the court. And although the New York court did cite the dark clothing as evidence of the cyclist's negligence, the court did not say that the cyclist had a duty to wear light clothing; instead, the court went on only to address the cyclist's statutory obligations: "Not only should the bicycle have been equipped with lights or reflectors, it also should have been operated on the right side of the road or on the usable right-hand shoulder thereof." So although the court suggested that wearing dark clothing in these circumstances was negligent, the court did not rule that the cyclist would have had to wear conspicuous clothing to avoid liability for negligence.

Now, you should understand that neither of these commentaries are the same thing as saying that a jury couldn't reasonably find a cyclist

50 *Spence v. Rasmussen*, 226 P.2d 819 (Or. 1951).

51 *Weise v. Lazore*, 99 A.D.2d 919 (N.Y. App. div. 3 Dept. 1984).

negligent for wearing dark clothing. The courts just haven't ruled yet on whether cyclists have a nonstatutory duty of conspicuity. On the one hand, a jury could find negligence for lack of conspicuity if that lack of conspicuity was the cause of injury to the cyclist or somebody else. For example, remember that dark clothing at night reduces perception distance to 75 feet, and driver reaction time to less than one second. On the other hand, it seems inconceivable that a cyclist who is riding in observance of the law's conspicuity requirements could nevertheless be found to be negligent for wearing dark clothing. After all, a cyclist who is equipped with lights and reflectors but wearing dark clothing is still conspicuous, even if the cyclist isn't as conspicuous as possible. It seems more probable instead that, if a cyclist was riding in violation of the law, a jury would consider dark clothing as *additional* evidence of negligence, rather than as evidence of negligence despite the cyclist's riding in observance of the law.[52]

And that raises an interesting issue. Suppose you're riding in low-light conditions; you're riding in observance of the law—with the required lights and reflectors—and you're also outfitted in fluorescent and reflective material, and your lights stop operating. Would a jury find you negligent in the event of an accident? In order to analyze whether a particular action might be considered negligence, the cyclist should ask herself two related questions: (1) "Would a jury consider this prudent"? and (2) "What would a reasonable person of ordinary prudence do in the same situation?" Remember, the "reasonable person" standard is an objective, rather than a subjective, standard; it doesn't have anything to do with what you personally believe to be prudent. It is neither the standard of behavior of the person who takes no precautions, nor of the person who takes excessive precautions; instead, it is the standard of behavior of the person who takes reasonable precautions, and it will depend upon what precautions a particular jury believes is prudent in a particular set of factual circumstances.

In the scenario outlined above, taking *additional* precautions beyond what the law requires, such as outfitting yourself with fluorescent and reflective material, might help convince a jury that you were not riding negligently, despite the failure of your lights. This would be an example of how you could introduce evidence contradicting the prima facie evidence of negligence. Of course, the courts would find a duty to be conspicuous where legislation requires it. However, there is currently no movement toward mandating more conspicuity through legislation; the

---

52 Note, however, that the law does not require anything more than reflectors at the rear–an inadequate standard for safety. Therefore, depending on the circumstances, a cyclist's compliance with the law would be insufficient to establish a motorist's liability.

states seem to be satisfied with the statutory requirements for reflectors and lights.

Of course, there's another, more important reason to take additional conspicuity precautions: preventing injury to yourself in the first place. Engineering studies have conclusively demonstrated that fluorescent and reflective materials significantly increase driver perception and recognition distances, and thus driver reaction time. This increased conspicuity occurs under both daylight and low-light conditions, especially when used in conjunction with lights and reflectors. Ultimately, preventing serious injury is by far preferable to arguing these points of law in court, even if you win the case. No amount of money can substitute for your good health.

Market demands have made conspicuity available to cyclists in the form of blinkies, taillights, and fluorescent and reflective clothing. However, most helmet designs ignore conspicuity, even though the helmet is often the most visible part of the cyclist. Even the Consumer Products Safety Commission declined to add a requirement for reflective material to the bicycle helmet standards when studies indicated that reflective tape on bicycle helmets actually appeared to *lengthen* motorist recognition times. Similarly, most bicycles are painted in drab, nonreflective colors that blend into the background, despite engineering studies demonstrating that fluorescent paint colors significantly increase a motorist's ability to recognize cyclists. Absent an increase in market demand for conspicuous equipment or a change in the statutes, it seems unlikely that manufacturers will make their products as conspicuous as they could be.

2-23 HELMETS

> **Oregon Revised Statutes Section 814.485. Failure to wear protective headgear; penalty.** (1) A person commits the offense of failure of a bicycle operator or rider to wear protective headgear if the person is under 16 years of age, operates or rides on a bicycle on a highway or on premises open to the public and is not wearing protective headgear of a type approved under ORS 815.052.
> **Oregon Revised Statutes Section 814.486.** Endangering bicycle operator or passenger; penalty. (1) A person commits the offense of endangering a bicycle operator or passenger if: . . . (b) The person is the parent, legal guardian or person with legal responsibility for the safety and welfare of a child under 16 years of age and the child operates or rides on a bicycle on a highway or on premises

open to the public without wearing protective headgear of a type
approved under ORS 815.052.
Oregon Revised Statutes Section 814.487. Exemptions from protective headgear requirements. A person is exempt from the requirements under ORS 814.485 and 814.486 to wear protective
headgear, if wearing the headgear would violate a religious belief
or practice of the person.
Oregon Revised Statutes Section 814.489. Use of evidence of
lack of protective headgear on bicyclist. Evidence of violation of
ORS 814.485 or 814.486 and evidence of lack of protective headgear shall not be admissible, applicable or effective to reduce the
amount of damages or to constitute a defense to an action for
damages brought by or on behalf of an injured bicyclist or bicycle
passenger or the survivors of a deceased bicyclist or passenger if
the bicyclist or passenger was injured or killed as a result in whole
or in part of the fault of another.

Twenty states have enacted statutes requiring the use of helmets
while bicycling.[53] Of the states that require helmet use, however, the requirement generally applies only to minors; no state requires adults to
wear helmets while bicycling (see Table 2.1). Seven of the twenty states
that have a statewide helmet statute also have local laws requiring adult
cyclists to wear helmets while riding. Another fourteen states have no
statewide statute requiring helmet use but do have local laws requiring
helmet use; eight of those states have local laws requiring adult cyclists
to wear helmets. Fourteen states have no helmet laws, local or statewide,
on the books. Despite these laws, compliance with the requirement is not
universal, which raises the question of whether a cyclist can be held liable for his own injuries if he or she is injured while riding in violation
of a helmet law.

In response to this legal tactic to shift blame to the cyclist, many states
have also enacted a "no-blame" provision in their helmet laws that prevents the legal lack of helmet use from being used against the cyclist in
court to prove contributory negligence or to reduce damage awards. Let's
say that motorist John Doe hits cyclist Jane Roe, and as a result, Jane
suffers $10,000 in injury. She is an adult, and in the state where this ac-
cident occurs, only cyclists under the age of 15 are required to wear helmets. Jane sues John for negligence and makes a strong case that she
was at fault. However, he argues that if Jane had been wearing a helmet,

---

53 Some countries require all cyclists to wear helmets when they ride; before you travel with your bike,
be sure to research the helmet laws of the countries where you will be riding.

TABLE 2.1 States with Bicycle Helmet Statutes

State	Ages	Date	City Laws
Alabama	16	1995	Yes
California	P5/18	1994	Yes
Connecticut	16	1997	No
Delaware	16	1996	No
Washington D.C.	16	2000	N/A
Florida	16	1997	Yes*
Georgia	16	1993	No
Hawaii	16	2001	No
Illinois	17	1997	Yes**
Louisiana	12	2002	No
Maine	16	1999	No
Maryland	16	1995	Yes
Massachusetts	P5/13	1994	No
New Jersey	14	1992	No
New York	P5/14	1994	Yes
North Carolina	16	2001	Yes
Oregon	16	1994	Yes
Rhode Island	16	1998	No
Tennessee	16	2000	Yes
West Virginia	15	1996	Yes

* Florida permits individual counties to opt out of the law; two have done so.

** Illinois requires all bike messengers to wear helmets.

Ages: All cyclists under this age must wear a helmet.

Dates: Date the law was enacted.

P: Passenger (for example, P4 means all passengers in child seats or bike trailers under four years old must wear a helmet.)

City Laws: The question answered in this column is, Do some cities and/or counties have separate laws?

The following states have no statewide law but allow local governments to enact their own bicycle helmet laws, and at least one locality in each state has done so: Arizona, Kentucky, Michigan, Missouri, Montana, Nevada, Oklahoma, Texas, Virginia, Washington, and Wisconsin.

she would only have suffered $5,000 in injury, so she should only have to pay her smaller amount. A no-blame clause prevents a wrongful driver from doing this. In some states, the no-blame clause is included right in the helmet statute, but in others it is buried in code sections dealing with negligence or rules of evidence. To find out whether your state has such a provision, consult the Bicycle Helmet Safety Institute website (www. helmets.org), local bicycle club websites, or websites run by state or local bicycle and pedestrian coordinators.

But what if helmet use is not required in your state? Can you be held liable for your injuries if there is no helmet law? Until very recently, if I had been asked whether a cyclist's legal lack of a helmet could be used against the cyclist in court, I would have responded with a resounding no. In a 1991 case, *Walden v. Montana*, an appeals court overturned the decision of a trial court that allowed the lack of a helmet to be considered as a factor by the jury in determining appropriate damages.[54] The appeals court said such evidence could not be used either to prove contributory negligence or to help determine appropriate damages.[55] In a 1997 New Jersey case, *Cordy v. Sherman Williams Company*, the U.S. District Court for the District of New Jersey concluded that because no state law required adult helmet use, a reasonable person would not be on notice that failure to wear a helmet could be unreasonable, and therefore such behavior could not be used to prejudice the cyclist's legal rights.[56] Helmet use could not be put before the jury as either evidence of contributory negligence or as a factor to be considered in calculating appropriate compensation.[57]

However, in *Nunez v. Schneider*, a 2002 case in the same court, a different judge disagreed with the ruling in *Cordy*.[58] In this case, a bicyclist was suing a truck driver. The court said:

> Evidence of plaintiff's failure to wear a helmet may go directly to the jury as evidence of comparative fault. . . . The jury must engage in a two step inquiry. It must decide whether a reasonable person exercising ordinary care would have worn a helmet to avoid or mitigate injury in the event of an accident. If the answer is yes, it must next decide whether the evidence establishes that failure to wear a helmet contributed to the severity of the injuries. Only then may

54 *Walden v. State*, 818 P.2d 1190 (Mont. 1991).

55 Ibid.

56 *Cordy v. Sherman Williams Co.*, 975 F. Supp. 639 (D.N.J. 1997).

57 Ibid.

58 *Nunez v. Schneider National Carriers*, 217 F. Supp.2d 562 (D.N.J. 2002).

the jury reduce damages to the extent that a helmet would have
decreased the injuries suffered.[59]

Normally, federal courts do not interpret state law. The federal court should have referred the issue to the New Jersey Supreme Court for consultation in a process called "certification." The fact that this court did not certify the issue of whether a cyclist can be blamed for the legal lack of helmet use may mean it is not good law. But the issue itself probably won't go away, and I would urge cycling advocates to try to add no-blame clauses to their states' bicycle helmet laws.

What is often missed in all of the debate surrounding helmet requirements is a discussion of what protection helmets are actually capable of providing. The typical noncycling proponent of helmet laws will point to a cycling fatality as evidence that cyclists should be required to wear helmets. In fact, as we will see in Chapter 5, §5-4, when reporting fatal cycling accidents, the news media typically mentions whether the cyclist was wearing a helmet even if the cyclist's injuries were not head injuries. This lack of critical thinking indicates a widespread belief that helmets somehow protect cyclists in *all* falls. The truth is, helmets don't even protect cyclists from *head* injuries in all falls, let alone protecting cyclists from the other serious injuries that sometimes prove fatal. This is because helmets are actually only designed to prevent injury during low-speed impacts—11 to 14 miles per hour, the type of low-speed impact a cyclist would expect to encounter while falling from his or her bike due to some defect in the road surface, or due to cyclist error.

In fact, these are by far the most common types of cycling accidents, so perhaps it makes some sense to require helmet manufacturers to at least produce helmets that are capable of protecting the cyclist from injury in a low-speed fall. And this may be supported by data from the National Electronic Injury Surveillance System (NEISS): In the one-third of all cycling accidents that resulted in helmet damage, 69 percent of the cyclists did not suffer head injuries.[60] Nevertheless, helmets are *not* designed to protect the cyclist from the type of high-speed impact associated with collisions between automobiles and bicycles. Despite this reality, proponents of helmet laws do not shrink from holding up fatalities in these collisions as evidence that cyclists should wear helmets. Again, according to the NEISS data, in cycling accidents that resulted in helmet damage, 31 percent of the cyclists nevertheless suffered head in-

59 Ibid.

60 Jeffrey P. Broker and Paul F. Hill, *Bicycle Accidents: Biomechanical, Engineering, and Legal Aspects* (Tucson: Lawyers and Judges, 2006), p. 177.

juries. Furthermore, even when head injuries are prevented, other types of serious injuries may be exacerbated because the cyclist was wearing a helmet.

Undoubtedly, those who draw a connection between high-speed automobile fatalities and helmet use are well intentioned, but they are also misinformed about helmet capabilities. However, because helmet safety standards are governed by extremely lax federal regulation, those who advocate for protecting cyclists from head injuries associated with automobile accidents will be most effective if they focus their attention on strengthening the lax federal helmet-safety standards, rather than on advocating laws that require cyclists to wear helmets that are not even designed to protect them from high-speed impact injuries in the first place.

Other Applicable Statutes

2-24 LITTERING

> **Chapter 415, Illinois Compiled Statutes Annotated Section 105/4. Dumping, deposit, etc., of litter prohibited.** No person shall dump, deposit, drop, throw, discard, leave, cause or permit the dumping, depositing, dropping, throwing, discarding or leaving of litter upon any public or private property in this state, or upon or into any river, lake, pond, or other stream or body of water in this state.

Littering bugs me. Maybe that's why people who litter are called litterbugs. Generally speaking, I am not the guy who feels it is his responsibility, or even his right, to "police" scofflaws. However, when a person litters in public, he is polluting the environment, which, of course, belongs to all of us.

I am loath to admit that I am as guilty of littering as any, unfortunately. In my racing days, I tossed out not only my unfinished food, but wrappers and cans as well. I rationalized my polluting as excusable because it occurred in the heat of battle—or maybe I thought the broom wagon would "sweep" it up as it trailed the race.

So what happens if, as you're riding, you toss out that food wrapper, or even something as seemingly innocuous as a banana peel or apple core? Could you be cited? The short answer is yes. Every state has an anti-littering statute on its books. Let's consider the anti-littering statute in Illinois as an example. The Illinois General Assembly addressed the issue of litter on public and state property statutorily, passing the Litter

Control Act, which became effective January 1, 1974. This act makes it a crime to litter on any public or state property.

Chapter 415, Illinois Compiled Statutes Annotated Section 105/3. Litter is any discarded, used or unconsumed substance or waste. Litter may include, but is not limited to, any garbage, trash, refuse, debris, rubbish, grass clippings or other lawn or garden waste, newspaper, magazines, glass, metal, plastic or paper containers or other packaging construction material, abandoned vehicle (as defined in the Illinois Vehicle Code), motor vehicle parts, furniture, oil, carcass of a dead animal, any nauseous or offensive matter of any kind, any object likely to injure any person or create a traffic hazard, potentially infectious medical waste as defined in Section 3.360 of the Environmental Protection Act, or anything else of an unsightly or unsanitary nature, which has been discarded, abandoned or otherwise disposed of improperly.[61]

As you can see, this list does cover food wrappers and drink containers, as well as garbage such as banana peels and apple cores. The Litter Control Act does not distinguish between biodegradable and nonbiodegradable items. Illinois passed the act in response to what the General Assembly determined to be "rapid population growth, the ever increasing mobility of the population and improper and abusive discard habits" of the people using the private and public property, including the state's highways and roads. Further determining that "litter is detrimental to the welfare of the people of this State" and that the government, industry, and public had so far failed to establish effective litter control, the General Assembly determined that it was necessary to have a uniform litter law and to provide for strict enforcement of litter control.

How strict? In Illinois, dropping that food wrapper, drink container, or banana peel somewhere other than a garbage can or other receptacle is a Class B misdemeanor, which is a criminal offense. A second conviction for littering pushes the offense to a Class A misdemeanor, and a third conviction would be a Class 4 felony. In addition to the fines that are applicable, a person convicted of violating the Litter Control Act can be ordered to remove and properly dispose of the litter, and the state may charge the offender the costs of supervising the litter cleanup.

As always, the penalties will vary from state to state, but as you can see, the consequences for being careless with the environment we all share can be quite serious—as they should be.

---

61 415 Illinois Compiled Statutes, Annotated Section 105/3.

2-25 ROADSIDE RELIEF

Here's one that most people never really think about: What happens when you're on that long ride and nature calls? A few places, mostly big cities, have a specific ordinance against urinating in public. Most of the time, however, taking a break for roadside relief has the potential to get you busted for indecent exposure or disorderly conduct.

You definitely do not want to get busted for indecent exposure (also called public indecency) because in many states it's a sex crime. And once you're convicted of a sex crime, your name goes on that list you don't want to be on—the sex offenders list. That's the list of the guys neighbors rally to protect their children against. If you are caught urinating in public, and you're charged with indecent exposure, you'd better hire an attorney. A conviction for a sex crime—even if *you know* it's something as innocuous as urinating in public—will follow you around for the rest of your life.

Fortunately, it seems as if it would be pretty hard to get convicted. *Indecent exposure requires a "lascivious exposure" of one's privates.* One Florida judge thoughtfully defined it as "an unlawful indulgence in lust, eager for sexual indulgence." That certainly doesn't leave much to the imagination. I don't know about you, but that's not what I have on my mind at 6:30 in the morning when I really, really need to get rid of some coffee. In fact, in *Cleveland v. Pugh* (1996), an Ohio appellate court specifically allowed "I've really gotta go" as an affirmative defense to a charge of public indecency. The court said, "The offense of public indecency was clearly enacted to punish 'sexual exposures,' not to punish a person for answering an urgent call of nature. . . . We find as a matter of law that merely 'answering an urgent call of nature alfresco' by urinating in public does not constitute public indecency."[62] This ruling was based on the legislative history of the state law, which noted that "answering the call of nature alfresco would not be an offense if the actor takes reasonable precautions against discovery, although if he is imprudent in choosing a site the act might constitute disorderly conduct."[63]

On the other hand, in *Columbus v. Breer* (2003), another Ohio appellate court disagreed with the *Pugh* court, holding that "appellee recklessly exposed his private parts, which exposure was viewed by and an affront to others. . . . Taking the usual, normal, and customary meaning of the words in [the ordinance], appellee's conduct constituted public in-

---

62 *Cleveland v. Pugh*, 674 N.E.2d 759 (Ohio Ct. App. 1996).

63 Ibid.

decency."[64] So, one Ohio court agreed with the "I really gotta go" defense, and another Ohio court disagreed. The best that can be said is that if you really gotta go, at least in Ohio, you'd better follow the advice of the Legislative Service Commission and take reasonable, prudent precautions against discovery. And really, although these are Ohio cases, that advice is probably good advice in any state.

But what if you are charged with disorderly conduct instead of indecent exposure? Fighting this charge could be a little tougher. Disorderly conduct is defined as "an act which creates a substantial risk of public inconvenience, annoyance, offense or alarm that was done for no legitimate purpose." There is no getting around the fact that relieving yourself in public is an act. So is your "act" annoying or alarming to anyone? That depends on where you go. As one judge put it, "Shouting, waving and drinking beer may be permissible at the ball park, but not at a funeral." (Yes, this was a public urination case. There are more out there than you would think. "Obscure law" is an oxymoron.) It was clear to another judge in Illinois, that relieving yourself in the playground area of a McDonald's did not qualify as "cheering on" the home team.

So, if you decide to relieve yourself in the middle of Chase County, Kansas (1,061 people, 120,600 head of cattle), you are probably going to be okay, but if you pick the starting line of the Tour Somerville just before the gun goes off, there may be a different result. But wait a minute; you're not out of the woods yet. Even if *nobody* sees you, you could still be in trouble if you create a condition that is "physically offensive to the public."

Once again, circumstances are everything. A man in Ohio who tinkled in the middle of a cabbage field got off without a conviction, while another man who leaked in the corner of a college classroom spent thirty days in the county jail getting remedial potty training. No one saw either person do the deed, but it was pretty hard to ignore the puddle in the classroom, whereas the Ohio judge wondered out loud how you could tell if someone had used a cabbage field for a bathroom.

Finally, *to be disorderly, the act must serve no legitimate purpose.* (I'm not talking about taking the leak here—it's pretty obvious what purpose taking a leak serves—I mean *where* you take the leak.) On one hand, a New York judge ruled that a man who got up from his restaurant table, walked past two perfectly functional men's rooms out the front door, and whizzed on the sidewalk did not have a *legitimate* reason for doing so. On the other hand, in the immortal words of Judge Daniel Markewich of South Nyack: "A persuasive defense of urgency, necessity or

---

64 *Columbus v. Breer*, 789 N.E.2d 1144 (Ohio Ct. App. 2003).

incontinence, at least when coupled with the unavailability of restroom facilities and with reasonable efforts by the defendant to conceal his act, negates some or all of the elements required for conviction under known laws."[65]

So go forth with your super-sized café latte, double extra shots, safe in the knowledge that if you really, really need to, and there's no potty, and it's where nobody is likely to see you or have to clean up after you, then you're probably going to be okay.

2-26 CARRYING IDENTIFICATION

"Our state law authorizes custodial arrests for violations of the Vehicle Code, but not in all circumstances. If the violation is declared to be a felony, the offender is to be dealt with in like manner 'as upon arrest for the commission of any other felony'. . . . For certain enumerated nonfelony offenses, the officer has the discretion to take the offender to 'the nearest or most accessible' magistrate with jurisdiction over the offense or to issue a citation and, upon the offender's signature of a promise to appear, release the offender. . . . For the remaining offenses (except driving under the influence), the officer must follow the cite-and-release procedure, unless the offender fails to present a driver's license or other satisfactory evidence of identity for examination, refuses to give a written promise to appear in court, or demands an immediate appearance before a magistrate, in which case the officer must take the offender to the magistrate. . . .

"There is likewise no dispute that at least one category of identification qualifies as 'other satisfactory evidence . . . of identity'–those forms of documentary evidence that are the functional equivalent of a driver's license. This would include a state-issued identification card and other current, reliable documentary evidence of identity that, like a driver's license, bears the person's photograph, physical description, current mailing address, and signature, and is serially or otherwise numbered."

People v. McKay, Supreme Court of California (2002)

Although bicycles are generally treated as vehicles, there is no statutory requirement for cyclists to be licensed in order to operate a bicycle. While some motorists grumble that cyclists *should* be licensed, a licensing requirement wouldn't change the bicycle's status as a vehicle; bicy-

---

65 *People v. Cooke*, 578 N.Y.S.2d 76 (N.Y. Just. Ct. 1991).

cles would still have the right to the road. What would change is that the bicycle would no longer be accessible to those too young to be licensed. Because bicycles are vehicles that many people, including very young children, operate in lieu of driving a car, licensing requirements have never been seriously considered.

However, bicycles are vehicles, and they are subject to the traffic laws. So what happens when you're on your bike and a police officer stops you for violating a traffic law? Can the officer require you to produce a driver's license for identification when issuing the citation? Depending on the laws of your state, perhaps. In general, if a law enforcement officer observes an offense being committed, and a statute authorizes that officer to make an arrest, the officer has "probable cause" to arrest. With a few limited exceptions, the statutes authorizing arrests give law enforcement officers a large amount of discretion as to whether to make an arrest or to release with a warning. Usually, when an officer observes you violating a traffic law, and stops you, the stop itself is investigative only, and not an arrest. However, once the officer decides against releasing you (usually with a warning), you are under arrest. Typically, the arrest will be a "non-custodial arrest" in the form of a citation.

By signing the citation, you're promising to appear in court to answer the charges against you; upon receiving your promise to appear, the officer releases you from custody. In contrast, in a custodial arrest the officer takes you into custody until you are either charged with an offense or released without charges.

Because you're being cited, the officer is entitled to know your identity (the alternative would be to place you under custodial arrest, which means a trip to jail). In some states, it may be sufficient legally to provide a verbal identification (however, be aware that failure to identify yourself, even if the "failure" is by providing a false identity, is a criminal offense.) In other states, you will be required to produce identification. Typically, this means presenting your driver's license to the officer, but you can substitute a state-issued identification card or other "reliable documentary evidence of identity." A military I.D., for example, might fit that description. In *People v. McKay* (2002), the California Supreme Court noted that in some instances, when the law-enforcement officer personally knows the person stopped, the officer could use that personal knowledge of the person as identification.[66] Ultimately, the officer has broad discretion in deciding whether to require proof of identification. The requirement to produce identification also may vary from state to state. But as a practical matter, if you are stopped for a traffic violation in

---

66 *People v. McKay*, 41 P.3d 59 (Cal.202).

a state where the officer has the discretion to arrest you for lack of identification, carrying identification while you ride may keep you out of jail. Finally, carrying some form of I.D. with you while you ride serves a practical purpose: assisting medical and law-enforcement personnel who might have to come to your aid if you are injured in a traffic accident.

Handling Your Own Traffic Ticket

Many legal problems are so complex and have such enormous consequences that you must have an attorney's assistance if you hope to have a successful outcome. Other problems, while perhaps unpleasant, are not as complex and have far less weighty consequences, so representing yourself is a realistic option. Usually, traffic citations fall into this category. Still, while they aren't as complex as some legal problems, they do involve legal issues, and they do have some consequences. Thus, while representing yourself is a realistic possibility, if you hope to *successfully* represent yourself, you must be prepared. Let's look at what's involved, and what you need to do to handle your own traffic ticket.

2-27 THE TRAFFIC STOP

So you're riding your bike, and suddenly a law-enforcement officer is pulling you over. Maybe you broke a traffic law because you always break that traffic law. Or maybe you broke a traffic law by mistake, or didn't realize you were breaking a traffic law. Maybe you didn't even break a traffic law, but the officer is stopping you because he or she doesn't understand the law but *believes* that you broke a traffic law. Now what? If you were driving an automobile, you'd want to get your driver's license and proof of insurance ready. But you're not driving an automobile. So what do you do?

The very first thing you must do is begin taking mental notes. What just happened? What were you doing? Was anybody else involved? Where did it happen? What are the road conditions? The weather conditions? Time of day? Make a quick mental note of all of the relevant circumstances, because the surrounding circumstances may all be relevant evidence at trial. The officer knows this and is making the same mental notes. You should too.

Before the officer tells you what you did, he or she will probably ask you if you know why you were stopped. There's a reason police officers ask this question: They want evidence. Your answer *can* be useful evidence, if you're not careful. If you admit to some violation, even if you didn't know it was a violation, you've just given the officer evidence that can be admitted against you at trial.

Let's see how that works. Let's say you are riding in a traffic lane, and the officer pulls you over, intending to cite you for failure to use a bicycle lane. The officer asks if you know why he stopped you, and you reply, "I think you pulled me over for failure to use the bicycle lane." Alternatively, you reply, "I don't know. I was just riding in the traffic lane." In both scenarios, you just admitted to failure to use the bicycle lane. Now maybe there's a defense for that, but for now, the important point is that you just gave the officer evidence that can be admitted against you at trial.

Sometimes, cyclists (and drivers) will attempt to talk the officer out of issuing a ticket. Some people claim to have a pretty good success rate with this approach. However, you should understand that when you take this approach, you are giving the officer evidence that can be used against you. The fact is, on most traffic stops the officer has already decided whether to warn you or cite you before you even start talking.

Of course, if an officer has decided to just let you off with a warning, you can always change the officer's mind with your attitude. Police officers report that of all their traffic stops, encounters with cyclists are the most abrasive. You should not be one of those abrasive cyclists. There is absolutely nothing to be gained, and everything to lose, by arguing with a police officer over a traffic stop. At the very least, you are giving the officer a reason to cite you, the evidence to convict you, the details to remember *this particular* traffic stop by, and an incentive to appear and testify at your trial. *Do not argue with the officer.*

Sometimes you're riding along, completely within the law, and the officer drives by and orders you to do something that you're not required to do. Usually, it will be something along the lines of "Get on the sidewalk!" It's rare, but it happens. In this situation, you're dealing with an officer who is either unschooled in the law or doesn't really care what the law is. It's your call. If you are absolutely certain that you are riding legally—remember, town ordinances may differ from state law—you will have to decide whether to comply with an illegal order or risk a citation that you will have to fight later.

If you know with absolute certainty that you are not violating the law, you will not be violating the law by refusing to comply with the officer's order. It is against the law to refuse to obey a *lawful* order; however, there's no requirement that you obey an unlawful order, so it's your call. If you're inclined to fight an unlawful order, this is one instance where you can politely discuss the law with the officer. Notice that I didn't say "argue." Now the tables are turned, because the officer is giving you evidence to be used at trial. If you know that the law doesn't require you to ride on the sidewalk, for example, you can ask the officer if you were doing something illegal. As always, take mental notes. If the officer says, "Yes, the law requires you to ride on the sidewalk," or "No, but it's not safe to ride in the street," you have gained some evidence to be used at trial. You can even disagree, if you wish, as long as you do it politely: "Officer, I've been riding for several years, and I'm familiar with all of the bicycle laws, and I know it's legal for me to ride here." Sometimes, an officer who knows the order is unlawful will just give up trying to intimidate you. In that case, you've won without having to go to trial. But sometimes, you may have to go to trial to assert your rights. Or you can just comply with the order. Again, it's your decision.

Okay, back to our traffic stop. You've been pulled over, you've made some quick mental notes about the circumstances, and the officer is approaching you. The officer asks, "Do you know why I'm pulling you over?" If you now know the officer is fishing for evidence, how *should* you respond? With a simple, polite "No, have I done something wrong?" By saying that, you have done two things. First, the only evidence the officer has is that you don't know why you were pulled over; second, you've now turned the tables by putting the officer in the position of having to give you evidence. Now let's say the officer says you were pulled over for failure to use the bicycle lane. Let's assume that, after reading this chapter, you were riding in compliance with the law, even if you weren't riding in the bicycle lane. Your next question should be, "Is that illegal?"

Once the officer says yes, it's up to you to decide whether you want to discuss the law at that point. If you decide to discuss the law, you may be able to talk yourself out of a ticket by pointing out the exception to the law about riding in bicycle lanes that lets you ride outside the lane. For example, you might have been avoiding debris, or you might have been preparing to make a left turn, or you might have been riding at the same speed as traffic.[67] If you were riding within the law, you might be able to convince the officer of that. If you weren't really riding within the law—if that debris you were "avoiding" was half a mile back, for example—then you're just giving the officer evidence to be used against you, and it would be better not to discuss the law at this point. Keep taking mental notes.

If the officer decides to issue a citation, you will probably be asked for some form of identification. Don't confuse this request with a requirement to have a driver's license to ride your bike. It's not quite the same thing. Any government-issued identification—for example, a state I.D. card, a military I.D. card, or a passport—should be acceptable (see

---

67 The exceptions may vary from state to state, so be familiar with the laws in *your* state.

§2-26 for recommendations on carrying identification). Remember, at this point the officer is making a noncustodial arrest and has the right to require you to provide acceptable evidence of your identity. Once you stray from government-issued identification, the officer has the discretion to decide whether the identification you are offering is "acceptable evidence."

Once you have been issued a citation, make one last mental note of everything that has happened and all of the surrounding circumstances. As soon as you can, write down everything that happened. The officer is doing the same thing to prepare for trial—although not as thoroughly as you're now doing—and your notes of what happened will be used to construct your defense.

2-28 Assess Your Legal Problem

Now you have to decide what to do next. Should you fight your ticket? Should you just pay your fine? Should you hire a lawyer? You need to assess your legal situation to know what to do. If you broke the law, and it's a minor violation, it might just be easier to pay your ticket. Or, you might be eligible for one of the new "cyclist diversion programs" that some jurisdictions are starting to implement. But if you believe that you did not break the law, you might want to fight your ticket. Or maybe you don't want another ticket on your driving record, so you need to fight this ticket. If the charges are minor—a traffic infraction—you have another choice to make: You can represent yourself, or you can have an attorney represent you. Even if you represent yourself, you can always consult with an attorney first.

If the charges are serious—for example, if you're being charged with a misdemeanor—you should seriously consider hiring a lawyer. A misdemeanor conviction will be entered on your criminal record. If you do not have a criminal record, you don't want to start having one now, and if you do have one, you don't want it any longer than it already is. If the charges are very serious—for example, public indecency, BUI, or worse— you had better hire a lawyer, because the consequences can be quite severe if you're convicted.

2-29 The Citation

When the officer issued you the citation, you were asked to sign the citation. This signature is not an admission of guilt, and the citation will say that. By signing the citation, you are making a promise to appear in court to answer the charges against you. The alternative to making that promise is for the officer to make a custodial arrest. So you signed the ticket, promising to appear. The first thing you must understand is that if you break that promise, a warrant will be issued for your arrest. Therefore, you are now bound to follow the traffic court's procedure for resolution of your ticket. You are not required to appear in court; you can just decide to pay the fine for your ticket and that will be the end of it. But you must do *something*.

That ticket will in fact be useful to you in two ways. First, it will give you the procedural information you will need for resolution of your case. It will inform you of the date and time of your court appearance, the location of your court appearance, the contact information for the traffic court, the offense you are being charged with, and the amount of bail you will need to pay. You can enter a plea in writing, which will save you the trouble of appearing in court to enter a plea, only to be given a later trial date. Second, the ticket will provide you with evidence for your case. The offense you are being charged with is evidence. The location of the offense is evidence. The date and time and weather conditions are all evidence. You will want to look at this evidence for any errors. For example, suppose you were cited for impeding traffic—a charge that you know does not apply to bicycles—instead of for failure to ride as close as practicable to the right. Or maybe there are two identical provisions in the vehicle code, one applying to bicycles and the other applying to motor vehicles. Failure to ride as close as practicable to the right is one of those charges. Take notes on everything that is relevant to your case.

2-30 PROCEDURE

If you decide not to contest your ticket, you can just send in your bail amount—essentially a fine at this point—to the address indicated before the deadline for responding, and you're done. Alternatively, you can plead guilty, with an explanation, in an attempt to have your fine reduced. If you decide to contest the charges, however, you must make a written plea and send in the bail amount with your plea. The exact procedure will vary by jurisdiction, so be sure to follow all of the instructions for entering a plea. You *must* do this within the time period required. Remember, if you fail to respond or fail to appear, a warrant will be issued for your arrest.

2-31 GATHERING EVIDENCE

Once you've decided to fight your ticket, you have another matter to settle: Do you need an attorney, or can you represent yourself? If the charges are serious, you should consult with an attorney, who will handle everything for you; if the charges are relatively minor, you can successfully represent yourself. If you're representing yourself, you have to start to do what a lawyer would do if you had one: research the law and gather evidence.

Let's talk about gathering evidence first. If it will be relevant to your case, you should return to the scene as soon as possible after the citation, because you will want to record the conditions existing at the time of your citation. Try to return at around the same time of day as well, so you can record traffic conditions. Bring a camera and a tape measure. Take photographs of the road conditions. For example, if you were riding outside the bicycle lane to avoid debris, take photos of the debris you were avoiding. Then take photos of where you were stopped. Measure the distance, if possible. In this instance, you may be arguing that riding outside the lane was legal because of the debris, and that you were stopped before you had a reasonable opportunity to return to the lane. Or maybe you were stopped for not riding as close as practicable to the right, so you take photographs of the road conditions (for example, the lane width, parked cars and their door zone, etc.) and make measurements of the lane width. In this instance, you may be arguing that because of existing road conditions, you were riding as close to the right as practicable. Or maybe there was some physical obstruction that prevented you from seeing that stop sign, or the officer's angle of view prevented the officer from clearly seeing what you were doing. You want to have photographic evidence of circumstances like that.

Of course, in order to gather evidence, you will also have to know what evidence you need to gather. And that will mean researching the statute you are charged with violating. For example, if you were riding outside the bike lane, you will need to read the text of the statute. Right there, in the text, it says you can ride outside the lane to avoid debris, and that is exactly what you were doing, so you know what your argument is and what evidence you need to gather. Or, if you're really lucky, you look up the statute, read it over, and smile—because you realize the officer cited you for an offense that applies to motor vehicles rather than to bicycles. For example, that citation for failure to ride as close as practicable to the right may be the motor-vehicle variant of the statute rather than the bicycle variant.

If you're a careful researcher, you'll use the annotated code book for your state, because there may be case law or a scholarly article addressing your issue. If there is, and the case law or article supports your argument, you can introduce that in support of your argument at your trial.

2-32 AT YOUR TRIAL

You've done your homework, you've gathered your evidence, and now your trial date has arrived. The first rule is *be on time*. If you miss your trial, it's a failure-to-appear charge. The second rule is to arrive prepared to argue your case. This means arriving with all of your evidence: the citation, any photographs you took, any measurements you made, the notes you took, copies of statutes, copies of case law, copies of scholarly articles, copies of dictionary terms. Basically, bring any evidence you will need to support your argument that you were not in violation of the statute.

Have we forgotten anything? How about witnesses who can testify as to what happened? If you were riding with somebody, that person can testify on your behalf. It's important to remember, however, that testimony must be truthful, so you should only offer the testimony of a witness if that witness can truthfully testify in support of your argument. This means two things. First, the witness shouldn't lie or be coached on what to say. Second, if the witness's truthful testimony will undermine your argument, do not bring the witness. When you're on trial, the officer will be trying to prove the case against you. You don't have to prove your innocence. Your only responsibility is to poke as many holes as you can in the officer's case. Therefore, if you have a witness, and if that witness's truthful testimony will help your defense, bring the witness. Otherwise, leave the witness at home.

The third rule is to arrive appropriately groomed and attired. Although it shouldn't matter what you look like, it does matter. The point here is to win your case, not to advance your right of personal liberty in matters of attire. You want to seem likeable and credible, so prepare for court as you would for a job interview: Wear clean clothing, wear appropriate clothing, and be appropriately groomed.

The fourth rule is to be respectful in court. Again, you are trying to win your case, so be polite, be respectful, and follow the judge's instructions. You address the judge as "Your Honor." You don't argue with the judge, and you don't say the judge is wrong. If the judge *is* wrong, you say, "Your Honor, the statute says . . ." or "Your Honor, the Supreme Court has held. . . ." The judge isn't supposed to be *trying* to convict you—after all, you are presumed innocent until proven guilty—but if you convince the judge that the officer is a likeable and credible person and you're not, you've got an uphill battle. The fact is, judges already tend to give more weight to an officer's testimony anyway, because the officer is presumed to have no reason to lie, while you are presumed to have a very powerful motivation for lying. There's nothing to be gained by tipping that advantage even further in the officer's favor.

If you're lucky, the officer will fail to appear, and you can move to have the charges dismissed. Oppose any attempt by the court to reset the trial date. It happens occasionally, but traffic court is bread-and-butter work for traffic officers, so it's more likely that the officer will appear. Remember, *you are not in court to prove your innocence.* You are in court because you've pled "not guilty." The officer is in court to prove your guilt. If the officer can't prove your guilt, you can't be convicted. Now, usually, that "proving your guilt" part will consist of the officer testifying that you committed the offense you are being charged with. If your only defense is to counter the officer's testimony with your own version of what happened, you will lose. Instead, you need to poke holes in the officer's case.

At this point, you've already entered a "not guilty" plea. You did that when you asked for a trial. But before we proceed to your defense, let's go back to that moment when you first entered your plea. You had a choice to plead "not guilty" or "guilty." If you had decided to plead guilty, you would have then been given an opportunity to explain any extenuating circumstances the court should take into consideration when sentencing you. For example, suppose you were cited for riding at night without a light. You plead guilty, but you explain to the court that your battery had just died, or that your light had just malfunctioned, and you present evidence, if possible, to back that claim up. Although you're guilty, the court will consider these extenuating circumstances. It may find you guilty, but reduce your fine. Or if you just can't afford to pay the fine, the court *may* be able to take that into consideration. However, many courts have had their hands tied by the legislature as to how much, if at all, they may reduce traffic fines.

But you pled "not guilty," which is why you're now on trial. Suppose you were cited for failure to ride as close to the right as practicable. Suppose also that the officer made a mistake and cited you for the motor-vehicle violation rather than for the bicycle violation. The court will enter your plea as "not guilty." Now it's up to the officer to prove the case against you. Again, you are not in court to prove your innocence. At this point, you are not supposed to explain why you're not guilty. The officer is supposed to testify that you are guilty. Until somebody has presented a case against you, you have no reason to present a defense. Now let's say that the officer testifies that you were not riding as close to the right as practicable. Now you present your defense. You produce a copy of the statute, from which you read, emphasizing that the statute applies *only* to operators of motor vehicles, and not to cyclists. Then you move to dismiss the charges against you. The court should dismiss the charges. It's possible that the court will allow the officer to amend the complaint against you, however. Or maybe the officer cited the correct statute in the first place. Now the officer testifies that you were not riding as close to the right as practicable, and you have to poke holes in that case against you. However, although that's your right, be aware that though this case is important to *you,* it's not important to the court. It's just one of many, many cases on an overcrowded docket, and the court doesn't have time for you to present a lengthy, complicated defense. Although it's patently unfair, traffic courts may pressure you to restrict your defense. Be respectful, but don't be intimidated. If your evidence is repetitive and you are pressured to hurry up, make a decision about what's most important to introduce and what's just overkill. If your evidence is necessary to your defense, insist that your line of questioning, or the evidence you are attempting to introduce, is necessary for your defense. If the court still won't let you continue, ask the court to enter your statement into the record that this evidence is necessary for your defense, and that you were denied the opportunity to introduce the evidence. Now, if you decide to appeal your conviction, you have at least one basis for appeal.

Question the officer if that will help your case. It's always good to have the other side introduce evidence in your favor. For example, if cars were parked at the curb, creating a hazardous door zone, you would want the officer to testify that cars were parked at the curb, so you ask the officer, "Did you happen to notice if there were any cars parked at the curb that day?" If the officer says yes, you produce your photograph of parked cars at the scene and ask, "Is this the location where the ticket was issued?" Officer: "Yes." "Does this photograph accurately depict the parking circumstances at that location?" Officer: "Yes." What's never good is assisting the other side in introducing evidence against you. Do *not* ask for the officer's opinion on whether riding in the door zone is safe. Do *not* ask for the officer's opinion on whether the lane is too narrow to share safely. Do *not* ask the officer to define "practicable."

Have the officer introduce evidence that will help you, such as admitting that there were parked cars at the curb, or agreeing that your photograph accurately depicts the location, or admitting that he was not in a position to accurately see what you were doing. Then introduce your own evidence to bolster your argument that under the circumstances, you were riding within the law. So you've got your research in front of you. You know what "practicable" means. You introduce evidence that "practicable" does not mean the same thing as "possible." You introduce evidence that there are exceptions to the rule. You introduce evidence that you were riding within one or more of those exceptions. For example, if the lane was too narrow to share safely with a vehicle, you introduce that evidence. If the only way to ride further to the right was to ride in the door zone, introduce that evidence, and also introduce evidence that door zones are a major hazard for cyclists. Use any evidence you have gathered to counter the officer's testimony that you were riding in violation of the law. There are traffic diagrams available in the courtroom, and if they will help the court understand your case, use them.

Congratulations, you've just poked some major holes in the case against you!

2-33 THREE MORE DEFENSES

There are three other possible defenses that may be relevant, depending on the circumstances. In these defenses, you're admitting that, while technically speaking, you did violate the law, you shouldn't be convicted.

The first defense, called *"mistake of fact,"* is one you would use where there was some physical circumstance beyond your control that led to the violation. For example, there may have been something obstructing your view of that stop sign. While it may be technically true that you ran through the stop sign, it was impossible for you to see the sign, and therefore, there was no way for you to know that there was a stop sign In order to make this defense, you should introduce evidence to support your argument.

The second defense, that you were *"legally justified"* in riding the way you did, applies when there is some fact that makes your otherwise unlawful action lawful. Typically, this will involve an action that might be unlawful, except that the law allows it under the circumstances. For example, if you are riding in the lane at the same speed as other traffic, but slow down to make a left turn, you are legally justified in slowing down, even though it would otherwise be unlawful to ride in the lane at a speed slower than other traffic.

Finally, if circumstances warrant, you can argue a *"necessity defense,"* in which you are arguing that there was some emergency that made breaking the law necessary to avoid harm to yourself or another person. For example, if it's against the law to ride on the sidewalk in your business district, but you swerved onto the sidewalk to avoid colliding with a car that cut you off while making a right turn, you have a necessity defense. Uh, just don't ride on the sidewalk for another five blocks after you were cut off. Right?

Constitutional Rights and Restrictions

So far, we've looked at where you can legally ride. However, if you think about it, the question of where you can legally ride implies the possibility that you can't necessarily ride everywhere. As we've seen, cyclists have rights under statutory law, under the common law, and under the Constitution. But as we've also seen, where you ride on the road itself may be limited, sometimes by the speed you can ride at, sometimes simply by virtue of being on a bicycle. Or, in particular jurisdictions, your right to ride a bike may be restricted by a prohibition against riding on the sidewalks. Obviously, then, your rights as a cyclist can be restricted. In fact, all rights are restricted in some manner. The most widely known expression of that principle comes from Justice Oliver Wendell Holmes, who observed that "the most stringent protection of free speech would not protect a man falsely shouting fire in a theater and causing a panic."[68]

The question we encounter, then, is, to what extent can the rights of cyclists be restricted? And this brings us to the U.S. Constitution and other founding documents, such as the Declaration of Independence. When the founding fathers declared their independence from Great Britain, they pointedly stated, "We hold these truths to be self-evident, that all men are created equal, that they are endowed by their Creator with certain unalienable Rights, that among these are Life, Liberty and the pursuit of Happiness.—That to secure these rights, Governments are instituted among Men, deriving their just powers from the consent of the governed."[69]

These were the founding principles of the nascent United States. The people have unalienable rights, and the powers of government are a grant from the people for the purpose of securing those rights. Those powers are limited to what is granted by the people to the government, and the U.S. Constitution is the law that defines exactly which powers the people grant to the government, and for what purpose. The Constitution itself states: "We the People of the United States, in Order to form a more perfect Union, establish Justice, insure domestic Tranquility, provide for the common defense, promote the general Welfare, and secure the Blessings of Liberty to ourselves and our Posterity, do ordain and establish this Constitution for the United States of America."[70]

The founding fathers were quite clear that one of the purposes of the Constitution was to "secure the Blessings of Liberty." Furthermore, the

---

68 *Schenck v. U.S.*, 249 U.S. 47, 52 (1919).

69 Declaration of Independence, 1776, paragraph 2.

70 U.S. Constitution, Preamble.

founding fathers were quite clear that the powers granted to the government were limited, stating, "The powers not delegated to the United States by the Constitution, nor prohibited by it to the States, are reserved for the States respectively, or to the people."[71] In addition to delineating the powers the people grant to the government, the founding fathers included a Bill of Rights, which they specifically said delineated some, but not all, of the unalienable rights of the people: "The enumeration in the Constitution, of certain rights, shall not be construed to deny or disparage others retained by the people."[72]

It's important to understand that although the people granted some of their power to the government, the government was not in return granting rights to the people. Rather, the government was acknowledging that it has a grant of limited powers from the people, and that the people have unalienable rights that the government must respect in exercising its grant of power. One of the powers the people granted to the government was the power to legislate: "All legislative Powers herein granted shall be vested in a Congress of the United States, which shall consist of a Senate and House of Representatives."[73] That grant of legislative power is limited, however: "This Constitution, and the Laws of the United States which shall be made in Pursuance thereof; and all Treaties made, or which shall be made, under the Authority of the United States, shall be the supreme Law of the Land; and the Judges in every State shall be bound thereby, any Thing in the Constitution or Laws of any State to the Contrary notwithstanding."[74]

Because the Constitution is the supreme law of the land, all other laws, whether local, state, national, or international, must not be in conflict with the Constitution, and all judges are bound to follow the Constitution in applying the law. Thus, all laws, whether passed by Congress or the state legislatures, must not be in conflict with the Constitution. Furthermore, each state has its own state constitution, and all laws passed by a state legislature or local government not only must be consistent with the applicable provisions of the U.S. Constitution, but must also be consistent with the state constitution.

Now let's return to our original question: To what extent can the rights of cyclists be restricted? When the legislature passes a statute stating that cyclists have all of the rights and all of the duties that are applicable to other vehicle operators, the legislature is granting those rights—although

71 U.S. Constitution, Tenth Amendment.

72 U.S. Constitution, Ninth Amendment.

73 U.S. Constitution, Article I.

74 U.S. Constitution, Article IV.

they may in fact be a statutory expression of an ancient and unalienable right of liberty—and thus, the legislature defines the extent and limits of those rights. However, the legislature cannot restrict the right in some way that would violate the U.S. Constitution (or the state constitution). Thus, if the U.S. Constitution guarantees the ancient right of liberty, including the right to travel, any statute that would restrict that right must do so in a way that is consistent with the limited powers of government and the constitutional right.

And that is where the courts come in. When the constitutionality of a statute is challenged, the courts must determine exactly what the legislature's intent was. The court must also decide whether the statute is being applied in a way that is consistent with the Constitution, or alternatively, whether the legislative intent itself is constitutional. At other times, when the court is interpreting a common-law right, the court must interpret whether a particular act was consistent or inconsistent with that common-law right. However, when the legislature sees fit to legislate on that subject, the statute then preempts the common law. As we've seen, in many states the legislatures have codified the common-law right into statutory law.

The right to travel is an unsettled area of constitutional law. All courts agree that there is a constitutional right to *interstate* travel (travel between the states); some courts, and virtually all constitutional scholars, have held that there is a corresponding right to *intrastate* travel (travel entirely within the state). This means that any statute limiting the right to interstate travel would be subject to judicial review for constitutionality. By the same token, a statute limiting the right to intrastate travel would be subject to judicial review in those jurisdictions that have held that there is a right to intrastate travel. And when we begin talking about judicial review, that raises a little issue called "standard of review."

When courts review a statute for constitutionality, they need some sort of standard by which to measure it. That standard will vary depending upon how important the constitutional right is. On one hand, if a state is interfering with a person's "life, liberty, or property," the standard the court uses to review the state's action is called *"rational basis."* This means the court determines whether the government has a constitutionally permissible interest in the activity being regulated and whether the statute at issue is rationally related to that governmental interest. This is the lowest level of scrutiny courts engage in, because once the government demonstrates that it has a constitutionally permitted interest, it is virtually certain that the legislation will be found to have a rational relationship to that interest.

On the other hand, if a state's action interferes with a constitutional right that is considered "fundamental," the standard the court uses to review the state's action is *strict scrutiny.*[75] This means that in order for the statute to survive judicial review, the government must demonstrate that three criteria have been met. First, the government must have a "compelling interest" in the issue being regulated. Second, the statute must be "narrowly tailored" to address the government's interest. Generally, this means that the law must be no broader than is necessary to achieve the governmental interest. And third, the statute must be the "least restrictive means" for achieving that governmental interest. This means that, given a range of competing methods for achieving the government's goal, the means chosen must be the one that is least restrictive of the fundamental right affected. If the government can prove that the statute meets these three criteria, the statute will survive judicial review. In practice, most laws that are subject to strict scrutiny do not in fact survive judicial review.

Here's how strict scrutiny would work with an ordinance that restricts cycling in some way. Suppose that, in the interests of traffic safety, a town decides to ban cycling on a road, or even within the town limits. The constitutionality of the ordinance is challenged in a lawsuit, and the court reviews it under the strict scrutiny standard. First, the court will inquire as to whether public safety is a "compelling governmental interest." The answer would be "yes, public safety is a compelling interest." Second, the court will inquire as to whether the ordinance is "narrowly tailored" to address the government's interest. This would mean that the ordinance must actually advance the government's interest in public safety. It would also mean that the ordinance could not be "overinclusive" or "underinclusive." For example, if the ordinance even banned cycling at the velodrome, it would be "overinclusive," because that would have no impact on traffic safety. On the other hand, suppose that restricting cycling in town has a minimal impact on traffic safety, because the safety issues are not really caused by cycling—an ordinance that restricts cycling without addressing the other traffic safety issues would be underinclusive. Finally, the ordinance must use the "least restrictive means." This means that in order for the ordinance to be constitutional, there would have to be nothing else the town could have done to promote traffic safety—the town couldn't lower the speed limits or enforce the existing speed limits; the town couldn't put in bike lanes, sharrows, or cycle paths, or designate alternative bike routes; the town couldn't have put in traffic signals at intersections, or installed traffic-calming measures. If the town couldn't

---

75 Strict scrutiny is a higher level of review than either "rational basis" or "intermediate scrutiny."

have done anything else, and the least restrictive way to promote traffic safety in this town would be to ban cycling, then the ordinance would pass constitutional muster. As you can probably see, because there would be a number of traffic safety alternatives to banning cycling, this ordinance would in fact most likely be found unconstitutional. Because the right to travel is considered fundamental, when that right is restricted the standard of review should always be strict scrutiny. Thus, all courts agree that laws restricting the right of *interstate* travel are restricting a fundamental right and therefore are subject to strict scrutiny review. And in those jurisdictions holding that there is a right to *intrastate* travel, the standard of review for when that right is restricted should also be strict scrutiny.

Then there's the real world. In *Lutz v. York*,[76] a 1990 case from Pennsylvania involving a challenge on a local ordinance banning "cruising," the Third Circuit Court of Appeals became the first court to recognize a right to intrastate travel. That *should* have meant that the court would then apply strict scrutiny to determine whether the cruising ban was constitutional. However, comparing the right to intrastate travel to the right of free speech, which is *not* a fundamental right, the court chose instead to apply "intermediate scrutiny." Remember what Justice Holmes said about the right of free speech? That it doesn't mean you can falsely shout "fire!" in a crowded theater? Justice Holmes was arguing that freedom of speech has limits.[77] In *Lutz*, the Third Circuit noted:

> "If the freedom of speech which is expressly enumerated in the First Amendment itself can be so qualified by mere intermediate scrutiny, then surely the unenumerated right of localized travel can be as well. The concerns underlying York's cruising ordinance seem to us highly analogous to the concerns that drive the time, place, and manner doctrine: just as the right to speak cannot conceivably imply the right to speak whenever, wherever, and however one pleases—even in public fora specifically used for public speech—so too the right to travel cannot conceivably imply the right to travel whenever, wherever, and however one pleases—even on roads specifically designed for public travel. . . .

76 *Lutz v. York*, 899 F.2d 255 (3rd Cir. 1990).

77 Remarkably, the reference to shouting "fire!" in a crowded theater had *nothing* to do with the case before Justice Holmes; he was just using an analogy to explain why even free speech has limits. Unfortunately, to Justice Holmes's discredit, he used a "straw man" analogy to explain why the government could imprison a man for speaking out against the draft during World War I. The decision in *Schenk v. U.S.* was a significant erosion of the right of free speech, but the Supreme Court later significantly reduced the restrictions on free speech that Justice Holmes devised.

"Therefore, in order to set out a workable jurisprudence for the newly recognized due process right of localized movement on the public roadways, we find it appropriate to borrow from the well-settled, highly analogous rules the Court has developed in the free speech context. The cruising ordinance will be subjected to intermediate scrutiny, and will be upheld if it is narrowly tailored to meet significant city objectives."[78]

For the *Lutz* court, time, place, and manner restrictions on the right of localized travel would be upheld if the government's interest is "plainly significant" and if the restriction is "limited in its scope" and leaves open "ample alternative routes to get about town without difficulty." Contrasting intermediate scrutiny with strict scrutiny, the *Lutz* court observed that "limited in its scope" means "the city need only write a narrowly tailored ordinance, not the least restrictive ordinance."[79]

Although the *Lutz* court was the first to recognize a right to intrastate travel, this is a bizarre formulation; the right to travel is fundamental, so the standard of review *should* be strict scrutiny. And in fact, all other courts that have recognized a right to intrastate travel have applied strict scrutiny. Clearly, the *Lutz* court got it only half right: There is a constitutional right to travel that is fundamental and of necessity includes the right to localized travel; however, the correct standard of judicial review for restrictions of fundamental rights is strict scrutiny, not the intermediate scrutiny applied in *Lutz*.

So where does that leave us? The mainstream view of constitutional scholarship is that there is a fundamental constitutional right to travel, and that right includes localized travel. Some state constitutions even explicitly guarantee the right of localized travel. All courts agree that there is a right to interstate travel. Many courts agree that the right to travel includes the right to intrastate travel. In these jurisdictions, the standard of review for any restriction on travel is strict scrutiny, which requires that the government have a compelling interest, that the law be narrowly tailored, and that the law use the least restrictive means to achieve the government's goal. Finally, in those jurisdictions that have not yet recognized a right to localized travel, the standard of review is "rational basis," which requires that the law be rationally related to a permissible governmental interest. If government can pass that bar—and it's such a low bar that it's almost impossible not to pass—then the statute will be upheld.

78 *Lutz v. York*, 899 F.2d 255 (3rd Cir. 1990).
79 Ibid.

All courts now agree that there is a right to interstate travel, and I believe that it is only a matter of time, and will, before all courts recognize a fundamental right to intrastate travel. Almost all constitutional scholars agree that the right to travel includes the fundamental right to localized travel. To the extent that some courts do not recognize this right, I believe the courts are wrong, and that over time the courts will shift toward the view that we all instinctively know is right, which is that *of course* the right to travel—the right to personal liberty, if you will—includes the right to local travel. As the Second Circuit Court of Appeals held in 1971, "It would be meaningless to describe the right to travel between the states as a fundamental precept of personal liberty and not to acknowledge a correlative constitutional right to travel within a state."[80]

80   *King v. New Rochelle Municipal Housing Authority*, 442 F.2d 646 (2nd Cir. 1971).

3

Bicycle Accidents and Other Hazards

INTRODUCTION

When Evylyn Thomas set out on her bicycle on Memorial Day, 1896, it was a well-settled point of law that her bicycle was a vehicle and that she had all of the rights, as well as all of the duties, that were applicable to operators of other vehicles. Among other things, this meant that she had as much right to the road as the operator of any other vehicle in the city, and that she was owed a duty of care by every other person on the street. It also meant that other operators of vehicles had as much right to the road as she did, and that she owed the same duty of care to every other person that was owed to her. This reciprocal relationship between all persons was the law in 1896, and it's still the law today. Like thousands of other New York cyclists that day, Evylyn Thomas was simply enjoying a ride on a beautiful spring day; it's unlikely that she was considering her rights and duties in the warm sunshine of the holiday as she pedaled south on Broadway.

Although Henry Wells was seated behind the wheel of a new type of carriage—a "horseless" carriage—that day, it was a well-settled point of law that carriages were vehicles, and that as the driver of a carriage, he, too, enjoyed the same rights, and was subject to the same duties, that all other carriage drivers enjoyed and were subject to. Although he was driving a type of vehicle that had never been seen in New York before, he had as much right to the road as any other carriage driver, and he was owed a duty of care by every other person on the street. And because the legal relationship was reciprocal, it also meant that every other vehicle had as much right to the road as he did, and that he owed the same duty of care to every other person that was owed to him. Mr. Wells was simply enjoying the capabilities of the new horseless carriage on a beautiful spring day; it's unlikely that he was considering his rights and duties in the warm sunshine of the holiday as he motored north on Broadway toward the King's Bridge checkpoint of the Cosmopolitan Race.

Neither Miss Thomas nor Mr. Wells expected to meet quite so dramatically that day. It's not that accidents were unheard of; every day, it seemed, the papers reported bicycle-related accidents. That day alone, seven people were reported injured in the New York area in four separate accidents: There was a collision between a bicycle and a wagon, a collision between two bicycles, a collision between a bicycle and a pedestrian, and two brothers who didn't collide with anything at all, but nevertheless managed to fall from their tandem. Traffic accidents were a common, everyday event, and yet people still went about their affairs, enjoying beautiful spring days when they could.

In short, Miss Thomas and Mr. Wells were not so different from us. But that day, something went amiss for both Miss Thomas and Mr. Wells—they had an accident, the first reported automobile accident resulting in an injury. As Miss Thomas, traveling south on Broadway, and Mr. Wells, traveling north on Broadway, neared the intersection with West 74th Avenue, witnesses reported that Mr. Wells lost control of his Duryea Motor Wagon and began to zigzag up the street toward Miss Thomas. They collided, and Miss Thomas was knocked from her bicycle into the street, where she lay unconscious, her leg broken. Miss Thomas was taken by ambulance to Manhattan Hospital; Mr. Wells was taken by paddy wagon to jail. The next day . . . well, that's anybody's guess. The record ends there, mostly. We know that Frank Duryea won the race, and that the prize money and the reputation thus earned gave the Duryeas the start they needed to begin selling the first mass-produced automobiles in America. The thirteen automobiles Duryea sold in 1896 represented the beginning of the American automobile industry. But that's another story.

Bicycle Accidents and the Law

Although the collision between Henry Wells and Evylyn Thomas was the first reported auto accident resulting in an injury, it wasn't exactly the first auto accident. In fact, the first automobile accident—well, actually, the first three automobile accidents—occurred six months earlier, on Thanksgiving Day, 1895, during the course of the Chicago Times-Herald Race, the first American auto race. One of the entrants in that race, a Benz car that was sponsored by the New York department store Macy's and driven by a hapless racer named Jerry O'Connor, had the misfortune to collide with a horse-drawn streetcar. And a horse-drawn sleigh. And a horse-drawn taxi, at which point his automobile was too damaged to continue and he called it a day. Frank Duryea went on to win the Chicago Times-Herald Race, a feat he would repeat six months later in the Cosmopolitan Race. The toll? Two auto races, four auto accidents, one injured cyclist.

Although we can't really be sure of the legal outcome of that toll, we can be sure that today, such a toll would trigger insurance claims and perhaps lawsuits for negligence. You've probably heard the term before, but what exactly is meant by "negligence"? And why would an accident raise issues of negligence?

3-1 NEGLIGENCE IN BICYCLE ACCIDENTS

Under the common law, every person owes every other person a duty of due care. Whether intentionally or not, from time to time someone ignores that. Let's break that legalese down into plain English.

First, all of the judicial decisions that have been handed down over the centuries, beginning in England and then continuing in the colonies of North America and later in the United States, are collectively what we call the *common law.* The courts use common law for guidance as to what the law is.

And yes, we really do follow legal principles that were established in England centuries ago, as well as the newer ones that were established in this country; in fact, some of these English decisions from earlier centuries survive in our own vehicular laws today.

Second, the *duty of due care* that every person owes every other person is the duty not to impose an "unreasonable" risk of harm upon the other person. As we've seen, the "reasonableness" of an act—or even a failure to act—is determined by the *reasonable person standard*—the objective legal standard of conduct of the ordinary prudent person who, under similar circumstances, takes "reasonable" precautions to protect others from unreasonable risk of harm. In short, the duty of due care is to behave as a reasonable person would under similar circumstances. A *breach of duty* occurs when a person acts or fails to act as a reasonable person would, exposing others to unreasonable risk of harm.

A *negligent act* comprises three key elements: Whenever these three elements are combined—an act or failure to act, a duty of care, and a breach of that duty—a negligent act has been committed. If injury results and the negligent act is both the actual and foreseeable cause of the defendant's injuries, the person breaching the duty is held liable for the tort of negligence, and the law provides a remedy—money, paid by the defendant—to right the wrong done to the plaintiff.

Gross negligence is more extreme than ordinary negligence but falls short of an intentional act. What separates gross negligence from ordinary negligence is a reckless disregard for the rights or safety of others; this reckless disregard is manifested by a conscious indifference to the consequences of the negligent act. Here's how it works: With ordinary negligence, the negligent conduct breaches a duty of due care that the defendant owes to every other person to behave as a reasonable person would under similar circumstances to protect others from unreasonable risk of harm. With gross negligence, that breach of duty is done with conscious indifference to the likely consequences. Sometimes, a statute will make gross negligence an element of a crime; when gross negligence is an element of a crime, it is called *criminal negligence.*

3-2 TORTS AND WHO'S TO BLAME

As we've seen, negligence is a tort. But what does the law mean by "tort"? Simply, a *tort* is a "civil wrong," rather than a criminal act, committed against another person. There are many types of torts besides negligence. For example, there are intentional torts, such as assault or battery, as well as torts that contain an element of intent, such as defamation or invasion of privacy. Even though a tort is a civil wrong, it may also be a criminal act under statutory law; this means that the legislature has made the act a crime. In a tort, the person who has been wronged files a civil lawsuit against the *tortfeasor*—that is, the perpetrator of the wrong—whereas when a crime has been committed, the "people," through the district attorney locally or the Department of Justice at the state and federal levels, conduct the prosecution. In a civil suit, if the defendant loses he is held "liable"; in a criminal trial, the defendant is found "guilty." In a civil trial, the remedy will usually be money damages payable to the *plaintiff* (i.e., the person filing the lawsuit against the defendant) while in a criminal trial the penalty will be a fine, imprisonment, or both.

RESPONDEAT SUPERIOR

Suppose somebody commits a tort while on the job. Obviously, the tortfeasor—again, the person actually committing the tort—can be held liable. But what about the employer? Can the employer be held liable? *Should* the employer be held liable? The answer is a qualified yes—under the legal doctrine of *respondeat superior,* the employer can be held responsible for an employee's tortious conduct if that tortious conduct is committed within the scope of employment.

Two factors will determine whether the employer shares responsibility. First, there must be an employer-employee relationship. This means that the person's work must be subject to the control of the employer. If the employer does not exert control over the work, the person is an independent contractor; there is no employer-employee relationship, and therefore the *respondeat superior* doctrine does not apply. If an employer-employee relationship can be established, the employee must also be acting within the scope of employment when the tort is committed for the *respondeat superior* doctrine to apply. This means that the employee must be acting to further the employer's business purpose; if this test is met, the employer may be held liable for the employee's tortious act— even if the act was specifically prohibited by the employer.

DISTRACTED AND INATTENTIVE DRIVERS

Distracted and inattentive drivers are an increasing hazard for all users of the road. Drivers who multitask while driving—whether grooming themselves, adjusting the stereo, or even reading—are twice as likely to be involved in an accident as drivers who are attentive to their task. And what if the driver is using a cell phone? That driver is four times as likely to be involved in an accident, even if the driver is using a hands-free device. In one infamous incident, a teen who was text-messaging a friend while driving collided with and killed a cyclist. Regardless of the driver's underlying action, the inattentiveness is negligent, perhaps even grossly negligent, depending on the extremity of the breach of the driver's duty of care.

IMPAIRED DRIVERS

In most cycling fatalities, alcohol impairment is a factor. Though not the most common hazard cyclists face, the impaired driver is certainly the greatest hazard. The impaired driver's actions are unintentional, and thus negligent. However, because the impaired driver is exhibiting the extreme carelessness and indifference to the likely consequences of her actions that are the hallmark of gross negligence, and because DUI is illegal, if you are injured by an impaired driver, that act may be criminally negligent.

ACTS OF GOD

Most of us try to be conscious of riding safely, but sometimes, despite our best efforts, we're subject to *Acts of God*. If we're lucky, we survive them. But sometimes, through nobody's fault, an Act of God causes injury. To be considered an Act of God, the event must be a natural event such as a hurricane or other storm, lightning, a tornado, a falling tree, or a flood. Other examples of Acts of God include earthquakes, fires caused by lightning, and the acts of wild animals. Acts of God do not include events that cause an injury if that injury could have been prevented through the exercise of due care. Thus, for example, although a falling tree or a flood could be considered an Act of God, it would not be an Act of God if somebody's carelessness contributed to it—for example, if somebody was negligent in maintaining a tree on his property, or in operating or maintaining a dam.

Sometimes, an Act of God is the sole legal cause of an injury. Sometimes, however, the Act of God leads to the injurious result threatened by

121

somebody's negligence. If reasonable care and foresight could have prevented the injury, the negligent person cannot avoid liability by claiming that an Act of God was the legal cause of the injury, even though an Act of God may have been involved.

3-3 ACCIDENT STATISTICS

There are three main sources for cyclist accident statistics: hospital emergency room reports, police reports, and cyclist surveys. None of these sources gives a completely accurate picture of cycling accidents because there isn't a single source that captures the full spectrum of accidents with consistency and objectivity.

Hospital emergency room statistics are reported to the National Electronic Injury Surveillance System (NEISS) of the Consumer Products Safety Commission. These statistics represent only those accidents serious enough to warrant a trip to the emergency room; thus, many cycling accidents are simply not reported. Nevertheless, more than 500,000 cycling accidents result in a trip to the emergency room each year.

Police reports are another source of cycling statistics; however, there are several problems with police report data. First, because police reports are typically filed only for automobile accident investigations, automobile-related cycling accidents are overrepresented in these reports. For example, one study based on emergency room reports indicated that automobile-related accidents accounted for only 15 percent of all bicycle accidents. Police report data are also questionable because, as we shall see in Chapter 5, police reports commonly reflect a bias against

FIGURE 3.1 Types of Cycling Accidents

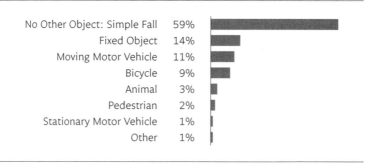

No Other Object: Simple Fall	59%
Fixed Object	14%
Moving Motor Vehicle	11%
Bicycle	9%
Animal	3%
Pedestrian	2%
Stationary Motor Vehicle	1%
Other	1%

(Source: William E. Moritz, "Adult Bicyclists in the U.S.: Characteristics and Riding Experiences," Transportation Research Board, 1998.)

FIGURE 3.2 Common Variables in Bicycle Crashes Involving Motor Vehicles

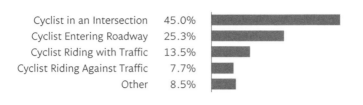

Cyclist in an Intersection	45.0%
Cyclist Entering Roadway	25.3%
Cyclist Riding with Traffic	13.5%
Cyclist Riding Against Traffic	7.7%
Other	8.5%

(Source: Highway Safety Research Center (using data from police reports) 1999.)

Note: Figures 3.2A–3.2D further break down the common scenarios for bicycle-motor vehicle crashes.

cyclists (see §5-2). This factor casts doubt on the validity of their conclusions. It is not uncommon in writing up accident reports for police officers to take the accident details from the motorist only, failing to interview the cyclist at all. Furthermore, safe—and more to the point, *legal*—riding practices may be reported by law-enforcement officers as "cyclist error." Nevertheless, if the police report data can be believed—and that's a *big* if—they indicate that cyclist error contributes to 80 percent of all reported accidents. Although of questionable value, the data from police reports are shown in Figures 3.1 and 3.2.

The third main source of data concerning cycling accidents is cyclist surveys compiled from organized cycling events and club riders. This does not include accident data from inexperienced cyclists, but it does provide data about cycling hazards faced by experienced cyclists. These data indicate that for experienced riders, 80 percent of all accidents occurred in the street; of these, only 21 percent were automobile accidents. And for these experienced riders, most accidents—nearly 37 percent—resulted from road surface conditions.

For many years, there was vehement debate over what types of bicycle accidents were most common. Virtually all statistics relating to bicycle accidents came from police accident reports, and critics maintained that this database systematically underreported bicycle accidents that did not involve a motor vehicle. Finally, in 1999, a team of researchers at the Highway Safety Research Center (HSRC) of the University of North Carolina at Chapel Hill performed a large-scale study of bike wrecks based on emergency room admissions. Their findings largely supported the critics: Only 320 of the 1,115 (28.7 percent) admissions resulting from bicycle accidents involved a motor vehicle. But there was also a surprise: Only 28 of the 1,115 (2.5 percent) incidents involved a bike-on-bike crash. This was contrary to the predictions of critics, who had assumed that bike-on-bike collisions constituted a much larger percentage of injury-producing bicycle accidents. A majority of the crashes that required an overnight stay in the hospital *did* involve a motor vehicle, however. Thus, even though less than one-third of all injury-producing bicycle accidents involve a motor vehicle, about three-quarters of all serious injuries result from car-on-bike accidents.[1]

3-4 OVERREPRESENTED VARIABLES IN CYCLING ACCIDENTS

The HSRC has also undertaken two large studies of car-on-bike crashes using police accident reports. In these studies, the center identified the various types of accidents that occurred and the accidents that resulted in very serious or fatal injuries (VS/F) to the cyclist. The results were interesting. Several types of accidents had identifiable characteristics that set them apart from the norm (in other words, they were "overrepresented variables"): accidents involving intersections, accidents involving riding at night, and accidents involving alcohol.

INTERSECTIONS

One study indicates that approximately half of all cycling accidents included in the study occurred in intersections; most of these accidents (84 percent) occurred while the cyclist was riding straight through the intersection.[2] However, NEISS data indicate that only 15 percent of all cycling accidents involve automobiles. There are two ways to interpret this discrepancy. One is to assume that intersection accidents account for no more than 8 percent of all cycling accidents. Another is to suppose that although intersection accidents account for half of all cycling accidents, those intersection accidents include collisions with automobiles, problems with defective or slippery road surfaces, and so on. Regardless of which interpretation is correct, it's important to note that although cyclists spend relatively little time crossing intersections, a disproportionate number of cycling accidents occur there.

---

1 Carol Tan, "Crash-Type Manual for Bicyclists," 1999, Federal Highway Administration, at http://www.tfhrc.gov/safety/pedbike/ctanbike/ctanbike.htm.

2 Jeffrey P. Broker and Paul F. Hill, *Bicycle Accidents: Biomechanical, Engineering, and Legal Aspects* (Tucson: Lawyers and Judges, 2006), p. 72; P. Garder, "Bicycle Accidents in Maine: An Analysis," *Transportation Research Record: Reserach Issues on Bicycling, Pedestrians, and Older Drivers*, no. 1438.

RIDING AT NIGHT

There is some evidence to indicate that riding at night—at least without lights—is a factor in nearly half of all cycling fatalities. In reviewing accident data, the Consumer Products Safety Commission found that 46 percent of cycling fatalities occurred at night. Only 8 percent of the cyclists in these fatalities were equipped with lights, suggesting that lack of conspicuity in night riding was a factor in most nighttime fatalities. There is some disagreement over the data, however, with a Johns Hopkins study claiming that 56 percent of all cycling fatalities occurred at night, and that 32 percent of those who sustained serious injuries in a cycling accident but did not die were involved in nighttime accidents.[3]

These data do not indicate whether nighttime accidents are more common than daytime accidents, or whether there is a greater per capita incidence of accidents for nighttime riders than there is for daytime riders. But they do demonstrate a correlation between decreased nighttime conspicuity, decreased nighttime perception and recognition distances, and increased fatalities.

Based on these data, there are basically two approaches you can take to reduce your risk of being seriously or fatally injured in a cycling accident. One is to limit your riding to daylight hours. Although this approach completely eliminates the risk, however, it may not be desirable, or even possible, for you to take this precaution, especially if you commute to work or school. The second approach is to increase your conspicuity. As we saw in Chapter 2, fluorescent clothing and reflective materials (see §2-22), used in conjunction with lights and reflectors (see §2-21), dramatically increase cyclist conspicuity and therefore driver perception and recognition distances.

ALCOHOL

Again, the majority of cycling fatalities have one other factor in common: alcohol. According to a Johns Hopkins study, one-third of all cycling fatalities involved a cyclist who was over the legal limit for blood alcohol content. It's unclear whether that number represents fatalities where only the cyclist is over the limit, or if it also includes fatal accidents involving a cyclist and a motorist who are both over the legal limit. However, the latter is quite plausible because the majority of the

---

3 "One in Three Fatal Bicycle Accidents Linked to Alcohol," Johns Hopkins Medical Institutions Office of Communications and Public Affairs, February 20, 2001. See also Broker and Hill, *Bicycle Accidents*, p. 288.

other two-thirds of cycling fatalities do involve a motorist who is driving under the influence.

Although these statistics may make it seem as if there's nothing you can do to protect yourself, there are in fact some steps you can take. First, you can lower your risk of being involved in a fatal collision by not mixing alcohol and riding. As the author of the Johns Hopkins study noted, "riding a bike requires a higher level of psychomotor skills and physical coordination than driving a car, so alcohol has an even stronger effect on bicyclists than drivers." Second, you can reduce your risk of encountering drunk drivers by avoiding nighttime riding. As mentioned above, this isn't always possible or even desirable. If you must ride at night, however, you can cut your risk of collision by increasing your conspicuity with fluorescent clothing, reflective materials, and lights and reflectors. It has been shown that a driver's perception is aided by the use of reflective materials even when the driver has elevated levels of blood alcohol.

The Most Common Cycling Accidents

Most cycling safety advice focuses on how to avoid "the most common" cycling accidents, which inevitably are presented as accidents with motor vehicles. Though it may be good advice, it creates the misleading impression that this type of collision is more common than any other type of cycling accident. Perhaps fortunately, this misleading impression is not actually true; as we've discussed, the vast majority of cycling accidents do not involve motor vehicles at all (see Figure 3.1). From a legal perspective, that raises a question, however: If you're involved in a bicycle accident, and there's no automobile or other vehicle involved, are you and you alone at fault? The answer to that question, as with all legal questions, is "It depends." Let's look at the categories of cyclist-only accidents to see why.

3-5 RIDER ERROR: HANDLING

If you ride long enough, you will eventually have an accident—it's inevitable, but hopefully, and with any luck, it will be a relatively minor one. Every rider occasionally makes a handling error while cycling. Some riders make handling errors because they're new, but more experienced riders can also encounter situations beyond their handling capabilities. Riders at any level can sometimes become distracted, have a lapse of judgment, or push themselves harder than they should have.

Even experienced riders with many thousands of miles and years of experience under their belts will occasionally make an error. For an accident where you've fallen *solely* due to your own handling error, you alone are at fault. For example, consider this actual accident: A cyclist was riding in the bike lane when an insect flew into his helmet vent. Thinking the insect might be a bee or wasp, the cyclist shook his head to dislodge the insect and failed to notice his wheel approaching the curb until it was too late. He fell and rolled end over end through thorns, gravel, and broken glass by the side of the road. This accident, which resulted in a case of road rash more painful and longer-lasting than any insect sting, was solely the fault of the cyclist. As Robert Hurst writes in *The Art of Cycling*, "Road rash is a precious gift. Road rash is your friend. Bask in it, appreciate it, love it. Above all, learn from it."[4] Hopefully, the cyclist in this accident learned a valuable lesson about distraction from the road rash he acquired in his battle with that housefly.

The question becomes more muddled when factors other than your own handling enter into the picture. For example, was there some defect in the road surface that you inexpertly attempted to avoid? Or did some other person on the road create a hazard that you inexpertly attempted to avoid? In these instances, even if your handling was the immediate cause of the accident, the legal cause of the accident may be another person's negligence. If there's any question about whether another person shares any of the fault in your cyclist-only accident, you should consult with an attorney.

3-6 RIDER ERROR: MAINTENANCE

You're riding along, and suddenly your wheel comes off, and down you go. Well, that doesn't happen often anymore, but it used to happen, and often enough that the industry eventually developed the popularly named "lawyer's tabs" to keep wheels from coming off when they were not properly tightened. Whether an accident resulting from improper maintenance is your fault or someone else's will depend on the particular circumstances. Did a shop do the maintenance? Did you do your own maintenance? Did the manufacturer have a duty to warn you about certain maintenance problems—for example, the proper way to tighten a quick-release mechanism? Were you aware of a maintenance problem, but did nothing about it? Was there a maintenance problem that you should have been aware of—for example, if the manufacturer advises you to perform certain maintenance functions at specific intervals—but

4 Robert Hurst, *The Art of Cycling* (Guilford, CT: Falcon, 2007).

you were not aware of it because you failed to maintain your bike? Depending on the circumstances, you may be entirely at fault, another person may be entirely at fault, or you may share some liability with another person. If the accident resulted from your failure to properly maintain your bike, you may be partially or entirely at fault; if another person owed you a duty to maintain your bike or to warn you about maintaining your bike, then that person may be partially or entirely at fault. Therefore, if you are involved in a maintenance-related accident, you should consult with an attorney to determine to what extent, if any, you or another party may be liable for your injuries.

3-7 BICYCLE FAILURE

You're riding along again, and this time, although your wheel is well secured in the fork end, your entire carbon-fiber fork snaps off, and down you go. Fortunately, you survive the face-plant—after all, some cyclists have been killed—but now you want to know if it's the manufacturer's fault. Was it solely the fault of the manufacturer? Did you know, or should you have known, of impending material failure, but did nothing about it? And will that affect your ability to recover damages? Or was there some hidden defect in the product that you couldn't possibly have known about? As with all accidents where another party may be liable, you will need to consult with an attorney to determine who might be liable and the extent of their liability.

3-8 ROAD DEFECTS

This time, you're riding along on a perfectly maintained bike, there are no defects in design or materials, and you're handling your bike properly. Everything is fine with the world. Then you hit a patch of gravel in the road, or a patch of oil, water, or ice. Maybe it was a pothole, railroad tracks, a utility cover, or a storm grate. Whatever it was, down you go. All of these categories can be loosely classified as road or surface defects. The question is, who, if anybody, is at fault? And, as always, the answer is, "It depends."

There are two questions to ask yourself in this scenario. First, did your own negligence contribute to the accident? If you'll recall from Chapter 2, cyclists have a duty to keep a proper lookout (see §2-6). If you rode into a road defect, such as a pothole, that you should have seen by keeping a proper lookout, then you may be at fault. But if you took reasonable precautions and nevertheless rode into the defect, the second question becomes relevant: Is somebody else at fault for the accident?

The answer may depend on who owns the land where the road defect occurs. If the land is private, and the landowner's lack of due care is the legal cause of the injury, then the landowner may be liable. If the landowner is a public entity, however, this may not be the case. The government enjoys immunity from liability for torts unless the government has waived liability. If the federal government is the landowner, immunity is waived under the Federal Tort Claims Act, and the government can be sued for negligence. If a state or local government is the landowner, its liability will depend on the state legislature, because no local or state government can be sued without its consent. Often, a government will waive this immunity by statute, but whether you can recover losses for governmental negligence will be entirely dependent upon the existence of a statutory waiver of immunity. Even if there is a statutory waiver of immunity, the governmental body may require that there be notice of both the defect *and* the accident before it can be held liable. *Notice of the defect* means that the governmental body must have been notified of the road defect before your accident and that it had a reasonable opportunity to correct the defect. *Notice of the accident* means that, following your accident, you notified the responsible governmental body within the required time limits.

In Illinois, a road defects case led to an Illinois Supreme Court decision that was a blow to cyclists' rights to the road. In September 1992, cyclist Jon Boub was crossing a one-lane bridge in DuPage County, Illinois, when his wheel became wedged in a gap between wooden planks on the bridge. Because of road-surface repairs that were in progress, asphalt had been removed from between the wooden planks under the road surface, creating the gap. Mr. Boub was injured and filed suit against Wayne Township, the local government responsible for the road repairs. *Boub v. Wayne Township* was appealed all the way up to the Illinois Supreme Court, which issued a controversial decision in October 1998.[5]

In *Boub,* the Illinois Supreme Court ruled that unless a road is "intended" for use by cyclists, as indicated by signs or surface markings, cyclists are not "intended" users of the road, and thus, government can't be held liable for their injuries. As you may realize by now, the statutory, common-law, and constitutional rights of cyclists are founded upon a right to use the roads; furthermore, the historical record conclusively demonstrates that cyclists are "intended" users of the road—the roads of America were paved because bicyclists demanded paved roads. Nevertheless, the Illinois legislature has granted immunity to the government through a statutory scheme that the Illinois Supreme Court interpreted

5 *Boub v. Wayne Township*, 702 N.E.2d 535 (Ill. 1998).

as dividing traffic into "intended" users of the road and "permitted" users of the road. The obvious problem with this dual classification is that *permitted user* implies that the use is not a right, but a privilege, and such use can be restricted or even denied by the state. This is obviously in conflict with cyclists' constitutional rights, but it will remain the law until its constitutionality is challenged.[6]

Regardless of whether the landowner is public or private, if the accident occurred on recreational land—a park trail or even a recreational bicycle path, for example—there may be a statute in place that grants recreational immunity to the landowner. Legislatures have passed these statutes in every state with the goal of encouraging the recreational use of land that might otherwise be closed to recreation due to liability concerns. The degree of recreational immunity will depend on what the specific state legislature has granted.

Remarkably, there's one other issue to consider in road defects cases: Some cyclists have had success recovering for their injuries from the manufacturers of storm grates on a theory of product liability. For example, if the grate's design is defective in a way that causes injury to cyclists riding over the grate—remember, storm grates are often located within the bicycle lane, and thus shouldn't be oriented in a way that will trap cyclists' wheels—the manufacturer might be held liable. To learn more about product liability law, see Chapter 7.

Because the law varies so widely depending on the state and circumstances, if you are injured in an accident resulting from a road defect, consult with an experienced attorney immediately. A personal injury attorney experienced in bicycle law can look at the facts to determine whether you have any rights under the law.

Common Accidents Involving Bicycles and Automobiles

Ask almost any cyclist about accident hazards, and accidents involving automobiles are inevitably what come to mind. Of course, we know that as cycling accidents go, collisions with automobiles are relatively rare. And yet these tend to be the most serious accidents, with alcohol-impaired drivers accounting for the majority of cycling fatalities. Even so, there are many more automobile-on-bicycle accidents that do not result in death, although the injuries may be severe. Well, that's the bad news.

6   Many, including myself, believe that the Illinois Supreme Court was wrong on the law; in fact, the Illinois Supreme Court itself was split 5-4 on the decision, with the dissent calling the decision an "absurd and dangerous proposition." Nevertheless, *Boub* is the law in Illinois until the court overturns its own decision.

The good news is that, unlike in some cyclist-only accidents, if you are injured by a driver's negligence, the driver can be held liable. Even better news is that the driver is legally required to be insured. That doesn't mean the driver will be *adequately* insured, and as we all know, it doesn't even mean the driver will actually *be* insured. However, most drivers are insured, and as we will discuss in Chapter 4, you can further protect yourself with your own insurance policy.

3-9 ACCIDENTS OCCURRING IN AN INTERSECTION

Intersections represent a relatively small portion of the cyclist's travel route; nevertheless, they are a particularly hazardous portion of that route. Cyclists are most at risk of being hit by an automobile when they are riding straight through an intersection. Perhaps that's not surprising, given the automobile-bicycle size ratio of 7 to 1. Whereas a motor vehicle is often difficult to miss, a bicycle is much smaller and may blend into the background, depending on a variety of factors, including the colors of the background, the bicycle, and the cyclist's clothing, as well as the ambient lighting, the angle of the sun, and the angle of the motorist to the cyclist. Additionally, motorists commonly underestimate the speed of cyclists, sometimes because they truly don't understand just

FIGURE 3.2A Frequency of Accidents: Bicyclist in an Intersection

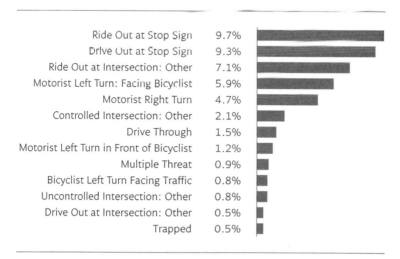

Ride Out at Stop Sign	9.7%
Drive Out at Stop Sign	9.3%
Ride Out at Intersection: Other	7.1%
Motorist Left Turn: Facing Bicyclist	5.9%
Motorist Right Turn	4.7%
Controlled Intersection: Other	2.1%
Drive Through	1.5%
Motorist Left Turn in Front of Bicyclist	1.2%
Multiple Threat	0.9%
Bicyclist Left Turn Facing Traffic	0.8%
Uncontrolled Intersection: Other	0.8%
Drive Out at Intersection: Other	0.5%
Trapped	0.5%

Note: 45 percent of bicycle-motor vehicle accidents occur in an intersection (cf. Figure 3.2).

BICYCLING AND THE LAW

how fast cyclists are capable of traveling, and sometimes because moving bicycles simply do not provide sufficient visual cues about speed, especially at night, when a single light often provides the only visual cue. Although motorists are required to keep a proper lookout and yield the right-of-way when turning, they may not see a cyclist, or may not even be expecting a cyclist to be there—for example, if the cyclist is riding against traffic while the motorist is turning into that lane. For the cyclist who is passed by a motorist, only to be cut off as the motorist makes a right turn directly in front of him, this seems absurd: "How could the motorist possibly have missed seeing me?" the cyclist might wonder.

Short of increasing the visual mass of the bicycle—perhaps possible with a fairing, or by towing a trailer, or by outfitting the bike with a safety flag—the cyclist can increase conspicuity through the use of a good lighting system that incorporates both a front and a rear lamp, conspicuous color selections, and reflective material (see §2-21–§2-22 for more suggestions). For daylight riding, cyclists should also consider the position of the sun: If the sun is at such an angle as to negatively impact the driver's ability to see you, you must take that into account when approaching intersections and take whatever precautions you think necessary to avoid being lost in the glare.[7] Many cyclists think of lighting as something they would use for nighttime riding. Consider, however, that motorcycles are much larger than bicycles, and yet many motorcyclists increase their conspicuity by riding with their lights on during the day. Of course, the benefits to be gained would be related to the effectiveness of the lighting system, with brighter lights more visible during daylight hours than dim lights.

Cyclists can also often avoid potential hazards by keeping a proper lookout. Remember, there's no legal requirement that you anticipate another person's unlawful behavior if you are riding within the law. However, even though there's no legal requirement to do so, it is nevertheless a good safety practice to ride defensively. If you are on a collision course with an automobile, you can sometimes avoid a serious collision by executing an emergency maneuver. However, your ability to execute such maneuvers will depend on knowing how to carry them out in the first place. Practicing those maneuvers regularly can enable you to act quickly if you're ever called upon to use them. Finally, as we will soon see, cyclists can increase their visibility and their safety simply by following the law, and sometimes simply by using common sense.

7 This is a good safety precaution, but it is not usually considered the legal requirement of the cyclist. There was a Georgia case in which the court decided the cyclist did have a duty to exercise due care when glare was present (*Duckwitz v. Manor*, 519 S.E.2d 483 (Ga. App. 1999)).

In addition to keeping a proper lookout for automobiles violating the right-of-way, you should keep a proper lookout for road-surface hazards such as gravel and slippery road conditions (including water, oil, utility covers, wide painted lines, and train tracks) as well as cracks and potholes in the pavement. Remember, most cycling accidents do not involve an automobile, so don't discount the importance of looking for and avoiding surface defects. As with imminent collisions with automobiles, you can sometimes avoid a surface defect by executing an emergency maneuver. Try to be aware of the traffic around you at all times—a rearview mirror can help with this—so that if a surface defect suddenly shows up, you will know instantly whether you have room to maneuver around it.

1. RIDE OUT AT STOP SIGN

The most frequent type of collision between motor vehicles and bicycles occurs at intersections where the cyclist has a stop sign, or a flashing red light, and the motorist does not. The cyclist rides out from a stop into the intersection as the motorist, who has the right-of-way, is approaching. It is often the case that the cyclist is under the age of fifteen.

The good news is that this type of intersection accident is almost entirely avoidable. However, because the cyclist involved in these collisions is typically quite young, it is not easily eradicated. Bicycle safety and handling programs directed at young riders can teach young cyclists the law and help them develop the cognitive skills to safely judge when they have the right-of-way. Such programs can also help children develop the bike-handling skills to avoid hazardous situations when they arise. In areas where such programs do not exist, cycling clubs and cycling advocacy groups should consider organizing them in cooperation with schools and police departments.

2. DRIVE OUT AT STOP SIGN

It stands to reason that if cyclists can screw up at an intersection, motorists can't be far behind, right? Right! Well, maybe not so right.

The second most common type of collision between motor vehicles and bicycles is the inverse of the "ride out at stop sign" type. In the "drive out at stop sign" accident, the cyclist has the right-of-way on a street with no stop sign, and the motorist is facing a stop sign. The cyclists typically involved in this scenario are fifteen to nineteen years of age or twenty-five to forty-four years of age.

At first glance, it may seem that there is little that cyclists can do to avoid this type of accident, because it is often attributable to driver error. But nothing is ever that simple. It turns out that 60 percent of the cyclists involved in this accident type are riding against traffic. It's not difficult to see why a driver would drive out into the intersection in those instances: The cyclist is riding the wrong way, entering the intersection from an unexpected position. The driver simply is not looking in that direction, because no one should be there. Legally speaking, the driver is required to look before entering the intersection. However, from a practical standpoint, the wrong-way cyclist may be approaching at such a close distance, and at such speed, as to make it difficult for the driver to perceive that a collision is imminent, thus compounding the driver's human error in not keeping a proper lookout. Of course, the wrong-way cyclist is also at fault in this collision, even if the driver hasn't kept a proper lookout. The key to eliminating 60 percent of these accidents is obvious: *Cyclists must ride with the flow of traffic.*[8]

It's not always the cyclist's fault, however. Sometimes the cyclist is riding in the direction of traffic, but the driver nevertheless does not see the cyclist. Even the "right-way" cyclist can take some steps to reduce the likelihood of being involved in this type of accident. First, make sure you are as conspicuous as possible. Pay attention to the color of your clothing and accessories, and ride with lights and reflectors, even during daylight hours. This is not a legal requirement, and you can't be held liable for failure to be as conspicuous as possible. However, as a practical matter, the more precautions you take, the greater your margin of safety. Second, you *must* keep a proper lookout when approaching these intersections. This *is* a legal requirement, and you can be held liable for failure to see something you should have seen, if only you had been paying attention. This is also a practical consideration; if you're riding legally, and you're keeping a proper lookout, you may be able to add some measure of physical safety because you're maintaining awareness of the situation when approaching these intersections. As always, a cyclist who is riding within the law does not have the duty to anticipate unlawful behavior, unless the unlawful behavior is obviously going to occur. Third, you may be able to reduce the likelihood of being injured by adjusting your lane position to the left when approaching these intersections; this makes you more visible to other drivers approaching the intersection. After clearing the intersection, you can adjust your lane position to the right again.

8 This is also a legal requirement. In an accident, failure to ride with the flow of traffic would be prima facie, or per se negligence, on the part of the cyclist.

3. RIDE OUT AT INTERSECTION: OTHER

And coming in third for intersection accidents, it's the cyclists again riding out at the intersection. This type of accident occurs at both controlled and uncontrolled intersections when the cyclist fails to yield. This is not a cyclist running the stop sign; rather it's a cyclist—typically under the age of fifteen—simply riding out into the intersection after stopping. Perhaps the cyclist doesn't see the approaching vehicle, or perhaps the cyclist simply misjudges the automobile's distance and speed. Either way, the result is a collision.

The good news—again—is that this type of accident is almost entirely avoidable. By following the law and yielding the right-of-way at intersections, cyclists can almost always avoid this type of accident, protecting themselves both physically and legally. However, once again, the challenge is the young age of the typical cyclist involved in such an accident.

If we could take these top three types of intersection accidents, and in three out of three, make a change for the better in cyclist behavior, we could almost entirely eliminate over 22 percent of all automobile-on-bicycle accidents. The key to changing cyclist behavior would likely be to establish bicycle safety and handling programs directed at young riders. By participating in such programs, they could learn about the laws pertaining to cycling and develop the skills they need to safely judge when they have the right-of-way. Even more accidents could be eliminated if adult cyclists could be taught not to ride against traffic. The remaining accidents are likely due to driver error, especially the driver's failure to see the cyclist; still, cyclists could reduce driver error through attention to conspicuity.

4. MOTORIST LEFT TURN: FACING BICYCLIST

In this type of accident, the motorist and the bicyclist are approaching the intersection from opposite directions, and as they enter the intersection, the motorist turns left, colliding with the cyclist. Usually, the motorist either doesn't see the cyclist or the motorist misjudges the cyclist's speed.

There are four ways to reduce your chances of falling victim to this driver's carelessness; note, however, that these four strategies are safety measures, not legal duties. You can't be held liable for failure to do any of these. As a practical matter, however, you will increase your margin of safety by taking these steps. First, do everything you can to maximize your conspicuity. This will mean choosing the appropriate colors for your clothing and accessories, and it will mean using lighting in daylight. Second, adjust your speed in the intersection to one at which you can quickly brake to a stop if necessary. Third, choose your lane position carefully. If you're riding to the right through the intersection, vehicles in the right lane may obscure you from the view of the left-turning motorist. If you take the entire lane through the intersection, you may be more visible. The trade-off will be that you may annoy the drivers of faster-moving vehicles behind you. You'll have to decide whether the perceived benefits of taking the lane outweigh that possibility. From a legal perspective, taking the lane would be practicable in an intersection if that is what your safety requires. Fourth, don't ride into the crosswalk from the sidewalk; this makes it more difficult for the motorist to see you, and that will decrease your safety.

5. MOTORIST RIGHT TURN

Typically, this type of collision occurs when a motorist passes a cyclist as both are approaching an intersection, and then the motorist makes a right turn at the intersection, cutting the cyclist off. A variant of this accident is when a cyclist is passing a slower motorist, and the motorist then makes a right turn. Another variant is when both the motorist and the cyclist are waiting at a light, and when the light turns green, the motorist turns right, cutting off the cyclist. In this last variant, if the motor vehicle is a big rig, the cyclist's life may be in danger as the truck crosses into the cyclist's lane to make that turn.

To avoid this type of collision, there are four strategies you can follow. First, keep a proper lookout. Check your mirror as you're approaching the intersection to see if any motor vehicles are approaching. If a motor vehicle is approaching you fast enough to pass you and turn right at the intersection, even if that turn would happen just as the vehicle passes you, you must be prepared for this possibility. It happens all the time.

Therefore, your second strategy is to be prepared for this possibility. This means you should either be prepared to brake in the event you are cut off, or you should adjust your lane position. You have a choice to either ride farther left, closer to the motor vehicle lane, or to take the entire right lane as you cross the intersection. If you ride farther to the left, but are not taking the lane, that will position you closer to any motor vehicle that is turning, and you will be able to anticipate and follow the turn sooner than if you are riding farther to the right. If you take the lane, you will make it impossible for a driver in the right lane to cut you off while making a right turn.[9] The safest position while waiting at a light will be to take the lane, in line with other vehicles; after you have crossed the intersection, you can adjust your lane position to the right again. The drawback to this "take the lane" strategy is that some motorists will not be turning right and will be extremely annoyed at having to slow down for you; even if they don't actually have to slow down, some motorists become annoyed at the mere possibility that they will have to slow down. There's no real way to explain to these motorists that you're taking an appropriate safety precaution based on a well-known traffic hazard, so you'll have to decide if you're comfortable with occasionally annoying motorists.

An alternative strategy, which will be far less annoying to motorists but will slow you down, is to cross the intersection at the crosswalk when you have the light. This is not the safest way to cross an intersection; you will need to press the pedestrian signal, wait for the light, and be cautious as you cross, because although you have the right-of-way, turning drivers may not be keeping a proper lookout. Never take a crosswalk riding against the flow of traffic, because this is how most crosswalk accidents occur.

The third strategy is never to pass a motor vehicle on the right; a slower-moving motor vehicle may be preparing to make a right turn, and the driver will not expect you and likely will not see you as the right turn is executed. You have two choices here. You can slow down to the motor vehicle's pace until the motor vehicle either makes a turn or resumes its speed, or you can take the lane and pass on the left when you can safely make the pass. Either way, avoid riding in the motorist's blind spot.

The fourth strategy is simply to avoid being in a motorist's blind spot while waiting at a traffic light. If the driver is planning to make a right turn, and you are in her blind spot, the driver won't see you. This is particularly important if the vehicle is a big rig, because the turning radius of the big rig means that you are putting your life in danger if you are stopped in the driver's blind spot at an intersection. If you just filter forward, instead of waiting in line, you will be passing vehicles on the right. This is legal, but it is unsafe because the drivers will not be expecting to be passed on the right, and therefore they will not be looking for you if they decide to turn as you're passing.

While waiting at a light, one alternative to passing vehicles on the right would be to pass them on the left, if you pass at all. Under traffic law, vehicles are generally required to pass on the left. Though bicycles

---

9 However, drivers irritated at the sight of a cyclist in "their lane" have been known to endanger the cyclist by making a right turn in front of the cyclist from the *left lane*.

are not generally subject to that requirement, as a practical matter no motorist would be expecting to be passed on the right if he or she is already in the right lane. Additionally, many motorists in the right lane will be preparing to turn right. Therefore, it's a bad idea to pass on the right, even if it is legal. With motorists preparing to turn left, it would also be a bad idea for you to pass them by filtering forward. You are safer waiting in line. The problem with waiting in line, however, is that the car in front of you is likely to obscure you from the view of oncoming motorists as you enter the intersection.

Another option exists in cities where cyclist safety has been accommodated through the use of "bicycle boxes," which position cyclists ahead of other vehicles at intersections. If there is a bicycle box at an intersection, you are safest positioning yourself there. When the light changes, you will be ahead of any right-turning vehicles. However, as you enter the intersection first, keep a lookout for any vehicles trying to beat that red light. This isn't a legal requirement—you can't be held liable if a motorist running a red light hits you—it's just another way to keep yourself safe.

6. CONTROLLED INTERSECTION: OTHER

This category is a kind of mystery bag of controlled intersection accidents that don't fit one of the other controlled intersection accident types. The studies do not tell us much in these cases, but we can still glean some information from what they do reveal—and what they do not reveal.

Let's start with what the studies do not tell us. The HSRC data are broken down neatly into a number of different accident types, some of which are not covered in this chapter—for example, children falling from their bicycles. As we've seen, the top three accident types are "ride out at stop sign," "drive out at stop sign," and "ride out at intersection." "Drive through" is another intersection accident category, which we'll cover next. And that leaves a gaping hole for "ride through." We know that mere stop signs and red lights constructed by mortals are no match for the superhuman cyclists who ride through those stop signs and red lights on a daily basis. We also know that some of those superhuman cyclists occasionally encounter SUV-shaped blocks of Kryptonite in the intersections they blow through. And yet, remarkably, there's no "ride through" category, just a mystery-bag category called "controlled intersection—other." I suspect that ride-through accidents are included in this category.

BICYCLE ACCIDENTS AND OTHER HAZARDS

Aside from this speculation, there are really only two pertinent pieces of information to be gathered from the data: Two-thirds of the cyclists were riding . . . well, I think you know where they were riding: against traffic. The other interesting bit of data is that in 24 percent of these collisions, the cyclist was riding in the crosswalk. So it's worth saying once again: You can significantly reduce your odds of getting hit by a motor vehicle if you ride in the direction of traffic. And if I told you that you could avoid some, perhaps most, of these encounters with SUV-shaped blocks of Kryptonite by not blowing through controlled intersections? Well, you probably knew that, too.

7. Drive through

We've seen that the second most common type of intersection accident is the "drive out at stop sign." In that accident, the motorist stops at the stop sign and then proceeds into the intersection and collides with the cyclist. In the "drive through" accident, the motorist runs the red light or stop sign and collides with the cyclist in the intersection. Most of these collisions occur after dark, and about one-third of them are hit-and-runs.

I could tell you to avoid red-light runners, but if life were that easy, these accidents wouldn't happen at all. Stay alert and practice your emergency maneuvers. It's a relatively rare type of crash (just 1.5 percent of all auto-bike crashes), so if nothing else, you've got the odds on your side.

8. Motorist left turn in front of bicyclist

I'm beginning to see a pattern to these; see if you can spot the pattern too. So the motorist and cyclist are traveling in the same direction, and the cyclist is on the other side of the road, riding against traffic. The motorist makes a left turn at an intersection, and he plows right into a cyclist that he likely never saw until it was too late.

And the reason the motorist never saw the cyclist? You know what to do, right? If not, I'll say it again: Ride with the flow of traffic.

9. Multiple threat

In this collision, the cyclist is still in the intersection when the light changes to red. Cars are waiting at the red light, and as the light changes to red for the cyclist, it changes to green for the cars. And it gets worse for this cyclist: The drivers in the right lane can't see the cyclist, because she's obscured behind the cars in the left lane, so the driver in the right lane proceeds into the intersection and drives right into the cyclist. The only sure way to avoid this accident is to clear the intersection before the light changes. Everything else just comes down to whether you're in the wrong place at the wrong time. Clear the intersection, and if there's any question about whether you can clear the intersection before the light changes, don't start through it. Wait for the next one.

10. BICYCLIST LEFT TURN FACING TRAFFIC

This one pretty much explains itself: The cyclist makes a left turn in front of an oncoming car. Typically cyclists involved in these accidents are under ten years of age. Other common factors: high speed of travel, high-speed road, rural area, wet road, and a moving or stopped vehicle obscuring the cyclist's vision of an oncoming car. Fortunately, it's another rare type of accident. Bicycle safety training programs might help make it more rare.

11. UNCONTROLLED INTERSECTION: OTHER

Lots of things can happen at an uncontrolled intersection. This category is for all of them, but the common denominator is that the cyclist rides out into an uncontrolled intersection. The cyclist is often under the age of ten, and often riding against traffic.

12. TRAPPED

In the "multiple threat" collision described above, the cyclist made it only partway through the intersection before the light changed. The same thing happens in the "trapped" type of accident, except that once the cyclist is "trapped," there is no line of cars obscuring the vision of the car that hits the cyclist. The light changes, the car proceeds, and the car drives right into the cyclist. Twenty-seven percent of these cyclists are riding the wrong way; the rest are riding with traffic. The motorist isn't really paying attention here, or this accident wouldn't happen. But we can't really force the motorist to pay attention, so the next best way to avoid this collision is to wait for the next light if you won't make it through this one, and if you do get "trapped" by a fast-changing traffic light, wearing appropriately conspicuous clothing and accessories, and riding with your lights on, even during daylight hours, may help you catch the attention of that motorist.

LEGAL ISSUES

The single most important legal issue raised in accidents occurring at intersections is right-of-way. To summarize the rules for right-of-way, at intersections that are not controlled by traffic signs or lights, when two vehicles arrive at the intersection at the same time, the vehicle to the right will always have the right-of-way. This rule also applies to intersections controlled by a stop sign. When one vehicle arrives before other vehicles at an uncontrolled intersection, the vehicle arriving first will have the right-of-way. There is an exception to these rules: If the intersection of a major street with a minor street is uncontrolled, then the traffic on the major street will have the right-of-way.

For intersections controlled by traffic signals, the right-of-way will be determined by the signal. This can create a problem for the cyclist if the signal sensor is unable to detect the presence of the bicycle. When this happens, the cyclist can choose to either cross at the crosswalk, after pressing the pedestrian signal, or wait until it is safe to cross against the light. Alternatively, the cyclist could wait for an automobile to arrive and trigger the sensor, but that is often not practical.

In most states, the motorist cannot use "the sun was in my eyes" as a defense for violating the cyclist's right-of-way. However, in Georgia, a court held that the cyclist was familiar with the angle of the sun on that road at that time, and that regardless of the cyclist's right-of-way, the cyclist still had a duty to exercise due care.[10] Other liability issues that have been raised by motorists who have collided with a cyclist at an intersection include:

- The cyclist was wearing dark clothes and blended into the background. The court held that the motorist did not have an absolute duty of due care; the duty is only to exercise the due care of a reasonable person.[11]

- The cyclist was riding too fast; the court affirmed the jury's finding.[12]

- The cyclist was riding in the wrong lane. The court upheld a jury finding that the cyclist was 33 percent responsible for his injuries.[13]

Whether a motorist or a cyclist, any person who disregards the right-of-way at an intersection is at risk of being held liable in the event of an

---

10 *Duckwitz v. Manor*, 519 S.E.2d 483 (Ga. App. 1999).

11 *Waring v. Wommack*, 945 S.W.2d 889 (Tex. App. 1997).

12 *Niel v. Griswold*, not reported in A.2d, 1992 WL 172138 (Conn. Supper.). Note that because this case has not been "reported," its precedential value is uncertain.

13 *Baker v. City of New Orleans*, 555 So.2d 659 (La. App. 1989).

accident. A cyclist held liable for disregarding right-of-way may not be able to recover for injuries, medical expenses, lost wages, or pain and suffering or receive any other monetary award for damages that would otherwise be available. In some states, if the cyclist does not come to a complete stop—and they mean a complete stop—the cyclist may be barred from any recovery, even if he or she came to an almost complete stop, and even if most of the liability for negligence would otherwise belong to the motorist. Real cyclists with real injuries are sometimes shocked to learn that by rolling through the stop sign at 1 mph, they have "assumed the risk" and may be unable to recover, even when their injuries are severe and the motorist holds most of the liability for negligence.

3-10 BICYCLIST RIDING WITH TRAFFIC

Cyclists face the greatest danger when negotiating an intersection because there's a lot of traffic going in different directions, passing through

FIGURE 3.2B Frequency of Accidents: Bicyclist Riding with Traffic

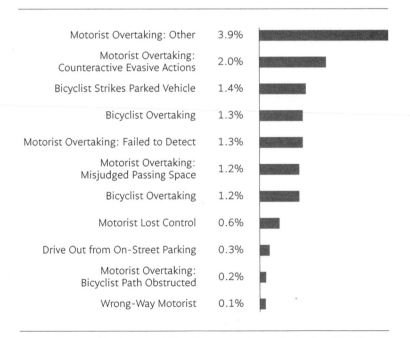

Motorist Overtaking: Other	3.9%
Motorist Overtaking: Counteractive Evasive Actions	2.0%
Bicyclist Strikes Parked Vehicle	1.4%
Bicyclist Overtaking	1.3%
Motorist Overtaking: Failed to Detect	1.3%
Motorist Overtaking: Misjudged Passing Space	1.2%
Bicyclist Overtaking	1.2%
Motorist Lost Control	0.6%
Drive Out from On-Street Parking	0.3%
Motorist Overtaking: Bicyclist Path Obstructed	0.2%
Wrong-Way Motorist	0.1%

Note: 13.5 percent of bicycle-motor vehicle accidents occur when a cyclist is riding with traffic (cf. Figure 3.2).

the same small plot of real estate. Bicycles are relatively hard to see because of their small size, and also very easy to push around, also because of their small size. So if a cyclist is on the open road, things should be easier, right?

Not really. Although accidents happen disproportionately in intersections, those that happen on the open road sometimes involve very high speeds, and that can make them, if not the most frequent accidents, the most deadly.

1. MOTORIST OVERTAKING: OTHER

Though it is the most common type of collision between cars and bikes traveling in the same direction, this category is another mystery bag. All we know for sure are a few details that don't add up to anything as instructive as some of the more specific types of accidents: Forty percent of these collisions occurred at night; most occurred on very high-speed roads; the majority of riders were between the ages of twenty and sixty; and 16 percent of the cyclists over the age of twenty-five and 6 percent of the motorists had been drinking.

Well, it may be a grab bag, but looking at the data, it's not too risky to say, "Don't ride at night on high-speed roads, especially if you've been drinking." If you must ride at night, and it must be on high-speed roads, do it sober, and wear reflective material to help the drivers (who've been drinking) to see you clearly.

2. MOTORIST OVERTAKING: COUNTERACTIVE EVASIVE ACTIONS

This type of collision occurs when a motorist is overtaking a cyclist and they both take evasive maneuvers that counteract each other. Cyclists from the ages of ten to fourteen are the most common victims of this kind of accident. The collisions occur most frequently on two-lane, high-speed county roads. In most instances, the cyclist and the motorist both swerved left. But in a few instances, both the cyclist and the motorist swerved right. This is a difficult accident for cyclists to avoid, because the motorist is contributing to the evasive actions responsible for the collision. That said, if cyclists swerve right to avoid an overtaking car on a collision course, in most instances the tactic will work because the driver will swerve left. The downside is that occasionally the driver will also swerve right.

3. BICYCLIST STRIKES PARKED VEHICLE

This is an interesting type of accident: A cyclist rides into a parked vehicle. Roughly half of these accidents—51 percent—involve cyclists who ride directly into a parked vehicle. Well, not actually *inside* the parked vehicle, usually, although that's happened too. The other 49 percent are "dooring" accidents. I'm going to discuss *dooring* accidents separately because there's a lot to say about getting doored that puts it into a somewhat different category (see §3-13). Let's focus here on just those accidents in which the cyclist rides directly into the parked vehicle.

How, you might ask, does one ride directly into a parked car? It's difficult to attribute percentages, but environmental conditions such as weather, glare, and obstructions to the cyclist's view are significant factors in these accidents. In one instance, a cyclist riding at night without lights was spooked by the sound of a dog barking, adjusted his position farther right, and rode into a parked vehicle that had not been there earlier and was not readily visible on a dark night.

There are two things cyclists can do to reduce the odds of riding into a parked vehicle. First, if you're riding at night, ride with a light. For one thing, you're required by law to have a light at night, and if you don't have one, you could be found liable for your own injuries. Sometimes cyclists aren't as concerned about that as they should be. But when you've been severely injured, and you don't know if you'll ever work again, liability is a very real and pressing concern. Follow the law, and you'll never have to sweat that one out. For another thing, riding with a light will likely prevent this type of accident from happening in the first place.

The second thing you can do is adjust your lane position farther left. If there are parked cars and other conditions, such as glare, that are making it difficult for you to see those cars, simply adjust your position left. This will help prevent both this accident and dooring. If something is obstructing your vision of the road ahead, you must either slow down or adjust your position left. Of course, if you can't see, neither can motorists, so adjusting to the left also has the potential to bring you right into their path when they can least see you.

4. BICYCLIST OVERTAKING

This situation is similar to riding into a parked vehicle, except that you may get bragging rights with this one, whereas you change the subject when the parked-car incident comes up. Here, the cyclist overtakes and crashes into a motor vehicle. How impressive is that? Well, it's much less impressive if you're injured, but those are precious bragging rights.

All levity aside, you can injure yourself just as much riding into a slow-moving or stopped auto as you can riding into a parked one. And the same environmental conditions factor in as in the parked-car incident. You cannot protect yourself by adjusting your lane position, however; preventing an accident of this type is all about keeping a proper lookout—though you'll want to make sure you don't follow too closely as well. Take care of those two duties, and you will significantly reduce the odds of this ever happening to you. Your ability to control the environmental factors—weather, glare, and obstructions to your view—is limited, but you can mitigate these factors. Get a good pair of sunglasses for riding, don't ride around an obstruction into that accident waiting to happen, and when you claim your bragging rights, make it about the one you caught that got away.

5. MOTORIST OVERTAKING: FAILED TO DETECT

This is "the Big One," the one cyclists always seem to fear the most: The motorist overtakes you from behind. Fortunately, the Big One, while not to be trifled with, isn't really all that big. Put in perspective, it's just 1.3 percent of all automobile-on-bicycle crashes. But when it happens, it's frightening: More than half of these accidents result in either serious injuries or fatalities.

Often, alcohol is involved. But before you go blaming the drunk driver, note that while 11 percent of the motorists involved had elevated blood alcohol levels, 17 percent of the cyclists involved also had elevated blood alcohol levels. The bad news is that there's absolutely nothing you can do to prevent somebody from driving down the road you're riding on after having "one more for the road." The good news is that you can cut your risks just by taking some simple precautions.

First, don't drink and ride; you're only putting yourself at risk. Second, most of these accidents happened under low-light conditions; you can substantially cut your risks by altering your riding time to avoid riding at night. If you must ride at night, pay attention to your conspicuity. Third, avoid riding at dawn or dusk, when sunlight can blind drivers. Fourth, avoid rural, high-speed roads under the aforementioned conditions.

But whatever you do, ride, and ride assured—the Big One is rare.

6. MOTORIST OVERTAKING: MISJUDGED PASSING SPACE

This scenario is the Big One redux, only this time it involves driver error. You know those annoying drivers who pass too close, coming within inches of taking your life? This is the accident you've narrowly missed every time you encountered one of them. Here, the motorist is passing the cyclist, but misjudges the passing space or distance, and down the cyclist goes. This type of collision is very dangerous—in 22 percent of the cases, the bicyclist receives serious or fatal injuries—but only half as dangerous as its evil twin. Unfortunately, we'll have to live with that inherently less deadly outcome, because there's not much you can do, aside from avoiding high-speed roads, to cut your risks on this one.

7. Bicyclist loses control

Picture this: A cyclist is riding down the street when suddenly, she loses control of her bike and swerves into the path of an oncoming car. How can you cut your risk for this one? That depends on how old you are. If you're under the age of ten, you're going to have to develop some bike safety and handling skills before you spend much time in the street. And what if you're over the age of twenty-five? Well, 42 percent of the cyclists over twenty-five who end up in an accident of this type had one— or a few—for the road before getting on their bike and losing control. To cut your risk, you know what you gotta do, right?

8. Motorist loses control

Okay, now that you're no longer losing control of your bike, your friends are amazed at the transformation, and you go out for a ride to celebrate your new bike-handling prowess.

And along comes this driver—the one who loses control of his car and hits you. Sound familiar? This is the accident that introduced Henry Wells to Evylyn Thomas. Although there's nothing in the record to indicate that Henry had been drinking, an astounding 65 percent of these drivers have been. Well, considering that they've lost control of their cars, maybe it's not such an astounding number. Fortunately, the overall incidence of this sort of accident is low; the type makes up just 0.6 percent of all car-on-bike accidents. The percentage of serious injuries and fatalities—37 percent—is relatively low, too. We're going to have to console ourselves with that good news, because there's nothing we can do to lower our risk of being involved in this type of accident.

9. Drive out from on-street parking

As with "motorist loses control," you can be thankful for the low incidence of this type of accident, because, once again, there's not much you can do to prevent it. In this scenario, the driver pulls out from an on-street parking space directly into your path. What can you do? You can hardly adjust your lane position; the driver is taking your lane. And you want to do more than just hope the drivers in their parked cars are paying attention. Fortunately, there is one thing you can do: Keep a hypervigilant lookout when you see a driver in a parked car preparing to leave. Be prepared for the drive out. Be prepared to brake. And be prepared to adjust your course.

10. MOTORIST OVERTAKING: BICYCLIST'S PATH OBSTRUCTED

One of the mantras of cycling safety is predictability. Be predictable. Among other things, that means riding in a straight, predictable line. Don't weave in and out between parked cars. And this accident is the case in point. A cyclist is riding along, hugging the curb, and up ahead there's a parked car in the cyclist's path; the cyclist rides out into the lane to go around the car, and he rides straight into the path of an overtaking vehicle.

It doesn't happen often, and statistically it doesn't result in serious injuries, but it does happen. The way to avoid this type of accident is obvious: Ride in a predictable, straight line, to the left of parked cars, and if you must adjust your position further to the left, look before you move left. Be aware of when a vehicle is overtaking you from the rear; if you have a rearview mirror, this isn't hard to do. Then, if you have to adjust your position left, you'll know if you have the leeway to do so. If there's an obstacle in your path and no leeway to adjust left, hit the brakes and slow down instead of swerving. It's always better to brake and slow down than to get hit and slow down.

11. WRONG-WAY MOTORIST

By now, you're doing everything right. You haven't been drinking, you're not running lights, and you're riding in the direction of traffic. Then along comes this guy, driving against traffic. There's a collision. Guess who takes the hit? This accident is not very common, and it's a good thing, because 33 percent of these accidents result in serious or fatal injuries.

Because this accident is not due to your own error, there's nothing you can do to lower the odds except take evasive action. If you see this driver coming, it's time to take evasive action. Ride off the road immediately, because it's the only option you have.

FIGURE 3.2C Frequency of Accidents: Bicyclists Riding Against Traffic

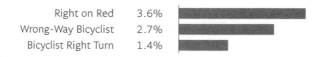

Right on Red	3.6%
Wrong-Way Bicyclist	2.7%
Bicyclist Right Turn	1.4%

Note: 7.7 percent of bicycle-motor vehicle accidents occur when a cyclist is riding against traffic (cf. Figure 3.2).

LEGAL ISSUES

When the behavior of cyclists contributes to their injuries, they are at risk of being found negligent. Bicycling Under the Influence is a case in point: Riding while intoxicated can be prima facie evidence of negligence if you are in a state where BUI is prosecuted; and even in states where BUI is not prosecuted, the intoxicated cyclist stands a strong chance of being found negligent in the event of a collision with an automobile. (See Chapter 2 for more on BUI, particularly §2-12.) Not every accident is preventable; sometimes there is just nothing you could have done to reduce your risk. But to make sure that you will not be found negligent—or grossly negligent—if you are ever in an accident, you must ride "within the law," taking the precautions of the "reasonable person." Riding in observance of the traffic laws and taking reasonable precautions will protect you legally, and may help you avoid injury altogether.

3-11 BICYCLIST RIDING AGAINST TRAFFIC

In nearly every state, bicycles are classified as vehicles, and in every state, cyclists are required to obey all applicable traffic laws. Of course, this means that cyclists are required to ride in the same direction as other traffic, and most cyclists do ride in the same direction as other traffic. Occasionally, a cyclist will ride against traffic. This is often a matter of misinformation; the cyclist has heard that cyclists are supposed to ride against traffic and conforms to that teaching.[14] If one thinks of bicycles as "not cars," it might even make sense, because pedestrians are

---

14 Some cyclists may be riding against traffic because it is a common practice in the country they emigrated from. For these cyclists, riding against traffic is what they've been taught, and it's what they believe to be the safest way to ride.

advised that it's safest to walk against traffic. According to this line of reasoning, if pedestrians are safer walking against traffic, cyclists must also be safer riding against traffic.

That line of reasoning is completely wrong. Cyclists are far safer—not to mention in conformance with the law—when they are riding with the flow of traffic.[15] Riding against traffic often puts the cyclist in a position on the roadway where motorists do not expect a bicycle to be, leaving the cyclist particularly susceptible to certain types of collisions. Furthermore, when a cyclist is riding against traffic, there will often be literally no time or room to maneuver if a collision with an automobile is imminent, and as we discussed earlier in this chapter, sometimes the driver and cyclist both attempt to evade each other, but end up counteracting each other's evasive maneuvers. Finally, when a cyclist is riding the wrong way, that cyclist is endangering all other cyclists on the road who are riding with traffic; when the right-way and wrong-way cyclists encounter each other on the road, they are at risk of collision with each other, and one of these cyclists may be forced out into the path of oncoming automobiles to evade an imminent bicycle-on-bicycle collision.

Fortunately, these accident types are entirely avoidable; cyclists can completely eliminate any possibility of being involved in one of these accidents by simply riding with the flow of traffic, as the law requires.

1. RIGHT ON RED

When a car is turning right on a red light, and a cyclist is riding against traffic and approaching the same intersection, the cyclist is moments away from disaster. The obvious problem is that the driver is not expecting a cyclist, or any other vehicle, to be coming from that direction. The driver stops at the intersection, looks to the left waiting for a break in the traffic, and turns right. Just before turning, a careful motorist will make sure no pedestrians are in the path of the automobile. This quick check won't protect the cyclist riding against traffic, though, because a cyclist travels at a much faster rate than a pedestrian. As the driver checks, sees no pedestrian, and then proceeds to make the turn, the automobile and the bicycle are in fact moving toward the point of impact at a faster rate of speed than either has time to detect or react to.

---

15   As this book was going to press, there were two separate accidents in Portland, Oregon, involving wrong-way cyclists. The first accident, on May 4, 2007, occurred when a wrong-way cyclist was struck by a vehicle entering the roadway from a commercial driveway; the cyclist was killed. Four days later, on May 8, another wrong-way cyclist rode straight into a light rail train that he apparently never saw coming. Miraculously, the cyclist survived the collision with superficial injuries, although he was reported to be coughing up blood at the scene.

Another variant of this accident occurs when the automobile is turning right on red, and the cyclist is riding in the crosswalk. In fact, almost 85 percent of these collisions involve a cyclist riding against traffic, and nearly half (45 percent) involve a cyclist riding in the crosswalk. As the automobile is preparing to turn right, the cyclist, who is riding on the sidewalk, rides out into the crosswalk *against traffic* and directly into the turning automobile. Even if the driver is careful and checks for pedestrians in the crosswalk, the driver never even sees the cyclist until the two vehicles have collided.

This accident is easily avoidable. First, cyclists should never ride against traffic. Doing so invites trouble. Second, cyclists should never ride against traffic on the sidewalk. Cars on intersecting streets will not be expecting you to be coming from that direction, and cars emerging from driveways won't be expecting it either.

2. Wrong-way bicyclist

This one speaks for itself: A wrong-way cyclist gets hit head-on by an automobile.

Nearly one-quarter of all cyclists over the age of twenty-five who were hit head-on while cycling against traffic had been drinking. Over one-quarter of these collisions happened "under conditions of darkness." Furthermore, in 7 percent of these collisions, the cyclist and the motorist both took evasive actions that counteracted the other. While that is a relatively small percentage of the total, it does demonstrate one of the hazards of riding against traffic. Every single one of these collisions is easily avoidable: Ride with traffic, not against it.

3. Bicyclist right turn

In this type of collision, a wrong-way cyclist is riding facing traffic on a two-way street and makes a right turn, heading right into the path of an automobile that is traveling in the same direction on the proper side of the street. Most cyclists involved in this type of collision are under the age of fifteen. This sort of collision is preventable, and the key is to teach young cyclists bicycle safety.

Legal issues

Cyclists riding against traffic are accidents waiting to happen. If they are riding in the street, they are in violation of the traffic laws; if they are riding on the sidewalk, they may not be in violation of the traffic laws, but they are no less of a hazard. Besides riding in violation of the law and endangering themselves and others, the wrong-way cyclist in the street is also handing the motorist prima facie evidence of his or her own negligence. Evidence of the cyclist's negligence has the potential to drastically reduce, or even eliminate altogether, any recovery the cyclist might otherwise be entitled to.

Motorists owe no duty of care to look for or anticipate wrong-way cyclists. The motorist does owe a duty of care to look before turning, but if the wrong-way cyclist suddenly rides into the "reasonably precautious" motorist's path, the motorist cannot be held liable for that cyclist's negligence. The motorist may also be negligent, of course, and if the cyclist is a minor, the motorist's own negligence may be greater than the cyclist's negligence. Nevertheless, the legal ramifications, as well as the potential for serious or even fatal injuries resulting from wrong-way riding, make a strong argument for riding with the flow of traffic and establishing more bicycle safety programs for children.

3-12 ACCIDENTS OCCURRING WHEN ENTERING THE ROADWAY

With two exceptions, the types of accidents that occur when a vehicle is entering the roadway usually involve children, and usually involve children riding out into the street from a driveway. A common feature in many of these accidents is a parked car or some other object that obstructs the child's view of an approaching car—not to mention obstructing the driver's view of the bicycle and child. Usually, when a child on a bicycle darts out into the street, the driver is not held liable. If the cyclist

FIGURE 3.2D Frequency of Accidents: Bicyclists Entering Roadway

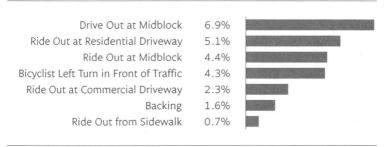

Drive Out at Midblock	6.9%	
Ride Out at Residential Driveway	5.1%	
Ride Out at Midblock	4.4%	
Bicyclist Left Turn in Front of Traffic	4.3%	
Ride Out at Commercial Driveway	2.3%	
Backing	1.6%	
Ride Out from Sidewalk	0.7%	

Note: 25.3 percent of bicycle-motor vehicle accidents occur when a cyclist enters a roadway (cf. Figure 3.2).

151

darting out is an adult, there is even less chance of the motorist being held liable.

One of the two exceptions to the general rule that these are children's accidents is the "ride out at midblock," a type of accident that can involve adults just as easily as children. Adult cyclists involved in this type of accident have often been drinking (45 percent of the incidents). The solution for this problem should be obvious: Don't mix drinking and riding.

The other exception is the "drive out at midblock," which occurs when a motorist is driving down a driveway or alley toward the street, intending to enter the street. The motorist crosses the sidewalk, preparing to stop at the street and check for traffic, when a cyclist, riding against traffic on the sidewalk, surprises the motorist by riding directly into the motorist's path. There's one easy way for you as a cyclist to avoid this accident: Ride with traffic, and when you're crossing where a driveway intersects with the sidewalk, do so at pedestrian speed. Well, maybe that's two easy ways, but you get the idea.

The rest of these accidents are variations on the all-too-common scenario where a child or youthful cyclist rides into the path of an approaching vehicle. As with all children's accidents, the key to reducing the likelihood of their occurrence lies in bicycle safety and handling programs.

LEGAL ISSUES

Children and adults are not held to the same standards when it comes to negligence and liability. Thus, even in situations where the child is negligent, that negligence is weighed by a lesser standard—the negligence of a child—against the motorist's greater standard of negligence as an adult. Nevertheless, a motorist will generally not be held liable when a child darts into the street. There are obvious exceptions, such as when the motorist's negligence—speeding, for example, or drunk driving—contributed to the accident. An adult cyclist who darts into the street, however, will fare even worse than the child. Thus, if the child generally can't dart into the street and then hold the motorist liable for negligence, the adult who darts into the street is on even less sure footing in court, because the adult is held to a higher standard. And, as is common in this type of accident, if the adult cyclist has an elevated blood alcohol level and darts into the street, he or she has virtually no chance of recovery, absent an equal or greater degree of negligence on the part of the motorist—for example, if the motorist also has an elevated blood alcohol level and is driving at excessive speed.

3-13 DOORING ACCIDENTS

In some European cities, bike lanes are separated from the parking curb, completely eliminating the possibility that an inattentive driver will door a passing cyclist. In those cities, the infrastructure needs of the cyclist are taken into account. Where cyclists are placed outside the door zone, doorings are unheard of. However, in the United States, bike lanes are positioned between the parking curb and the traffic lanes, and getting doored is a very real and common problem.[16] I have represented numerous cyclists who have been "doored." In some doorings, the cyclist strikes the door at high speed and is severely injured. Sometimes, the cyclist's collision is cushioned by the softer-than-the-door motorist. For many cyclists, this is considered the lesser of two evils and is even seen as instant karma for the negligent motorist. Sometimes, the cyclist takes evasive action, and as we shall see, rides straight from the frying pan into the fire. While getting doored is sometimes depicted humorously in films, the reality of getting doored is not at all funny. A staff member at the University of Michigan has compiled a number of news accounts of cyclists who were doored, and though the collection does not amount to what anyone would call a scientific study, the results are interesting, to say the least.[17] In this survey, there are seventeen news accounts of cyclists getting doored; eleven of those cyclists were killed, and five were seriously injured. How the injuries occurred is perhaps the most revealing part of the articles.

Of the eleven cyclists who were killed, nine of them were actually killed by another vehicle passing by. One of the nine swerved to avoid getting doored, lost control of his bike, fell, and was struck by a passing eighteen-wheeler. The other eight were knocked into the path of another vehicle after first striking the door. The other two cyclists who were killed died after striking the door and being thrown to the pavement. One died of head injuries, while the other "lapsed into a coma" before dying. The accounts do not indicate whether these two cyclists were wearing helmets when they were thrown to the pavement.

Of the five cyclists who were injured, one struck the door and was thrown into the path of another vehicle, suffering a crushed pelvis. The other four cyclists sustained injuries from striking the door. One suffered a broken collarbone and facial injuries, another sustained a torn rotator

---

16 In a "dooring" accident, the cyclist is riding along, "as close as practicable to the right," when the driver or a passenger sitting in a parked car inadvertently opens the car door just as the cyclist approaches, threatening to cause or actually causing an imminent collision between the cyclist and the door.

17 Riin Gill, "The Door Zone Project," at http://www.riinsrants.info/bikes/doorzone.htm.

cuff and a badly bruised head, the third received serious head injuries, and the fourth is now a quadriplegic.

The newspaper clippings are informative. Striking a door in your path can lead to serious injury, but getting nailed by a passing vehicle is far more deadly. To protect yourself from being involved in a dooring accident, safety experts generally suggest riding outside the door zone, which means keeping a distance of 3 to 5 feet between your handlebars and the parked vehicles. However, this riding strategy can potentially place you in the traffic lane instead of the bike lane. In many states, the traffic laws require you to ride in the bike lane, which effectively puts you in the door zone. So how do you cope with that contradiction between safety and the law? You need to read the statutes in your state and see what they require and what they allow. For examples, let's look at what the laws say in California, Oregon, and Washington.

Let's look first at California:

> **21202. Operation on Roadway.** (a) Any person operating a bicycle upon a roadway at a speed less than the normal speed of traffic moving in the same direction at that time shall ride as close as practicable to the right-hand curb or edge of the roadway except under any of the following situations . . . (3) When reasonably necessary to avoid conditions (including, but not limited to, fixed or moving objects, vehicles, bicycles, pedestrians, animals, surface hazards, or substandard width lanes) that make it unsafe to continue along the right-hand curb or edge.
>
> **21208. Permitted Movements from Bicycle Lanes.** (a) Whenever a bicycle lane has been established on a roadway pursuant to Section 21207, any person operating a bicycle upon the roadway at a speed less than the normal speed of traffic moving in the same direction at that time shall ride within the bicycle lane, except that the person may move out of the lane under any of the following situations . . . (3) When reasonably necessary to leave the bicycle lane to avoid debris or other hazardous conditions.

Although at first glance it may seem that the law requires you to ride to the right, in fact it only requires you to ride as close to the right as "practicable," and only when you're riding "at a speed less than the normal speed of traffic moving in the same direction at that time." As noted in Chapter 2 (see §2-13–§2-14), this means that you must ride close to the right if conditions make it feasible to do so. However, unsafe conditions are an exception to that requirement. After reading about the injuries and fatalities involved in dooring accidents, is there any doubt in your mind that cars parked next to a bike lane present a hazardous condition? In effect, because of unsafe conditions, it is not feasible to ride in the door zone. However, there's another statute cyclists have to consider when determining where they can legally ride. The bicycle lane statute requires cyclists to ride in the bicycle lane, but again, if "hazardous conditions" are present, cyclists are permitted to leave the bicycle lane to avoid those conditions. Thus, in California, you are not required to choose between safe riding and obeying the law.

Now let's see what Oregon says. The Oregon Revised Statutes (ORS) require cyclists to use a bicycle lane:

> **814.420. Failure to use bicycle lane or path.** (1) . . . a person commits the offense of failure to use a bicycle lane or path if the person operates a bicycle on any portion of a roadway that is not a bicycle lane or bicycle path when a bicycle lane or bicycle path is adjacent to or near the roadway . . . (3) A person is not in violation of the offense under this section if the person is able to safely move out of the bicycle lane or path for the purpose of: . . . (c) Avoiding debris or other hazardous conditions.

So, although you are required to ride in the bicycle lane when one is available in Oregon, you are not in violation of this section if you are riding outside of the lane to avoid hazardous conditions. Oregon also makes it illegal to open your car door unless it is reasonably safe to do so, so arguably, the law eliminates that hazardous condition. But realistically, people are still going to open their doors as cyclists are passing. At best, the hazardous condition is illegal, but still hazardous.

Washington's laws are similar:

> **46.61.770. Riding on Roadways and Bicycle Paths.** (1) Every person operating a bicycle upon a roadway at a rate of speed less than the normal flow of traffic at the particular time and place shall ride as near to the right side of the right through lane as is safe.

That's an interesting statute. Although it appears to require you to ride to the right, it actually has two exceptions. First, you are required to ride to the right only if you are "operating a bicycle upon a roadway at a rate of speed less than the normal flow of traffic"; this is the same requirement as the California statute. Generally, that means that you don't have to ride to the right as long as you can keep up with the flow of traffic (for a more detailed discussion of "normal flow of traffic," see §2-13).

Second, you are required to ride only as far to the right "as is safe." Because a door zone is demonstrably "not safe," you are not required to ride in the door zone.

In addition to riding outside of the door zone, there are two simple precautions you can take to protect yourself from getting doored. First, if you are riding in a door zone, you should scan the parked cars for any drivers who may be about to open a door. If there is anyone in the driver's seat, or on the driver's side of the backseat, be cautious. Although you always have a duty to keep a proper lookout, in this situation scanning ahead is more about staying safe than it is a legal requirement. The liability for a motorist or passenger opening a door without first looking will remain with the motorist or passenger, even if you didn't see him or her preparing to open the door. However, if you are riding within the door zone, watching the parked vehicles for signs of drivers or passengers inside who *may* be preparing to open a door will allow you to take appropriate precautions for your own safety; you might, for example, adjust your lane position left, or prepare to brake if necessary. Keep in mind that if you are riding within the law, you are not required to anticipate somebody else's unlawful behavior; however, if you are aware of a driver opening a door, or if you should have been aware because it was obvious that the door was about to be opened, then you may have a duty to anticipate that illegal behavior.

The second thing you can do to protect yourself is to get a mirror. There are several types available; some attach to your helmet, and others attach to your bars. Experienced cyclists swear by their mirrors, and using a mirror soon becomes second nature for these cyclists. If you're not riding with one now, I would encourage you to start today.

LEGAL ISSUES

Most cases involving cyclists getting doored revolve around who bears the liability—usually, the motorist, a passenger, a cab company, a passing motorist, or the cyclist. These cases are all just typical negligence cases, with different outcomes based on different sets of facts. However, there is one case that every cyclist should be aware of, and it concerns insurance issues. In *Government Employees Ins. Co. v. Herring*, the cyclist was doored and injured.[18] The motorist did not report the accident to his insurance company. He explained: "I didn't think that it was my fault in the accident and I didn't think that my insurance company was involved in it. Being a parked vehicle that was run into, I regarded it the same as

18 *Government Employees Ins. Co. v. Herring*, 477 P.2d 903 (Ore. 1970).

if somebody had run into a tree or something, a fixed object, I didn't re-alize that my insurance was involved at all."

Because the motorist didn't report the accident to his insurer, the in-surer denied the claim, and the court upheld the insurer. This left the cy-clist unable to be compensated by the driver's insurance, and like many people, the driver didn't have the means to pay for the cyclist's injuries. Eventually, the cyclist was compensated by his own auto policy's cover-age for uninsured motorists. But he could easily have lost out altogether, because he didn't report the accident to the driver's insurance company either. The lesson to take away from this case is that if you are injured in a dooring accident, you must make sure that both insurers—the driver's insurer and your own—are notified within the time limits of the respec-tive policies.

3-14 Projecting Loads

Loads projecting from vehicles can be deadly. A projecting load can be as small as a sideview mirror or as large as a load of lumber; it is simply some item projecting from the vehicle that poses a danger to a cyclist when the vehicle passes the cyclist too closely. Most cyclists have expe-rienced vehicles passing within inches of their bike; imagine that vehi-cle passing too close, only this time with a projecting load that clips the cyclist, and instead of experiencing a near miss, the cyclist is sent flying. In some cases, cyclists struck by a projecting load have been killed. For-tunately, it's a relatively rare occurrence.

Unfortunately, there's not much you can do about this type of acci-dent; it's the driver, and not you, who is negligent. There's a growing movement in the state legislatures to clarify the minimum passing dis-tance; these statutes provide an extra margin of safety for cyclists and should reduce the number of projecting-load accidents as motorists be-come more aware of safe passing distances. However, there will always be some motorists who will not observe the law. Therefore, one step you can take to help reduce your likelihood of being hit by a projecting load is to outfit yourself with a mirror and get in the habit of using it. There's no guarantee that you will see the projection coming, but if you are using your mirror, you might see it coming. If you do, get out of the way, be-cause the kind of driver who doesn't give you enough room to begin with isn't likely to realize that he's about to clip you.

Legal Issues

Generally, it's against the law for a driver to operate a passenger vehicle with any load that is projecting more than 6 inches from the right side of the vehicle. Unless you're riding against traffic, and therefore *should* have seen the projecting load coming, you generally cannot be held liable for an accident of this type. This exception for wrong-way cyclists should not apply to cyclists riding with the flow of traffic and using a mirror; if you're equipped with a mirror, it should be presumed that you were keeping a proper lookout, but that's not the same thing as saying that you should have seen the load coming from behind you. Although using a mirror is not legally required, it will help you to be aware of what's happening behind you; nevertheless, you cannot possibly be held responsible for knowing what's happening behind you at all times.

3-15 SIDEWALKS, CROSSWALKS, AND PATHS

To inexperienced riders it may seem safer to ride on the sidewalk, where there are no cars, and to cross intersections in the crosswalk. However, riding on sidewalks isn't as safe as it seems. Cyclists riding on sidewalks are at increased risk of colliding with motorists who are entering or exiting a driveway, particularly when the cyclist is riding against traffic. It may seem counterintuitive, but riding on the roadway, "as close as practicable to the right," and in the same direction as the flow of traffic, is, without a doubt, the safer way to go.

Approaching an intersection from a sidewalk or bike path is particularly hazardous for a cyclist. If the cyclist is riding against traffic, it is even worse: There is a good chance the cyclist will ride straight into the path of a motorist who is not expecting to encounter a fast-moving vehicle coming from that direction. Pedestrians present another hazard to a cyclist on the sidewalk—and the cyclist is a hazard for the pedestrians as well. Although you have the same rights as pedestrians in relation to automobiles, in some jurisdictions there's still a hierarchy of duties owed, and pedestrians are at the top of that hierarchy. Depending on the jurisdiction, when you are riding on the sidewalk, the pedestrian will often have the right-of-way, and you must respect that right-of-way. If that's a problem for you, don't ride on the sidewalk, because in any collision where the pedestrian has the right-of-way, you will be held liable if you violate that right-of-way. In some jurisdictions, cyclists will have the same rights on the sidewalk as pedestrians. However, even in these jurisdictions, cyclists owe a duty of care to pedestrians, and the cyclist who violates that duty of care will be held liable.

We're all creatures of habit, and motorists are no exception. When you're riding on the sidewalk against traffic, motorists simply aren't expecting to see you there. They aren't looking in that direction to watch for fast-moving vehicles. And they don't take the same care to look for a bicycle riding against traffic on the sidewalk as they take to look for oncoming cars from the right direction. Blame motorists all you want; that's still the reality of how they enter traffic. You can accept that reality and ride where motorists expect to find you, or you can court disaster. If you're going to ride on the sidewalk, then you must ride with the flow of traffic if you expect to be seen. This is not generally a legal requirement; it is a commonsense requirement. Even when riding in the direction of traffic, you should also ride at a slow enough pace that a motorist entering or exiting a driveway has time to see you and react. Again, blame motorists all you want, but if you are riding on the sidewalk, and suddenly appear in front of a car crossing the sidewalk, you're not likely to be seen, and you're likely to be found negligent to boot. Ride with the flow of traffic, and ride at pedestrian speeds when crossing in front of driveways; it's common sense, and it will save you some needless grief.

Even if you are riding with traffic, you must take care that you have the right-of-way when entering an intersection. This means that you must have the light, or, at an intersection that is controlled by stop signs, or is uncontrolled, that you are not entering the crosswalk when approaching vehicles are so close as to constitute an imminent hazard. Even when you are entering the intersection legally, for your own safety you must make sure that any motorists who are turning are aware that you are entering the intersection. The best way to do that is to avoid surprising a motorist by riding out into the intersection. Yes, it may be legal, but it's not safe. If there's any doubt about whether motorists will see you, walk out into the intersection. Walking your bike through the intersection is far safer than suddenly appearing out of nowhere on your bike and taking a motorist by surprise. If you do ride out, slow to a walking speed. It's safer than riding out at high speed, and it may be required by law.

Finally, when you're riding on the sidewalk, you must yield the right-of-way to pedestrians in those jurisdictions where they have the right-of-way, and you owe pedestrians a duty of care in those jurisdictions where pedestrians and cyclists have the same right-of-way. In some jurisdictions, you must also warn pedestrians of your approach with a bell. Violate these duties at your peril; in the event of a collision, there will be a presumption of negligence against you if you have violated the law, and it will be your responsibility to prove you were not negligent.

LEGAL ISSUES

Generally, riding on sidewalks is legal, except where it has specifically been prohibited. In most states, that will mean that riding on the sidewalk is legal except in towns that have prohibited sidewalk riding, either in the central business district or, less often, throughout the town. In Wisconsin, however, it is illegal to ride on sidewalks unless a local government permits it. This approach is the opposite of the approach other states use. Regardless of your home state, know the laws wherever you ride; this means knowing the laws where you live and knowing the laws where you ride, because they will vary from jurisdiction to jurisdiction.

If it is legal for a cyclist to ride on the sidewalk in a particular jurisdiction, the cyclist generally has the same rights and duties as a pedestrian; however, in some jurisdictions, the cyclist who rides on the sidewalk must yield the right-of-way to pedestrians, and in all jurisdictions, cyclists who ride on the sidewalk owe a duty of care to both pedestrians and other cyclists.

As we saw in Chapter 2 (§2-18), a crosswalk is an extension of the sidewalk; this means that when you're in the crosswalk, you have the same rights that you have on the sidewalk. The only exception to this is if there is a statute specifically prohibiting you from riding in the crosswalk. Regardless of whether you may ride in a crosswalk or must walk, you have the same rights and duties as a pedestrian when you are in the crosswalk with your bike.

In some localities, there are mandatory bike-path laws requiring you to ride on a parallel bike path if one is available. On a bike path, you have the same rights you would have on the sidewalk. One area of law that is unsettled is whether a recreational immunity statute applies where bike paths are mandatory. These statutes, enacted to encourage the recreational use of lands, waive or severely limit landowner liability for negligence. Can a cyclist be required to ride on a path if the government accepts liability for surface defects on the roadway, but not on the bike path? It's possible, but such a requirement would obviously be discriminatory against cyclists. It's an issue that would need to be tested in the courts. At the very least, where cyclists are required to use bike paths, that use should not be considered "recreational."

Other Cycling Hazards

3-16 BICYCLE-ON-BICYCLE ACCIDENTS

There's no question that the attention of most cyclists is focused more on collisions with automobiles than on any other type of accident. It stands to reason that probably every cyclist quite reasonably believes that in an encounter with an automobile, she will be the only one injured.[19] Based on this belief, some cyclists claim that if they violate the right-of-way at an intersection, they are the only one who will be injured. This claim can be true only if the cyclist is the only cyclist on the road; in fact, it reflects the societal bias toward the automobile, because, as we all know, we are sharing the road with many users, including other cyclists. Because we're sharing the road with many other users, including other cyclists, the claim that the cyclist is the only person who will be injured if she violates the right-of-way is wrong.

There are in fact a number of cases involving bicycle-on bicycle collisions representing a variety of circumstances, ranging from accidents where a cyclist violates another cyclist's right-of-way at an intersection to accidents where two cyclists sideswipe each other or accidents where cyclists have a head-on collision. In the right-of-way cases, liability will tend to lie with the cyclist violating the right-of-way. In the other cases, liability is often found in both parties, typically because both were riding in the wrong place on the road or because one or both of the cyclists were not equipped with a light.

If you are injured in a collision with another cyclist, consult with an attorney. Although motorists are required to carry insurance, cyclists are not. Nevertheless, if one of the cyclists is covered under a homeowner's or renter's policy, the injured cyclist may be able to recover damages.

3-17 BICYCLE-ON-PEDESTRIAN ACCIDENTS

Cyclists have been colliding with pedestrians since the early days of cycling. The danger in the nineteenth century was the silent approach of the bicycle, in contrast to the clattering of horses' hooves that signaled

---

19 The likelihood that a cyclist would be the only one injured in a collision with an automobile is certainly greater than the likelihood that the motorist would be injured. Nevertheless, there is some possibility that a motorist would also be injured, especially if the motorist crashed into something else while attempting to avoid hitting the cyclist. Furthermore, the motorist could injure another person while attempting to avoid hitting the cyclist. And of course, "injury" does not just include bodily harm—it also includes property damage. Based on these factors, the belief that a cyclist is the only person who could possibly be injured in a collision with an automobile is mistaken.

traditional vehicles; many an unsuspecting pedes-
the ground by a silently approaching scorcher.

on-pedestrian accidents are rarer today than they
wing to a combination of fewer bicycles, fewer pe-
comprehensive traffic laws, pedestrians are still
d down and injured, or even killed, by cyclists. A collision wiiι ι ι ͺ trian may put the cyclist at a legal disadvantage, because the cyclist owes the pedestrian a higher duty of care than is owed
to vehicles. Although pedestrians owe a duty not to step out into traffic
if an approaching vehicle is so close that it is impossible for the driver
to yield, drivers must nevertheless "exercise due care to avoid colliding
with any pedestrian," even if the pedestrian has violated the duty not to
step out into approaching traffic.

This legal disadvantage does not relieve the pedestrian of a duty to
keep a proper lookout. Nevertheless, the cyclist is required both to keep
a proper lookout and to exercise due care to avoid colliding with the pedestrian. Generally, this will be a statutory requirement, which means
that there will be a prima facie presumption of negligence on the part of
the cyclist if, in an accident case, it is proved that the cyclist did not keep
a proper lookout or exercise due care to avoid colliding with the pedestrian. In order to overcome this presumption of negligence, the cyclist
will need to introduce contradictory evidence.

When a cyclist is approaching a pedestrian from the rear, the cyclist
should alert the pedestrian and exercise due care to avoid colliding. In
one case, a cyclist who did neither was held liable for knocking a child
down when the child stepped into the cyclist's path just as the cyclist
was passing.

The doctrine of *respondeat superior*, which holds the employer liable
for the negligence of the employee (see §3-2), has been raised in some
cases involving bicycle messengers colliding with pedestrians. In one
New York case, for example, the jury found the messenger to be an independent contractor, and therefore the messenger company was *not* held
liable.[20] In another case, also in New York, however, the jury found the
messenger to be an employee of the messenger company, and therefore
the messenger company *was* held liable. In any case involving a cyclist
who is "on the job," the liability of the company will depend on whether
the cyclist is an employee and is acting within the scope of employment.
This will vary on a case-by-case basis.

The vast majority of bicycle-on-pedestrian cases, however, involve a
child riding into a pedestrian. In these cases, the issue of parental liabil-

---

20 *Sorrenti v. The Go Between*, 548 N.Y.S.2d 503 (N.Y. App. 1989).

ity is raised, because although children can be held liable for their actions, they will be held to a lower standard than adults for exercising a duty of care.[21]

3-18 ACCIDENTS CAUSED BY DOGS

It's an old story: As long as there have been cyclists, there have been dogs chasing cyclists. Nearly every cyclist has been chased by a dog at one time or another.

Although dog bites can be a serious injury in their own right, the real danger a cyclist faces when chased by a dog is a collision with the dog and a subsequent fall. You really can't blame the dogs; they're just following their instinct to give chase to fleeing prey, and when you're riding by, you resemble fleeing prey.

When a dog runs out and starts to chase a cyclist, the cyclist's first thought is usually to try to outrun the dog, just as it is for the fleeing prey. Maybe that's part of why the cyclist resembles prey in the first place. Sometimes it's relatively easy to outrun a chasing dog, but sometimes it's a real race; even the smallest of dogs can be remarkably persistent in the chase, and with bigger, more aggressive dogs, the consequences can be dangerous if the cyclist loses the race. The second thought, therefore, is often of self-defense. If you are being attacked, you have the right to defend yourself. Be aware, however, of the limitations of self-defense. Generally, with a human assailant, you have the right to defend yourself with a force that is proportionate to the threat and that is necessary to end the attack. Once the attack has ended, you cannot continue to fight. With animals, there is no similar set of common-law rules. However, pet owners are increasingly turning to the courts for redress when their pets have been injured, whether through negligence or through intent. If you want to avoid the risk of losing a lawsuit, you should restrict your self-defense to the level of defense that you're entitled to with a human assailant. That is a legally defensible position; if you go beyond that with somebody's pet, you could find yourself being held liable for the damages.

There's a third avenue of response for the cyclist, however—one that is far too rarely pursued—and that is to turn to the law. Under the law, the cyclist has rights and the dog owner owes a duty of care to the cyclist. When the dog begins the chase, the dog owner may be breaching that duty. In most states, the dog owner will have a common-law liability for the dog. Under the common law, it is presumed that the dog is a pet, and

---

21 The standard that children are held to will be that of reasonable conduct for a child of the child's age, intelligence, and experience. Thus, as a child matures, the standard for duty of care approaches closer and closer to the adult standard.

harmless, and therefore is not required to be locked up and may roam at will. Even if the dog injures you, the owner will not be held liable, unless the owner had some sort of knowledge that the dog has a vicious nature. This prior knowledge would include a previous attack, and might also include aggressive behavior, or even the reputation of the breed. Once the owner has prior notice of the dog's vicious nature, the owner will be held liable for any attacks the dog makes.

In a large minority of the states, however, the legislatures have adopted "strict liability" statutes. In these states, there is no need for the dog's owner to have had prior notice of a dog's vicious nature in order to be held liable for its actions. Typically, if the dog makes an unprovoked attack, and the person attacked is not a trespasser, the dog's owner will be held liable.

Increasingly, the owners of dogs are being held liable for the injuries their dogs cause in an attack. Although a cyclist's first instinct is often to run, and the second instinct is self-defense, the most powerful weapon cyclists have for dealing with dogs may be their ability to hold an irresponsible dog owner liable for their injuries. If you've been injured by a dog, whether through collision or a dog bite, consult with an attorney to determine the extent of the owner's liability for your injuries. Of course, holding the owner accountable for the dog's actions can take place only after the fact, so in the meantime, just ride safely as you try to win that race with the dog—and don't go beyond allowed self-defense, or the dog owner can win on countersuit.

What to Do If You Are Involved in an Accident

As we've seen, most bicycle accidents *do not* involve a motor vehicle. Nevertheless, accidents with motor vehicles are the most feared, presumably because they hold the most potential for serious injury, or even death, for the cyclist. If you are involved in an accident while riding your bike, the decisions you make in the immediate aftermath of the accident will be important. They can be crucial in determining the outcome of any lawsuit that may stem from the accident, and thus can affect whether you can recover for damages; they can even affect whether you end up being held liable for the accident yourself. So, if you are still conscious, what do you do? And what should you do later when you have time to sort things out?

If you've been injured in a bicycle accident that does not involve a motorist, you will need to make an initial decision about whether you or somebody else was at fault. For example, if the accident was caused *solely* by your error or lack of bicycle-handling skills, you are at fault. If the accident is the result of some defect in the road surface, somebody else's carelessness, or a defective bicycle product, somebody else *may* be liable. If you're injured in one of these types of accidents, the police will not respond. Since there will be no police report, you will need to conduct your own initial investigation. The first thing you will need to do is preserve your evidence: Take some photos of the road condition that caused your accident; if the accident was the result of a defective bicycle product, take some photos of the defective product and preserve your evidence (see Chapter 7).

You may not be sure whether the road defect is somebody else's fault. Or you may wonder if a bicycle product is defective, but you just aren't certain. If this is the case, take pictures and preserve the evidence anyway. If there's a possibility that some defect or someone's carelessness caused your accident, you need to preserve the evidence of the possible defect or carelessness. Once you've done that, you can consult with an attorney, who can help you determine whether someone else's carelessness caused your injuries.

Now, what about that minority of bicycling accidents capturing most of our attention: the accidents involving automobiles? What should you do if you're involved in one of these accidents?

1. *Always wait for the police to respond to the accident scene so that an official report will be filed.* Some cyclists do not realize that they have been injured until several hours after the accident. Seemingly minor injuries can develop into serious and permanent injuries. By then, it may be too late to identify the at-fault driver. Keep in mind that many times the law-enforcement officer responding to the scene will take a statement from the motorist and write the police report without even bothering to talk to the cyclist. It's no surprise, then, that the police report will often blame the cyclist for the accident even when the motorist was at fault.

   To remedy this, try to get your version of what happened in the original police report. However, even if the police seem hostile, be polite and cooperate with the officer. If you're injured, even slightly, this is not the time to be stoic. Report your injuries to the police officer, no matter how minor they may seem; remember that after a few hours or days they may worsen, and you want it on the record that you did sustain injuries. If the police report contains only the motorist's version of the accident, you can have the police report amended later, if necessary. Also, try to get the names and contact information for any witnesses. This might be difficult if you've been injured, and of course it may be impossible if you're being carried away unconscious. If you are conscious but unable to get up and talk to the witnesses, ask a bystander to do it for you. Make sure you have the driver's name, address, phone number, driver's license number, vehicle license number, and insurance information. Although all of this information *should* be in the police report, don't assume that the police will include it. And often, police reports do not include witness information. If you can, make mental notes about the accident as well: Note anything you can about what happened, how it happened, where it occurred, when it occurred, and road, traffic, and weather conditions. As soon as you can, write down everything that happened.

2. *Seek prompt medical treatment for your injuries.* Seeking medical attention is proof that you were in fact injured, and the records generated by the medical provider will help establish the extent of your injuries. Have several photos of your injuries taken from different angles, and with different lighting, as soon as possible after the accident. Start a journal (injury diary) of your physical symptoms and make entries every couple of days.

3. *Preserve your evidence.* Take photos of your damaged equipment and accessories. Leave your bike and other damaged property in the same state that it was in right after the accident. This is critical. All elements of the crash must be preserved. That means that you must not move or bend anything. Do not take anything apart and put it back together. Do not have anyone look at, examine, or inspect it. Do not wash the clothes you were wearing. Most importantly, do *not* send *any* part of the bicycle, helmet, or components to anyone. Do *not* release custody of your damaged bicycle to anybody other than your attorney.

4. *Get professional advice.* Many automobile-on-bicycle accidents are too complex a legal problem for you to handle on your own. This is one of those legal situations where you will need some professional assistance to navigate the mazes successfully. You should not attempt to negotiate with the at-fault driver. He or she may not give you accurate information about his or her identity, insurance coverage, or vehicle ownership. Many drivers who cause accidents will initially apologize and accept blame for the accident, but later, after they've had time to consider the ramifications, they will deny that they were negligent. They may even deny that they were present at the accident scene, or tell a different version of events.

The accident report will include the driver's statements as well as all other witness statements. Additionally, the responding officer may decide to ticket the driver, and this can be useful when trying to settle the case with the insurance company. *Do not* attempt to communicate with the insurance company before consulting with an attorney. Most cyclists want to be fair and reasonable with insurance companies. However, insurance companies are not trying to be "fair and reasonable" with you. They are gathering information. And, unfortunately, your fair and honest account of the accident can and will be turned around and used against you later. As you will see in Chapter 4, there are some legal pitfalls to signing a settlement agreement in even the simplest of accidents. Therefore, you should consult with an attorney who is experienced in handling bicycle accidents, even if it's just for advice on how to proceed. Sometimes, a letter from an attorney to the insurance company will resolve the issues while avoiding any legal pitfalls; in fact, most injury cases are settled without ever going to trial.

Although many attorneys are competent to handle general injury cases, make sure your attorney has the following qualifications:

- Expert knowledge of bicycle traffic laws
- Skill and experience in negotiating bicycle accident cases with insurance companies
- Skill and experience in trying bicycle accident cases in court
- Understanding of the prevailing prejudice against cyclists by motorists and juries
- Knowledge of the names and functions of all bicycle components
- Understanding of bicycle traveling speeds, as well as braking and cornering
- Understanding of bicycle-handling skills, techniques, and customs
- Knowledge of how to get the full value of property damage estimates for your bicycle
- Knowledge of how to establish the value of lost riding time
- Access to leading bicycle accident reconstruction experts
- Access to licensed forensic bicycle engineers
- Understanding of how to establish the value of permanent diminished riding ability

The accident scene should be investigated for information about how the accident occurred. The investigation should include obtaining skid mark measurements, photographing the accident scene, speaking with additional witnesses, and measuring and diagramming the accident scene. If you've retained the services of an experienced bicycle accident attorney, the attorney will have this investigation conducted on your behalf by an investigator if the case warrants it: For example, if the motorist's liability is being questioned by the insurance company, or if the damages are very high, an experienced bicycle accident attorney will retain a bicycle accident expert to assist with your case. This is essential when there is a need to reconstruct the accident to prove what actually happened.

Be aware, however, that not all bicycle accident reconstructionists are equally qualified. Many are retired law-enforcement officers who become accident reconstructionists after taking a short course. These "experts" get destroyed on the witness stand. Experienced bicycle accident attorneys know the difference and retain a bicycle forensics engineer instead. In my own practice, I have often retained Jim Green,[22] one of the leading experts in the field and author of a bicycle accident book for forensic engineers. Jim is a particularly valuable member of a bicycle accident legal team, because in addition to being a well-known and respected engineer with expertise in the forensics of bicycle accidents, he brings an understanding of bicycling from his own racing pedigree. In fact, Jim continues to compete in triathlons. A bicycle accident engineer will generate an expert report on the accident and then provide expert testimony in depositions and in court on your behalf; the defense team will hire their own expert. For this reason, having a real expert on your team will be necessary if you want to receive just compensation for your injuries.

22 See http://www.bikereconstruction.com.

4

A Cyclist's Guide to Insurance

by Steven M. Magas

INTRODUCTION

It's indisputable: Every person owes every other person a "duty of care." If Henry Wells breaches his duty to Evylyn Thomas, and she is injured as a result of his breach of duty, he is liable for the injury he has caused. The same goes for Evylyn Thomas: If she breaches her duty to Henry Wells or to any other person, she will be held liable for the injuries she has caused.

It's one thing to say that Henry is liable to Evylyn for the injuries he has caused; it's another thing, however, to get Henry to pay for her injuries. The simple reality is that most people just do not have the financial resources to pay for the injuries that could potentially result from their negligence. Even when people do have assets to attach, the potential damages resulting from a breach of duty may be financially ruinous. So what happens if there's an accident, then? Do we simply let Henry escape liability for his breach of duty, because we know he can't pay? Do we find Henry liable, sell off whatever assets he has, and garnish his wages for the rest of his life?

Or do we find a way between those extremes—one that holds Henry liable for his breach, and ensures that Evylyn will be compensated for her injuries, even though Henry can't possibly pay for his breach?

This third way—via what we call "insurance"—is the means by which we ensure that Henry will be held liable and Evylyn will be compensated. Simply put, insurance is probably the most important factor in every collision involving a car and a bicycle. No insurance usually means no recovery, no ability to pay current or future medical bills, no way to recover wages lost, and no funds to compensate for your pain and suffering. However, insurance policies and insurance issues frequently become extremely complicated, particularly for the uninitiated. Understanding insurance policies and the laws of insurance takes some study and practice.

Health, auto, homeowner's, and life insurance policies all may come into play if you are involved in an injury-causing crash while operating your bike. More exotic products, like "excess" or "umbrella" coverage, can also be triggered in more catastrophic incidents. However, once you tap into insurance coverage, the insurance representatives or lawyers may begin to make references to obscure legal concepts such as "subrogation," "medical payments coverage," "uninsured/underinsured motorist," and "no fault" or "PIP." They are not trying to confuse you—these terms all have specific meanings and implications that may indeed apply to your case—but trying to figure out how they affect your situation may be frustrating. The purpose of this chapter is to give you a brief law-

TABLE 4.1 Four Insurance Systems

No Fault

Florida	Massachusetts	North Dakota
Hawaii	Michigan	New York
Kansas	Minnesota	Utah

Hybrid

Arkansas	Maryland	South Carolina	Texas
Delaware	Oregon	South Dakota	Virginia

Choice

Kentucky	New Jersey	Pennsylvania	District of Columbia

Tort Liability

All remaining states are tort liability states.

---

yer's-eye view into the wacky world of insurance in order to help you understand how it all fits together. If you are in an accident, it is essential to consult an attorney. However, the more you understand insurance and the issues you will be facing in the event of an accident, the better prepared you will be to select appropriate insurance policies in the first place and to avoid any pitfalls that would be looming in dealing with insurance companies. In the event of an accident, you will also be in a better position to understand what your attorney is talking about as you discuss your case.

There are four basic types of insurance systems used in the United States: the tort liability system, the no-fault system, the hybrid system, and the choice system. You probably won't have to deal with all four of these, unless you are in the rather unfortunate position of getting injured in a lot of different states, because each state uses only one system. Therefore, you will likely be subject to only one of these four systems, and the system you're subject to will depend on which state you're riding in. Nevertheless, it's important to understand what system your state uses, because it will determine how you will be compensated, and what your rights are, if you are injured in a cycling accident.

The Four Insurance Systems

4-1 THE TORT LIABILITY SYSTEM

A tort liability system is the traditional system for handling personal injury and property damage. In a tort liability system, if somebody's negligent act causes injury, that person is liable for damages to the injured person. Damages are compensation for losses such as:

→ ECONOMIC LOSS. *This includes medical expenses, lost earnings, and other out-of-pocket expenses incurred as a result of the injury.*

→ PHYSICAL PAIN. *These damages include pain already suffered as well as pain expected to occur in the future.*

→ MENTAL DISTRESS. *These damages include the fright and shock experienced at the time of the injury; humiliation due to lasting effects of the injury, such as disfigurement or disability; and depression resulting from the inability to continue one's former life due to the seriousness of the injury.*

→ LOSS OF THE ABILITY TO ENJOY LIFE. *This is the loss incurred when the injured person is unable to enjoy aspects of life that were enjoyed prior to being injured. For example, an avid cyclist who can never ride again following an accident may be able to recover damages for this loss.*

→ LOSS OF CONSORTIUM OR COMPANIONSHIP. *These are the losses suffered by the spouse, parents, and children of an injured person.*

→ WRONGFUL DEATH. *These are losses suffered by the survivors of a person who was killed as a result of somebody's negligent act.*

→ FUTURE DAMAGES. *These are damages resulting from the negligent act that the injured person can be expected to sustain in the future. Future damages are awarded because the injured person cannot file a separate future lawsuit to recover later damages.*

→ PUNITIVE DAMAGES. *These are damages awarded to the injured person to penalize the person who committed the negligent act and to deter others from acting in a similar manner, where the conduct of the person who committed the negligent act is particularly outrageous.*

Twenty-nine states have a tort liability system for traffic accidents; in one of these states, if you're involved in an accident, there will be an attempt to determine fault. Depending on which state the accident occurs in, one of the following negligence systems will be in effect:

→ PURE COMPARATIVE NEGLIGENCE. *In a pure comparative negligence system, the injured person can recover damages for injuries received and is liable for damages for injuries inflicted. For example, if the cyclist is 40 percent negligent and the driver is 60 percent negligent, the cyclist can recover 60 percent of his or her damages but also is liable for 40 percent of the driver's damages.*

→ MODIFIED COMPARATIVE NEGLIGENCE. *In a modified comparative negligence system, if the injured person is determined to be 50 percent or more negligent, he or she cannot recover damages.*

→ CONTRIBUTORY NEGLIGENCE. *In a contributory negligence system, if the injured person's own negligence contributed to the accident in any way—even if he or she was only 1 percent negligent—then he or she cannot recover damages.*

Now, let's assume that you're involved in a collision with an automobile. Following an accident in a tort liability state, the initial determination of fault will be made by the insurance company of the driver who hit you; there are three possible determinations of fault:

1. The insurance company will determine that the driver who hit you is 100 percent at fault.

2. The insurance company will determine that you are 100 percent at fault.

3. The insurance company will determine that you're both at fault.

Once the insurance company has made this determination, its representatives will inform you of the amount, if any, that the company will reimburse you for your expenses, as well as the amount, if any, that the company expects you to reimburse the motorist for damage to the car.

The type of negligence system in effect in your state will then determine who pays what. On one hand, for example, if the insurance company decides you are 100 percent at fault, you will not be reimbursed for your expenses, and you will be expected to pay for the damage to the car. On the other hand, in a comparative negligence state, if the insurance company determines that you are 40 percent at fault, you will be offered reimbursement for 60 percent of your expenses, and you will be expected to pay for 40 percent of the damage to the car. If your state follows a system of modified comparative negligence, and your liability in the accident is 50 percent or more, you will not be reimbursed for your expenses, and you will be expected to pay your liability percentage of the driver's damages.

TABLE 4.2 Three Negligence Systems

Pure Comparative Negligence

Alaska	Kentucky	New Mexico	Washington
Arizona	Louisiana	New York	
California	Mississippi	Rhode Island	
Florida	Missouri	South Dakota	

Modified Comparative Negligence

Arkansas	Iowa	New Hampshire	Texas
Colorado	Kansas	New Jersey	Utah
Connecticut	Maine	North Dakota	Vermont
Delaware	Massachusetts	Ohio	West Virginia
Georgia	Michigan	Oklahoma	Wisconsin
Hawaii	Minnesota	Oregon	Wyoming
Idaho	Montana	Pennsylvania	
Illinois	Nebraska	South Carolina	
Indiana	Nevada	Tennessee	

Contributory Negligence

Alabama	North Carolina	District of Columbia
Maryland	Virginia	

In a comparative negligence state, the insurance adjustor will almost always claim that the bike rider did something wrong. She will likely argue that the cyclist was not riding "as far right as practicable," failed to signal a turn, or committed some other infraction rendering the cyclist "negligent" or "comparatively negligent." This shifts at least some of the burden for paying the costs of the accident onto the cyclist. One key point is that the alleged negligence by the cyclist must actually play *some* role in causing the crash. For example, if a car/bike accident occurs at night, the motorist may argue that the cyclist had no front headlight and was thus in violation of state law and negligent. However, if the accident was a "rear-ender," the cyclist could counter that the absence of a front headlight played no role in causing the motorist to strike the cyclist from behind. Thus, the cyclist would argue, there can be no reduction for comparative negligence.

Finally, if you happen to be unfortunate enough to live in a contributory negligence state, and you are negligent to any degree—even if the driver was 99 percent negligent, and you were only 1 percent negligent—you will not be able to recover for any damages. There are defenses available to contributory negligence that can act to mitigate your negligence and allow you to recover damages for your injuries despite your negligence. However, these defenses raise complex legal issues; you must consult with an attorney if you are injured in a contributory negligence state and hope to recover damages for your injuries.

Based on these determinations—that is, the insurance company's *determination of fault*—the company may decide that you can recover damages and will make an offer to settle your claim. Whether you accept this offer is entirely up to you. For example, if you feel that the offer does not adequately compensate you for your damages, you are not required to accept the offer. Similarly, if you do not agree with the insurance company's determination of your own degree of fault, you are not required to agree with them. If you decide to reject the insurance company's determination of fault and/or their offer, you have two options: You can either negotiate further with the insurance company or file a lawsuit. Ultimately, if you and the insurance company cannot come to an agreement through negotiation, it will be up to a jury, not the insurance company, to determine liability and damage awards.

1.3 THE NO FAULT SYSTEM

Nine states have abandoned the tort liability system for a no-fault insurance system. There are two main features of a no-fault system. First, if you are injured in a collision, you will be compensated for your injuries and property damage by your own auto insurance policy, without regard for who was at fault. However, that compensation would be limited to your economic damages, such as medical expenses and lost income; none of the noneconomic damages, such as "pain and suffering" damages, would be available to you. This can have the effect of dramatically limiting recoveries, particularly if the injuries are very painful and debilitating but where there is little that can be done—for example, if the cyclist suffers fractured ribs, disfiguring injuries, or loss of the "enjoyment of life."

Second, if you're injured in a no-fault state, your right to sue for severe injuries and pain and suffering is severely restricted by the state's "threshold"—the level that your injuries must meet before you are allowed to file a lawsuit. Some states use a *verbal threshold,* whereas others use a *monetary threshold.* A state that uses a verbal threshold will not permit you to sue for your injuries unless your injuries meet the state's description of the severity of injury necessary for a lawsuit to proceed.

A state that uses a monetary threshold will allow you to sue for your injuries only if your expenses exceed the dollar amount of the monetary threshold. The thresholds will vary from state to state; in states that have decided to severely limit litigation, the thresholds are set high, thereby eliminating most lawsuits. Because monetary thresholds set a dollar "target" that encourages fraud, some states have instead opted for the verbal threshold. Again, the law is different everywhere: If you live in a no-fault state and have been injured, you will need to consult with your friendly neighborhood "bike lawyer"—or, lacking that, a lawyer specializing in personal-injury cases—to determine what damages you are entitled to under the law.

The insurance industry is the driving force behind no-fault insurance; the industry's theory is that by restricting litigation, costs and delays are reduced, resulting in benefits to consumers. Proponents of no-fault point to a study indicating that states with strict limits on litigation have lower average bodily injury claim costs than other states. Another study, however, indicates that states with no-fault insurance have consistently higher premiums than traditional tort liability states, so those lower bodily injury costs are not being passed on to consumers in the form of lower premiums. The real losers in no-fault states, however, are the injured parties, because they are severely restricted in recovering damages for their injuries.

If you're injured in a collision, the claim for your medical expenses and lost income will be submitted to your own auto insurance company. If you live in a no-fault state and don't have an auto insurance policy—if, for example, you're a bicycle commuter who doesn't own a car, and therefore you don't have insurance for one—there are other rules determining who pays your damages. The driver's insurance company may be required to compensate you, or if the driver is uninsured, the insurance company of another driver in your household may be required to compensate you. If there is no other driver in your household or in the driver's household, the state may have an uninsured driver's fund to compensate you.

4-3 THE HYBRID SYSTEM

Nine states have adopted a "hybrid system" in which the first-party benefits—that is, your own insurance policy benefits—of the no-fault system are "added on" to the traditional tort liability system. In these states, there are no restrictions on lawsuits, but the first-party insurance coverage may not be mandatory, as it is in the no-fault states, and the first-party benefits may be lower than in the no-fault states.

4-4 THE CHOICE SYSTEM

The remaining three states offer a choice between no-fault and tort liability. In these states, consumers choose whether they want a policy with a threshold limit on lawsuits or a policy with no restrictions on lawsuits. In New Jersey, the consumer is presumed to have accepted a verbal threshold on lawsuits unless he or she specifically rejects the verbal threshold and retains the right to sue. In Pennsylvania, by contrast, the consumer is presumed to have retained the right to sue unless he or she specifically requests a verbal threshold on lawsuits. In Kentucky, the consumer must specifically request to retain the right to sue, as in New Jersey, except that Kentucky's threshold is monetary.

Finally, in the District of Columbia, consumers may choose either no-fault or fault-based (tort liability) coverage; however, if a driver with a no-fault policy is involved in an accident, that driver has sixty days to decide whether to accept the no-fault compensation or to file a lawsuit.

How Insurance Works

Now that we've sorted all that out, let's see how insurance works. Say you are in a crash—a particularly ugly crash—in which you are significantly and permanently injured. You may miss days, weeks, or months of work. You may not be able to work in the future, you may be forced to retire early, or you may have to change the way you work and live. You incur huge medical bills and suffer intolerable pain. You have disfiguring scars and debilitating, permanent medical problems. And it's all the other guy's fault . . . mostly. In short, from a lawyer's warped perspective, you have a good case. How does insurance come into play? One more assumption for this part of our discussion is that you are *not* in a "no-fault" state.

Again from the lawyer's perspective, the question really is how you will get paid (and how the lawyer will get paid), because that's the attorney's job. The answer almost always lies in the insurance equation, because compensation for injured victims of another's negligence almost always comes from an insurance company. Many of the questions that arise in the aftermath of an accident have to do with insurance, and one of the best ways to be prepared for an accident is to make sure you have the right type of insurance.

What if the motorist who hit you has no insurance? Where can you get money to pay your medical bills or living expenses? What if the motorist who hit you has some insurance but not enough insurance to cover your claim? What if you have great health insurance and disability insurance through your job, but all of a sudden you start receiving "subrogation" letters that seem to say you have to pay back your insurers all the money they paid to your doctors if you get a settlement? Can they do that? What if you are at least partially at fault for causing the crash? How does this affect your ability to obtain money or your negotiations with various insurers? What steps do you have to take to protect the rights of your various insurance companies when you look to settle your claim?

All of these questions illustrate the overlap of insurance law into bicycle crash cases. As soon as that car hit you, *a lot* of insurance policies were triggered. Let's take a look at some of the issues raised above.

4-5 THE MOTORIST'S AUTO POLICY

The first, and most obvious, insurance policy that comes into play when you are hit by an errant motorist is the motorist's automobile insurance policy—assuming you are "lucky" enough to be hit by someone who has insurance. The typical automobile insurance policy is designed to pay money to those injured by the motorist's "negligence" or carelessness. If you are involved in a collision with an insured motorist, the motorist (or you, the cyclist) must provide timely "notice" to the motorist's insurer of the crash. Typically, the insurer then assigns an "adjustor" to handle your claim. The injured cyclist presents a "claim" against the motorist to the adjustor by providing documentation to support the claim, and the claim is then considered by the insurer. The insurer has the right under the policy to "settle" the claim by paying a sum of money to the injured party. This sum of money, which is based on the law of the particular jurisdiction's relative "tort claims" or "personal injury" claims, usually covers medical bills and wage loss along with other out-of-pocket expenses and monies to compensate for "pain and suffering." The insurer usually has separate coverage to pay any "property damage" claim arising out of the crash. If the insurer makes an "offer" to settle, negotiations may ensue and the claim may be settled. If a settlement cannot be reached, a lawsuit may be necessary. That's the claims process in a nutshell; now let's look at some critical issues.

NOTICE TO EACH INSURER

To trigger the insurance claims process, the injured cyclist or his or her lawyer typically notifies the motorist that a claim is being presented. The smart motorist provides that letter to his or her insurance agent or reports it directly to the insurer. This notification to the insurer is critical. Failure to notify the insurer in a timely manner may give the insurer the right to deny the claim, depending on the terms of the particular policy. The cyclist's lawyer should not only notify the motorist but also contact the motorist's insurer. Frequently, the name of the insurer is listed on the police report, and every insurer has a toll-free number for reporting claims.

THE ADJUSTOR: FRIEND OR FOE?

The insurer then assigns the claim to one or two people, known as "adjustors" or "claims representatives." Some insurers have separate adjustors for the "property damage" and "personal injury" claims, but some use the same adjustor for the entire package. Some insurers have adjustors who are actually employees of the carrier; others retain a separate company to handle the claim.

Let me offer a few words of perspective about insurance adjustors. For the most part, they are highly trained professionals who are extremely adept at protecting the insurance company's assets by paying as little money to the injured bicyclist/claimant as possible. They are professional cynics—that's their job. They handle dozens or hundreds of claims at a time. In virtually every case, someone wants more money than the insurer wants to pay. They've heard every story on the planet. They demand documentation to support every element of a claim. They take nothing for granted and nothing at face value.

Adjustors are trained in property damage, accident investigation, witness interviewing, the law of torts, medical issues, insurance law, subrogation, and negotiation. They are professional negotiators. The adjustor has likely handled hundreds, even thousands, of claims, whereas you probably have been involved in only one accident. Remember that they know more than you do and are very good at what they do.

The personalities of adjustors run the gamut from sugary-sweet to mean and ornery. Some adjustors make life so miserable for claimants that they take less money than their cases are worth just to not have to deal with them anymore. Some adjustors befriend the claimants, such that the injured victim feels the adjustor has his or her best interests at heart. For you, the victim of a negligent motorist, the most important thing to remember is that the adjustor's job is to make sure the insurer pays you the smallest amount of money it possibly can to resolve your case. The adjustor is not your friend but your adversary. Treat him or her professionally. If the adjustor does not treat you professionally, document it in a letter and send it to a supervisor. If the treatment is bad enough, you can report it directly to the state insurance commissioner.

A SECRET ABOUT ADJUSTORS

Let me tell one huge secret about dealing with adjustors. I learned this secret, sometimes the hard way, during negotiations with hundreds of different adjustors over the past twenty-five years. I also learned it during my days as an employee with an insurance company, where adjustors were my colleagues and friends. I learned it as the lawyer hired by the adjustor to defend the case. The secret is this: *Do not tick off your adjustor over stupid stuff.*

An adjustor's caseload is huge. Hundreds of claim files may be on his or her shelves at any given time. The adjustor usually has no emotional attachment to a particular case. Do not give the adjustor reason to have a very negative emotional attachment to your case. You, unlike the adjustor, have only one claim, and you may well have a very strong emotional attachment to that claim. You may wonder why the motorist never called to check on you in the hospital. You may be angry because the insurer gave you only one-third of what you felt your property damage claim was worth. However, if you let that anger spill into the negotiations, you may sour the claim forever.

The claimant's or attorney's relationship with the adjustor is critical. Try to be professional, precise, prepared, and thorough in dealing with adjustors. Establish a good rapport, and try to be realistic about your case—don't sell a $500 claim as a $50,000 claim. Document everything, and make sure you can back up every comment you make about a case with reference to a piece of paper. Know how to read the medical records and know how to read between the lines of the medical chart. If you can keep the adjustor's caseload and motivation in mind and treat the adjustor professionally and courteously, you will be more likely to succeed.

If you are working with an adjustor, you should never be condescending, arrogant, abusive, or grossly unreasonable—even if you feel the adjustor is acting that way. Each adjustor has his or her own personality, but if you anger your adjustor by arguing over things that ultimately aren't important, you may ruin any opportunity for obtaining a reasonable settlement. Adjustors are tough and sometimes difficult to deal with—they have to be in order to protect the insurer's assets. You can argue points, present your views, and engage in professional "puffery" as you would in any negotiations—for a car, a house, or a used tuba! But once it goes beyond professional negotiation and into personal attacks, *you* lose. The adjustor controls the purse strings, and if your file is "red-flagged," it will be difficult to gain an edge in negotiations. Negotiate fairly, aggressively, and professionally to get best results. Once the purse strings are drawn shut, you are stuck either taking an unreasonably low settlement or filing a lawsuit. The adjustor is asserting the insurance company's position, and it's necessary for you to assert your position. However, having the negotiations reduced to arguing serves only the interests of the insurance company—especially if you become upset. Some adjustors will deliberately try to manipulate you into making that mistake, so don't get suckered into that ploy. Pick your battles wisely, stand firm on the important issues of your case, and always negotiate in a calm, professional manner.

Your attorney should negotiate hard, trying to get the best possible deal for you. If I think an adjustor is being unreasonable, I say so—but, I always have data to back me up. This may consist of my personal experience, a series of reported cases, or some jury verdict research I have conducted. I also use my experience of working inside an insurance company for several years to try to see what's driving the insurer's position. Occasionally, I've had to get more experienced claims representatives involved when a particular adjustor was unusually obnoxious, but that is very rare.

PRESENTING YOUR CLAIM: THE PAPER TRAIL

So what do you need to present your insurance claim? The one-word answer is *"paper!"* You need to obtain every single piece of paper related to your case: the police report, witness statements, photographs of the scene, and property damage documentation, along with any additional analysis of the crash to show you were not at fault. You need every single piece of paper in your medical care provider's files relative to your injuries—every office note, test result, X-ray report—and the record should be "certified" such that the insurer knows you are providing all the records. If your X rays or other films show the injury, then you should order copies of the actual films. Professional photographs of scars, bones, disfiguring bony protrusions, or other deformities related to the crash, as well as of the scene of the crash, the vehicles, and all property damage, should also be obtained.

If you have an attorney, he or she should wait until you are fully healed—or your recovery has plateaued—before presenting the complete package of documentation for your claim. Once that occurs, the attorney will make sure all the documents are on hand, organize them in a package, and prepare a "demand" letter. This lengthy letter reviews and analyzes all aspects of the case—the liability or legal issues, the nature and extent of the injuries, a summary of all medical care, and a spreadsheet showing all medical bills and wage loss. At the end of the demand letter, your attorney will set forth the opening "demand"—the amount of money you would accept to settle. This is always at the very highest end of "reasonable."

The first "offer" from the insurer is always at the very lowest end of reasonable (or downright unreasonable), and from there the negotiations proceed much like the dickering over a used car—both sides poking at the weak spots of the other's position, kicking the tires, and trading offers and counteroffers until the case is either resolved or an impasse is reached.

If the motorist's insurance policy has sufficient policy limits, the case may then resolve. If the value of your case is greater than the policy limits, the insurer should, but probably will not, tell you this and offer the policy limits. Where do you go if the motorist's policy is not enough? How do you know what the policy limits are if the insurer won't tell you?

In some jurisdictions, the insurer is required to tell you the policy limits. In many jurisdictions, lawyers who handle personal injury claims know which companies are most likely to sell policies with lower limits. If you have any type of "big" case involving significant injuries, such as fractures, burns, scars, surgery, and the like, you need to consult with a lawyer. You should not be trying to recover from those injuries and stay on top of a complex personal injury claim.

4-6 THE MOTORIST'S EMPLOYER'S AUTO POLICY

One thing to determine in every case is whether the negligent motorist was "at work" at the time of the crash. If so, the motorist's employer may very well have insurance coverage you can tap into to pay your claim.

How do you find out whether the motorist was working for someone else at the time of the crash? Sometimes it appears on the police report. Sometimes, when the insurance adjustor contacts you, the "Insured" listed on the letterhead may tip you off. For example, it may say "Joe Schmoe Trucking, Inc.," or some other business name. Sometimes you can infer that the driver was working from the circumstances of the crash. Sometimes you can just call the driver and ask.

The nice thing about commercial automobile policies is that they almost always have large policy limits—$500,000 and $1,000,000 are typical policy limits. Due to the "notice" requirements mentioned above, though, you need to do this detective work quickly and put the carrier on notice right away.

A motorist who negligently injures you while acting in the course and scope of his employment generally also causes his employer to be liable as well. There has been a lot of litigation over the limits of this rule, however, and you are well advised to consult with an attorney if any issues arise. For example, if the driver was supposed to be working but was actually on what early cases referred to as a "frolic" (for example, stopping off at a bar for a drink), then the insurance company could avoid coverage.

4-7 THE CYCLIST'S AUTO POLICY

Your own auto insurance policy may come into play if you are the cyclist in a bike/car accident, particularly if the motorist who hit you is uninsured or has insufficient insurance coverage. This is all too common a problem, because states have very low requirements for liability coverage, and insurance companies aggressively market policies with low liability limits. Such policies are like free money to these insurance companies—they sell policies, collect premiums, and if they ever have to pay out on a claim, the low liability limits protect the insurance company from paying out any more than the policy limit. Thus, many drivers have only minimal liability coverage—in other words, they're "underinsured," because if one of these drivers hits you, her insurance policy can't even come close to paying for your injuries.

An example of a state with low liability limits is my home state of Ohio, which has one of the lowest "minimum" coverage requirements in the nation, at $12,500. This means that a motorist who hits you in Ohio only has to have "Twelve Five" coverage to be "legal." Almost any significant injury requiring more than minimal medical care will have a value in excess of this amount. Numerous other states also have minimum coverage amounts that may be insufficient for many claims that occur in bike/car accidents. As a result, I frequently end up filing an "uninsured/ underinsured motorist" (UM/UIM) claim against the cyclist's own automobile insurance carrier. There are two provisions that are very important on your policy and could come into play in an accident: The first is UM/UIM, and the second is the medical payments provision.

UNINSURED AND UNDERINSURED MOTORIST COVERAGE

If it appears likely that the cyclist's damages will be in excess of the motorist's available policy limits, the cyclist will have to open a claim against his or her own policy's UM/UIM provision. If the motorist who ran into you has *no* coverage, then "uninsured" coverage comes into play. If the motorist has some coverage, but not enough to pay the full value of your claim, then the motorist is deemed to be "underinsured." Either way, the claim is handled the same way.

It is a good idea to buy as much UM/UIM coverage as you can afford. Do not let an insurance agent cut the cost of your insurance bill by deleting your UM/UIM coverage. This coverage protects you in the event of an encounter with someone who lacks sufficient insurance or assets to pay you.

UM/UIM issues can be complicated. In Ohio, for example, in the past ten years or so, there have been hundreds of appellate decisions on UM/UIM issues. Pro-insurance company forces try to change laws to limit recoveries. Pro-plaintiff groups argue for expanding the law. Let's look at what you should do if you find yourself turning to your UM/UIM coverage.

The UM/UIM Trap

The UM/UIM trap arises when the motorist's insurer admits to you that your claim exceeds the motorist's policy limits. The insurer then offers you the policy limits, and all of a sudden there's this pile of money sitting there for you—all you have to do is sign a release and the money is yours! What harm can possibly come from this? The answer is simple: If you don't know what your UM/UIM policy says, and what you must do to protect your claim and your carrier's rights, you could destroy your UM/UIM claim.

First, do *not* sign that release—at least not until you have consulted with legal counsel.

To protect your claim, you must comply with every possible requirement under your UM/UIM policy and the statutory and case law of your particular jurisdiction relative to these claims. Your failure to do so may close off your ability to collect any additional money under your auto policy. For example, signing a release without obtaining the approval of your UM/UIM carrier can lead to the loss of your UM/UIM coverage.

A concept in the law known as "subrogation" arises in virtually every bike/car crash claim. "Subrogation" is the right of an insurance company to "stand in the shoes" of its insured once it pays money to the insured. This means two things. First, if you receive money from the person who ran into you, you may have to pay back the insurer that paid your medical bills, your UM/UIM claim, your disability claim, or your wage-loss claim. (This is discussed later.) Second, subrogation permits an insurer that paid money to you to file a lawsuit against the motorist that ran into you to try to collect back that money.

How does your signing a release screw all that up? Once you sign a release, your claim is dead—a lawsuit can never be filed against the motorist relative to this particular accident, by you or by anyone who "stands in your shoes." Signing that release effectively destroys the ability of any other interested party to go after the motorist, including your health insurer, your UM/UIM carrier, and your disability insurance provider. Because your claim against the motorist dies when you sign the release, the claims of these "subrogated" insurers also die.

By signing a release without the knowledge or consent of the subrogated insurers, you have prevented those carriers from getting their money back. If you sign the release and take the money, you may not be permitted to present a UM/UIM claim against your own insurer, and you have thereby robbed yourself of an additional significant recovery.

Each jurisdiction has a manner of dealing with this problem. In many jurisdictions, and under the terms of many auto policies, you are required to notify *all* subrogated parties when you receive an offer of money from the motorist's insurer. The subrogated parties then have a "reasonable" time to tell you whether it is okay for you to accept the money and sign the release.

The subrogated parties are supposed to investigate the assets of the motorist during this "reasonable" period of time. If a subrogated party thinks it may be possible to sue the motorist to recapture some of the money, that party may offer to pay you the same amount of money offered by the motorist's insurer. That way, you get the money, but you do not have to sign a release, thereby keeping the claim against the motorist alive. The insurer can sue the motorist later, should it so choose.

Complicated? You betcha! That's why this "trap" snares many unsuspecting injured victims, as well as many lawyers who do not regularly deal with personal injury or insurance claims.

UM/UIM Policy Limits

Let's assume you took my advice and purchased automobile insurance coverage with $250,000 UM/UIM policy limits. The person who ran into you also has a policy limit of $250,000. Let's say your claim is worth in excess of $500,000. So you get $250,000 from the guy who hit you and $250,000 from your UM/UIM carrier, right? Wrong!

In many states, you can use "underinsured" motorist coverage only if the other guy's coverage is *less* than yours. Furthermore, you can recover only the *difference* between your policy limits and the other policy limits. Thus, if the motorist has $100,000 in coverage and you have $250,000, you can recover $150,000 from your own UM/UIM carrier—assuming your case has significant value. In our example, though, because your coverage ($250,000) was equal to the motorist's coverage, you would get zero from your own policy, even though you paid for $250,000 of coverage and even though the $250,000 from the motorist is only one-half of the value of your claim.

Again, this is complicated stuff. You are well advised to consult with an attorney well versed in insurance law in any such case.

MEDICAL PAYMENTS COVERAGE

"Medical payments" coverage is another provision on your policy. This coverage pays *your* medical bills if the policy terms are met. The limits are usually relatively low, often $10,000 or less, sometimes only $1,000. The "med-pay" coverage can pay your out-of-pocket expenses, "co-pays," and the like.

The requirements for presenting a med-pay claim are contained in the policy; the policy language is complicated and can be difficult to understand and interpret, so I'll give you just the highlights, using some standard language from my own automobile policy as an example. My carrier states that it "will pay the reasonable expenses incurred for necessary medical services received within three years from the date of a motor vehicle accident because of bodily injury" so long as the injuries were

- sustained by an insured person, and
- caused by that motor vehicle accident.

Following this broad "we're happy to pay your medical bills" language is a list of fifteen "exclusions." Exclusions are an insurer's way of saying "We're *not* paying you" for certain types of claims.

What does all this mean? Clearly, if you are riding your bike and are actually struck by a car, the coverage applies. But what if the car never hits you? For example, say the motorist cuts you off, and you hit the brakes and go head over handlebars. A very strong argument can be made that this accident is covered under med-pay (as well as triggering the UM coverage).

A "phantom motorist" claim may also be covered. In this case, an unknown motorist causes a wreck and leaves the scene. Typically, a phantom motorist is the cause of the accident but doesn't actually collide with the cyclist. For example, a phantom motorist may cut another car off, causing that other car to swerve and collide with you. Or perhaps the phantom motorist cuts you off, causing you to swerve and have an accident as the phantom motorist continues down the road. Some states have a "physical contact" requirement, meaning the phantom motorist must actually hit the cyclist. Others require proof of some sort other than the victim's statement—some "corroborating" evidence of the presence of a phantom motorist. Here, you must not only read the policy but know the case law and statutory law of your particular jurisdiction. Sounds like a trip to the lawyer's office is in order!

4-8 HOMEOWNER'S AND RENTER'S COVERAGE

Automobile policies are not the only source of insurance coverage for cyclists to consider; homeowner's or renter's policies will cover cyclists in some types of accidents. For example, what if a can of soda is thrown from a passing car and injures the cyclist? Courts have gone both ways on this type of assault. Some courts have found that your automobile insurance coverage applies, some have said no. But if a passenger tosses an object out the window that causes you to crash, then the passenger's *homeowner's* insurance can come into play. (However, no insurance policy in the world covers intentional or "criminal" acts, and if the act of throwing an object at a cyclist is deemed a criminal act, then there may be no coverage available.)

Or what if you, the cyclist, are at fault? You run a stop sign, broadside a Porsche, and cause a $10,000 dent. What if you're on your bike and you negligently injure another cyclist or a pedestrian? This time, it is *your* homeowner's policy that comes into play to cover your negligence.

4-9 EXCESS OR UMBRELLA COVERAGE

The vast majority of bicycle insurance claims do not involve catastrophic losses. However, every once in a while there is a bicycle/car crash that paralyzes or kills the rider or causes loss of a limb or other injuries that can devastate the rider's ability to live a normal life, or that require a lifetime of medical care. What kind of insurance protection can you purchase to protect yourself in the event of such an accident?

"Excess" or "umbrella" coverage is available from many insurers. This is a highly specialized type of insurance coverage with very large policy limits that comes into play only when all other available coverages are exhausted. You must carry a particular level of "underlying" coverage, perhaps $250,000 or more, before you can purchase an excess or umbrella policy. The cost of umbrella coverage is relatively low in comparison with other types of coverage—primarily because it is only rarely used. When you need it, though, it is invaluable.

As I write this, I have a relatively new case sitting on my desk. A cyclist, a professional man in the prime of his earning potential, suffered a broken neck when a pickup truck backed out of a driveway directly in front of him. His unstable fractured neck was treated by fusing his neck at two levels—a very complex operation that leaves him at risk for future problems. Fortunately, he was not paralyzed. His medical bills are approaching $100,000, and his wage loss will likely reach a similar figure, assuming he is able to return to work effectively at some point.

The driver of the pickup truck carried only Ohio's minimum coverage—$12,500. My client carried UM/UIM coverage of $300,000—pretty good coverage. Using the math from the explanation above, we should be able to obtain $287,500 ($300,000 – $12,500) from my client's UM/UIM carrier. Where does he go for compensation for the rest of his claim, assuming the value is in excess of $300,000?

Fortunately, my client carried an umbrella policy with policy limits of $1,000,000. As I explained to him, this incident illustrates exactly why I encourage people to buy an umbrella policy. Instead of looking at a lifetime of poverty or bankruptcy due to six-figure medical bills, the client's insurance choice will provide him with the money he needs to keep his life relatively "normal" in the face of his current level of disability.

Does he just "get" a million bucks? No. At the appropriate time, we will present a thoroughly documented claim to the insurer. Our maximum recovery from the umbrella policy will be $700,000 ($1,000,000 – $300,000). We will try to negotiate an appropriate settlement based on the injuries, recovery, losses, and other relevant factors.

4-10 CYCLIST'S HEALTH INSURANCE

Health insurance seems like it should not present any complicated legal issues. You got hurt. You submit a claim for your medical bills. The bills get paid. Life goes on. However, the "subrogation" concept we discussed earlier can complicate almost every injury case.

Health insurers have become extremely adept at figuring out which of their insureds have been involved in accidents, and then sending out "subrogation notices" demanding repayment of the bills it paid out of any settlement. Many insurers have entire "subrogation departments" whose job it is to ferret out potential claims of this type. Other insurers retain the services of outside companies devoted to pursuing such claims.

The problem for cyclists arises when they handle their own claims. It seems as if the subrogation notices get stuffed in the back of the drawer because they are not understood. Injured cyclists negotiate what seems like a decent settlement with the motorist's insurer, and later they are shocked to discover that they have to pay back their own insurer. If they have negotiated a deal that did not take the subrogation claim into account, they may have to give up all or most of their settlement to the health insurer.

4-11 CYCLIST'S EMPLOYMENT BENEFITS

This may come as a shock to some, but many cyclists not only have jobs, but actually have good jobs with benefits, such as short-term or long-term disability insurance, accident insurance, or "PTO" (paid time off). However, as you can probably guess by now, although these benefits can help you when you are injured by a negligent motorist, the insurance companies underwriting these benefits have "subrogation" rights. When negotiating with the motorist's insurer, the cyclist must keep these subrogation rights in mind.

One area of potential recovery that many people overlook when they negotiate their own claims is the ability to recoup employee benefits used due to injury. If you accumulate "leave" or time off as you work and have to use that leave as a result of your injuries, you should include this in your negotiations. You worked for it. You earned it. Now you've had to use it due to someone else's negligence, and the time off is no longer available if you get pneumonia, have a heart attack, or otherwise need time away from work.

4-12 CYCLIST'S STATE OR FEDERAL BENEFITS

Many people today do not have health insurance. If their income is low enough—if they're not the "working poor" who have no access to health insurance—they may be able to rely on benefits provided by state or federal government programs. Benefits such as Medicare (federal) and Medicaid (state) provide health insurance for millions of Americans today.

Like private health insurance companies, the federal government has provided a special mechanism for Medicare to recoup money in situations where a motorist runs over a cyclist and the cyclist utilizes Medicare to cover medical expenses. The "Medicare lien" has been referred to as a "super lien" by some lawyers. The code provisions that define the lien, how it is calculated, and issues concerning the responsibilities and potential liabilities of the parties are incredibly complicated. Long seminars for lawyers covering only Medicare lien issues are not uncommon.

What you need to know is that the super lien is dangerous. The government can come after you for payment of its "subrogation" at any time. You *must* notify the government within sixty days of settlement. It can take weeks, months, or years for the government to get back to you. If you ignore this lien and choose not to pay it, there can be civil or even criminal penalties.

4-13 WHAT IF YOUR CLAIM IS DENIED?

The fact that your claim is "denied" by an insurer is not the end of the story. If you have handled the claim yourself, you should consult with competent insurance or personal injury counsel to determine your rights. Many cyclists simply decide not to present their claim when they are told by an insurer that their claim is meritless. However, a denial is not the end.

Sometimes you can go above the current adjustor's head to a different adjustor, or to a committee of adjustors. Sometimes you can find new facts, witnesses, or information and present that to the insurer to try to reopen negotiations. But sometimes, the only way to find out if the insurer was right in denying the claim is to challenge the decision in court. If the court determines that the insurer unreasonably denied the claim and acted in "bad faith," you may be entitled to additional damages. Sometimes all of these issues can be stacked into one lawsuit against both the motorist and your insurer, but two separate actions may be required. Again, the particular laws and court rules of your jurisdiction would need to be followed. If your claim has been denied, it will be essential for you to find a good lawyer.

CONCLUSION

Every motorist is required by law to demonstrate "financial responsibility." For most motorists, this will mean being insured against liability.[1] Most motorists meet this requirement. However, just as some people do not take their duty of care seriously, some people do not take their financial responsibility requirement seriously: They drive without insurance. With that in mind, no cyclist can afford to assume that, in the event of a collision with a motorist, the motorist will be insured. Even if the motorist *is* insured, many motorists meet the letter of the law by insuring themselves for the minimum amount the law requires. In many states, the minimum amount required is simply inadequate. As we saw, for example, the minimum amount of coverage required in Ohio, $12,500, is so low that you can literally use it up in the first crucial minutes of a serious accident.

So what's a cyclist to do? Unfortunately, you can't force every motorist to have adequate insurance coverage, just as you can't force every motor-

---

1 Alternatively, motorists may demonstrate financial responsibility by posting a bond; however, most motorists simply do not have the financial means to post the required bond.

ist to exercise the duty of care owed to you. Clearly, in order to protect yourself, you should make sure that *you* are insured.

If you have automobile insurance in a state with first-party benefits, your insurance policy will cover you in collisions with a motor vehicle. In particular, in those states that offer it, you will want to make sure that you have adequate coverage for personal injury protection (PIP), because this will pay your medical bills and lost income if you are injured. In those states where medical payment coverage is available, make sure that you have adequate coverage in your policy. You should also make certain that you have adequate uninsured motorist (UM) and underinsured motorist (UIM) coverage, because these coverages will pay both your economic and noneconomic losses if you are hit by an uninsured or underinsured motorist. When you assess the adequacy of your coverage for PIP, UM, and UIM, make certain that you have high coverage limits; the cost of coverage for these parts of your policy is modest, and having an adequate amount is the only way you can be certain that you will be covered if you are involved in a serious collision with a motorist.

Unfortunately, if you don't have an auto insurance policy, these coverages won't be available to you. Increasingly, many cyclists are choosing to make the change from an automobile-centered lifestyle to an automobile-free lifestyle. The hidden danger in this choice is that you lose your insurance coverage if you have no automobile to insure. For this reason, some auto-free cyclists choose to continue to own and insure an automobile, even one that they never use, in order to retain access to insurance coverage. Of course, this strategy works only for those cyclists who have the option of owning an automobile. For those who do not have this option, a good health insurance policy is the next best plan. But what if you don't have—or want—an automobile, and you don't have health insurance? Should automobile ownership even be a prerequisite for access to insurance?

In our automobile-centric society, the answer appears to be yes. The fact is, most cyclists *do* own automobiles, and so, embedded as we are in an automobile-centric society, even many cyclists see no problem with requiring automobile ownership as a prerequisite for access to insurance. But for many cyclists, the social acceptance of this prerequisite, even among cyclists, is symptomatic of the pervasiveness of an anticycling bias in our culture.

The obvious solution would be comprehensive "bicycle insurance," similar to the comprehensive automobile insurance available to motorists. This insurance would cover you and your bicycle for both liability and loss, just as motorists are covered with their automobile policies. For many cyclists, this would be the only source of medical coverage they have when they ride, particularly if they were hit by an uninsured, underinsured, or hit-and-run driver. Unfortunately, there's no such thing as comprehensive "bicycle insurance" in the United States at the present time. For those who think it isn't necessary, consider that 46 million Americans—the "working poor"—have no medical insurance and no means of paying for medical care. Some of those 46 million Americans ride bicycles. For those who think it's an unfortunate situation but that nothing can be done, consider that comprehensive bicycle insurance is available in England. Clearly, if the British insurance industry can offer comprehensive bicycle insurance, there's no rational reason that the American insurance industry can't or shouldn't do the same. The fact that comprehensive bicycle insurance isn't available in the United States can only be attributed to one thing: a pervasive bias against cycling in an automobile-centric society, which manifests itself in many ways, including the irrational requirement of car ownership as a prerequisite for insurance coverage.

As a society, we can do better than to acquiesce to the anticycling bias. The insurance industry can, and should, offer cyclists the same kinds of policies it offers motorists. As cyclists—equal users of the road under the law—we must demand the equal treatment we are entitled to.

5

Cyclist Harassment and What You Can Do about It

INTRODUCTION

Although some accidents are truly unforeseeable—those called "Acts of God," for instance—most accidents result instead from the failure to exercise due care. When that failure results in injury, we call it "negligence." But whether the accident results from a simple failure to exercise due care, or from extreme carelessness and indifference to the likely consequences, every injury resulting from a negligent act is still unintentional. Not every injury is unintentional, however; some injuries—even injuries that were themselves unintended—result from intentional acts.

Longtime riders often agree that cyclist harassment, once an almost unknown phenomenon, has reared its antisocial head over the past few decades and is on the rise. That common wisdom is both right and wrong. Harassment of cyclists is as old as cycling, as nineteenth-century incidents amply demonstrate. Sources from that era record the following examples:[1]

- Children made a sport of knocking cyclists off their bicycles with rocks, tin cans, and sticks in the spokes. They also took delight in puncturing bicycle tires with pins, and mysterious miscreants commonly left roads strewn with tacks, glass, and sharp wires.

- Riding in a horse-drawn cab one day, New Yorker Samuel F. Scott took the opportunity to kick a passing cyclist off his bike.

- While driving his wagon on a Long Island road one day, Jacob Heltz refused to pull over to let a group of cyclists pass, going so far as to block the width of the road with his wagon. The cyclists dismounted and walked their bikes around him, but after they remounted, he charged his team at them, knocking several of the cyclists off their bikes.

- One spring day in New York City, a coachman named Andrew Weiss shot five cyclists. A man and a woman riding a tandem were his first victims, followed by two men and a boy. He was arrested while taking aim at a sixth cyclist.

Unfortunately, harassment of cyclists has increased in recent years, as longtime riders often attest. The phenomenon seems to mirror the rising popularity of cycling; as more cyclists appear on the crowded roads, other users of the road begin to retaliate for the inconvenience—real or imagined—of having to share the road with them.

---

1 Robert A. Smith, *A Social History of the Bicycle* (New York: American Heritage Press, 1972).

If you ride a bike, you have probably been harassed. Cyclists have been harassed by drivers who have yelled at them to "get off the road," thrown beer cans at them, assaulted them with baseball bats from moving vehicles, and intentionally run them off the road. Motorists have shot cyclists with paintball guns and with real guns; cyclists have been assaulted by pedestrians in bad neighborhoods, and in college towns they have been pelted with objects thrown from frat houses. Harassment of cyclists isn't limited to road ragers and pranksters; cyclists have been intentionally "cut off" by city buses and wrongfully pulled over by police officers.

This harassment is more than a nuisance: It violates cyclists' rights to the road, it is often illegal, and it poses a real danger to the life and limb of cyclists everywhere. So if harassment violates cyclists' rights, and is even illegal, is there something cyclists can do when confronted by a harasser?

By now you know the answer is yes. After all, I wrote this book both to help you understand your duties—what you need to know to stay out of trouble—and to help you understand your rights—what you need to know when your rights have been violated.

So yes, when your rights have been violated, you can do something about it. In fact, I will argue that when your rights have been violated, you not only *can* do something about it, you *must* do something about it. But first, in order to fully understand what we can do about harassment, it's necessary to understand *why* cyclists are harassed—where the bias against cyclists comes from—as well as to understand and distinguish among different types of harassers and different forms of harassment. Only then can we fully understand *what* we can do to stop cyclist harassment.

The Social Bias against Cyclists

It's a sad fact of the contemporary milieu: Cyclists, once seen in the bike boom of the 1970s as the health-conscious, environmentally responsible good guys, are now more often scorned as "Public Enemy Number 1." And it's not just in the United States—it's happening in such places as Canada, the United Kingdom, and Australia as well. But why is that? As one report commissioned in the United Kingdom by the Transport Research Foundation found, motorists view cyclists as members of an "out-group."[2] This means, according to the social-identity theory developed by social psychologists Henri Tajfel and John Turner, that motorists cat-

2   Will Storr, "Braking Point," *The Observer*, June 4, 2006.

egorize cyclists as a group that is different from the group motorists belong to. In-group prejudices against the out-group lead to stereotypes and to subtle and not-so-subtle forms of discrimination.[3]

The stereotyping, prejudice, and discrimination directed at "outgroups" are all too familiar to cyclists today. And as we'll see, it's not limited to the occasional foaming-at-the-mouth road-rager; that's just the most obvious tip of the iceberg. Rather, the bias against cyclists is institutionalized, permeating every level of society. Most often, that bias takes the form of discrimination against cyclists on the road or in the legal system; sometimes, it explodes into violence. Understanding this bias and knowing how to counter it are essential if we are to counter cyclist harassment—the more dangerous expression of the trident of hate, which sometimes results in violence, and always results in a violation of the cyclist's rights.

5-1 INFRASTRUCTURE BIAS AGAINST CYCLISTS

When a motorist yells "Get off the road!" at a cyclist, the implicit message is "The road is for cars." Well, we know that that's not an accurate statement from a legal perspective, of course, but it's not historically accurate either. Of course, roads predate both the automobile and the bicycle, but one of the problems tackled early on by cyclists was the condition of the roads. Albert Pope of Columbia Bicycles and A. H. Overman of Victor Bicycles, together with the League of American Wheelmen (known now as the League of American Bicyclists), led the way with the Good Roads Movement, footing the bill for lobbying the cities and states to pave the roads. By the time the automobile arrived on the scene, the roads of America were well on their way to being paved, paid for sometimes by cyclists out of their own pockets, sometimes by taxes on bicycles, and sometimes by the combined efforts of property owners, counties, and states.

"Well," motorists might counter, "the roads of today are paid for by motorists!" While that makes for a nice, soothing fairy tale for the anti-cyclist crowd, it's not an accurate statement. All roads are paid for by taxes, tolls, or development fees, and the source of financing depends upon the type of road. Generally, new streets in residential subdivisions are paid for by developers, and those costs are then passed on to the homeowners in the purchase price of the house. The maintenance of roads, however, is generally paid for from property-tax general funds. The state highways are usually paid for from each state's general funds, which

3 Ibid.

typically come from sales taxes, income taxes, and property taxes. Interstate highways are jointly funded by the federal and state governments, again from the general fund. Although motorists do pay gas taxes, those taxes are paid into the general fund rather than into a "roads fund"; the general funds always pay for a variety of government services, including roads. Thus, all of us, motorists and cyclists alike, pay for the construction and maintenance of roads. In any case, most cyclists also own cars, and they pay fuel taxes every time they buy gas for their cars.

So, cyclists were the first to lobby for paved roads and to pay for the paving of roads, and they continue to pay for the construction and maintenance of roads today along with every other taxpayer. And what do they get in return? A road infrastructure that is heavily biased in favor of the automobile, with accommodations for bicycles added in as an afterthought, if at all. Lanes that are too narrow to safely share mean that cyclists must "take the lane," thereby irritating drivers who mistakenly believe the practice to be both illegal and rude; alternatively, cyclists who feel intimidated by taking the lane must abandon roads with narrow lanes altogether. Where bicycle lanes are added to roads, they are usually located in the "door zone" of parked cars, making the bike lane especially hazardous when cars are parked on the side of the road. Furthermore, cars crossing the bike lane to get to or from parking often violate the cyclist's right-of-way in doing so. Cars making right turns are notorious for violating the bike lane right-of-way. Many intersections make use of four-way stops as a traffic-calming measure for automobiles, but no thought is given to what cyclists need. Where stoplights control traffic at intersections, the sensors that trigger the light changes are often capable of detecting only an automobile. Once cyclists enter an intersection, they're on the terrain that accounts for approximately half of all cycling accidents, even though the intersection represents only a small fraction of the spatial and temporal components of a cyclist's travel.

WHAT CAN BE DONE

Infrastructure bias against cyclists is real, and it inevitably leads to conflict and accidents. Fortunately, it can be addressed through better transportation planning that takes the needs of cyclists into account. For example, where lanes on arterial roads are too narrow and too high-speed to safely share with automobiles, "bicycle boulevards" on adjacent streets, designed to meet the needs of cyclists, can relieve the competition for space. On narrow streets where the speed limit is slower, sharrows[4] can alert motorists that they are sharing the lane with bicyclists. On wider streets, bicycle lanes can be redesigned to move them outside of the door zone. In bicycle-friendly European cities, cyclists have their own lanes, physically separated from automobile traffic, door zones, and sidewalks, and complete with traffic signals that let cyclists proceed first; there's no reason that successful innovation can't be applied here. Intersections can and must be redesigned to make them safer for cyclists. Where bike lanes are used, solid blue colors in the bike lane at high-conflict intersections, such as where lanes from converging roadways merge, have been shown to be safer for cyclists than the traditional use of white striping alone on the pavement. These blue bike lanes alert the motorist that cyclists have the legal right-of-way, and motorists have been shown to respect that right-of-way where it is clearly demarcated. The use of "bicycle boxes"—a marked space at the intersection—gives bicycles a priority starting place when lights change and prevents the kind of right turns that often cause cycling accidents. Traffic signal–controlled intersections can be made more bike-friendly through the use of signal sensors that are capable of detecting a bike. An even friendlier intersection can be biased in favor of cyclist safety through the use of "scramble signals," "HAWK signals," and "pedestrian half-signals."[5]

In short, bicycle-friendly infrastructure helps level a playing field that is currently heavily biased in favor of the automobile; such measures actually reduce conflict between cyclists and motorists and help to create a safer road environment for all. The benefits for cyclists are obvious; less obvious are the significant benefits to motorists in the form of reduced conflict with cyclists for space, safer roads, and ultimately fewer cars competing for space. I believe the reduced conflict over road space would lead, in turn, to a lessening of the bias against cyclists, which has been brought about in large part by the automobile-biased infrastructure, and to a more cooperative road environment for all.

5-2 POLICE BIAS AGAINST CYCLISTS

In 1998, the local media in Austin, Texas, reported that a "helmetless cyclist died in a collision at MLK and Lavaca."[6] It's unclear from that

---

4 A *sharrow* is a lane shared by motorists and cyclists and marked to alert road users that the lane is to be shared. The word is derived by combining "share" and "arrow," referring to the road markings of a directional arrow and a bicycle, to denote the shared use of the lane.

5 A scramble signal stops all automotive movement at an intersection and allows pedestrians, cyclists, and others to move through the intersection in any direction; HAWK signals–a "High-intensity Activated WalK" signal–and pedestrian half-signals allow pedestrians and cyclists to cross major streets from a minor intersecting street.

6 Michael Bluejay, http://bicycleaustin.info/index.html.

BICYCLING AND THE LAW

story whether the cyclist's lack of a helmet was relevant to his fatal injuries or not; what's particularly appalling about the reporting, however, is
that the media neglected to mention that the driver ran a red light. The
"slant" that was given to the story is that the irresponsible cyclist was
responsible for his own injuries. And where did that slant come from?
It came straight from a police news release about the accident, which
omitted the fact that the driver ran the red light, but included the information about the cyclist not wearing a helmet. The police bias against cycling was then picked up and echoed by the media. The circle of bias was
completed when the public read the slanted news, reported as a factual
account of a cycling accident.

You'd think the police department was trying to present a version of
the truth that was slanted—and you'd be right in thinking so. This should
not come as any surprise; after all, law-enforcement officers are no more
immune to bias than anybody else. That anticyclist bias is nowhere more
obvious than in the conflict between motorists and cyclists. Consider the
following incidents: A motorist warns a cyclist that he "had better get
out of her way or else" and then purposely runs the cyclist down. After
the cyclist picks himself up, he throws his bike at the motorist's car and
breaks her windshield. When the police arrive, they arrest the cyclist
for assault but take no action against the motorist who deliberately ran
him down. In another case, I represented a cyclist who was arrested for
using his bike lock to break off the sideview mirror of a driver who had
intentionally and repeatedly swerved into him, putting the cyclist's life
in danger. The police arrested the cyclist; the motorist was not charged
with any violation.

Even when a cyclist has done nothing in self-defense or retaliation,
the police don't always respond to harassment by motorists in a serious
way. If you contact the police about a dangerous and harassing motorist,
it is often difficult to get them to conduct anything beyond a cursory investigation, if they do anything at all. When you try to follow up on a case
they're not interested in pursuing, they will tell you it is under investigation, and that their policy is not to comment on ongoing investigations.
On the other hand, when the police are interested in solving a case, the
offending motorist is charged within hours of the incident.

Even when law enforcement does investigate a harassment problem,
the anticycling bias is impossible to miss. In one case, a cyclist was riding legally in a marked and signed bike lane when he was struck from behind and killed.[7] The sixteen-year-old driver of the vehicle was estimated
to be speeding at about 80 mph—in a 55 mph zone—when he struck the

7 Ibid.

cyclist, and tested positive for cocaine, marijuana, and alcohol. The police blamed the cyclist, telling his family that he should not have been riding there. I believe that many officers, even those sympathetic to cyclists, subconsciously blame the cyclist in accidents because they feel it was the cyclist's presence on the road that caused the accident and that it was foreseeable that a disaster could occur. This kind of injustice must be changed.

Another disturbing trend is law enforcement's unwillingness to charge the proper infraction or crime against drivers who hit and injure cyclists. Even in cases where the cyclist is riding legally, and is hit and killed by a driver who drifted onto the shoulder, the police commonly find no fault on the part of the driver; at best, the driver may receive a citation for a minor traffic infraction. For example, a fourteen-year-old was riding his bike home from a neighbor's house when he was run down by a driver who was doing an estimated 50 mph in a 30 mph zone.[8] Before hitting the cyclist, the driver honked his horn, but he didn't bother applying his brakes until after the collision. The driver received three tickets: two for speeding and one for negligent driving. It was as if the police didn't realize that a child had just been killed. Though it may be hard to believe that an anticyclist bias could prevent officers from pressing appropriate charges that would reflect the seriousness of an incident, case after case shows this to be true.

The bias becomes even more evident when the police arrest a cyclist for a minor traffic infraction. Motorists receive plenty of tickets, but they are hardly ever arrested for a simple traffic infraction or have their vehicles impounded. Yet being handcuffed and thrown into a squad car is not an unheard-of occurrence for cyclists. For example, in one case, two cyclists on a group ride were run down by a driver who ran a red light.[9] The cyclists were both injured, sitting dazed and bleeding in the road, when the police arrived on the scene; the driver was not even cited, because the police blamed the cyclists for riding on the shoulder of the road. In another case, a cyclist was stopped for riding her bike on the sidewalk. She asked the officer to clarify the law for her, and he arrested her.[10] These are not isolated incidents; there are dozens more, making the anticyclist bias held by law enforcement glaringly evident.

One serious and consequential effect of police bias against cycling is spotlighted by the way accident reports involving cyclists and motorists are completed. It's common for police officers to leave out critical

8 Ibid.
9 Ibid.
10 Ibid.

information about how and where the accident occurred, to fail to interview all witnesses, or to fail to take proper accident-scene measurements. It's as if they're thinking that the reason for the collision is obvious: Someone on a bike got in the way of someone in a motor vehicle. I have represented both motorists and cyclists in my injury practice, and the difference in the way police handle motorists and cyclists is remarkable. Starting at the accident scene, the officer will first interview the driver for his version, while the paramedics attend to the injured cyclist. Next, the officer will interview other witnesses, who are usually other motorists. It is not uncommon for the first contact between the officer and the injured cyclist to be in the hospital when the cop presents the cyclist with a ticket. In many cases, the cyclist's version of events is not contained anywhere in the police report, and the cyclist, along with his or her attorney, has to file an amendment to the original report. If it were two motorists involved in a collision, the officer wouldn't even consider ticketing one driver without at least getting that driver's version of the incident.

The question remains, however: *Why* would the police have a bias against cyclists? I believe that one simplistic response won't really answer the question; the bias stems from a variety of causes. One inescapable reality is that, despite the fact that many police departments have a bike patrol, most police officers are motorists, and they see the world from that perspective. And maybe some officers hold the societal view that the roads are for cars, period. The growing sentiment in public discourse seems to be that "if you get hurt on a bike, you shouldn't blame anyone but yourself." It's not hard to see this sentiment mirrored in the comments of the law-enforcement officers who blamed the cyclist killed by a speeding, impaired teenager who veered into the bike lane.

Another factor is job-related. Police officers on patrol are in constant contact with cyclists and may come to see them as a nuisance making their difficult job even harder. When cyclists disregard the traffic laws that the police are supposed to enforce, it will reasonably lead to some resentment of cyclists. Of course, given the regularity with which motorists blatantly disregard the traffic laws, the police would have to hold a preexisting bias against cyclists—one that has nothing to do with scofflaw behavior—in order to be biased against lawbreaking cyclists but not against the far more numerous lawbreaking motorists. Police do report that cyclists are far more abrasive than motorists during traffic stops, and this could be a factor in police bias against cyclists.

Another source of police bias may be their clashes with aggressive and demanding bicycle-mounted protest groups. The media is full of stories of protesters clashing with police officers; some of these protesters are on bikes out of convenience, and some, like members of Critical Mass, by design. The police are on the front lines of the law, and repeated clashes with bicycle-mounted protesters can help reinforce a bias against cyclists in general. On one hand, given the current state of public hostility toward cyclists, one has to commend these groups for demanding in a public way that their legal right to the road be respected; silently being mistreated by drivers, the police, and the legal system has not worked to make the roads safer for cycling. On the other hand, deliberately antagonizing other users of the road is probably not winning cyclists many friends either, and when law-enforcement officers come into the fray, it's not hard to see how their biases could be reinforced.

WHAT CAN BE DONE

What can you do if you encounter police bias? It can be difficult to know how to respond to a situation that seems unfair, especially if you are the one being mistreated. Police officers have a lot of power in our society—and they know it. If you're on the receiving end of police bias, however, there are some ways of responding that are better than others; exactly what those are depend in part on the situation.

Let's say you've been stopped for a traffic violation. Maintaining control of a situation is at the core of law-enforcement training, and any attempt on your part to wrest control of the situation from the officer will only cause an escalation in tactics as the officer continues to assert control over you. In short, except under circumstances where the police officer acts outside the law, you cannot win in a confrontation with police officers. Even where the officer is acting outside the law, if you choose to confront the officer at that moment, you will lose, at least in the short run, and you may lose in the long run—many law-enforcement officers do not hesitate to lie under oath if that's what it takes to get the job done. In their worldview, after all, they're "the good guys" in a world full of bad guys. I don't mean to paint an overly harsh portrait of police officers, because like any other microcosm of society, their ranks range from the decent, hardworking, community-oriented guys who will give you a break if you deserve one all the way to some really rotten apples in the barrel.

If you've been stopped, first, don't argue with the officer. If you've just committed an offense, the officer is not going to be impressed with your angry verbal assault as you explain why you shouldn't have to obey the law. You have nothing to gain, and everything to lose, if you decide to confront the officer. Second, if you've actually committed the offense, shut up. Shut up now. You do not want to have the officer testifying at the hearing about your twenty-minute tirade in which you admitted to the offense. Save your argument for court, if you decide to go to court.

Suppose, however, that you're stopped for something that's perfectly legal. Suppose, for example, the officer tells you that the law requires you to be on the sidewalk, and you know with absolute certainty that it does not.[11] Be respectful. Don't argue with the officer; save your argument for court, where it will do some good.[12]

Now let's say you've been injured or attacked by a motorist, and you want the police to do something about it. You can report the matter, but unfortunately, with some limited exceptions, you can't force them to do anything. They have the discretion to decide what to investigate and how to investigate it. If you want the police to conduct an investigation or to issue a citation, and they refuse, be polite but firm. Many times, police officers will attempt to talk you out of asserting your rights. They might tell you that filing a police report won't do any good, because the suspect has left the scene and can't be found.[13] Or they might tell you that if they press charges against a driver who just assaulted you, the driver can also press charges against you, so it's better just to let the whole thing drop.[14] The key to dealing with this type of bias is to stand your ground: Be polite but be firm. Insist—politely—that the officer file a report on the incident. Politely decline the officer's suggestions to "let the matter drop." Be respectful but persistent.

There are a couple of reasons for insisting on a police report, despite an officer's best attempts to dissuade you from filing one. First, if a police report is completed, there's a record of the incident, which you can then use to press charges against the miscreant motorist. If the police aren't interested in pressing charges, you can ask the district attorney to press charges. In some states, you can even press charges yourself. Even if neither the police nor the D.A. is willing to press charges, and there is no statute that allows you to press charges, you can still file a

---

11 By "absolute certainty," I mean that you know both the state laws and the local laws. Many cyclists make the mistake of knowing only the state laws and are often surprised by variations in the local laws.

12 See §2-27 for a discussion on how to discuss the law during a traffic stop.

13 Although this may be technically true, it should not be relevant to whether the police department decides to investigate. It is possible that the suspect went on to commit another offense against somebody else five minutes down the road, and that the next bicyclist could contribute more information about the suspect, or that the suspect might be apprehended tomorrow, or next week, doing the exact same thing. With a proper investigation, repeating offenders could be caught.

14 In one incident in Portland, Oregon, on November 7, 2006, a driver buzzed a cyclist, who rapped a warning on the passenger-side window as the driver buzzed him. The driver—who was driving on a suspended license—pulled over, got out, and assaulted the cyclist. Witnesses were present to verify what had happened, but the responding officer told the cyclist that because he had rapped on the window, he could be charged with harassment, which was an offense equivalent to the assault, in the officer's reasoning. The officer concluded that it would be better if the cyclist didn't file a police report.

civil suit against your attacker, and a police report is a record of the incident that can be used as evidence at trial. So, if law enforcement attempts to persuade you not to file a police report, politely but firmly insist on filing one anyway.

The second reason to file a police report is to establish a record of the motorist's behavior. Suppose, for example, that a motorist deliberately endangers your life in an attempt to harass you. Then suppose that motorist deliberately endangers another cyclist's life five minutes later, or the next day, or the next week. Suppose, then, that the motorist injures or kills a cyclist and claims that it was an accident: She didn't see the cyclist; the cyclist swerved into her path. She might actually get away with this line of defense—unless there's a paper trail out there documenting a history of cyclist harassment. If your life is endangered by a motorist intent on harassing you, file a police report. Insist on it, politely but firmly, no matter how much the officer may try to dissuade you.

Now let's say you've been injured in a collision with a motorist. It's not uncommon for responding officers to neglect to interview the cyclist, gathering the "facts" from the motorist only. The police do not have a right to present a slanted version of an accident to the court; you do have a right to a fair and impartial account of an accident. If the responding officer fails to interview you, or fails to include relevant information in the report, you will need to get your version of the accident in the police report.[15] Your first preference should be to make sure that the officer interviews you and includes the relevant information in the report; this is preferred because it's the responding officer's report of the accident. But if the officer doesn't interview you, or doesn't include relevant information, you will need to file an amendment to the police report.

There's one more thing that cycling advocacy groups can do to reduce anticycling bias in law enforcement: Educate police officers. Officers can and must be educated about cycling—about the statutes and case law regarding cycling, the hazards of cycling, and safe cycling practices. This education should be mandatory; if it isn't mandatory for your law-enforcement agencies, it's a policy that bicycling advocates in your area should address in order to improve the cycling environment.

---

15   By "relevant information," I mean information that would tend to affect the outcome of the case. For example, if the officer fails to report that the driver ran a red light, that is relevant information. If the officer fails to report that you had a bicycle light, that is relevant information (cyclists have had their insurance claims denied because the police failed to report that the bicycle was equipped with a light).

5-3 JUDICIAL SYSTEM BIAS AGAINST CYCLISTS

The law-enforcement bias against cyclists doesn't end at the precinct station. It permeates the entire justice system. *If* the police decide to investigate, they have the choice of closing the case, filing charges, or presenting the district attorney with the evidence in the case. Let's assume it's the latter; the police conduct an investigation and then turn their case over to the district attorney. Now it's up to the D.A. to decide what, if anything, to do. You should understand that the D.A. is under no obligation to do anything—the D.A. has "prosecutorial discretion." This means that he or she can choose whether or not to file charges, and if charges are filed, what to charge the offender with. The D.A. also has discretion to plead the case down or even to dismiss the charges, although this discretion is tempered by "victim's rights" legislation that requires prosecutors to consult with victims before making these decisions.

What would motivate a D.A. to take a case less seriously than the facts warrant? One factor is the nature of the job; the D.A. is actually the elected public official who oversees a staff of attorneys who prosecute cases for the local jurisdiction. Because the D.A. is an elected official, there is always one eye kept on winning reelection. For the D.A., this means winning cases. D.A.s with low conviction rates always run the risk of losing the next election to another attorney who promises to do a better job. This creates pressure to prosecute cases that are sure wins, which means pressing charges that are easy to prove, or even declining to prosecute altogether if the case is hard to prove. Additionally, the criminal justice system is notorious for "plea bargains," another way for the D.A. to get a sure win. Here's how it works: The D.A. charges the accused with several offenses, some of which are very serious indeed. The D.A. and the defense both know that it will be difficult to prove the more serious charges. But they also both know that it will be easy to prove that the accused did commit some sort of offense. So they bargain; the defense agrees to plead guilty to a lesser charge if the D.A. agrees to drop the more serious charges. On one hand, nobody has to spend resources on going to trial; on the other hand, it's not exactly justice either.

Bias enters the picture when the D.A. refuses to charge drivers for offenses that would never be tolerated if committed against another driver. Remember that driver who ran down two cyclists when he ran a red light? He wasn't even ticketed. Do you suppose the D.A. would have tolerated a red-light runner who injured two motorists?

Unfortunately, the bias against people on bikes extends to judges and juries as well. Far too often, the first question a cyclist hears from the judge is "What were you doing riding in the street?" If the judge, who is supposed to be fair and impartial not to mention "up on the law," doesn't understand, or worse, believe, that cyclists have a right to the road, cyclists have already begun with a disadvantage in the courtroom—one that continues right through trial and into jury deliberations. Experienced attorneys report that in trials they *should* be winning, juries are finding "no liability" on the part of drivers who had no defense to hitting a cyclist who was riding legally. In 2001, a jury found for a truck driver who had made an unsafe pass, injuring a cyclist.[16] It later surfaced that in deliberations, the jury had discussed an issue not presented at trial: whether the cyclist should have pulled off the road to let the truck pass. The jury verdict was eventually overturned on appeal, because there is nothing in the law that requires the cyclist to be responsible for the safety of the motorist's pass. That jury prejudice against cyclists was uncovered only because one of the jurors was troubled that the jury had discussed the issue. How many other jury verdicts against cyclists are based on an anticyclist bias? According to experienced trial attorneys, too many.

WHAT CAN BE DONE

There is absolutely nothing you can do to force the D.A. to press charges if he or she doesn't want to press charges. However, if you've been the target of criminal behavior, you can always attempt to persuade the D.A. to press charges. If the D.A. seems disinterested in pressing charges, it will be up to you to make your case—as is always the case when you're trying to convince somebody to take some discretionary action. Be polite but firm. You won't convince anybody to do what you want if you're not polite, and you won't convince anybody to take a stand if you're not firm. Be persuasive: Marshal your facts, and the law, and demonstrate to the D.A. why the law fits the facts of your case. Be prepared to discuss what statutes were violated, as well as case law interpreting those statutes. If you can't convince the D.A. to press charges, your only recourse will be to prosecute your own case (see "Using the Legal System" later in this chapter).[17]

In court, be respectful when addressing the judge. Like police officers, judges have a lot of power, and they are well aware of that. When you're in the courtroom, you are in a world that the judge has almost complete

---

16 *Previs v. Dailey*, 180 S.W.3d 435 (Ky. 2005).

17 However, once the D.A. has decided to prosecute, "victim's rights" legislation does give you some limited rights that act as a check on the D.A.'s discretionary power. For example, the D.A. must consult with the victim of a crime before making a decision to make a plea bargain. Although the D.A. is not required to do anything beyond "consultation," the crime victim has the right to ask the judge not to accept the plea bargain.

control over. As with your interactions with the police, you have nothing to gain, and everything to lose, by angering a judge. Therefore, you must follow the judge's courtroom instructions, and you must be respectful. Do not argue with the judge, do not interrupt the judge, do not use disrespectful language, do not wear inappropriate attire, and do not neglect personal grooming. If you understand that the judge controls the courtroom, and that you must be respectful in court, you will have done a lot to avoid angering the judge. That doesn't mean that you've eliminated any preexisting biases the judge has about cycling; however, it does mean that you haven't confirmed the judge's biases through inappropriate behavior. You may still have some persuading to do. For example, if the judge interrupts you to ask, "What were you doing riding in the street?" you must persuade the judge that you were in fact riding in the street legally. Be prepared with copies of the statutes; argue your legal points respectfully and persuasively. These guidelines are not about "how to win your case in ten easy steps"; rather they're about how to disarm any anticyclist biases the judge may hold so that you can have your case heard and decided as fairly as possible.

Top Ten Things News Gets Wrong about Crash Reports
by Evan Manvel, Executive Director, Bicycle Transportation Alliance

In today's *Oregonian*, I read that a vacationing cyclist was hit head-on by a sleepy driver in Newport. The newspaper story noted that the cyclist wasn't wearing a helmet. That probably wouldn't have made a difference in a head-on crash, yet is always included in bike crash reports. That's just one bee in my bonnet about crash reports.

Journalists are busy folks. TV, radio and newspapers are working with fewer staff, fewer resources, and on quicker deadlines than before. So I'll cut them some slack.

But consider the following news account:

*"Roman G. Zaytsev, 81, of Vancouver died Tuesday in a Vancouver hospital of **chest injuries** received four weeks earlier in a bicycle-car collision, according to the Clark County medical examiner's office. Zaytsev was riding his bike southbound in a northbound lane of Andresen Road when he rode into the side of a car pulling onto the road near 25th Street. Zaytsev was*

(continues)

(continued)

> *not wearing a helmet. The driver of the car, Shaynne Goodwin, 29, of Vancouver was cited for driving while his license was suspended and for not having proof of insurance."*
>
> —The Oregonian, *March 11, 2006*

So, I thought, someone who dies of chest injuries is blamed for failing to wear a helmet (on his chest)?

Inquiries into the report received the response, "we get a lot of calls about the story if we don't include certain information." But that's simply bad reporting–reporters should include what's pertinent to the report, and exclude what's not, period. And the reason readers want to know whether a chest-injury fatality was wearing a helmet is because the media has taught them that helmet use is what's important.

Enough exposition. Time for my list of Top Ten Things the News Gets Wrong About Crash Reporting, which undoubtedly will evolve over time:

1. **Failure to include speeds in the report.** Vehicle speed is the top factor in a crash's seriousness, and excessive speed is a leading cause of crashes. While speeds might not be available immediately, journalists should at least mention if cars were speeding or appeared to be speeding.

2. **Failure to mention distracted or sleepy driving.** Drowsiness and distractedness make drivers as crash-prone as intoxicating [sic]. While drunk driving is reported by the news, other risky actions such as cell phone use, eating, putting on make-up, driving while overly tired, etc. are rarely reported.

3. **Mentioning whether the cyclist was in a bike lane, when she/he has a right to not be in one.** Cyclists are allowed by law to be outside bike lanes for various reasons (turning, to avoid debris and hazards, to pass, etc.).

4. **Mentioning that the cyclist wasn't in a bike lane, when there was no bike lane on the road.** Cyclists have the right to the road. Mentioning this implies they don't.

(continues)

(continued)

5. **Noting that the pedestrian wasn't in a crosswalk, when she/he was in an unmarked crosswalk.** All intersections are legal crosswalks unless marked otherwise. The lack of a "zebra stripe" or marked crosswalk doesn't put blame on the pedestrian.

6. **Noting the pedestrian was over the legal limit for alcohol use.** There's no legal alcohol limit for walking. Focus on the behavior (swerving into traffic) if there was unpredictable behavior, instead of implying a law that doesn't exist.

7. **Calling crashes "accidents" instead of "crashes."** The term "accident" absolves responsibility. "Crash" is a more neutral term.

8. **Repeating driver claims that the driver "didn't see the pedestrian/cyclist," or that the pedestrian/cyclist "darted" out.** These are a common factor–what it often means is that drivers aren't paying enough attention to the road and just noticed the cyclist or pedestrian at the last minute. Repeating the claim based on the driver's perspective gives the driver credence she/he doesn't deserve.

9. **Talking about people's choice of clothes.** On a related note, pedestrians and cyclists shouldn't be required to wear a certain color of clothes just to get around, and shouldn't be blamed as victims if drivers hit them while wearing dark clothing. The color, reflectivity, or visibility of the car is virtually never reported.

10. **Including information about helmet use unnecessarily.** Bicycle helmets aren't required by Oregon law for those 16 years or older, and including information about helmet use focuses on post-crash facts instead of focusing on the factors causing the crash. In the Netherlands, very few cyclists wear helmets and yet the fatality rate is one-fifth that of the U.S. And in many crashes–most crashes at 40 mph or more–helmets won't save the life of the cyclist.[1]

Reprinted with permission by Evan Manvel

1 Evan Manvel, *Top Ten Things News Gets Wrong about Crash Reports*, at http://www. bta4bikes.org/btablog/2006/09/18/top-ten-things-news-gets-wrong-about-crash-reports/.

Like police officers, judges and prosecutors can and must be educated about cycling—the statutes and case law, the hazards, and safe cycling practices. If this education isn't already ongoing in your community, it's an area that bicycling advocates should address in order to improve the cycling environment.

5-4 MEDIA BIAS AGAINST CYCLISTS

A final note: most of these news releases are just run directly from statements developed by the Sheriffs' Offices or Oregon State Police. Those offices need to shape up their acts, too.

What's your pet peeve about crash reporting?

In this day and age of "infotainment," can we be surprised by the lack of accurate reporting about cycling? Unfortunately, it's just "easier" for the media to cover minor yet sensationalistic news like cycling tragedies by parroting the police version of events. And equally unfortunately, this often means that the media simply gets the story wrong.

Do you remember the news story I mentioned about a helmetless cyclist in Austin, Texas, who was killed in a collision with a car? As we saw, when the media reported that story, they left out one detail—in fact, the most important detail of the story: The driver had run a red light. That story came straight from a police-department news release, which took pains to highlight the cyclist's lack of a helmet while neglecting that one crucial detail that told the truth about the story.

The fact is, the "mainstream media" does an abysmal job of covering cycling. Media outlets tend to ignore important cycling stories or get them completely wrong; it's apparent that cycling is simply not important to most media outlets. In short, cars are still the "mainstream" vehicles in America, and the "mainstream media" has a bias toward them and against cycling. When the media does cover cycling and cycling politics, it takes its cue from the establishment. The bias comes through, for example, in stories about Critical Mass being "unruly, illegally riding cyclists." That is, the media parrots the police version of events justifying the draconian tactics police employed at a protest event. When cyclists are killed in a crash, the stories often make it sound like the accident was the cyclist's fault before an investigation has even begun.

There are more people who drive automobiles as their primary form of transportation than there are who ride bicycles; the media, like any business, targets this audience, and therefore a bias toward motorists should come as no surprise. Media bias is on the rise in the United States; cycling is not a power player in modern America, and when cycling-related stories are covered that involve conflict or controversy, the cycling side of the story will come out on the bottom, especially if the "other side" of the story is being supported by business interests or government.[18]

WHAT CAN BE DONE

The First Amendment to the Constitution guarantees the "freedom of the press"; this guarantee of a free press is made to the owners of the press—their freedoms cannot be abridged by Congress. This means that the press is free to cover whatever it wants, and to cover those things however it wants to, as long as its reporting isn't libelous;[19] and unless you own a media outlet, you can't force one to report a story the way you want it reported.

However, the Society of Professional Journalists maintains a code of ethics, which holds that "public enlightenment is the forerunner of justice and the foundation of democracy. The duty of the journalist is to further those ends by seeking truth and providing a fair and comprehensive account of events and issues. Conscientious journalists from all media and specialties strive to serve the public with thoroughness and honesty. Professional integrity is the cornerstone of a journalist's credibility."

Thus, although you can't force the media to cover a story the way you want it covered, you can try to persuade the media to cover a story by the standards of the code of ethics: truthfully, by providing a fair and comprehensive account of events and issues. The best approach to persuasion, of course, is to avoid an accusatory tone or condescension—journalists are people, too, after all, and respond to a negative approach just as any of us would be expected to respond. Instead, appeal to their journalistic sense of ethics without condescending to them by telling them what their code of ethics requires. Just be polite and informative. Write a letter to the editor, politely setting the facts straight on a story. If you're a persuasive writer, talk with the editorial staff about writing an op-ed piece. If a media outlet has presented a biased story, ask the editor about covering the other side of the issue. If it's a broadcast media outlet, and its reporters or their supervisors refuse to present balanced coverage, go to the outlet's competitors and ask them to present a balanced story.

18 By "media bias," I mean the bias of mass media journalists and news producers in the selection of which events will be reported, and how they will be covered.

19 *Libel* is the intentional or negligent publication of a falsehood about a person that injures that person's reputation.

With a little polite and friendly persuasion, you may be able to convince a reporter or editor to present a different perspective.

5-5 PROFESSIONAL DRIVER BIAS AGAINST CYCLISTS

Professional drivers—usually taxi drivers and bus drivers, but including anybody who drives for a living—may also hold biases against cyclists. For these drivers, the road is their workplace, and if they hold an anti-cyclist bias, they will see cyclists as being "in their way." They may also see other motorists as being in their way—for example, cabbies are notorious for violating the right-of-way for motorists and cyclists alike—but when they hold an anticyclist bias, they may freely violate the cyclist's right to the road while respecting other motorists' right to the road.

WHAT CAN BE DONE

One step that can be taken to reduce conflicts between professional drivers and cyclists is for bicycle advocacy groups to work with cab companies and transit agencies on education. Both are required by law to provide training for their drivers, and therefore, cyclists have an opportunity to help educate these drivers about cycling—including education about statutes and case laws, cycling hazards, and safe cycling practices. This education should be mandatory, and if it isn't mandatory for your cab and public transit agencies, it's a subject that bicycling advocates in your area should address in order to improve the cycling environment.

5-6 PUBLIC BIAS AGAINST CYCLISTS

This is the big one, the visible tip of the bias iceberg that immediately comes to mind for most cyclists. I say "visible" because, as we've seen, anticyclist bias is socially institutionalized; while most cyclists readily recognize anticyclist bias when it's expressed by passing motorists, and they may even recognize that the transportation infrastructure is not ideal for cyclists, they don't necessarily recognize that the anticyclist bias in the transportation infrastructure exacerbates cyclist-motorist tensions. It's virtually certain that most motorists do not understand this point. Yet, motorists do understand at some intuitive level that the infrastructure is biased against cyclists; thus, when a motorist yells "Get off the road!" at a cyclist, the implicit message is "The road is for cars."

Anticyclist attitudes create a vicious negative feedback loop—the road is for cars, the reasoning goes, so we don't need to accommodate bicycles, and because we don't accommodate bicycles, the road is for cars—

and so the anticyclist bias continues. But as many motorists have noted, we cyclists are not blameless in the antagonism between motorists and cyclists.

Members of the noncycling public tell remarkably similar tales of frustration with cyclist behavior: tales of cyclists who ride as if the law doesn't apply to them, of cyclists with no regard for other users of the road, and of cyclist aggression against those who complain of illegal behavior. This cyclist aggression is as old as the harassment of cyclists and may be a contributing factor in that harassment; and though some motorists verbally express their frustration with cyclists, others take matters much further. These observations, while anecdotal, all point to one inescapable fact: Our own lawless behavior on the road is identified by large numbers of otherwise reasonable motorists as the source of their disgust with cyclists. These motorist concerns are consistent with the results of a British study, conducted by Dr. Ben Fincham of Cardiff University, concluding that "anger towards cyclists derives from a 'hierarchy of vulnerability,' meaning that while a bike user might make a mistake, it will be a driver that injures them."[20] The boorish behavior of some cyclists compounds that fear of injuring a cyclist into a loathing of all cyclists.

Cyclists correctly observe that motorists themselves *also* break the law when it's convenient for them. As one poster on an Internet forum wrote: "Stopping at red lights, reducing speed when necessary, using turn signals; these are all things regular motorists fail to do every second of every day. I think the rolling stop has been around ever since the invention of the automobile." And as bicycle advocate Michael Bluejay observed: "Put this into perspective the next time motorists complain how cyclists won't get respect until they start following the law. Hit & running someone with a motor vehicle is far more illegal than rolling a stop sign, but when was the last time anyone suggested that motorists as a class don't deserve to be on the road until they start acting lawful?"[21]

Clearly, road safety is a two-way street. However, from the standpoint of what *we* as cyclists can do to reduce public bias against us, arguments that motorists are also culpable miss the point. Of course, as many experienced cyclists know, cyclists who ride as if they have only rights—but no corresponding responsibilities—also deny that their behavior creates any negative impression of cyclists in the noncycling public. This denial is nothing more than self-serving justification for boorish behavior; the truth is, it's destructive to cycling, and unfortunately, it tars all cyclists with the same brush in the eyes of the noncycling public. As one pedes-

---

20 Paul Rowland, "Why Drivers Really Hate Cyclists," *Western Mail*, April 26, 2006.

21 Michael Bluejay, http://bicycleaustin.info/justice/.

trian who is "sick to the back teeth of the sickos on cycles" put it on the Internet, "Naturally, they all deny their guilt. All regular bike riders condemn 'kamikaze cyclists' who 'give the rest of us a bad name.' In fact, finding a cyclist who admits to willfully ignoring the rules of the road is as difficult as finding a white South African who will admit to having supported apartheid. 'No mate, not me. Never do a thing like that. Terrible.'"

Cyclists who do obey the law, and who are courteous to other users of the road, confirm the anger. One cyclist reported: "While stopped at a stoplight or stop sign, I've been personally taken to task by drivers infuriated by misdeeds of our fellow cyclists (the fact that I bike safely has often seemed immaterial to road-weary drivers at these times). I've appreciated the opportunity to help educate those with whom we share the road (although saddened—and even afraid for my safety—at such anger I've seen)."

The ill will generated by the scofflaw and boorish behavior of some cyclists isn't just directed at cyclists on the road; it also affects cyclists in the courtroom, as cyclists who have been injured by motorists are finding to their dismay when juries decide their cases. As bicycle attorneys are increasingly discovering, that negative public impression of cyclists is real, and it is resulting in lost cases in the courtroom. Attorneys must struggle to overcome prejudice against cyclists in cases that should be, and would have been, won in less antagonistic times.

WHAT CAN BE DONE

The public bias against cyclists derives from several sources, and in order to effectively combat that bias, each source must be addressed. The infrastructure bias in favor of automobiles is fundamental because it leads to conflict with motorists and helps fuel other forms of anticyclist bias. Eliminating the automobile-centered bias in our infrastructure would reduce conflict between bicycles and automobiles. It would also make the roads safer for cyclists and reduce motorists' fears of injuring cyclists.

But another major source of anticyclist bias is the riding behavior of some cyclists. One obvious solution to the problem of cyclist harassment is for cyclists to remember that with rights come responsibilities, and that by riding within the law, they are helping to create better public perceptions of cyclists. If we're going to turn the bias against cyclists around—in how cyclists are accommodated in the transportation infrastructure, how cyclists are accommodated in the legislature, and how

PHOTO 5.1 1896 Army Bicycle

cyclists are treated on the road and in the courtroom—we must, as Mahatma Gandhi said, be the change we wish to see in the world.

Harassment of Cyclists

Anticyclist bias is one thing, but when those who are biased against cyclists take the law into their own hands, the bias escalates to harassment. Cyclist harassment violates the rights of cyclists and is potentially life-threatening. It covers a wide range of actions and may stem from different sets of motivational factors. In other words, there are many types of harassers, whether they are police officers, representatives of the media, professional drivers, or regular motorists, and they harass cyclists for different reasons and in different ways.

Some harassers may be motivated by a desire for revenge stemming from an earlier encounter with a different cyclist. Or maybe the harasser is simply frustrated with being late for an appointment and taking out his anxiety on the nearest easy target. The cyclist who is being harassed might not care about why it is occurring; he or she might be more concerned about stopping the immediate incident of harassment, and perhaps seeking redress afterward. However, from the larger perspective of improving the relationship between cyclists and the rest of society, it is important to understand what motivates the harassers. From understanding who the harasser is, we can begin to understand what steps must be taken to improve the cycling environment—perhaps in some circumstances, the solution is education; in others, it may be expanded facilities. But in order to know what ameliorative measures are needed, we need to understand what is going on in the mind of the harasser.

5-7 POLICE HARASSMENT OF CYCLISTS

The police are charged with protecting society, and they are, first and foremost, considered "peace officers," so why include them as potential harassers of cyclists? The truth is that some police *do* harass cyclists.

Consider the 2004 Republican National Convention held in New York City. The monthly Critical Mass ride, which had occurred peacefully for years, was the site of mass arrests and violence against cyclists. After getting their marching orders from above, New York's finest kicked, tackled, and dragged cyclists off their bikes before arresting hundreds of them for no offense other than being on a bike in the street. This illegal and authoritarian type of behavior has led to a downward spiral of continuing animosity between police and cyclists. *And Still We Ride*, a documentary film,[22] captures the police brutality, harassment, and bias against cyclists in the summer of 2004. Instances of similar police brutality toward cyclists can be found in many cities across the United States.

Another way police officers harass cyclists is to ticket them for nonsensical violations, such as not using the bike lane on roads where there is no bike lane. Another tactic is to order cyclists off roads on which they have a legal right to be riding, under threat of arrest. If a police officer ordered a driver commuting to work to get his or her car off the road— NOW!—or face arrest, no one would find this acceptable. It would probably make the national news, and the officer could be suspended from his job while an investigation took place, or even fired. No one would feel that the order was lawful. But this type of thing is not that uncommon for cyclists, even though they also have a legal right to the road. Police have harassed cyclists in other illegal ways; for instance, cyclists have reported being "buzzed" by law-enforcement officers.

Even when the officer's behavior is technically "legal," the bias against cyclists may mean that an officer is engaging in a low level of harassment. Maybe the officer doesn't interview the cyclist at an accident scene, or asks the injured cyclist only accusatory questions, such as "Where's your light?"—to which more than one cyclist has responded, "It's lying there

---

22 See http://www.stillweridethemovie.com/.

in the street, still on, after it was knocked off my bike in the collision!"—
before concluding that the motorist was not at fault. Or maybe the officer refuses to arrest a motorist who has just assaulted a cyclist, or tries
to talk the cyclist out of filing a complaint. While these police behaviors
may be technically legal, depending upon department regulations, they
may nevertheless amount to harassment.

WHAT CAN BE DONE

Everyone—cyclists included—is entitled to equal protection under the
law; when that constitutional right is violated by the government—by
police officers, for instance—a citizen has recourse under the law. Under
Section 1983 of the Civil Rights Act of 1871, "Every person who, under
color of any statute, ordinance, regulation, custom, or usage, of any
State or Territory or the District of Columbia, subjects, or causes to be
subjected, any citizen of the United States or other person within the
jurisdiction thereof to the deprivation of any rights, privileges, or immunities secured by the Constitution and laws, shall be liable to the party
injured."[23]

That is, no law-enforcement officer may deprive you of your constitutional right to use the road. This doesn't mean that you have a constitutional right that somehow outweighs the requirement to obey the traffic
laws. What it does mean is that if you're riding in compliance with the
traffic laws, you can't have your constitutional rights infringed "under
color of law"—in other words, by a law-enforcement officer purporting
to enforce the law by ordering you to abandon your right to the road,
whether by ordering you off the road when you have a legal right to be
on the road, by ticketing you with a nonsensical violation, or by pulling
you off your bike and arresting you simply because the order has gone
out to arrest all bicycle riders, as happened during the 2004 Republican
Convention.

If law enforcement is harassing you with these illegal methods, it
is not only your right, but your duty, to hold them accountable. To my
knowledge, Section 1983 lawsuits against law-enforcement harassers of
cyclists are few and far between. One case was prosecuted in Boston, but
the cyclist lost that case, in my view because the facts of the case—an arrest after the cyclist was ordered off the roadway—were muddied because it occurred during a Critical Mass ride; the officer testified that
the ride was blocking traffic and that the cyclist refused repeated orders

23 42 U.S.C. 1983 (2000).

to get off the road.[24] Despite this loss, I believe that under the right circumstances, where the order is clearly unlawful and there are no confusing circumstances, such as were alleged in this case—cyclists blocking all lanes of traffic—a Section 1983 case could be won.

What if the harassment isn't a civil rights violation, however? Suppose it just takes the form of law enforcement dragging their feet in an investigation. In one Austin, Texas, case, a drunk driver killed a cyclist; police sat on the investigation for six months, until a TV news report described as "scathing" revealed that no action had been taken on the investigation, while another investigation, in which a police officer had been killed, had been completed in ten hours. Shortly after the news report aired, the police completed the investigation and the case was submitted to the D.A.[25]

I would recommend giving the police the chance to do their job before you turn to the media, but if it becomes clear over time that the police have no intention of doing their job, going to the media or, alternatively, to your elected representatives with your story is one effective avenue for exerting some pressure on the police.

5-8 MEDIA HARASSMENT OF CYCLISTS

One particularly egregious form of cyclist harassment comes from the media through the anticyclist tirades of "shock jocks." Periodically, a radio talk-show host will begin a bitter outburst against cyclists. These denunciations go way beyond "I wish cyclists weren't on the road," or even "I don't like cyclists"; typically, the talk-show host will boast of illegal acts he has committed against cyclists, encourage others to phone in to the show to boast of their illegal acts, or even suggest that illegal acts should be committed.

In July 2006, for example, a radio talk-show host in Portland, Oregon, encouraged listeners to phone in with stories of cyclists who had been injured by cars. The cohost then said that she had intentionally cut off a cyclist the previous day, and that the cyclist had punched her rear window. Because of that incident, she said, "Now I carry extra water bottles in my car to throw at them." Her cohost then talked about how much he hated cyclists, and remarked that "when I hear on TV that a cyclist has been hit and killed by a car I laugh, I think it's funny.... If you are a cy-

---

24 The cyclist, Peter Rowinsky, disputed the officer's account, claiming that he was attempting to comply with the officer's order when he was arrested.

25 Michael Bluejay, http://bicycleaustin.info/index.html.

clist you should know I exist, that I don't care about you. That I don't care about your life."[26]

The most notorious media harassment incidents consisted of a group of broadcasts from stations owned by broadcast media giant Clear Channel, beginning with a February 13, 2001, broadcast from KSJO, a Clear Channel station in San Jose, California. The two shock jocks hosting the show urged their listeners to "door" passing cyclists or to run them down.[27] Cyclists objected to the broadcast, and the station apologized, promising to air bicycle safety messages as mitigation for the harm done.

The big brouhaha was yet to come, however, over broadcasts made at three separate Clear Channel stations during one three-month period in 2003. The first broadcast was from WMJI, a Clear Channel station in Cleveland, Ohio, on June 30, 2003. One of the shock jocks complained about being held up in traffic by a group of bicyclists; soon, the shock jocks were suggesting that cyclists should be rammed off the roads. They fielded three hours of anticyclist phone calls from listeners. When bike-shop co-owner Lois Cowan called in, she was "repeatedly called a buffoon, an idiot and a PMS sufferer who couldn't take a joke."[28] The show was rebroadcast on July 2 and 3, 2003.

The second broadcast was at KLOL, a Clear Channel station in Houston, Texas. On August 30, 2003, a driver had lost control of her pickup truck and crashed into a twenty-bike pace line, killing two cyclists and injuring eight others; one of the injured cyclists had to be life-flighted to the hospital. Three days later, on September 2, 2003, the shock jocks at KLOL broadcast a show on which they advocated that their listeners should hit cyclists with their sideview mirrors. Houston cyclist Frank Karbarz commented that "they did it almost like a tutorial. It wasn't humorous. It was how to hurt someone."[29] The show was rebroadcast on September 5, 2003, apparently against orders, and allegedly by accident.

The third broadcast occurred at a Clear Channel station in Raleigh, North Carolina, on September 22 and 23, 2003, during which the show's hosts talked about hitting cyclists with Yoo-hoo bottles and urged listeners to phone in with their own stories of cyclist harassment. According

---

26 See http://bikeportland.org/2006/07/14/local-radio-show-promotes-hatred-toward-cyclists/.

27 The shock jocks were encouraging motorists to open their car doors as cyclists passed their cars, with the intent of injuring the cyclist. Usually, this type of incident, commonly known among cyclists as "dooring" or "getting doored," is a dangerous, but unintentional, act by the motorist. In this instance, the shock jocks were encouraging their listeners to intentionally batter and injure passing cyclists.

28 J. Michael Kennedy, "Mikes vs. Bikes," Los Angeles Times, October 7, 2003.

29 Ibid.

to a *Los Angeles Times* article, "In the course of the program, listeners flooded their telephone lines to vent about cyclists, including one woman who boasted that her father intentionally hit one while they were on the way to church."[30]

Following these broadcasts, the League of American Bicyclists informed the Federal Communications Commission that, in the opinion of the league, the broadcasts by the Clear Channel stations were tantamount to inciting listeners to commit felonious assault. The outrage over these incidents went all the way to the top of Clear Channel, but Clear Channel's response was ambiguous. CEO John Hogan issued a statement: "We deeply regret that comments made by on-air personalities were misinterpreted. Clear Channel does not condone violence in any form and we are committed to working with the cycling community to improve cycling safety."[31]

The statement did not mollify cyclists—after all, Hogan was essentially defending the broadcasts by claiming that cyclists had "misinterpreted" calls for attacks on cyclists as advocating attacks on cyclists—and Hogan was able to defuse the situation only by meeting with two representatives of the League of American Bicyclists, Executive Director Elissa Margolin and Communications Director Patrick McCormick, on November 5, 2003. Following that meeting, Hogan issued a letter making it clear that further broadcast incidents would not be tolerated. The producer who re-aired the Houston show was terminated, and a program of corrective measures was announced, including on-air public apologies at each of the stations involved, a partnering program with local cycling organizations, and a series of "share the road" public service announcements at each of the three stations. Clear Channel also donated $10,000 to EcoCity Cleveland for a "safe routes to school" program. Nevertheless, some industry analysts believe the chain is pushing a "lowest common denominator" strategy in hotly contested market areas, an analysis given some weight by reports that Clear Channel's national director of programming is a former shock jock.

As unbelievable as it may seem, these broadcasts *may* be protected free speech under the First Amendment of the Constitution. The First Amendment provides very broad protection, and courts have treated it accordingly. However, as Justice Oliver Wendell Holmes famously said, the right of free speech doesn't let you stand up in a crowded theater and yell "Fire!" There are certain limits, and for our purposes, three particular limitations are important to analyze: advocacy of illegal conduct,

30 Ibid.

31 "Clear Channel DJs Encourage Drivers to Harass Cyclists," AP Report, November 1, 2003.

aiding and abetting illegal acts, and regulation of speech in electronic media.

So what do those terms mean to the courts? Let's take a look.

ADVOCACY OF ILLEGAL CONDUCT

Until some relatively recent cases, it was much easier to control speech advocating or promoting illegal conduct than it is now. The original doctrine for controlling speech was the "clear and present danger" test put forth by U.S. Supreme Court Justice Oliver Wendell Holmes in a 1919 case, *Schenk v. United States:* Does the speech constitute a probable danger of an evil so great as to warrant government restraint?[32]

By 1951, the Supreme Court further expanded the "clear and present danger" test to consider if "the gravity of the evil, discounted by its improbability, justified such invasion of speech as necessary to avoid the danger." The problem was that this test, called the "Dennis Doctrine" after the case it was formulated in—*Dennis v. United States*—was used to prosecute individuals who had joined the Communist Party.[33] The accused man, Eugene Dennis, never said anything about the overthrow of the government—his membership in the party alone was considered to be advocating illegal conduct.

Given the abuses of the McCarthy era, the Dennis Doctrine became unacceptable over time, so in 1969 the Supreme Court reversed itself in *Brandenburg v. Ohio.*[34] The new doctrine strongly protected free speech: "Advocacy of the idea of illegal conduct, without more, is constitutionally protected. Only where such advocacy is directed to inciting or producing imminent lawless conduct and is likely to produce such actions may the speech be suppressed."

Today's "shock jocks" may sound like troglodytes, but most of them know their First Amendment law better than most lawyers. If you were to listen to a tape recording of the offending shows, you would probably never hear a single sentence or string of sentences that contains the three essential *Brandenburg* elements needed to be unprotected speech advocating illegal conduct:

1. The speech must direct, not just advocate, unlawful conduct. (For example: Do it! Go now—do it!)

---

32 *Schenk v. United States*, 249 U.S. 47 (1919).
33 *Dennis v. United States*, 341 U.S. 494 (1951).
34 *Brandenburg v. Ohio*, 395 U.S. 444 (1969).

2. The unlawful conduct must be imminent or at a certain time in the future, not in the indefinite future. (For example: Go out *now*! Today, this morning, on your way to work, *do it*!)

3. The speech must be likely to produce lawless action.

Unless the shock jock has somehow managed to meet these three elements—an unlikely event—the "advocacy of illegal conduct" exception won't be able to rein the shock jock in.

AIDING AND ABETTING ILLEGAL ACTS

Suppose someone runs you off the road, or hits you with a bottle, and then claims that he was encouraged by the radio station. In general, one who commands, directs, advises, encourages, procures, instigates, promotes, controls, aids, or abets a wrongful act by another is considered as responsible as the person who physically committed the act. In *Halberstam v. Welch* (1983), the Federal Circuit Court for the District of Columbia considered the case of Linda Hamilton, the live-in companion of Bernard Welch.[35] Welch was a career burglar who, during one of his robberies, killed a man. Although Hamilton participated in none of her paramour's crimes, she lived off the proceeds of his burglaries and encouraged his activities. The family of the murdered man sued her and won. The court reasoned that "a person who encourages another to commit a tortious act may also be responsible for other foreseeable acts done by such other person in connection with the intended act."

There have been a great number of cases where an accused criminal tried to claim he or she was "intoxicated" or "deranged" by a movie, song, or exposure to violence on TV. Generally, such "media" cases have gone nowhere. However, in a 1997 case, *Rice v. Paladin Enterprises,* a young man, James Perry, killed three people.[36] Perry admitted that he did it, and he confessed that he did it because he was paid by the husband of one of the victims. But he also told the police that he would never have taken up the offer if he had not been inspired and instructed by two books, *Hit Man* and *How to Make a Silencer,* published by Paladin Press. Perry followed the instructions in *Hit Man* when he killed his three victims. The victims' family sued the publisher for encouraging and aiding Perry in his crime. Although the trial court denied liability, a federal appeals court reversed the judgment and sent the case back to the trial court so a jury could determine how much Paladin Press owed the family.

---

35 *Halberstam v. Welch*, 705 F.2d 472 (D.C. Cir. 1983).

36 *Rice v. Paladin Enterprises*, 128 F.3d 233 (4th Cir. 1997).

The appeals court determined that freedom of speech was a nonissue in cases where a media entity aids or abets in a crime or tort. Relying on the logic used in the Linda Hamilton case, the court formed a three-prong test for determining if a media entity "aided or abetted" a criminal:

1. The party whom the media outlet aids must perform a wrongful act that causes an injury.

2. The media outlet must be generally aware of its role as part of an overall illegal or tortious activity at the time that it provides the assistance.

3. The media outlet must intentionally and knowingly assist the principal violation.

It may be worth exploring: Would a radio station that encourages its listeners to commit violent acts against cyclists meet that test? So far, this is a matter that has not come before the courts; however, it would make an interesting legal challenge.

SPEECH IN ELECTRONIC MEDIA

Because the airwaves over which the media corporations broadcast are publicly owned, the government regulates those broadcasters. This government power to regulate the use of the publicly owned airwaves is another potential avenue for challenging broadcasters advocating violent assaults on the civil and legal rights of cyclists.

For example, in *F.C.C. v. Pacifica* (1978), the Supreme Court upheld a Federal Communications Commission (FCC) civil fine levied against a radio station that played a monologue by the comic George Carlin, called "Seven Dirty Words," at 2:30 in the afternoon.[37] The court agreed that of all forms of speech, electronic media is the most limited because it is "a uniquely pervasive presence in the lives of all Americans." And in a 2002 case, *Planned Parenthood of Columbia v. American Coalition of Life Activists,* a U.S. Circuit Court of Appeals extended government regulation of speech to the Internet, ruling that an Internet site that listed the names of physicians it accused of providing abortion services, and that crossed out the names of physicians that had recently been murdered, was in violation of a federal statute and could therefore be regulated by state and federal authorities.[38]

---

37 *F.C.C. v. Pacifica*, 438 U.S. 726 (1978). The monologue contained many obscenities but was not itself hurtful or insulting. Carlin's basic premise was that there are no inherently dirty words, just unkind thoughts.

38 *Planned Parenthood of Columbia v. American Coalition of Life Activists*, 290 F.3d 1058 (9th Cir. 2002).

It remains to be seen whether the government power to regulate scarce bandwidth will provide a means of reining in the shock jocks. Certainly, the power is there, if the government has the will to use it. However, during the past two decades, that government power has been sharply curtailed by deregulation. Even so, under deregulation the FCC retains the authority to issue and renew broadcast licenses, and this authority does give the FCC the power to deny licenses to stations that abuse their licensing requirements.

WHAT CAN BE DONE

There are three approaches to dealing with media harassment of cyclists: community dialogue with the media outlet, an FCC licensing challenge, and a civil suit.

Community Dialogue
In the first approach, when cyclists have heard a radio program advocating illegal acts against cyclists, they have protested to the station management. Following the anticyclist broadcast in Portland, the local cycling community protested to the station. At first, the show's host insisted that his comments had been "taken out of context." However, the station refused to provide a recording of the show, despite the fact that all shows are recorded, and despite the fact that all other shows were podcast on the station's website. If the show had been "taken out of context," it should have been easy for the station to prove—something that neither the talk-show host nor the station manager ever did.

Under mounting pressure, the station manager finally apologized, saying, "We all make mistakes, it's how you deal with them and grow that matters." The show's host apologized on air and rode a bike with a reporter for the local weekly paper, which ran a story on the ride. In meeting with local cycling advocates, the station manager was reported to have repeatedly remarked, "What can I do to make this stop?! I will do anything you ask," and he informed local cycling advocates that he would be happy to perform a number of services for the local cycling community, including running public service announcements, giving away free bikes, and donating to the Bicycle Transportation Alliance, Oregon's cycling advocacy organization.

FCC License-Renewal Challenge
The second approach is to challenge a station's broadcasting license with the Federal Communications Commission. Periodically, broadcast

stations must renew their licenses because they operate, at least theoretically, on the "public's airwaves." Under the Communications Act of 1934,

> If the licensee of a broadcast station submits an application to the Commission for renewal of such license, the Commission shall grant a license renewal application if it finds, with respect to that station, during the preceding license term—
>
> A the station has served the public interest, convenience, and necessity;
>
> B there have been no serious violations by the licensee of the Communications Act or the Commission's Rules; and
>
> C there have been no other violations of the Act or the Commission's rules which, taken together, would constitute a pattern of abuse.[39]

If you want to file an objection with the FCC regarding a station's license renewal, there are two basic methods: the informal "objection" and the formal "Petition to Deny."

Informal Objection ▶ The informal objection process is a means of establishing an official record of public dissatisfaction with a broadcast station's obligation to serve the public interest. One objection to a broadcast station's public service record isn't likely to get the attention of the FCC. Hundreds of objections, however, will get noticed, by both the FCC and station management. After all, the FCC does retain the power to put the station out of business, even if that power is rarely used.

First, if you want to file an objection, you will need to know when stations in your state are required to renew their licenses.[40] Once you have this information, you can file your objection. Generally, the best time to file this objection is between two and four months before the station's current license expires; however, you may file it at any time between the day the station applies for its license renewal and the day the FCC grants the renewal.[41]

Second, you will need to document the station's abuses of its licensing requirements. If a station is broadcasting shows that encourage listeners, either directly or indirectly, to commit acts of harassment and violence against cyclists, document the show: Record the date, the time,

---

39 47 U.S.C. 309(k) (200).

40 Currently, broadcast stations are required to renew their licenses every eight years; you will need to know when stations in your state are up for license renewal.

41 The status of broadcast license renewals can be checked on the FCC's Consolidate DataBase System website at http://gullfoss2.fcc.gov/prod/cdbs/pubacc/prod/cdbs_pa.htm.

exactly what was said, and who said it. You may be able to access the show in question from a podcast on the station's website. If the station has podcasts of all of the other shows, but not of the show in question, document that. Document whether the station's programming is fair and balanced: Does it present only negative portrayals of cyclists? Or does the station also present positive portrayals of cyclists and cycling? You are entitled by law to look through the public file that the station is required to keep. This file documents the station's programming, including its educational, political, and community affairs programming. Again, document whether the station's programming is fair and balanced.

Third, you will need to send a letter to the FCC.[42] The first page of your letter will need to include the station's call letters, the city and state the station broadcasts from, the station's facility number, and the station's license-renewal application file number.[43] Once you have provided the FCC with this information, your letter will need to specify your objection to the station's performance and explain why its license should not be renewed; here, use the information you've gathered by documenting the station's broadcasts as well as information that you found in the station's public file. You must mail two copies of your objection: one to the FCC and the other to the station's general manager.

Formal Petition to Deny ▶ The second method for objecting to a station's license renewal is through a formal Petition to Deny. To file this type of objection, you must be a "party in interest" and have "standing." This means that you must be a regular listener or have some other contact with the station that gives you a real stake in the outcome of the renewal process. The petition must include a signed original and two copies, mailed or delivered to the appropriate FCC address. Additional "courtesy copies" may be sent directly to the Audio Division, License Renewal Processing Team. The petition must be supported by an affidavit of a person or persons with personal knowledge of the allegations of fact contained in the petition. The filing must also be "timely"—the petition must be filed no later than one month prior to the license expiration date[44]—and you must include a certification that a copy of the petition was mailed to the station.

A Petition to Deny is a more serious challenge to a station's license renewal than the informal objection. However, because the requirements for a formal petition are more stringent, you should work with an attorney if you decide to pursue this option.

---

42   Again, an objection to a license renewal should include as many letters as possible.

43   This information will be available on the FCC's CDBS website.

44   The filing date is the date the petition is received by the FCC.

Unfortunately, decades of deregulation of the airwaves in favor of free-market ideology—owing to sustained attacks on the Fairness Doctrine in the courts, in Congress, and at the FCC—have left broadcast licensees largely unanswerable to the public that actually "owns" the airwaves.[45] Thus, license-renewal challenges tend to be very long, expensive affairs that usually end in a renewal of the challenged license. Nevertheless, because there is at least a nominal threat hanging over the heads of broadcast licensees, you may have an opportunity to influence station management through community dialogue, with the unspoken threat of an FCC license-renewal challenge held in reserve for recalcitrant station managers.

Civil Suit

The third approach is to file a civil suit against the station. There are two different types of suits that can be filed. The first would be a suit where, although the cyclist was injured by somebody other than the station, that person is alleging that he or she was encouraged by the station to engage in illegal conduct and acted on that encouragement, as in *Paladin*, where the hit man read a book that inspired and instructed him, or the case of Linda Hamilton, who was held liable for the tortious acts she encouraged Bernard Welch to commit. In this type of civil suit, the cyclist would be reaching the conduct of the station—encouraging the commission of illegal acts—through the conduct of the person who actually committed the illegal act.

The second type of suit that can be filed is a civil rights claim against the station under Section 1985 of the Civil Rights Act of 1871.[46] Under this act, if two or more persons conspire to deprive "either directly or indirectly, any person or class of persons of the equal protection of the laws, or of equal privileges and immunities under the laws"—for example, if they conspire to harass or injure cyclists on the road—they can be held liable for their conspiracy because the right to travel is a civil right protected under the Constitution. The problem with this type of lawsuit is that, while encouraging others to go out and commit illegal acts might sound sort of like conspiracy, unless there is a more tangible connection

45 The Fairness Doctrine called for broadcasters "to operate in the public interest and to afford reasonable opportunity for the discussion of conflicting views on issues of social importance." One regulation under the Fairness Doctrine was the "personal attack rule," which required that persons or groups subjected to attacks on their character, honesty, or integrity during the broadcast of opinions on controversial issues of public importance be offered "a reasonable opportunity to respond." The personal attack rule was eliminated by court order less than two months before the 2000 presidential election. One of the most visible results of the rise of broadcaster unaccountability has been the concurrent rise of the shock jocks who encourage the commission of crimes against cyclists.

46 42 U.S.C. 1985 (200).

between the talk-show host and the listener, the conversation probably doesn't amount to conspiracy in a legal sense. Still, if it looks as if they crossed that threshold, it's an approach worth exploring.

5-9 PROFESSIONAL DRIVER HARASSMENT OF CYCLISTS

The "professional" is the motorist who drives for a living—a taxi driver, a bus driver, a delivery person, a trucker, or anyone else who sees the road as his working space. We have all experienced pressure and frustration at work; some of these drivers have come to see cyclists as an impediment to their work. In addition, spending a lot of time on the road means they have had many encounters with people on bikes. If some of these encounters turn negative, the frustrated driver may develop an attitude of disrespect and enmity toward all cyclists. Some of the most consistent and brazen abuse of the rights of cyclists comes from public employees: the public-transit bus drivers. These drivers are notorious for ignoring right-of-way, for cutting off cyclists, and for forcing cyclists into oncoming traffic—and it's often intentional.

WHAT CAN BE DONE

The response to harassment by professional drivers will depend upon the type of professional driver: delivery or truck driver, cabbie, or bus driver. But there is one legal doctrine that will apply to all professional drivers. This legal doctrine, called *respondeat superior,* holds that an employer may be held liable for *any* tortious conduct—whether negligent or intentional—of an employee. In fact, an employer may be held liable for tortious conduct even if the employer has expressly forbidden the tortious conduct. That might seem unfair, but it prevents the kind of winking "disapproval" of tortious conduct that might otherwise occur. If the conduct furthers the business of the employer, even if the conduct is forbidden, the employer may be held liable.

In order for *respondeat superior* to apply, certain conditions must exist. First, the person committing the act usually must be an employee; persons who hire independent contractors usually aren't held liable for the tortious acts of the independent contractor. Many employers prefer to operate under the fiction that their employees are actually independent contractors. However, the mere assertion by an employer that a worker is not an employee doesn't prove that the worker is not an employee. Rather, there are legal tests for distinguishing between employees and independent contractors; generally, if the person who has hired a worker exerts control over the work, the worker is an employee.[47]

Second, the tortious act must be committed within the scope of employment. This means that the employee must be acting with the intent to serve her employer, rather than from purely personal motives.

Delivery or Truck Drivers

A delivery or truck driver may be an employee or an independent contractor, depending on the company he or she is driving for. If the driver is an employee, and if the driver is harassing you in furtherance of the business of the carrier, you can hold the carrier liable in a civil suit, which I will discuss in more detail in §5-10, "Public Harassment of Cyclists."

Regardless of the employment status of the driver, if you have been intentionally endangered by a delivery or truck driver, you should report that driver to the company. Another avenue for disciplining dangerous drivers is through the state. Motor carriers are regulated by state law and must hold a permit issued by the state's Department of Transportation. If you have been intentionally endangered by a delivery or truck driver, check your state laws regulating motor carriers, because these statutes will vary by state; when you are familiar with what state law requires, you can take appropriate steps to have the Department of Transportation discipline that driver.

Cab and Limousine Drivers

Generally, cab companies maintain that their drivers are independent contractors. However, cabbies themselves have been challenging this assertion, claiming that they are, in fact, employees of the cab companies. In some challenges made by cabbies, the National Labor Relations Board has ruled that cabbies are, in fact, employees of the cab companies. Nevertheless, there is no clear answer as to whether cabbies are employees or independent contractors. If a cabbie is an employee, and if the cabbie is harassing you in furtherance of the business of the cab company, you can hold the cab company liable in a civil suit. This approach is discussed in more detail in the next section, §5-10.

Because both cab companies and taxi and limousine drivers are licensed by the city they operate in, you can also exert some pressure to discipline or revoke the licenses of dangerous drivers with the city agency that licenses them. The rules for licensing will be specific to each

---

47 While an independent contractor must perform the contract, he is free to perform it as he sees fit, as long as he performs the contract as specified. Thus, for example, while an independent contractor may have a completion date, he chooses his own hours and is not subject to employee rules on hours, breaks, dress code, and the like.

city, so you will need to check your local ordinances regulating the cab industry.

Bus Drivers

Bus drivers include drivers for private bus lines as well as public-transit employees. In both instances, the drivers will be employees of the company or agency they are driving for. Thus, the company or agency can be held liable for the driver's tortious conduct in a civil suit (see the next section, §5-10).

Although public transit bus drivers are often notorious for intentionally endangering cyclists, you should be aware that state law may require you to yield the right-of-way to buses under defined circumstances. For example, in Oregon, Section 811.167 of the Vehicle Code states that

> a person commits the offense of failure to yield the right-of-way to a transit bus entering traffic if the person does not yield the right-of-way to a transit bus when:
> (a) A yield sign . . . is displayed on the back of the transit bus;
> (b) The person is operating a vehicle that is overtaking the transit bus from the rear of the transit bus; and
> (c) The transit bus, after stopping to receive or discharge passengers, is signaling an intention to enter the traffic lane occupied by the person.

Despite this requirement to yield, the law does not absolve bus drivers of their responsibility to you. The same Oregon law, for example, states,"This section does not relieve a driver of a transit bus from the duty to drive with due regard for the safety of all persons using the roadway."

Thus, whether you are in violation of the law or not, a transit bus driver may not endanger your safety. If a transit driver has endangered your safety, you can report that driver to the agency; the regulations for each agency will be specific to that agency, so you should check those regulations before you file a complaint.

5-10 PUBLIC HARASSMENT OF CYCLISTS

Cyclist harassment covers a wide range of actions. The first step to understanding the phenomenon is to recognize that not every driver who endangers your life is doing so intentionally. The second step is to understand that among those who do intentionally harass cyclists, there are different reasons for the behavior. "Harassers" are actually a disparate group of people who simply have in common the behavioral traits of being uncivil, rude, and dangerous to cyclists. The third step is to understand what you can do and what you must—and mustn't—do when you are being endangered on the road.

THE UNAWARE DRIVER

Entering a long, winding valley, I saw a large combine-tractor coming toward me, the driver safely ensconced in his modern climate-controlled cabin. By habit, I turned around to see if I might be overtaken by another motorist approaching from the rear. Having seen nary another traveler for hours, I was somewhat surprised to see an old station wagon bearing down on me. Judging by our respective speeds, I estimated that, as bad luck would have it, all three of us would be sharing the same twenty-foot section of country road at the same time. I decided not to take the lane, moved to a tiny ribbon-width of roadway, and held my line. I didn't dare turn around, and at that time, I was too cool to use the bar-end mirror I now rely on. I didn't hear any sounds from behind and thought the wagon driver had slowed and was waiting to pass me. Just as the large tractor—using more than half the roadway—passed, the wagon whooshed within an inch of my elbow—so close I could feel the turbulence through my jersey. He was moving so fast he was a quarter of a mile ahead of me before I could manage to throw my arm up in a display of anger.

His brake lights came on, and I readied myself for battle—youth, adrenaline, and righteous indignation on my side. He pulled his faux-wood-sided beast to the shoulder and lumbered his large heavy frame out of the driver's seat. I rode straight up to him, threw my bike on the ground, and walked directly up to him and stood nose to nose. He seemed genuinely confused by my rage and had a big smile on his face. I knew something was wrong with this scenario. I yelled something like "Why the *#%@ did you just do that?" "Do what?" he replied. "Almost kill me!" He stared at me with a perplexed expression and shook his head. "I'm sorry, did I hit you?" he asked in earnest. It turned out that he liked to ride his own bike, and inexplicably, didn't realize that a cyclist wouldn't appreciate such a close pass—after all, roads were for motor vehicles and anyone riding a bike knew that. I calmed down and even apologized for being so enraged. He honestly didn't think it had been a dangerous pass, pointing out that cars heading in opposite directions are within a foot or less of colliding as a matter of course.

This type of driver doesn't mean to harm you and is genuinely unaware of the effect his driving has on the cyclists with whom he shares the road. Sometimes, as with the driver I confronted, the unaware driver will pass too closely without realizing that the pass is unsafe.

There are two other types of drivers who, while also unintentionally endangering you, fall into a slightly different category from the unaware driver. The first is the inattentive driver—the driver who is so absorbed with a task that he or she fails to notice you. This driver could be talking on a cell phone—or even text messaging!—or fiddling with the stereo controls, or talking with a passenger, and simply fail to notice that he or she has just endangered your life. Whatever the cause, although this inattentive driver is endangering your life, that endangerment is the result of negligence rather than an intentional act. This driver is not harassing you, although when your life is flashing before your eyes you may not see it that way.

The second type of driver is more dangerous. This driver's actions, while unintentional and thus not harassment, are so extreme that they become criminally negligent. This driver will be driving while under the influence of alcohol or drugs and is simply incapable of safely operating a vehicle; because driving under the influence is illegal, the driver is exhibiting the extreme carelessness and indifference to the likely consequences of her actions that are the hallmark of gross negligence. However, unless this driver actually intends to frighten or otherwise harm you, her actions are negligent, not intentional.

Regardless of whether this driver is simply negligent, grossly negligent, or criminally negligent, it's important to understand that she is not intentionally endangering you, because the legal response to her actions will not be the same as the legal response to the actions of drivers who are intentionally harassing you.

The unaware driver means no ill will in terms of intent, but the consequences for the cyclist are no different from the consequences when a driver intentionally harasses people who are legally riding a bike on the public roadway. Perhaps these drivers cut their driving teeth at a time when there were few cyclists to share the road with (or in a place where cyclists were uncommon). This excuse becomes more and more unacceptable, however, as new drivers are made well aware of cycling through driver's education training, driver exams, and handbooks published by the states. Additionally, many states have posted signs commanding motorists to "share the road" with an illustrated cycling figure centered in the sign.

These drivers may simply lack information about cycling, but their ignorance will put cyclists at risk wherever they go. They may pass within inches of a cyclist because they mistakenly believe they are not allowed to cross a double yellow line. Instead, they will squeeze past the cyclist, coming too close and risking the cyclist's life, or stay behind the cyclist, causing a queue of irate drivers, who then vent against the innocent cyclist once it is their turn to pass. Or the uneducated driver may pull out directly in front of a cyclist, violating the cyclist's right-of-way with no malice intended, or turn without signaling, creating a deadly hazard for the cyclist. You know you are dealing with an unaware driver by the befuddled look on the driver's face and the genuine regret and palpable fear he exudes as he tries to set you back on your bike *á la* Tom Simpson style—as if getting you up and started again will erase the consequences of his negligent driving.

The solution for this confused driver is education. These drivers need to be apprised of the law—informed that cyclists are legally operating a vehicle and have the same rights to the road as they do in their mini-van or SUV. Unfortunately, the cyclist who has just been knocked off his or her bike is not likely to have the proper frame of mind to deliver a measured elocution of the law. Berating this kind of driver in an effort to embarrass and humiliate him into adherence will not likely succeed in doing anything but turning him into an anticyclist. If, for instance, the driver pulled out directly in front of a cyclist, causing an accident or near miss, it may not have been his intent to do any harm. Perhaps he didn't keep a reasonable lookout, or perhaps the driver underestimated the closing speed of the cyclist. The cyclist who discusses the event with the driver in a calm voice has the best chance of successfully educating the driver about cyclists' rights and not creating another anticyclist. Of course, if the driver did pull out intentionally, he might just be an anticyclist, and not unaware, and the measured response can be accompanied by other remedial legal actions.

FOUR TYPES OF HARASSERS

Unlike drivers who are merely unaware of the danger they're putting you in, or those who are merely careless or negligent drivers, the harasser is aware of what she is doing—she is intentionally attempting to intimidate you, frighten you, or even harm you.

That's the one common thread of all harassers: The harassment, or worse, is intentional. Nevertheless, the motivations for the harasser will vary from driver to driver; some common examples of cyclist harassers include the frustrated driver, the opportunity harasser, the anticyclist, and the road rager. Let's take a closer look at each of these types before discussing what you can do in preparation for harassment, and what you must do if you've been harassed.

The Frustrated Driver

This is the driver who is battling traffic, is perhaps late for work or an appointment, and now finds himself "stuck" behind a cyclist. As his anxiety rises, he projects his feelings of frustration outward toward others—it's their fault he's late! It's their fault he's stuck in traffic! His enmity could be directed at construction delays, other motorists, his passengers, or anyone or anything that he feels is working against him. A cyclist who "gets in his way" is a natural target for his enmity. He may not know that the cyclist has the same legal right to the road as he does, and he decides his imagined "superior legal status" on the road justifies his actions of harassment against the cyclist. He might sound his horn or yell out the window as he passes. Worse still, he might aggressively pass as closely as he can, forcefully demonstrating his displeasure to the unsuspecting cyclist who had the nerve to "get in his way." I have no doubt that, like many of these categories of harassing drivers, the frustrated harasser has hit and killed cyclists while attempting to intimidate them.

The Opportunity Harasser

If you seek the thrill of "messing with" someone, you need a victim. For the opportunity harasser, happening upon someone who is vulnerable to attack and in no position to respond is an ideal situation for achieving the thrill. Unfortunately, cyclists are often in the ideal vulnerable position for this harasser, whether they are cycling in a city bike lane or out on a lonely country road.

The mildest form of harassment in this category typically comes from teenagers out for pranks. When this opportunity victimizer attacks, it can come in the form of a flying beverage container or a banshee-like scream, timed perfectly to startle the cyclist. Other teens "out for fun" haven't been so mild—some have actually shot cyclists with frozen paintballs as they drove by; others have knocked cyclists off their bikes with a baseball bat as they drove by. All of these "pranks," no matter how "mild" or how "wild," are offensive, dangerous, and illegal. I have caught up to some of these miscreants myself and been witness to their well-honed apology act. Their parents and other apologists will typically use phrases like "caught up in the moment" and "a good kid."

The middle territory of convenience harassers is composed of drivers of all ages who simply cannot abide the right of cyclists to the road. They will, in an almost offhanded way, throw a can of beer or cup of ice at a cyclist as they pass, just to mess with them, because they don't like seeing people out riding on bikes. Or sometimes, more sinisterly, they will veer their vehicle in a menacing and threatening way toward a cyclist with the intent to intimidate—again, just to mess with the cyclist.

The most serious type of opportunity harasser is the sociopath—a person with a psychiatric disorder characterized, among other things, by a failure to conform to law-abiding behavior, by irritability and aggressiveness, by reckless disregard for the safety of others, and by lack of remorse for his or her actions. The sociopath is a very dangerous person to encounter, whether on or off the road. He or she may choose a cyclist to harass and victimize for the same reason he or she chooses his or her other victims—because cyclists are vulnerable. Fortunately, sociopaths are rare, but be aware that they are out there.

The Anticyclist

Some drivers just don't like cyclists. As we saw previously, many drivers are genuinely fearful of injuring cyclists, and that fear transforms into a loathing of cyclists. Many drivers are offended by rude and scofflaw behavior, especially when the cyclist is in the wrong and blames the motorist. Even among these drivers, however, it's possible to discern separate categories.

The "Get Even" Driver ▶ The "get even" driver has a vendetta to settle with people on bikes. There may be many different reasons for these drivers to feel such enmity toward cyclists, but in the typical case, the "get even" driver has had some prior negative interaction with a cyclist or group of cyclists. Perhaps he made a driving mistake and was taken to task by a cyclist. Some "get even" drivers see cyclists as a loathsome group of scofflaws who are making the roads dangerous—this feeling can stem from perceived scofflaw behavior when the motorist simply doesn't understand the law. The "get even" driver sees cyclists riding on the road, which he assumes—incorrectly—is illegal; some drivers simply cannot accept that riding a bike on the roadways is legal, and they are motivated by wanting to show the cyclist, through words or actions, who really "owns the road." The feeling that cyclists are scofflaws can also stem from actual scofflaw behavior on the part of cyclists; the "get even" driver sees cyclists running red lights, for example, which he assumes—this time correctly—is illegal. Then the "get even" driver begins to think of cyclists as thumbing their collective noses at the law every time they get on a bike. This driver wants to settle a score, and harassing a cyclist—any cyclist—will do.

The "get even" driver assumes a vigilante-like code of behavior toward cyclists. This might come in the form of making a close pass or by screaming invectives or throwing objects at cyclists. Unfortunately, however, this attitude of treating cyclists as second-class members of our driving society can have tragic results. The number of negative encounters between drivers and cyclists is on the rise. Stories of battles turning tragic are everywhere in the media. Cyclists are intentionally forced off the road and even purposely hit by vehicles. Accounts of cyclists being shot by motorists have been reported in several states.

To the harassed cyclist, how the "get even" driver came to dislike people on bikes is irrelevant in terms of response. A distinction should be made between being harassed and being simply irritated. For instance, if a cyclist and a motorist both arrive at a four-way stop at nearly the same time, and the motorist decides to go first, this is likely not harassment. The motorist who fails to yield the right-of-way to a cyclist may or may not be harassing. Screaming and yelling at a cyclist to "get off the damn road!" is harassment.

The Social/Political Harasser ▶ Some harassers see cyclists as a seditious group trying to push a social agenda on society and may believe that people who ride bikes belong to a particular political group they despise. They come to associate people who commute by bike as somehow "un-American," and they see those who wear colorful cycling clothing as a threat to traditional dress and proper attire. They see the legal right to the road as a kind of "zero-sum game" and view "cyclists' rights" as diminishing their own rights. These drivers can be quite vocal about their views and may even act on their feelings. Such behavior, in their minds, is justified because they see cycling as countercultural behavior that should not be tolerated.

This stereotype is ridiculous, of course, but it is nevertheless repeated in letters to the editors of local newspapers and rants on call-in radio programs. The fact that cyclists' rights groups take to the streets to demand their rights also adds to the belief that people on bikes are troublemakers and a nuisance.

Drivers who are convinced that the "end of civilization" is being hastened by people on bikes are typically passive harassers. For instance, they might use their vehicles in a way that makes riding past them difficult, or they may confront random cyclists to engage in unprovoked shouting matches.

The Road Rager
I once represented a cyclist who was intentionally knocked off his bike by an irate motorist. The client was a very nimble and proficient rider in the mold of a big-city bike messenger. He was riding his fixed-gear bike in the inside lane of a four-lane roadway that had a posted speed limit of 25 mph. Traffic was heavy, and he took the entire lane and was keeping up with traffic and not even close to his limit. The cyclist heard a vehicle gunning its engine directly behind him. He ignored the driver and continued riding without turning around. When the outside lane

opened, he moved to his right. The motorist zoomed into the vacated opening and sounded his horn. The cyclist flipped him off, and the motorist veered quickly into the cyclist, knocking him to the ground, which shattered his helmet. The motorist continued without stopping and returned only when another driver caught up to him and insisted he return to the accident scene and wait for the police. The cyclist ended up losing his sight. The driver had a record of hit-and-runs, threatening neighbors with guns, and other road-rage incidents.

Road ragers come from all walks of life, but they have one trait in common: They rage. They rage against other drivers who break their personal code of driving etiquette, tailgate tailgaters just to teach them a lesson, and block others from switching lanes but go to fists if someone does the same thing to them. They are equal-opportunity offenders when behind the wheel, and in addition to menacing other drivers, they will take their rage and anger out on cyclists with disregard for life and limb. They are very dangerous drivers whose actions cannot be predicted. We have all met such persons in traffic. We might even *be* this person in traffic.

What Is Road Rage? ▶ Road rage can be categorized by the different levels of rage or aggression perpetrated by the operator of a vehicle against others. The seed of road rage is the feeling of anger and hostility toward others in traffic. Escalating from there, the rager communicates her displeasure and/or hostility through verbal and/or demonstrative gestures toward a target. When screaming or gesturing doesn't quell the rager's anger, it's time for her to take action. This may involve tailgating, blaring the horn, or zooming in and out of traffic lanes. If that doesn't work, *or if the other driver responds in kind,* things begin to escalate. The rager may swerve toward the target of her enmity or slam on the brakes. In this internal zone of frustration, the rager feels she is still acting within the law; later, she will defend such actions with the claim that it was necessary to swerve to avoid another driver, or that by hitting the brakes it was possible to avoid running into a slowing vehicle ahead. The rager is unlikely to admit that she was trying to intimidate a cyclist.

The last and most extreme level of road rage is all-out aggression. This can involve the rager basically using his vehicle as a weapon to spar with an unfortunate foe as if in the "ring of death." Only instead of bloodthirsty ringside fans, the only witnesses are the other drivers, cyclists, or pedestrians who happen to be present, who may be caught up in the battle but are often simply alarmed. This is a rampage: Someone may die because of the rager's vendetta, but that doesn't even register with the rager . . . unless he must go through a trial to relive the event or has to spend years behind bars to ponder the consequences of his actions. These drivers are seeing red and seemingly unable to stop, and they often act as if they are willing to die along with their foe if it is required to make their point. Why does society tolerate these maniacs on the road? Because *they are us*.

Driving and road rage go hand in hand on today's roadways, and many a commute is filled with hostility, stress, antagonism, territorial competitiveness, and fear. Humans are imitative animals, and it is currently culturally acceptable to point a bad driver out to your passengers and verbally assail them or worse. Venting and hurling insults at another member of our society, someone you have never met and know nothing about, is considered acceptable behavior, and if we act in this way we should not be surprised to learn that our children practice the same behavior when they come of age to drive. It's a behavior we've learned as children, watching how Mom and Dad drive, and passed on to our children as they watch us drive.

What Causes Road Rage? ▶ The hurried pace of modern living, the competitive nature of our society, the anonymity of driving, the status of another driver as a "thing" instead of a person—these all contribute to the development of road rage. The loss of control experienced by commuters stuck in traffic breeds frustration, contempt, and anger toward those whom we blame for our bad feelings. Recently, road rage has been identified by some researchers as an expression of Intermittent Explosive Disorder (IED), sometimes called Militant Episode Disorder (MED). This disorder is an impulse-control disorder categorized in the *Diagnostic and Statistical Manual of Mental Disorders* (DSM-IV) with other impulse-control disorders, such as kleptomania and pyromania. Persons with an impulse-control disorder experience impulses that are difficult, or perhaps even impossible, to control; when the impulse-control disorder is characterized by aggressive impulses, the aggression is disproportionate to the "provocation" triggering the aggression.

WHAT CAN BE DONE

If there's anything more annoying than a driver who yells, "Get off the road," it's got to be the drivers who have appointed themselves and their vehicles to be the ones to get you off the road. These drivers are not only wrong about the law, they're a deadly menace to society; and the more we can do to remove them from the roads, the better for all of us. It's simply too dangerous to leave these drivers free to assault another cyclist—even if you haven't been physically injured in a confrontation. Think of it this way: The longer one of these drivers is on the road harassing cyclists and getting away with it, the greater the chance that he or she is going to seriously injure or kill a cyclist someday. For that reason, I argue that when your rights have been violated, not only *can* you do something about it, you *must* do something about it.

The first step you must take in any road-rage incident is to avoid escalating the attack. This goes against instinct—we all tend to feel aggressive when the adrenaline is flooding into our bodies after we've been attacked. But responding to road rage leads only to escalation, and when you're on a bike and locked in combat with the driver of a multiton machine, you will always lose if the situation escalates. This escalation of tactics is what typifies road rage, and so, if you're being assaulted, *don't escalate the situation.* Keep your finger where it belongs: on your handlebars. If you absolutely must use your finger, use it to dial the police. Likewise, keep your tongue in check. If you feel an irresistible urge to say something, say it to the police—just keep it polite. If you've got a sudden adrenaline rush surging through you, put that power into your spinning. Whatever you do, *don't make the situation worse.*

Second, you can prepare beforehand for the inevitable confrontational encounters. For example, many cyclists ride with cell phones and use them when harassed. Sometimes, they even take photos of the driver's license plate with their camera phone. Other cyclists ride with miniature video cameras mounted to their helmet; if they are assaulted, they have video evidence of the incident. Many cyclists ride with another person; though this doesn't necessarily stop assaults, it does mean that there are witnesses to testify in what would otherwise be a "he said, she said" situation. If you are commuting by bike, see if there is anybody else who is making the same commute and who would be interested in having a commuting partner. Finally, if you witness the harassment of another cyclist—whether you're on your bike, in a car, or walking—step forward and offer to testify. They'll need the help, just as you would need the offer if you were alone on your bike and being harassed.

5-11 A WORD ABOUT SELF-DEFENSE

So far, we've looked at responses *after* an incident has occurred. What about responses *during* an incident? Can a cyclist defend herself if attacked? The answer is a qualified yes. Generally, if you are assaulted, you have the right to defend yourself and your property; this right also extends to defending another person from assault. However, the law places limits on this right to self-defense. First, it is not "self-defense" if you intentionally provoke the other person to attack you so that you can fight back and cause injury. Likewise, if you are the person who started the fight, you cannot claim that you acted in "self-defense" unless your actions occurred after you had withdrawn from the fight; even then, you must have effectively communicated your withdrawal to the other person. If you have withdrawn and communicated your withdrawal, and the other person continues to attack, you are entitled to defend yourself. The other person's attack must be under way or "imminent" for your actions to qualify as self-defense. This is an objective standard and means that a "reasonable person" would believe the attack was under way or imminent. For example, if the person is lunging toward you, a reasonable person would believe that an attack was imminent.[48]

Say you're in a situation that clearly requires self-defense: What type of self-defense is allowed, and what other limits apply? Generally, you are allowed to use the force that a reasonable person would believe to be necessary to stop the threatened, imminent, or actual attack. There's that word again—"reasonable." As we've seen in other contexts, "reasonable" force is an objective standard: It means what the "reasonable person," as determined by a jury, would believe is necessary to stop the attack. Thus, it does not include force that would go beyond what a "reasonable person" believes is necessary to stop the attack. To that extent, a "reasonable person" would use force proportionate to the threat of harm. "Reasonable force" *may* include lethal force if the "reasonable person" believes that lethal force is necessary, due to the *threatened or imminently lethal* nature of the attack, to defend against the attack. Let's repeat that point, just so it's clear: Lethal force can be used only where the force against you is either threatened to be lethal or is imminently lethal. Once an attack has been broken off, any further violence on your part would not be considered self-defense. You are allowed to use reasonable force, however, to hold the person while waiting for law enforcement to arrive.

The thing to keep in mind with self-defense is that you don't want to shift from being the victim of a crime to becoming the perpetrator of a crime. Defend yourself if you must, but let the other guy get arrested.

Your right to self-defense will be determined by the laws of the state you live in, so you should consult those laws if you think that you may have occasion to defend yourself. They will determine under what circumstances you can defend yourself and how much force is appropriate. They may also regulate the carrying and use of weapons. Some cyclists ride with a container of pepper spray in case they need to defend themselves. If you decide to carry pepper spray, be sure to check on the legality of carrying and using the spray in your state. Cyclists have also used a bike lock or chain in self-defense; if you carry these with the intent of using them in self-defense, check your state laws to see what is allowed.

---

48 In fact, the word "assault" is derived from the Latin *saltare*, meaning "to jump."

Some cyclists have even used their bike itself as a self-defense weapon; I think it's safe to say that no state regulates bicycles as a weapon. Some cyclists ride with knives or firearms for self-defense; if you decide to do this, check your state laws to be sure that you are in compliance with the law. The key thing to remember in choosing a method of self-defense is the "reasonableness" of the self-defense: What would a "reasonable person" do in a similar situation?

Using the Legal System

So far we've talked about what you can do before and during an attack. Now let's take a look at what you can do after you've been attacked. The legal response to cycling harassment depends on the facts and circumstances of each individual case as well as the state law under which the encounter occurred. It also depends upon which system of justice the case is proceeding through: the criminal justice system or the civil justice system. In the criminal justice system, when a law is violated, the police conduct investigations, gather evidence, and make arrests. The district attorney's office considers the evidence and the alleged crimes and decides whether there is enough evidence to go forward with a trial. If there is a trial, the D.A. prosecutes the alleged crime, representing the people of the state. That's why in the criminal justice system a case will have a name like "*State v. Smith.*" In that sense, a crime is an offense against the people of the state, rather than being an offense solely against the victim.

In the civil justice system, you are prosecuting your own case through your attorney; you conduct your own investigation, gather your own evidence, and bring your own case to trial. That's why in the civil justice system a case will have a name like "*Jones v. Smith.*" Another difference between the two systems is in the burden of proof required: In a criminal trial, the prosecutor must prove the case "beyond a reasonable doubt." This is an objective "reasonable person" standard; there may always be some minuscule nagging doubt, like a voice suggesting "what if," in a juror's mind, but if a reasonable person would have enough doubt to believe that the defendant may not be guilty, then the prosecution has not met its burden of proof and the defendant must be found "not guilty." In a civil trial, you need only prove your case by a "preponderance of the evidence." This is a simple probability standard: If it seems more likely than not that the defendant committed the offense, then you have met your burden of proof. In a civil trial, this means that the defendant will be found "liable," and will receive a judgment of damages against him; to satisfy the judgment, the defendant will be required to pay you money damages to compensate you for your injuries.[49] This differs from the outcome in a criminal trial, where, if the prosecutor proves his or her case, the defendant is found "guilty" and will be sentenced to jail time and/or a fine. Often, the defendant will receive probation as a part of the sentence. If the defendant is placed on probation, and then violates the terms of the probation, he or she will have to serve the sentence.

There is nothing to keep you from asking the D.A. to file criminal charges against a harasser while you also file a civil complaint (legalese for a "lawsuit") yourself. It's entirely up to you how you proceed. You can ask the D.A. to file charges, or you can file your own lawsuit, or you can do both.

5-12 TRAFFIC AND CRIMINAL CHARGES

Let's consider an act of harassment that is prosecuted in the criminal justice system. Assume that a driver is following you down the road, tailgating you and honking his horn, in an attempt to intimidate you into abandoning your right to the road. Then, while waiting at a stoplight, the driver intentionally taps you with his car to further intimidate you. You call the police, and the driver is apprehended.[50] The first thing you must do is be sure that a police report is accurately completed. Once the police report has been completed, it's time for the next step, pressing charges. There are a variety of traffic and criminal charges that the D.A. can bring in a case like this. Although it's possible that some of the following statutes may not have been violated, these are the kinds of violations you should be thinking about when discussing this case with the prosecutor.

Because the laws will vary from state to state, let's assume that the harassment occurred in Maryland. We'll start with the violations of Maryland's Transportation Code:

Section 20-103. *Requires the driver to remain at the scene of an accident*

Section 20-104. *Requires a driver to give information and render aid*

Section 20-105.1. *Requires insurance information to be given*

---

49 *Injuries* is legalese for any violation of your legal rights, including, but not limited to, physical injuries to your person.

50 The police will cite or arrest a driver only if they (1) witness the incident themselves, (2) have sufficient evidence if they didn't witness the incident themselves, or (3) the driver confesses to the incident. Because police rarely witness anticyclist road-rage incidents, the only certain way police will press charges against your harasser is if you have video footage, witnesses, or both.

Section 21-303. *General rules governing overtaking and passing vehicles*

Section 21-310. *Prohibits following too closely*

Section 21-901.1. *Prohibits reckless and negligent driving*

Section 21-901.2. *Prohibits aggressive driving*

Section 21-1117. *Excessive noise prohibited*

Section 21-1209. *Requires drivers to exercise care to avoid collisions with bicycles*

Section 22-401. *Prohibits use of horn except when necessary to ensure safe operation*

During the course of his harassment, the driver committed potential violations of each of these sections of the Transportation Code. But there's more; there are also criminal violations at issue here. Let's look at some of the Maryland Criminal Code violations you should be discussing with the prosecutor:

Section 3-203. *Assault in the second degree (misdemeanor)*

Section 3-204. *Reckless endangerment (misdemeanor)*

Section 3-802. *Stalking (misdemeanor)*

Section 3-803. *Harassment (misdemeanor)*

Section 6-301. *Malicious destruction (misdemeanor)*

Every state will have statutes on the books that make assault and battery a crime. In addition to being offenses in the criminal justice system, assault and battery are tortious acts in the civil justice system. Every state also has reckless driving statutes that may be applicable, depending upon the circumstances of the case. A few states have statutes specifically targeting road rage and cyclist harassment. For example, Oregon recently enacted a statute making vehicular assault of bicyclists or pedestrians a criminal offense.[51] In Maryland, it is illegal to "throw any object at or in the direction of any person riding a bicycle." The same Maryland statute also prohibits opening "the door of any motor vehicle with intent to strike, injure, or interfere with any person riding a bicycle."[52]

When you are discussing the case with the D.A., remember that it's your responsibility to impress upon the D.A. the seriousness of the harassment incident. That's not a legal standard; the D.A. should take every

51 O.R.S. 811.060, Vehicular assault of cyclist or pedestrian (2001).

52 Annotated Code of Maryland, TR Section 21-1209, Throwing object at bicycle, motor scooter, or EPAMD.

case seriously. But sometimes the D.A. doesn't take every case seriously, and that is why it's your responsibility. If the D.A. seems disinterested in pressing appropriate charges, it will be up to you to make your case—as is always the case when you're trying to convince somebody to take some discretionary action. Be polite but firm, and be persuasive: Marshal your facts and the law, and demonstrate to the D.A. why the law fits the facts of your case. Be prepared to discuss what statutes were violated as well as case law interpreting those statutes.

If you've been assaulted, your first step must *always* be to contact law enforcement. As noted above, many cyclists now ride with camera cell phones, and even helmet-mounted video cameras, and if they are assaulted by a motorist—whether it was an attempt to harass them off the road or to force them off the road—they report the incident to law enforcement, complete with evidentiary record.

5-13 VICTIM'S RIGHTS STATUTES

In the criminal justice system, the people are represented by the prosecutor, and the defendant is represented by his or her attorney.[53] This raises a question, however: Who represents the victim of the crime? Until recently, nobody represented the crime victim; her interests were simply not taken into consideration in the criminal justice system. With the advent of victim's rights statutes, the criminal justice system has slowly begun to allow crime victims a limited role in criminal prosecutions. Generally, once criminal charges are filed, the crime victim's rights are triggered. These rights typically include, among others, the right to confer with the prosecutor, the right to be notified of hearings, and the right to be present at hearings. Although the prosecutor still has discretion on how to prosecute the case, the crime victim has the right to be represented by an attorney who will advocate on the crime victim's behalf with the prosecutor and the court, and to contest prosecutorial decisions that do not take the crime victim's interests in justice into account. Thus, by allowing a crime victim the right to be represented by counsel and to contest prosecutorial decisions that are not in the interests of justice, crime victims, through the court, have some limited checking power on prosecutorial discretion.

Today, there are victim's rights statutes in every state; in some states, these rights are enshrined in the state constitution. At the federal level, there are several crime victim's statutes, including the federal Crime

---

53 Depending on the crime, a defendant may even have a constitutional right to be represented by an attorney. Thus, even if the defendant cannot afford an attorney, the court will appoint an attorney to represent the defendant when the defendant has a constitutional right to representation.

Victims Rights Act (CVRA).[54] If you are the victim of a crime, and you want your interests represented in court, consult with an attorney to determine what your rights are in your jurisdiction.[55]

5-14 CITIZEN-INITIATED PROSECUTIONS

Another innovative Oregon statute is the citizen-initiated prosecution. The decision to prosecute is usually made jointly between the D.A. and the law-enforcement officer investigating the offense. But what happens when a cyclist is injured and the authorities decide against pressing charges? Under Oregon's statute, which was enacted in 1999, the cyclist, a pedestrian, or anyone who has witnessed a traffic violation may prosecute his or her own case if the authorities decline to prosecute. This statute has resulted in at least two successful prosecutions by cyclists recently.[56] Although these cases were simple driver error rather than cyclist harassment, the statute is a powerful tool for any cyclist who is harassed by an irate motorist.[57]

5-15 HATE CRIMES

In most states, hate crime legislation addresses crimes committed against what the law calls a "suspect class." Typically, this will include

---

54 Federal Crime Victims Rights Act, 18 U.S.C. 3771 (2000).

55 For more information on victim's rights legislation at the federal and state levels, visit the National Crime Victim Law Institute's online library at http://www.ncvli.org/ncvlilibrary.html. If you are the victim of a crime, you can contact the National Crime Victim Law Institute (NCVLA), at http://www.ncvli.org, for assistance with questions about your rights.

56 Portland, Oregon, bicycle law attorney Ray Thomas was behind the effort to bring this statute to the attention of Oregon cyclists. As a result of that effort, Portland cyclist Mike Reuter became the first cyclist to attempt a citizen-initiated prosecution. On September 22, 2005, Reuter was severely injured by a motorist who ran a red light; the police did not issue a citation to the motorist, so Reuter filed his own complaint, and he successfully prosecuted the motorist on April 5, 2006. This victory was followed by a second victory eight days later, when Portland cyclist Sean Barrett successfully prosecuted the motorist who had injured him when the motorist made a sudden right turn from the left lane, colliding with Barrett in the bicycle lane. Police had refused to issue a citation, so Barrett filed his own complaint and won. These citizen-initiated prosecutions are very useful tools for cyclists, because when the police fail to issue a citation, the motorist will often lie about the accident to his or her insurance company, which makes it more difficult, perhaps even impossible, for the cyclist to be compensated for the motorist's negligence. When the cyclist successfully prosecutes the motorist, that prosecution serves as evidence to the insurance company that their insured motorist was negligent, and the motorist's insurance carrier is likely to stop disputing liability and begin negotiating the amount of compensation to the cyclist. Although the process has been used so far to issue citations to motorists who weren't harassing the cyclists involved, there's no reason that a cyclist who has been intentionally endangered by a motorist who is violating traffic laws (to harass the cyclist) couldn't also prosecute a citation.

57 Citizen-initiated prosecutions may be filed only on traffic violations (they can also be used to prosecute boating violations, wildlife violations, commercial fishing violations, and weights and measures violations), and not for nontraffic criminal offenses.

crimes against persons based on the person's race, religion, ethnicity, gender, and, depending on the state, disability or sexual orientation. Utah takes a different approach. Under the Utah hate crimes statute,[58]

> assault and some acts of criminal mischief [59] qualify as hate crimes if
> - they are committed with the intent to cause a person to fear for his physical safety, or with the intent to damage property, or if
> - they are committed with reason to believe that the act would cause a person to fear for his physical safety, or with reason to believe that it would damage property; and if
> - the act was committed with the intent to cause a person to fear to freely exercise or enjoy any statutory or constitutional right.

It's that intent to cause a person to fear to freely exercise or enjoy any statutory or constitutional right that makes Utah's statute different from statutes in other states, and which brings cyclists under the protection of the hate crimes statute. Typical rights that, if infringed, might transform an assault into a hate crime would include the generic right to the road that is found in most state statutes. Under the laws of Utah, "a person operating a bicycle . . . has all of the rights and is subject to the provisions of [the Traffic Code] applicable to the operator of any other vehicle."[60] The Utah constitution guarantees, among other rights, that "all men have the inherent and inalienable right to enjoy and defend their liberties"[61] and that "no person shall be deprived of life, liberty or property without due process of law."[62] The Constitution of the United States also guarantees that "no person shall . . . be deprived of life, liberty, or property, without due process of law,"[63] and as we saw in Chapter 1, the right to travel is a fundamental personal liberty guaranteed by the U.S. Constitution.

---

58 Found at Utah Code Annotated Section 76-3-203.3.

59 Criminal mischief, where the person "intentionally and unlawfully tampers with the property of another and as a result recklessly endangers human life or human health and safety," may qualify as a hate crime if it is intended to "intimidate or terrorize" another person, under the meaning of the hate crimes statute.

60 Utah Code Annotated Section 41-6a-1102.

61 Constitution of Utah, Article I, Section 1.

62 Constitution of Utah, Article I, Section 7.

63 Constitution of the United States, Fifth Amendment.

If any of these (or other rights) are infringed within the requirements of the hate crimes statute, the crime would meet the definition of a hate crime and could be prosecuted as such.[64]

5-16 CIVIL SUITS

One powerful legal tool that has to this date been underutilized is the civil rights statutes, commonly known as "Section 1983" and "Section 1985"; these monikers refer to the U.S. Code section for the federal civil rights statutes.[65] What's particularly interesting about these statutes is that the person whose rights have been violated prosecutes the case. There is no need to convince a prosecutor that your rights have been violated; you need only convince a jury.

As noted earlier in this chapter, Section 1983 makes it a federal crime for "every person who, under color of any statute, ordinance, regulation, custom, or usage, of any state" to deprive any person of "rights, privileges, or immunities secured by the Constitution and laws." Section 1985 makes it a federal crime "if two or more persons in any state or territory conspire or go in disguise on the highway or on the premises of another, for the purpose of depriving, either directly or indirectly, any person or class of persons of the equal protection of the laws, or of equal privileges and immunities under the laws."[66] Thus, if two or more persons conspired to harass cyclists—for example, two guys driving down the road decide to harass a cyclist—it would constitute a federal crime. There is no corresponding civil rights statute for civil rights violations by individuals, however; there must be a conspiracy in order for this statute to be applicable.

Despite its patina of federal civil rights law, a civil rights suit is simply a civil suit alleging a tortious act: the violation of your civil rights. You don't have to allege a civil rights violation in order to file a civil suit. For example, if you've been injured in an accident, you can file a suit for negligence. But as we've seen, negligence is an unintentional act, while harassment is an intentional act. The difference between negligence and an intentional act is, as you might guess, one of intent. With an intentional act, the defendant must have acted with the intent to cause a tortious injury to the plaintiff, even if the injury suffered wasn't intended. There are several types of intentional torts; the main two that cyclists typically en-

64 Under the Utah hate crimes statute, a hate crime is classified as a third-degree felony.

65 These sections of the Civil Rights Act of 1871, dating back to the post-Civil War Reconstruction era, are codified at 42 U.S.C. 1983 and 42 U.S.C. 1985, respectively, thus their common monikers "Section 1983" and "Section 1985."

66 Section 1985 was also discussed previously under "Media Harassment of Cyclists."

counter when harassed are assault and battery. We've already looked at criminal charges for assault and battery; the next section examines civil lawsuits for assault and for battery.

ASSAULT

Assault is an intentional act by the defendant that creates an apprehension in the plaintiff that a harmful physical contact is imminent. Let's look at a typical kind of tortious assault to see how the law and the facts interact. Suppose you're riding along on your bike, and a motorist comes up fast behind you and lays on the horn; she continues tailgating you while blasting her horn for nearly a mile. Have you been assaulted? There are four elements to assault, each of which must be proved in order to win a judgment for assault:

1. An act by the defendant

2. Intent

3. Apprehension

4. Causation

The first element, an act by the defendant, refers to the willful physical movements by the defendant. For example, suppose a motorist decides to "teach you a lesson" by swerving into you, but without actually making contact with you. In this case, you would have to prove that the defendant was using her arms and hands to steer her car, and to sound her horn, and was using her legs and feet to operate her pedals. Showing the defendant's willful physical movements of operating the vehicle would be required to prove the first element of assault.

To prove the second element, intent, you would need to show that the defendant's act was done with the intent to either (1) inflict a harmful or offensive touching of the plaintiff, or (2) put the plaintiff in apprehension of an imminent harmful or offensive touching. The defendant's intent is a subjective standard, rather than the objective "reasonable person" standard found in a lawsuit for negligence. If you're trying to prove that the defendant intended to inflict a harmful or offensive touching, for example, you must show that the defendant acted with the desire to cause the harmful or offensive touching or believed that the harmful or offensive touching was certain to occur as a result of her act. Alternatively, you must show that the defendant acted with the desire to cause you to believe that a harmful or offensive touching was imminent. It is this desire or belief of the defendant that makes intent a subjective standard.

The third element in a lawsuit for assault is apprehension; this means that the plaintiff was aware of the threat of imminent harmful or offensive touching at the time of the threat. If the motorist swerved at you, intending to scare you, but you were distracted by the scenery and didn't even notice, the necessary apprehension hasn't been created. Note that the harm threatened must be to the person, rather than to property. Thus, the motorist would have to create an apprehension of harm to your person, rather than merely creating the apprehension that she intends to destroy your bike while you're not even riding it.

The final element in a lawsuit for assault is causation; you would need to show that the apprehension was caused by the defendant's act.

If the plaintiff can prove those four elements, the plaintiff will receive a judgment against the defendant for assault. The plaintiff does not need to show emotional distress caused by physical injuries to collect damages, although a showing of these types of damages means the plaintiff can recover damages for those as well.

Now, let's apply the facts of this case to a lawsuit for assault: The driver comes up fast behind you and lays on the horn, and then continues tailgating you while blasting her horn for nearly a mile. You would have to show that the defendant was engaged in the willful physical act of driving her car, that she intended either to inflict a harmful or offensive touching of your person or to put you in apprehension of an imminent or harmful touching, that you were aware of the threat, and that the defendant's act was the cause of that apprehension. If you can prove those elements, the defendant will be held liable for assault and will owe you damages—read: money—for that assault. But what happens once there is physical contact?

BATTERY

In tort law, battery is an intentional act by the defendant that causes a harmful or offensive physical contact. Now let's take a closer look at battery, using a slightly different set of facts. You're at a stoplight, and the driver behind you is honking his horn at you, presumably because he doesn't think cyclists belong on the road. Then it happens: Determined to get your attention, the driver taps your rear wheel with his bumper. Have you been battered? As in assault, there are four elements to battery, each of which must be proved to win a judgment for battery; however, the elements for battery are slightly different from the elements for assault. They are:

1. An act by the defendant

2. Intent

3. Harmful or offensive touching

4. Causation

The first element, an act by the defendant, is the same as for assault; it refers to the willful physical movements by the defendant. In this case, the defendant was using his arms and hands to steer his car, and he was using his legs and feet to operate his pedals. Showing the defendant's willful physical movements in operating the vehicle would be required to prove the first element of battery.

To prove the second element, intent, you would need to show that the defendant's act was done with the intent to inflict a harmful or offensive touching of the plaintiff. As in assault, the defendant's intent is a subjective standard, rather than the objective "reasonable person" standard found in a lawsuit for negligence; you must show that the defendant acted with the desire to cause the harmful or offensive touching or believed that the harmful or offensive touching was certain to occur as a result of his act.

The third element in a suit for battery is harmful or offensive touching; this is different from the third element in assault—apprehension of imminent harmful or offensive touching. In assault, you have apprehension that you will be subjected to harmful or offensive touching; in battery, you have actually been subjected to that harmful or offensive touching. What does the law mean by "harmful or offensive touching," though? Simply, harmful touching is a touching that causes injury, while offensive touching is a touching that would offend a reasonable person's sense of dignity. Although harmful or offensive touching generally refers to a harmful or offensive touching of a person's body, it can also occur if the defendant touches something so closely associated with the plaintiff that the touching is equivalent to touching the person. For example, knocking a person's hat off his head would be a harmful or offensive touching.

The final element in a lawsuit for battery is causation; you would need to show that the harmful or offensive touching was caused by the defendant's act.

Now, let's apply the facts of this case to a lawsuit for battery: After you ignore the driver's honking, he hits you with his vehicle. You would need to show that the defendant was engaged in the willful physical act of driving his car; that he intended to inflict a harmful or offensive touching of your person, including your bicycle; that there was a harmful or offensive touching of your person; and that the defendant's act was the cause of that harmful or intentional touching.[67]

Now, one final point to keep in mind. No police officer was present to witness events, so how will you be able to bring charges? Simple. You are the witness, so it is your testimony that will be introduced as evidence. Although you are not required to step forward with corroborating witnesses (witnesses who will support your testimony), the more witnesses who can support your testimony, the more believable your testimony will be, and the less believable the driver will be if he denies your account of events.

CONCLUSION

The average automobile is 7 times the size of a bicycle with rider; the automobile typically weighs between 1 and 2 tons, whereas the typical bicycle with rider weighs between 175 and 275 pounds. This mass differential makes the cyclist a vulnerable user of the road, leaving cyclists at the mercy of motorists. When motorists are sometimes negligent— an inevitable fact of life—it is cyclists who bear the brunt of the damage. More sinisterly, when the motorist's mass differential is coupled with the widespread bias against cyclists, and the sometimes murderous rage directed against them, the cyclist's life—not to mention the cyclist's right to the road—is in danger.

As we've seen, cyclists are not entirely defenseless. They do have recourse under the law, and as I've argued, they must use that recourse when their rights are violated. Nevertheless, cyclists do not receive equal treatment under the law, beginning with the inequities in the design and execution of the transportation infrastructure. In turn, those inequities create a vicious feedback loop of bias against cyclists, which is expressed in the continuing treatment of cyclists as second-class users of the roads. Therefore, one fundamental step toward leveling the playing field for cyclists must be to accord cyclists equal consideration in the design and execution of transportation infrastructure. When transportation planners design infrastructure, cyclists must not be treated as an

---

67 Note that a "harmful or offensive touching" does not require that a physical injury result, although if a physical injury does occur as a result, the touching will certainly be considered "harmful." In a case for battery, the touching can be "offensive" rather than "harmful." In fact, offensive touching is not limited to offensive touching of the person's body; it can include offensive touching of something so closely associated with the person–for example, knocking the hat off somebody's head–that the touching is considered the equivalent of an offensive touching of the person's body. Because the bicycle is so closely associated with the cyclist's person, I believe it can be proved that an offensive touching of the bicycle *while the cyclist is mounted* is the equivalent of an offensive touching of the cyclist's person, and thus constitutes one of the elements of battery.

afterthought; their needs must receive the same consideration that is accorded the needs of motorists.

That does not mean that cyclists must be treated exactly like motorists—far from it. Instead, it means that the needs of cyclists must be addressed. In some instances, this will mean that cyclists will receive *more* consideration than motorists, reflecting the vulnerability of cyclists in those instances. For example, cyclists are particularly vulnerable to collisions with motorists at intersections. "Equal consideration" in the design of infrastructure will take this vulnerability into account, rather than leaving cyclists at the mercy of the hordes of distracted drivers. Finally, "equal consideration" will mean that where road conditions are suitable, cyclists and motor vehicles will share the road, and where sharing the road puts cyclists at a disadvantage, the infrastructure will provide cycling facilities that can mitigate that disadvantage.

Cyclists also receive unequal treatment in the enforcement of laws. Law enforcement can and must do more to eliminate the anticycling bias that results in the unequal treatment of cyclists; to that end, police departments must establish procedures requiring law-enforcement officers to impartially investigate bicycle/car accidents.

Cyclists also receive unequal treatment in the enforcement of laws when the criminal justice system fails to take cyclist harassment seriously. Violent physical attacks against cyclists, whether intended to merely frighten the cyclist or to actually injure the cyclist, are directed against the cyclist's exercise and enjoyment of fundamental rights, and they must be recognized as such by law-enforcement agencies and the criminal justice system and dealt with accordingly. As it now stands, an indifferent justice system too often leaves cyclists to defend themselves against violent efforts to remove them from the road. In what other context would either law enforcement or the criminal justice system tolerate assault with a deadly weapon? This must change. "Equal treatment" must also mean a concerted effort to protect cyclists from those who would use violence—or even the threat of violence—to violate their civil and legal rights. To that end, the state legislatures must recognize cyclists as vulnerable users of the road and establish prohibitions against assaulting them that reflect the seriousness of the crime; in turn, law-enforcement agencies and prosecutors must take these assaults seriously, investigating cases and bringing the offenders to trial. Although cyclists have had the right to the road for over a century, that right will not be secure until cyclists receive equal treatment under the law.

6

What You Need to Know about Bicycle Theft

INTRODUCTION

The "Denver Ring" was notorious—although nobody really called these mysterious thieves the "Denver Ring" until they were arrested in Denver in November 1895—for stealing bikes in towns throughout the Midwest, breaking them down for shipment, and selling them in other towns throughout the region. The first known bike thief in the Midwest—though not part of the same ring—had been arrested the year before in Minneapolis, after he had switched from stealing buggies to stealing bicycles. He was apprehended with several bicycles that had been repainted after the serial numbers were filed off. The next bike-theft ring to hit the Midwest operated out of Chicago, which had an estimated 200,000 bicycles on the roads in 1896. Stealing bikes in Chicago, the members of the ring would then sell the bikes in Cincinnati, St. Louis, and Indianapolis.

In New York, some bike thieves simply loitered around, watching and waiting, until somebody left a bike outside "for just a minute"—and that's less than the time it would take the thief to ride off. Other thieves simply rode off with bikes they were "test riding"; one notorious thief's M.O. was to make a gentlemanly offer to fix a nonexistent problem on a passing woman's bike; the last sight she'd have of the bike would be the "gentleman" riding off with it.

The situation called for measures to be taken, and American business stepped up to the plate. Yale and Towne Lock Company increased production of its locks in response to increased demand, and the National Bicycle Protective Company began selling theft insurance for $2.50. In fact, if a cyclist wished, for an extra $1.50 he could purchase collision insurance; as a result, when automobiles began appearing on the roads, the concept of collision insurance had already been established, and it was soon adopted by motorists. The Wheelman's Protective Society offered a different type of service: registration for bicycles, with claims of a 40 percent recovery rate for those that were registered and then stolen. The League of American Wheelmen began selling their own theft protection, issuing plates identifying members' bicycles and offering rewards for the recovery of members' stolen bikes.

Bicycle theft continued, of course. Holdup men began to realize that bicyclists were easy prey, cycling as they often were out on lonely roads, even after dark. In response to rampant robbery, cyclists began to arm themselves for their rides. Again, American business stepped up. Sears, Roebuck and Company began offering a "bicycle rifle" in 1898; it could be either fired as a rifle or "collapsed" as a pistol, in which form it was carried in a holster when it was not warding off highway robbers. This was perhaps the most ingenious bicycle armament, but cyclists had begun arming themselves before the bicycle rifle became available; the *New York Post* reported in 1896 that so many cyclists had begun carrying guns that the arms industry was experiencing a boom it hadn't anticipated.

Bicycle theft continues today. In most large cities, a bicycle is stolen every thirty seconds. In 1994, the FBI reported that bike theft was up 10 percent, even though theft overall had decreased by 14 percent. College campuses are particularly popular with bike thieves. A four-year college student had a 53 percent chance of having a bike stolen in 1994. By 2001, however, bike theft at one university campus—the University of California at Davis—had decreased by a dramatic 73 percent. This drop was attributed to a combination of increased campus police attention, improved bike racks, and an on-campus bike-theft education program.[1]

It is estimated that somewhere between 800,000 and 2 million bicycles—worth an astounding $50 million, an amount higher than the annual take from bank robberies[2]—are stolen annually. The precise number is difficult to determine, because a relatively low proportion of these thefts—somewhere between 20 and 33 percent—are reported to law enforcement. Remarkably, 48 percent of stolen bikes are recovered by police; however, only 5 percent of stolen bikes are returned to their owners. This low rate of return results from problems in existing bicycle registration systems; few bicycles are registered to begin with, and when they are registered, police departments are able to identify only those registered with their own department. There is no shared registration database through which law enforcement may match bicycles with owners, even among nearby jurisdictions, and so recovered bicycles usually remain unclaimed in police impoundment until they are auctioned off. The high rate of bicycle theft creates a chilling effect on bicycling; counter to intuition, bicycle sales—particularly sales of high-quality bicycles—and interest in bicycling are reduced because of the fear and perceived risk of theft.

Many cyclists give the topic of bike theft little real thought, sometimes not even buying a lock. That's a big mistake, because when it comes to bike theft, an ounce of protection is easily worth more than a pound of cure. Study stolen bike listings, and you'll begin to see a pattern: The stolen bikes were locked with cheap locks, locked improperly, and most often, simply not locked at all. There are, in fact, many simple steps that you can take that will not only greatly decrease your chances of falling

---

1   "Patrols, Tips, Precautions Help Put Brakes on Bike Thefts," *Dateline UCDavis*, June 15, 2001.

2   "Chasing My Stolen Bicycle," *San Francisco Bay Guardian*, February 13, 2007.

victim to bike theft, but also greatly increase your chances of recovering your bike if it is stolen.

How Bike Thieves Operate

"The problem here is that we have so many bikes, high-dollar bikes, and these kids are not getting good locks. The thieves, they're going after cheap locks, not cheap bikes."

—*University of Texas Police Sergeant Donna Maga*[3]

Bike thieves run the gamut from kids to opportunists, from drug addicts looking for quick money to semiprofessional and professional bike-theft rings. Thus, the level of sophistication—both in recognizing which bikes to target and in being able to defeat the locks—will vary from thief to thief. Common theft locations vary by time of day; schoolyards and playgrounds are popular daytime theft locations, while lawns, porches, and garages are popular nighttime theft locations. Bicycle theft can happen anywhere, but college towns, and in particular college campuses, are prime operating areas for bike thieves. Although most people never see the theft of their bike in progress, bike thieves often operate in the open, stealing bikes despite the presence of witnesses. Bike thieves have even stolen bikes under the watchful eyes of security cameras, security guards, and law-enforcement officers.[4] For bike thieves, the key to a successful theft is the ease, speed, and nonchalance with which they can take the bike. Consider these eyewitness accounts of bike theft:

"The thieves were two men. In broad daylight, with people around, they used bolt cutters and cut my cable lock, then put my bike in their SUV and drove off. The theft was called in to the police before I even knew about it. The man who took my bike actually looked right at a passerby and said hello all nice and nonchalantly, then stole my bike anyway."

"My bike was stolen—it was 7:00 P.M., bright out, and busy on the street. A woman who was parking right beside the thief challenged

---

3 "Stop Thief!" *Austin Chronicle*, November 26, 1999.

4 A good lock and good locking technique are necessary for bike security; if you always use a technique as your primary security method *and* supplement it by locking your bike in the presence of security personnel or law-enforcement officers, you *may* increase your margin of security. If you leave your bike unlocked or poorly locked, but in the presence of security guards or law-enforcement officers, your bike is not secure. You may return to find that your bike has been stolen and that there are no witnesses. Bike thieves work quickly; sometimes they brazenly cut locks and steal bikes even though they know they've been spotted by a witness.

*him when she saw his bolt cutter, and he gave her the finger and
rode away. He cut through a wire rope lock quickly. I called the
police about 10 minutes after it happened. I spoke with the witness
and learned the man's identifying features, thinking the cops could
cruise around the neighborhood with their eyes peeled since the
crime had just occurred. It took the officer TWO HOURS to arrive. I'd called 3 times in those 2 hours and talked with whomever I
could, and was told by one unsympathetic officer that all of the cops
were out catching the "bad guys." When the officer finally arrived,
he showed some empathy and expressed frustration at the increase
of this kind of crime. He said the thief would almost definitely not
do jail time if caught, that he'd be put on probation, and probably
be required to do community service. Not much of a deterrent."*

*"A friend and I were sitting outside a pizza place—it was still light
out. We had our two bikes locked to a bike rack about twenty feet
away. I saw someone walk up to the rack and squat down in front
of my bike. I ran up to him, yelling, and saw that he had a pair
of eighteen inch bolt cutters on my lock (it was one of the stout,
inch-thick cable locks, but who knows if it would have held up). He
jumped up and cocked the bolt cutters back to swing at me. The
confrontation was pretty intense. We yelled at each other for a
minute, and then he hopped on his beater bike and rode off. Another
guy was standing around, and he started telling me he had just
met this guy, and had no idea he was a thief. Someone sitting at a
table (ten feet away from the bikes!) pulled me aside and said that
these two had been hanging out together and seemed to know each
other well. Further, this second guy had been riding back and forth,
scouting out these bikes for several minutes. He hopped on his bike
and rode away while the witness was telling me all this. Both men
were late thirties to early forties, pretty scroungy looking, on beat-
up mountain bikes."*

*"I had stopped for coffee at the end of my morning bike commute.
While in line at the coffee shop, I saw someone ride up on another
bike, pull out a pair of cable cutters and snip through the cable lock
on my bike. I rushed outside, pushed him off my bike just as he was
about to ride away, and confronted him. We got into a fight (in his
corner: 6 foot 2-ish, around 200 pounds and alleged to be high on
methamphetamine; in my corner: 5 foot 9, 150 pounds and I hadn't
even had my morning coffee yet), and he hit me in the head with his
cable cutters. It took three "Good Samaritans" to intercede, stop the*

*beating and hold him down until the police arrived. I ended up with
six stitches in my head, $700 in out-of-pocket medical expenses and
a missed day of work to make up. One of the Good Samaritans got
bitten—fortunately, the thief appears to be HIV and Hepatitis C
negative. The police pulled a six-inch knife out of the guy's pocket—
lucky for me that he didn't think to use it. The thief pled guilty to
assault and got nine months in jail, of which he had served over
half at the time of sentencing. One of the defense's main arguments
appeared to be that I had provoked the attack, and he had merely
defended himself. The case never went before a jury, so I have no
idea how that would have played, but the experience of having to
face the thief in court and be cross-examined on the whole thing
was extremely unpleasant."*

Each of these eyewitness accounts has at least one element in common. The thief had targeted a bike locked with an easily cut cable lock.
It's clear from these and other accounts that, unless you're standing right
there watching your bike, a cable lock won't prevent the theft of your
bike; at most, the cable lock might alert you, or a witness, that a theft is
in progress. That's only slightly more protection than not locking your
bike at all.

In fact, any bike lock—no matter how well constructed—can be defeated by a determined professional. One popular video making the
rounds on the Internet shows a "thief" stealing a bike in New York City
in broad daylight. The "thief"—actually, the owner of the bike, who is
making the video—uses various bolt cutters, hand tools, and power tools
to defeat the locks on the bike. At one point, a passerby even stops to
help. Clearly, from watching this video, there's nothing that can be done
to stop a thief from stealing your bike, right? Well, not quite. There's a
world of difference between the psychology of a guy who's noisily cutting the lock on his own bike and the psychology of a thief who's trying
to steal your bike before you come back and catch him in the act. It's an
interesting video about the psychology of passersby, but it shouldn't be
taken as proof that your bike can't be protected.

It is true that a professional bike-theft crew can defeat any lock, given
enough time and motivation. However, it's also clear from the vast majority of theft reports that most bike thefts do not involve professional crews
noisily cutting the best locks in broad daylight. According to most bike-
theft reports, the owner left the bike unlocked and unattended, often
"just for a minute" while going into a store. Shocking, isn't it, to think that
a bike thief would take advantage of you like that? Nevertheless, the fact
that this is actually the most common method of bike theft should give

you some indication of the relatively rare threat of a professional bike-theft crew taking ten minutes to cut through your U-lock with power tools in broad daylight.[5]

The next most common type of theft is where the owner had the bike locked with a cable lock, which the bike thief defeated with a pair of bolt cutters. As eyewitness accounts confirm, this method of bike theft is shockingly easy; a pair of bolt cutters can cut through a cheap padlock in less than a second, with no noise to attract attention. One second to cut the lock—a slight bit longer perhaps to cut a cable if there's no padlock—and your bike itself is the getaway vehicle.

A much smaller number of bike-theft reports indicate that the victim was using a U-lock but did not use proper locking technique. For example, one theft victim reported using a U-lock to lock together the two ends of a cable lock. Although the U-lock cannot be cut with a pair of bolt cutters, the cable can be cut, and thus, the U-lock was being used improperly. One very common improper locking technique is to "lock" the bike with a U-lock securing the front wheel only. A bike locked this way isn't really locked at all; a thief can easily release the quick release on the front wheel and walk off with the rest of the bike.

Bike thieves regularly take advantage of other improper locking techniques. One common bike-theft technique is to lure a bike owner into locking a bike to something that looks secure but isn't. For example, thieves have been known to remove bolts on bike racks and walk off with the bike. In fact, some thieves set traps for unsuspecting cyclists, removing the bolts beforehand, sometimes even replacing the bolt heads so the rack looks secure—and waiting for a cyclist to lock up to the rack and walk away. Once the cyclist has left, the thief lifts the rack, takes the bike, and then replaces the rack, setting the trap for the next unsuspecting cyclist. Thieves have used this technique on street signposts as well, lifting the post—called a "sucker pole"—and removing the bike, then setting the trap for the next cyclist. Another technique they use on street signs is to disassemble the sign from the post and slide the bike over the top of the pole. Aluminum poles, chain-link fences, and wooden objects such as small trees and wooden railings can all be—and are—easily cut by thieves.

5 Bikes left locked outside overnight are at much greater risk than bikes left locked in broad daylight. Sergeant Doug Schulz of the University of Washington Police Department, for example, reported that bike thieves have been caught on the UW campus "with everything from portable power saws to blow torches." "Bike Thieves Beware: Officer of the Year Excels at Recovering Stolen Bikes," *University Week*, August 18, 2005.

PHOTO 6.1 Improper Lockup, Front Wheel Only

What's rarely, if ever, seen in the theft reports is a thief taking a bike that's been properly locked with a high-quality lock. That doesn't mean it can't happen; it's just rare.

So what happens to all of these stolen bikes? Many thieves are looking for quick money to buy drugs; for these thieves, the fastest way to get that money is to take the stolen bike to a pawn shop or bike shop that sells used bikes. When they run out of pawn shops—pawning lots of bikes kind of raises red flags, after all, because the pawn shop loses its money, at least in theory, if the police discover a stolen bike in the shop—they sell them at bargain rates on the street.

Bike-theft rings will also sell stolen bikes on the street and at flea markets. On the street, stolen bicycles are used as a form of currency, easily traded for drugs, cash, and sex.[6] Many stolen bikes are resold in the same city they were stolen in, or nearby, often stripped of their components, which are replaced with components from other stolen bikes to make them harder to identify. Others, however, are shipped by "fences" to other cities, where they will be sold on the street, at flea markets, and even online, parted or whole. In 2004, San Francisco police discovered one bike thief with auctions for over twenty stolen bikes in his eBay account, and another twenty in storage awaiting sale.[7] Large numbers of

6 "Chasing My Stolen Bicycle."

7 Ibid.

stolen bikes are reportedly shipped out of Miami and New Jersey for export to Mexico and Southeast Asia.

Preventing Theft

6-1 DOCUMENTING YOUR BIKE

Preventing theft must begin as soon as you acquire your bike. Before you do anything else, you must begin to document your bike. The very first piece of documentation will *always* be your receipt. If you buy the bike new, the bike shop will give you a receipt. If you buy a used bike, ask for a receipt. The receipt should include:

1. The date of the sale
2. The name and contact information of the seller
3. The name and contact information of the buyer
4. A description of the bike, including the make, model, year (if known), serial number, color, condition, and any other relevant information about the bike
5. The purchase price
6. Any additional information that would be relevant to the sale

Establish a rule for yourself: There's no excuse for not having a receipt for your bike. Once you have your receipt, begin a file and place the receipt inside; having a receipt won't be much help to you if you can't find it when you need it. If it's a new bike, you will also receive an owner's manual with your bike. Keep your owner's manual in the file with your receipt; it will be an important document if you have a product liability problem with your bike. If you buy a used bike, ask the seller for the owner's manual. Often the seller won't know where it is even if he or she does have it, but it can't hurt to ask.

This is a good start, but you're not done documenting your bike yet. Now you will want to establish a photographic record of your bike. Take several photos, documenting the entire bike, as well as close-ups of significant identification features. Anytime your bike's appearance changes—for example, if you paint it, or (ouch!) gouge a major scratch into it, or change a component—you should update your photographic record. These marks will help you identify your bike if it is stolen.

So now you've got a receipt that proves you own your bike, an owner's manual, and photographs that show what the bike looks like. Now you need to protect your record. Keep digital copies on your hard drive, and remember to back them up. Keep print copies in a file, and place that file in fireproof storage with your other valuable documents, such as deeds, automobile titles, insurance policies, and passports. Anytime you have your bike serviced, save the receipt. This is especially important if you don't have a receipt for your bike; a record of service receipts will help establish ownership when you don't have a purchase receipt. In addition, if you make expensive upgrades to your bike, save the receipts, because they will help establish the value of your bike. Add all of your receipts to your documentation file.

6-2 IDENTIFYING YOUR BIKE

Let's say you own a bike—a white ACME 2000 Pedalmaster—and it is stolen. You report the theft, but you don't know the serial number because you never got around to writing it down. Unfortunately, there are several hundred white ACME 2000 Pedalmasters in your town. Even if a stolen white ACME 2000 Pedalmaster is recovered by the police department, you can't prove it's *your* stolen white ACME 2000 Pedalmaster, and the police department will not release the bike to you without that proof.

Every bike will have an identifying serial number stamped into its frame by the manufacturer. Most serial numbers are located on the underside of the bottom bracket shell, where the crankset passes through the frame. This serial number *must* be documented in your records, either on a purchase receipt or on a separate document—you can just record the number on a piece of paper and place it in your document file, if necessary. The important point is that you must record the serial number now, while the bike is in your possession, as soon as you've begun your documentation file.

This *should* be enough to identify your bike if it is stolen and then recovered. However, there's no guarantee that the serial number will be reported properly by a pawn shop, or that the police department will take the time to match the reported serial number with the stolen-bike reports. In some instances, bike thieves have been known to file serial numbers off, thus making it impossible to identify the bike as stolen if it is found in their possession.

For these reasons, it is often suggested that bicycle owners also make unique identifying marks on their bicycles. For example, some college police departments and national bicycle registries suggest engraving a unique identifying number, such as your driver's license number, into your bike frame.[8] If any police department in your state recovers your bike, officers will be able to match the driver's license number to you, which means they will be able to notify you that your bike has been recovered. On the other hand, the thief can file that mark or number off as well. For this reason, some people even engrave the number or mark in two locations on the bike in the hope that the thief will miss one of them. If the police recover your bike, and it has an engraved number or other distinguishing mark—something that a thief might not recognize as an "identification" mark—in a hidden location, you will have proof that the bike is yours even if the serial number is filed off.

If you do engrave a unique identifying mark into your frame, remember to document it. Record your unique number in your documentation file, and take photographs of any unique distinguishing marks or numbers to make sure you have all the evidence you may need, should you end up having to prove ownership later on.

6-3 REGISTERING YOUR BIKE

Now that you've got your bike fully documented, you will want to register your bike. First, make sure that you add your bike to your homeowner's or renter's insurance policy. If you are a renter and don't have renter's insurance, get some. It's surprisingly affordable, and it will protect you against loss of your possessions, including your bike. Adding the bike to your homeowner's or renter's policy will also provide you with liability coverage in case you cause an accident. Coverage limits will apply—your bike will be insured only for the maximum amount specified in your policy—but you can get optional expanded coverage for an additional fee. Alternatively, the better lock companies offer guarantees with coverage that will far exceed the coverage limits on your insurance policy. There are several drawbacks to the lock guarantee coverage, however: The coverage is for a limited duration of only one to three years; the guarantee covers only your bike and not your accessories; the coverage is limited if you also have homeowner's or renter's insurance; and, most important, the lock guarantee doesn't cover you for liability the way an insurance policy does. For these reasons, you should be sure to have a homeowner's or renter's insurance policy with the amount of coverage you need specified.

You should also register your bike with several sources. The better bike locks will come with an antitheft guarantee, and when you register your bike with the lock company, the guarantee covers your bike against

---

8   A unique identifying number is called an "Owner Applied Number," or OAN.

theft. When you pay the higher price for the better lock, you have the option of accepting this guarantee—usually for an additional fee, and for a limited period of one to three years, however—so take advantage of this service and register your bike with the lock company. If your bike is covered by homeowner's or renter's insurance, the lock guarantee will cover the deductible on your claim—typically $250 to $500.

In some states, bike dealers are required by law to provide you with registration materials when you buy a bike. However, bike shops don't always comply with this requirement; if your state law requires bike dealers to provide registration materials, but your bike shop does not do this, ask them for the registration forms. Whether your state requires bike shops to provide registration materials or not, you should register your bike with your local police department (or fire department, depending on the city). In some jurisdictions, you're required by law to do this, but even if you are not, it is a good idea to register. The police will record your bike's serial number and your personal information—name, address, and so on—which will help them match the bike to you if it is stolen and recovered. Additionally, you will be issued a "license number" on a sticker that is to be applied to your bike. The sticker may help convince a thief to steal somebody else's unregistered bike instead of yours, and evidence of a sticker that has been scratched off serves as probable cause for a police investigation of bike theft in some jurisdictions. Remember, however, that registration with the police department is for a limited period of time—often five years—and must be renewed when it expires for your bike to remain registered.

Despite the benefits of registration, some people are under the mistaken impression that if they don't have identifying marks on their bikes, and don't register their bikes, the police won't be able to identify them during a stop for a traffic violation. This idea is nonsense. The police are fully authorized to demand proper identification if they have probable cause to issue a citation, and they can place you under custodial arrest if you fail to produce proper identification. In short, there is no real reason *not* to register your bike.

If you're a college student, your campus police department may also require you to register your bike. If your bike is stolen and campus police catch the thief with your bike—it happens more than people realize—they can prove theft if your bike is registered. Campus police departments are often far more aggressive about finding and recovering stolen bikes than are their city counterparts; recording your serial number and registering your bike with your campus police department will vastly increase your odds of recovering your bike if it's stolen. Many thieves work college campuses precisely because the pickings are so easy and the risks are so low. Even if the police catch the thief in the act, however, and thus know the bike is stolen, they can't match it with the owner if it's not registered. Again, there's no real reason *not* to register your bike with campus police, so get it registered.

Also consider registering your bike with a national bicycle registry. For an inexpensive fee, you receive national registration of your bike, which can permit coordination among multiple police agencies across the country.

If your bike is stolen, state law governs how long police must hold it until it is disposed of. Typically, that period will be from three to six months. If the police can determine with a reasonable level of assurance that you are the owner of the bike, they are required to return it to you; otherwise, they will have some means of disposing of it, such as through public auction or a giveaway program. One little-known fact is that many cyclists accidentally leave their bikes on public-transit vehicles; the transit agencies also hold the bikes for a specified period before disposing of them. Your stolen bike may be accidentally left on the bus by a drugged-out thief—so even if you know you didn't leave your bike on the bus, you should check with your local transit agency in case your bike is sitting in the agency's impound yard. Whether your bike is stolen or simply lost, be sure to check with any appropriate agencies to see if it has been recovered.

6-4 TAKING SECURITY MEASURES

There are many approaches to bike security, but they all have one philosophy in common: If a bear is chasing you and your friend, you don't have to run faster than the bear; you just have to run faster than your friend.

What? Bears? Running? Here's what experienced cyclists mean. A bike thief is going to look for the easiest bike to steal. And if there are two equally easy bikes to steal, the thief is going to steal the better of the two. Now, depending on the sophistication of the thief, the "better" bike might mean the flashiest-looking bike, or it might mean the more expensive bike. But regardless of the thief's level of sophistication, the thief will always target the easier of the two bikes to steal.[9] And that is analogous to the bear chasing you and your friend. In order to keep the thief at bay, your bike needs to be more difficult to steal than other bikes in the immediate vicinity. The thief gets the easier bike, just as the bear gets the

9 This will not necessarily hold true for professional thieves targeting a specific bike; some thieves even "steal to order." Nevertheless, the vast majority of bike thefts are committed by thieves looking for an easy target.

slower runner. Now let's look at some strategies that experienced cyclists use to "run faster than their friend" in the urban forest.

PROPER LOCK SELECTION

The first, most obvious strategy for keeping your bike safe is to choose a high-quality lock. If your bike is an expensive, top-of-the-line model, the cost of a high-quality lock in relation to your bike is negligible. Even if your bike is a modest commuter that isn't worth much more than the cost of the lock, spend the extra money and buy the best lock you can; it is a small investment, but it could save you from having to spend an even greater amount of money to replace your stolen bike.

Your lock should be a name-brand lock, made from tool-hardened steel, from Kryptonite, Onguard, Abus, or an equivalent manufacturer. Avoid low-cost "look-alikes," because they don't "perform alike." One good source for lock information is http://www.soldsecure.com/Leisure. htm, which publishes an annual review of locks based on solid testing data. The locks that receive a "gold" rating from Soldsecure will be the best-quality locks. Of course, these locks are the most expensive locks, but you get what you pay for. In this case, you get a lock that will defeat all but the most determined professional thief, and a bicycle replacement guarantee that will supplement your homeowner's insurance policy by covering the cost of your deductible, which can be as high as $250 to $500. The higher the lock quality, the higher the guaranteed replacement value. Be sure to read the guarantee, though, because certain rules apply. First, you will have a limited period in which to register your bike (usually two weeks), and this includes sending in a copy of your sales receipt or a bike dealer's appraisal of your bike's market value.[10] Second, the guarantee will be for a limited period of one to three years.[11] Third, the guarantee may be limited to paying your deductible if you have homeowner's insurance on your bike. And fourth, if your bike is stolen, you will have to follow the company's instructions for proving the theft—they don't just hand out new bicycles to anybody and everybody who claims to have lost a bike.

There are two basic lock types that you should consider. One is a chain lock; the high-quality chain locks are *very* heavy-duty, with links and locks that can't be cut with a pair of bolt cutters. The other type is a

10 Insurance companies always prefer to pay you Actual Cash Value (ACV) on your loss. ACV is an estimated value that considers the age and condition of the bicycle at the time of the loss. When you make a claim on your policy, be sure to submit an appraisal of "Replacement Value"–what it would cost you to replace the bike– instead of accepting the insurance company's lower ACV offer.

11 Due to state law, in New York the program is an insurance program, rather than a guarantee.

PHOTO 6.2 Brand-Name U-Lock

U-lock. If you choose a U-lock, select the smallest size that you can lock your bike with. The idea is to prevent thieves from gaining a hold from which to leverage your lock open.[12] Make sure it is the flat-key type and not the cylinder-key type; the cylinder-key types are older and were removed from the market when it was discovered that they could be picked with a ballpoint pen.

Regardless of which type of lock you choose—and some people use both, to further hamper thieves—there is one other type of lock you should consider: locking skewers to replace the quick release on your wheels and seatpost. Many people who have locked up a bike have nevertheless returned to discover a wheel or saddle missing. Replacing your quick releases with locking skewers will keep these parts where they belong—on your bike. If you don't use locking skewers, you should remove your front wheel and lock it to your rear wheel with your U-lock,

---

12 Although U-locks are strong, they can still be defeated with enough leverage. Thieves can place a car jack in the "U" and slowly force it to break, or put a lever into the "U" and twist it. Thieves have also used the bike itself as a lever to pry the lock open, twisting the bike until the lock breaks. This works only with cheap U-locks, though; with expensive ones, the bike frame bends first. Thieves have been known to hammer against U-locks on the ground in an attempt to smash them open, and there have been reports of the earlier U-locks—the ones with barrel-type lock cylinders—being picked with a ballpoint pen. In addition to these simple techniques for breaking U-locks, there are more extreme methods that professional thieves sometimes use, such as freezing the lock mechanism with liquid nitrogen in order to shatter it with a hammer, or cutting it with power tools. In its rating tests, Soldsecure noted that it took ten minutes to cut the best locks with portable power tools. Others have claimed to cut U-locks in forty seconds with the best power tools.

and take your saddle with you. Obviously, locking skewers are easier to deal with.

PROPER LOCKING TECHNIQUE

Once you have selected a lock, you need to use proper locking technique to secure your bike. If you're using a U-lock, you should secure your bike as shown in Photo 6.3. Do not place the U-lock so low that it touches the ground; a lock in contact with the ground can be smashed with a hammer in an attempt to force it open. Securing your bike with two U-locks, or a U-lock and a chain lock, will prevent a thief from using your entire bike as a lever to pry open the lock and will really slow a thief down. Select a sturdy steel rack that is set in concrete. If the rack is thin steel or aluminum tubing, look for a better rack. Thieves have been known to cut through flimsy racks. If the rack is not set in concrete, inspect the bolts to make sure they haven't been tampered with. Also make sure that the rack can't easily be disassembled. If it's held together with just nuts and bolts, don't lock up to it. Likewise, don't lock up to street signs, because they are easily disassembled by a determined thief.

Choose a public, visible, well-lit area with pedestrian traffic in which to lock up. If you lock up to a rack that has numerous bikes attached to it, the rack will likely draw the attention of bike thieves; however, your securely locked bike will be a tougher target than the poorly locked bikes

PHOTO 6.3 Proper Lockup Method

next to it, so a thief looking for easy prey will move on to the poorly locked bikes. If you have an expensive bike, you will have to add an extra layer of caution into your strategy to guard against that one thief who might think your bike is worth the extra effort. Never lock up at the same time and place day after day; vary your routine. If a real professional—the kind who can defeat any lock—sees your expensive bike, he's going to study it to see what type of lock you use and what your routine is, then come back with the proper tools to break your lock when he knows it is safe to do so.

BEATER, CAMOUFLAGE, OR LOUD AND PROUD?

Many people simply refuse to let an expensive bike out of their sight even when it's locked. If they must leave a bike unattended, they have a "beater" bike for that purpose.[13] They still lock it securely, but it's a less tempting target. Others go so far as to camouflage their expensive bike, spray-painting it, scratching it, and covering it with tape or stickers, all in an effort to disguise its true nature. This probably works for the unsophisticated thief, but a true professional bike thief will recognize the thoroughbred beneath the uglified exterior. Just as you would.

THE ARMS RACE

Say you've invested in a proper lock, and you're using proper locking technique. Is there anything else to worry about? Unfortunately, yes. Anything that can be removed from your bike—basically everything that attaches to the frame—and isn't locked can be stolen. Though you can take some measures to defeat this—removing your accessories when you lock up, and filling in the Allen bolt heads with silicone, for instance—you can only slow down the unprepared thief. It's an arms race, really, between cyclists and thieves. And even when you defeat the thief, some thieves will take revenge on you by vandalizing your bike. For these reasons, it's not a good idea to leave your bike locked up unattended for long periods, and if you must, it's probably a good idea to lock up your beater instead.[14] Even at home, proper security techniques dictate that

---

13 A "beater" bike is a low-value bike that cyclists ride instead of their higher-value bike when a threat of theft or poor weather conditions exist.

14 If parts are stolen from your bike, *do not* leave your vandalized bike locked where it is; once a bike has had a part stolen, it seems to bring thieves out of the woodwork. If one wheel has been stolen, they seem to figure, why not the other wheel? And then the seatpost. And then the brakes. Until there's nothing left to steal . . . so then they start bending the frame, until there's absolutely nothing usable left on the bike. Eventually, the city sends a crew out to cut your bike free and send it off for disposal–a sad end. If you've had a part stolen, you should remove your bike immediately, before more damage is done.

your bike should be locked when you're not riding it; remember, theft from balconies, garages, and even from inside homes, apartments, and buildings does happen.

Okay, you've followed all of these precautions. Is that all you need to do to protect yourself? The answer, as you might suspect, is still no.

THE ROUGH STUFF

A man who allegedly opened fire on two San Francisco police offi-cers who were responding to a reported bicycle theft over the week-end was charged Tuesday with two counts of attempted murder. Francisco Valle, 50, also faces felony burglary and firearms charges, and if convicted could spend life in prison. He was arraigned Tuesday in Superior Court, where bail was set at $1 million. He remains in custody. Police say they received a call early Saturday from a resident on the 2000 block of the Great Highway who re-ported that a man was in the building's garage stealing a bicycle. When officers arrived at [the scene], they spotted the suspect on the bicycle and confronted him, according to police accounts. Police say the suspect fired at the officers and missed, but hit their patrol car. One of the officers returned fire, hitting Valle, who fled. He was found later hiding in some bushes at Santiago Street and the Great Highway, according to police. Valle was treated for minor injuries. The two officers also sustained minor injuries when they dived for cover. Valle, who police say lived in San Francisco and Daly City, is scheduled to return to court Thursday to enter a plea.[15]

There's one more security problem you have to think about: robbery. The difference between theft and robbery is whether the criminal is tak-ing the bike while you're not there—that's theft—or while you're in phys-ical possession of it—that's robbery. Being robbed isn't ever a pleasant experience, but some robberies are more dangerous than others. Some robbers pose as curious admirers of your bike; they seem harmless when they ask to take your bike for a spin, but the last sight you catch of your bike is under the "friendly admirer" racing off with it. Others may phys-ically assault you to gain possession of your bike, or even threaten you with a weapon; if you're threatened by a robber with a weapon, that is "armed robbery."

15   "Police Arrest Man in Bike Theft, Shooting," *SF Gate*, May 23, 2007.

Generally, a robber will restrict his activities to isolated areas, although this may not be true in the "bad" parts of town. Unless you're prepared to defend your bike with violence—and to be better armed for violence than the robber—the best protection against robbery is common sense.[16] First, be sure that your bike is insured. Second, use common sense to avoid unsafe areas: isolated parks when you're riding alone, unsafe parks, parks at night, poorly lit streets, streets in the wrong neighborhood, and isolated sections of town, such as business or shipping districts after dark. When you're riding in areas where there *could* be somebody lurking in the dark, or in the bushes in the daytime, you have to remain alert to that possibility. Ride at a fast clip; this may discourage opportunistic robbers, and if someone decides to attempt robbery anyway, it gives you an advantage. If you see a group of guys hanging around who *seem* like they're looking for trouble, use your common sense and assume that they *are* looking for trouble. More than one cyclist has been knocked off his bike as he rode too close to a group of troublemakers. Don't ride into trouble, and if trouble comes running at you, be prepared to outrace it. In addition to being alert, this means keeping your bike in good working order. There's not much worse than having a breakdown just as a robber starts sprinting after you.

If you or another person is assaulted, you have the right to defend yourself or that other person, whether the other person is somebody you know or a complete stranger. However, you should understand the limits to self-defense. Generally, you are allowed to use the force that a reasonable person would believe to be necessary to stop the threatened, imminent, or actual attack. "Reasonable" force is an objective standard: what the "reasonable person," as determined by a jury, would believe is necessary to stop the attack. It does not include force that would go beyond what a "reasonable person" believes is necessary to stop the attack. To that extent, a "reasonable person" would use force proportionate to the threat of harm. Once an attack has been broken off, any further violence on your part would not be considered self-defense. You are allowed to use reasonable force, however, to hold the person while waiting for law enforcement to arrive.

"Reasonable force" may include lethal force if the "reasonable person" believes that lethal force is necessary, due to the threatened or im-

---

16 Some cyclists ride with pepper spray in case they need to defend themselves. If you decide to carry pepper spray, be sure to check on the legality of carrying and using it in your state or the states where you are traveling. Another "tool" cyclists have used in self-defense is a bike lock and/or chain. Some cyclists have even used the bike itself as a self-defense weapon. None of these methods will work against a robber armed with a gun; though pepper spray *might* disable a knife-wielding robber, a lock or bike chain might not. The key to remember in choosing a method of self-defense is the "reasonableness" of the self-defense. What would a "reasonable person" do in a similar situation?

minently lethal nature of the attack, to defend against the attack. In some states, lethal force is also legal to defend against a burglary in your dwelling; thus, for example, in those states it would be legal for you to use lethal force against a thief who has broken into your home to steal your bike.

Although you have the right to self-defense, common sense still applies. If somebody is threatening to shoot you unless you hand your bike over, does it make sense to refuse to comply? After all, in the end, it is just a bike. If your life is in danger unless you defend yourself, of course it makes sense to defend yourself, but you should always let your common sense prevail.

If Your Bike Has Been Stolen

The unthinkable has happened: Your bike has been stolen. This is when all your preparation will pay off.

6-5 FILING A POLICE REPORT

First, file a stolen-bike report with the police department for the jurisdiction in which the bike was stolen and any other police agency or service with which the bike is registered. Use all of the documentation you've saved for just this moment to help the police identify your bike. The police report will do four things:

1. It will alert law enforcement that your bike has been stolen; after all, you can't expect law enforcement to look for your stolen bike if they don't know it's been stolen.

2. It will help law enforcement to identify the bike's lawful owner—that's you—if it is recovered.

3. It will serve as proof that your bike was stolen if it's found in somebody else's possession. A police report won't prove, by itself, that the person in possession of your bike is the thief. But it will allow the police to recover your bike and provides evidence of theft, which may help convict a thief if other evidence is available. It will also be proof that your bike was stolen if you need to recover your bike from a third party, such as a pawnbroker or bona fide buyer.

4. It will serve as proof of theft if you file an insurance claim.

6-6 GETTING THE WORD OUT

Second, place a stolen-bike listing online. The Portland, Oregon, bicycle website www.bikeportland.org has developed an innovative stolen-bike listing service in concert with www.finetoothcog.com. When you list your stolen bike, the service scans Craigslist and eBay for "bicycle for sale" ads describing your stolen bike and e-mails you with possible matches. This service has several other interesting features. It includes a search function, and each bike listing contains data about the bike and the theft, as well as an e-mail link to alert the owner. You can also access a Google map from these websites showing the location of every reported bike theft in Portland, if you're interested in figuring out where the bike-theft hotspots are. If there is a similar online service in your area, list your stolen bike with that service. Also place a stolen-bike listing with online services such as Craigslist. If people who read your listing see your bike, they will know whom to contact. Next, make the rounds of all the bike shops and pawn shops in your town with a flyer describing your bike, and asking people to contact you and the police department if it is spotted—thieves *have* been apprehended with the help of alert bike-shop employees. Depending on how you feel about it, you might consider posting a "reward, no questions asked" flyer around town. If the bike thief has an enemy looking for some payback, he might take your reward and turn in the thief. Of course, there's also the possibility that you'll be buying your bike back from the thief, so you'll have to decide if that matters to you.

6-7 BEGINNING YOUR SEARCH

Now that you've gotten the word out, you might want to start combing through local police and transit agency warehouses to see if your bike has been confiscated. One thing to keep in mind is that if your bike is still in town, it may have been repainted to disguise it, so in addition to looking for your white ACME 2000 Pedalmaster, you might want to keep an eye out for bikes that *might* be a white ACME 2000 Pedalmaster underneath that coat of paint. This is obviously harder to do, but a repainted bike will be obviously repainted—not necessarily a bad job, but you should nonetheless be able to tell that the bike has been painted. Telltale signs might be as subtle as the lack of identifying decals and badges or, on a hasty spray-paint job, as blatant as the original paint showing through in places.

6-8 Filing an Insurance Claim

You can also file a claim with your insurance company or lock manufacturer at this point; be sure to check with your policy and lock guarantee to see if you have time limits for making a claim. Although the insurance company will most likely want to pay you the "Actual Cost Value"—an estimated value that considers the age and condition of the bicycle at the time of the loss—rather than your replacement cost, you're not obligated to accept a lowball offer. When you submit your claim, be sure to ask for your "Replacement Value," the amount it would cost you to replace your bike. Be prepared to submit evidence of its replacement value in the form of a "Replacement Cost Estimate" from a bike dealer familiar with your make and model of bike. Request that the dealer provide the estimate on the shop letterhead, and have the dealer sign the estimate. If your bicycle is no longer being made, have the dealer choose a comparable make and model for use on the estimate. Be sure to provide a list of all upgrades to the bicycle, as well as any component replacements you have made. Furthermore, list all accessories that were on the bicycle—for example, if your bike was equipped with a computer, pump, spare tubes, fenders, saddlebag, or water-bottle cages, you would want those included in the estimate.

If your bike is insured *and* you had a lock with a guarantee, the lock manufacturer will likely limit its liability to paying your deductible; be sure to read your lock guarantee so you understand the process before you file your claim.

You should be aware that once you've been paid, the bike no longer belongs to you; instead it belongs to the insurer, and if it's recovered, and you still want your bike, you will have to buy it back from the company. Furthermore, making claims against your insurance policy has a tendency to cause your rates to rise, so you may want to consider that before you make a claim. If you think of insurance as covering losses you can't cover yourself, that will give you some idea of when you should cover the loss yourself and when you should submit a claim.

Recovering Your Stolen Bike

Your bike was stolen, and you've done everything you can. Then one day, out of the blue, there's your bike: What can you do? Let's look at some different scenarios.

6-9 Scenario 1: The Police Recover Your Bike

You just had some good luck; the police have recovered your stolen bike. Through diligence, the police may connect the bike to you and contact you. Alternatively, through your diligence, you discover your bike in police impound. Either way, because you have taken the proper steps to document your bike and to report the theft, you have proof that the bike is yours and the police release it to you. Case solved. If the thief has been apprehended, you may want to encourage your district attorney's office to prosecute in order to put a dent in bike theft in your community.

6-10 Scenario 2: You Find Your Bike Advertised Online

You can't believe what you're seeing: You discover your stolen bike for sale in an online ad. This should be a no-brainer—contact law enforcement immediately. Law enforcement should help you in recovering your bicycle. I say "should" because some law-enforcement agencies have been reported to be extremely indifferent to stolen bicycles being sold in their communities if the thefts occurred outside their jurisdiction. Hopefully, you will encounter a more professional law-enforcement agency. If you do encounter local law-enforcement indifference, report the advertised sale of your stolen bike to the state police. If the bike is being offered for sale in another state, report the offered sale to the FBI. Although one bicycle may seem to you like a low priority for these agencies, the seller may be part of an organized theft ring that is significant enough to warrant state or federal attention.

In addition to seeking criminal charges and the return of your bike, you can pursue the seller for damages in civil court. Although you can theoretically subpoena the bike even if it is sold to someone else, don't count on being able to find it. Unless there is an online record of the sale, the seller is likely to develop a sudden case of amnesia when questioned about the buyer. If there is an online record of the transaction—for example, on eBay—you will be able to subpoena the stolen bike from the new, unsuspecting owner. But in the rare event that the police won't help, you should buy your bike back before it's sold to someone else, unless you know for certain that you can subpoena the bike later. Here are the steps you should follow:

1. Preserve a copy of the ad listing your bike for sale.

2. Buy your bike back. Use a cashier's check or money order, and bring a friend or friends who are willing to serve as witnesses.

3. Get a receipt.

By following these steps, you're collecting and preserving evidence. You have copies of the ad, a record of the payment, and a receipt; you also have the stolen bicycle in your possession, and you have witnesses to the transaction. This is all evidence. Now you can take your evidence—including the original police report and your original proof of ownership—to a prosecutor and ask that criminal charges be filed. Absent any other evidence, the "fence" will likely be able to claim that he "found" your bike. But that story won't hold up if there are other stolen bikes in his possession (remember that fence with twenty stolen bikes in his eBay account, and another twenty in storage?). You can also file civil charges against the seller, either in addition to criminal charges or instead of criminal charges. If you want to pursue civil charges against the seller, you should consult with an attorney.

6-11 SCENARIO 3: YOUR BIKE IS IN A PAWN SHOP

Let's say the police discover your bike in a pawn shop. Or maybe you do your own investigation: You walk into a pawn shop, and there's your bike for sale. Or maybe you find your bike for sale online, and it turns out the seller is a pawn shop. What do you do?

Before we get to that, let's make sure we're on the same page about what pawn shops are and how they work. A pawn shop is a business that makes short term, high interest loans to low-income people who have no access to other lines of credit.[17] These ninety-day loans are secured by personal property that the borrowers leave as collateral, and which is returned to the borrower when the loan and interest are paid. If the borrower fails to repay the loan, or alternatively, to renew the loan at the end of the ninety-day period, the collateral becomes the property of the pawn shop, which is then free to sell the property for significantly more than the value of the original loan. Sometimes, depending on the personal property offered, a pawn shop will prefer to purchase the property outright rather than make a loan. In this regard, pawn shops are similar to secondhand shops, which will purchase property only for resale and will not make loans.

Both pawn shops and secondhand shops are regulated by state and local laws and are subject to law-enforcement oversight. When a pawn shop buys a used bicycle from somebody purporting to be the owner, the shop is required by law to record the identity of the seller and report

---

17 There's no requirement that borrowers be low-income; however, the simple reality is that pawn shop loans are typically for very small amounts of cash loaned at very high interest rates. Thus, the borrowers are inevitably low-income borrowers who are desperate for a few dollars to tide them over for a short while. That easy access to cash is obviously also very attractive to drug addicts with stolen items to sell.

both the sale and the identity of the seller to the police.[18] In addition, the pawn shop is required by law to hold the bike for a specified waiting period—typically fifteen to thirty days—before putting the bicycle up for sale. This waiting period is designed to prevent the sale of stolen merchandise before the police can inspect pawn shop records of purchases. It is illegal for a pawn shop to sell stolen merchandise, and under the law, if the pawn shop has purchased your stolen bike from a thief, the pawn shop can be ordered to return your stolen bike to you. You are under no legal obligation to pay the pawn shop for the return of your bike.

The law and the reality are two different things, however. Some pawn shops are legitimate, reputable businesses; some, particularly secondhand shops, operate merely as fronts for "fencing" operations. Depending on the jurisdiction, pawn shops may adhere to the law, or they may openly and blatantly engage in illegal practices. These illegal practices may include putting your stolen bike up for sale immediately, before the waiting period has expired, or attempting to sell your stolen bike after being notified that the bike is stolen.[19] Some police departments will not tolerate pawn shops selling stolen merchandise, let alone these illegal practices, and will assist you in recovering your bike. In these jurisdictions, pawn shops are more likely to adhere to the law. Inexplicably, other police departments *will* tolerate the sale of stolen merchandise and other illegal activities; as you might guess, in these jurisdictions pawn shops are less likely to adhere to the law. One shady but nevertheless legal practice that pawn shops engage in is refusing to return your stolen bike to you until you've paid the pawn shop for it. In jurisdictions that tolerate illegal pawn shop activity, police departments will actually assist pawn shops by advising you that the fastest way—indeed, the only sure way—to get your stolen bike back is to buy it back from the pawn shop. You may even be advised that it's "only fair" to the pawn shop.

Whether you pay for the return of your stolen bike is up to you. While it's true that buying your stolen bike back will be the fastest way to recover it, police departments that advise you that it's the only sure way of recovering your bike are misleading you. That might be difficult for some people to accept, but it's a sad fact of life that some police departments "coddle and enable" illegal pawn shop activity.[20]

18 Some jurisdictions only require pawn shops to make these records available for police inspection, rather than requiring them to report the information.

19 A pawn shop with a stolen bicycle in its possession faces the prospect of losing both the bike and the money it paid the thief; for this reason, disreputable pawn shops may attempt to sell the stolen bike, once they have been notified that the bike is stolen, in an attempt to pass the loss on to the unsuspecting buyer.

20 In September 2005, a Portland police detective wrote in an internal memo to Police Chief Derrick Foxworth that "an impression has developed among a significant number of investigators that we as a

Buying your bike back is *not* the only sure way to recover your bike. It's not even "only fair to the pawn shop." That argument is pure nonsense, legally and morally. There's nothing fair about requiring you—the rightful owner—to pay for the return of your stolen property. There's nothing fair about allowing the seller of stolen property to transfer the loss for his mistake to you, the innocent victim of a crime. Whether the pawn shop is a legitimate, reputable business that was merely careless in buying stolen property—a risk of the business—or a "fencing" operation, the loss properly, fairly, and legally belongs to the pawn shop. Don't let anybody tell you differently.

In any case, if you find your bike for sale in a pawn shop, notify the police. The police, in turn, will notify the pawn shop that the bike is stolen. At this point, the pawn shop will likely refuse to return your bike unless you pay for it, and the police may advise you that you should pay the pawn shop. Again, whether you follow that advice is up to you. If you want your bike returned, but you don't want to pay the pawn shop, you are under no obligation to pay—as long as you can prove ownership and have filed a police report. When a pawn shop refuses to surrender a bike, its proprietor is hoping that you will not be able to prove ownership, or that you will not be able to prove that the bike was stolen. But because you've documented your bike and filed a police report, you *can* prove ownership *and* that the bike was stolen.

If you don't want to buy your bike back from a pawn shop, you can refuse to pay and insist—politely but firmly—that the police department assist you with recovery of your bike. In some jurisdictions, the police department will confiscate the stolen bike pending a hearing. Although the police department will have physical possession of the bike, the pawn shop will still retain a property interest in the bike until a court hears the matter. In other jurisdictions, the police department will place a police hold on the stolen bike; the pawn shop will retain physical possession of the bike but will be ordered not to sell the bike pending a hearing. By law, the pawn shop can't sell your bike once the police department has placed a hold on it.[21]

Regardless of whether the police or the pawn shop has physical possession of the bike, it won't be returned to you without a court order. So how do you get a court order? Easy—you file an *action in replevin*, requesting a *Writ of Replevin* from the court. Whoa! An action in replevin? A Writ of Replevin? That doesn't sound easy; it sounds more like legalese.

police bureau 'coddle' and enable the second hand industry in Portland."

21   In some jurisdictions, the police may simply confiscate the stolen bike and return it to you; the trend, however, appears to be to require a hearing before the bike is returned to its owner.

That's because it is legalese, but the action it describes is easy enough to understand. An action in replevin is a lawsuit for the return of personal property wrongfully taken or detained; a Writ of Replevin is simply an order from the court authorizing the retaking of personal property wrongfully taken or detained. In an action for replevin, the court is being asked to decide who owns the property—in this case, your stolen bike. On one hand, the pawn shop will try to convince the court that it is the lawful owner of the bike; as evidence, it will submit the paperwork documenting its purchase of the bike. You, on the other hand, will try to convince the court that you are the lawful owner of the bike. As evidence, you will submit your receipts, photos, recorded serial number and Owner Applied Number, insurance policy coverage, proof of registration with police and national registries, and the police report. Whom do you think the court will decide for? If *you* were the judge presented with that evidence, whom would you decide for? The pawnbroker with a receipt documenting a sale from "some guy," or the guy with extensive documentation of ownership? Faced with that evidence, there isn't a court in this country that would decide for the pawn shop. In fact, most hearings result in an order to return the stolen property to its lawful owner. Do you see now why there's no need to pay the pawn shop for the return of your bike? More importantly, do you see the value of documenting your ownership of the bike so thoroughly from the start?

So how do you file an action in replevin? When you request police help in recovering your bike from the pawn shop, the police should assist you with filing the action. If the police department is not helpful, the clerk of your county court should be able to assist you. If you want, you can hire an attorney to file the action for you; however, there's no requirement to be represented by an attorney.

Suppose the pawn shop is disreputable, and it sells your stolen bike, either after it has been notified that the bike is stolen or even after the police have placed a hold on it pending a hearing. Are you powerless to do anything about it? Absolutely not. In that situation, you can still recover your bike from the person who bought it, again through an action for replevin, or even an "action for conversion." You can also file a lawsuit for conversion against the pawn shop, seeking the full value of your bike. Conversion is a tort that includes theft, but it is much broader than theft. For example, somebody who interferes with your attempt to recover your stolen property may be found liable for conversion. If you think that you might want to file an action for conversion against the pawn shop—or any other party involved in the unlawful interference with your right to your property—you should consult with an attorney.

There's one more thing you can do if the pawn shop violates any law or regulation in its handling of your bike—for instance, putting your bike up for sale before the waiting period has expired, or selling your bike after it has been notified that the bike is stolen or after it has had a police hold placed on it: You can have the pawn shop's license revoked, both through the state agency that regulates pawn shops and through the police department that issues licenses to pawnbrokers in its jurisdiction. If a pawn shop has violated the law in its handling of your bike, you may have the power to put it out of business, and that will act as a deterrent on bike theft in your community.

6-12 SCENARIO 4: YOUR BIKE IS FOR SALE AT A FLEA MARKET

Suppose you're making the rounds at the flea market and you spot your bike for sale. This one is also a no-brainer. Call the police immediately. Flea markets are less rigorously regulated than pawn shops and second-hand shops; nevertheless, law enforcement is aware that stolen items can be found for sale at flea markets, and the police do investigate flea markets for stolen merchandise. Although the law allows you to recover your own property, you should wait for the police. First, you can recover your property yourself only under certain circumstances: You must be absolutely certain that it's your property, and you must be in fresh pursuit of your property. Recovering your property later, after the theft, won't qualify as "fresh pursuit." If the person selling the bike purchased it in good faith, you must use the legal process to recover your bike. Although you still retain title to the bike, even if a thief has sold the bike to a "bona fide" or good-faith purchaser, the good-faith purchaser has title in the bike against everybody except you. Therefore, you will have to prove your ownership of the bike. Although you may be able to defend a self-recovery against criminal or civil charges, it's not a certainty, so you shouldn't risk these charges if you can have the police recover the bike for you. Second, there is a very strong probability that this seller has other stolen items for sale, and the police will want to investigate the person selling your bike for evidence of other crimes. Unless the police are unable to help, let them recover the bike for you.

6-13 SCENARIO 5: YOUR BIKE IS FOR SALE ON THE STREET

It's unlikely, but suppose somebody on the street offers to sell you a bike at a bargain price, and it's your stolen bike. Again, call the police. There is virtually no chance that this person is a bona fide purchaser, and virtually every chance that this person stole your bike. Under the law, you are entitled to recover your own property and even to use "reasonable force"—the force a "reasonable person" would find necessary to recover her property. Deadly force would not be considered "reasonable." However, you are allowed to recover your own property only if you are absolutely certain that it's yours, and only if you are in "fresh pursuit" of a thief. If you have spotted your bike some time after the theft, you are no longer in "fresh pursuit." Therefore, you should call the police unless there is no opportunity to do so and your only opportunity to recover the bike is to forcefully take it—for example, if the thief begins to ride off on your bike after you've started dialing the cops.

There are several good reasons for getting the police involved at this point and having them recover your bike, instead of taking matters into your own hands and forcefully taking your bike yourself. First, you may be insulated from any legal actions—in other words, lawsuits—by the person selling the bike.[22] Second, it is less likely that you will become involved in a violent struggle with a potentially armed and dangerous criminal. Third, you will not be exposing yourself to potential criminal charges. Fourth, the police may be able to press criminal charges against the suspected thief. If you see your bike for sale on the street, call the police, for the sake of your safety *and* your bike.

6-14 SCENARIO 6: YOU SEE SOMEONE WITH YOUR BIKE

Say that one day you discover your stolen bike with somebody else riding it. By now, you should know what to do: Call the police. Understandably, bike theft is an emotional issue with cyclists, and many cyclists have advocated the use of violence against the person caught riding a stolen bike.

That is the worst advice possible.

This situation is a bit more ambiguous than some of the other scenarios. The person riding your bike could be the thief, but he or she could just as easily be an unsuspecting innocent buyer—what the law calls the *bona fide* purchaser. A violent attack against a bona fide purchaser is not only morally wrong, it's unlawful. Whether the person riding the bike is a thief or a bona fide purchaser, however, there is no legal defense that justifies the attack; in either case, the attack exposes the perpetrator to both criminal and civil charges, so let's put that bad idea to rest.

---

22 Generally, you will have a defense against lawsuits unless you intentionally provide false information to the police or instigate an unlawful arrest.

So what can you do? *Call the police.* Remember, if the person riding your bike is a bona fide purchaser, he or she has rights to the bike against everybody but you, the lawful owner. This means that if you can prove your ownership of the bike, and that it was stolen—by showing the court all that documentation of ownership you have and the police report you filed—you will be able to obtain a court order allowing you to recover your bike.

What if you just confiscate the bike, because you know you can't prove that it's your bike and that it was stolen? Now you've just committed a crime—either larceny or robbery—and you may face both criminal and civil charges. Ironic, isn't it, that *you* could go to jail, or be ordered to pay a fine or to pay damages to the person in possession of your bike? That's why your first step in theft prevention is always going to be documenting your ownership.

But what if you were prepared, and you *can* prove ownership, but you just confiscate the bike anyway? This is still a tricky situation. Under the law, a person cannot be convicted of stealing his own property, and a proof of title is usually sufficient to defend against an accusation of theft. In addition, in most states a reasonable, good-faith belief that one is the owner of property is an affirmative defense against theft; however, a "reasonable mistake" won't protect you against civil charges—you must be absolutely certain that the bike is yours. Additionally, the law allows "recapture" of your property only if you are in "fresh pursuit" of your property. Clearly, spotting your bike some time after the theft won't qualify as "fresh pursuit." If you can prove that you are the legal owner of the bike, and you can call the police and recover your bike through legal means, why expose yourself to criminal charges, and possibly civil charges, by recovering the bike yourself? The only time you should attempt to recover your bike yourself in this situation is if the police either can't or won't help you recover your bike; your only recourse then may be to recover it yourself.[23]

However, you should be aware that there are many exceptions and reservations to the general rule that you can recover your own property. For example, as we saw, you must be absolutely certain that the property is yours—it's possible you will be found liable for conversion, or even convicted of theft, if you take a bike that looks like yours but isn't. It gets even trickier. Let's say the person bought a new set of wheels and put them on your stolen bike, and then you recovered the bike yourself. Depending on the state, you could be convicted of either stealing the wheels

23 One cyclist in Portland, Oregon, reported that a responding police officer advised her to recover her stolen bike—which she had spotted locked to a bike rack—herself, because the bike was locked and the officer didn't have tools or the time to help her break the lock.

or even—because it wasn't the specific property taken from you—stealing the entire bicycle.

In addition, although you can use "reasonable force" to recover your property if you are in "fresh pursuit," the use of force, threat of force, or a retaliatory act to recover property when you are not in fresh pursuit almost always nullifies the defense of good-faith self-help in every state. Although one New York judge noted that his state permitted a limited right of self-help recovery, he cautioned that "the availability of such remedy does not countenance self-help which involves the threat or actual use of force."

Finally, if your insurance company has given you a settlement on the stolen bicycle, the insurer, and not you, may be the owner of the bicycle, which would mean you have no right of self-recovery, because it's not your bike. Moreover, if you have signed a settlement agreement with the insurance company, a prosecutor may be able to argue that you had notice that the bicycle no longer belonged to you, so you lacked even a reasonable, good-faith belief that you were recovering your own property.

For all of these reasons, unless you are chasing a thief who has just now stolen your bike, your first option should always be to have the police recover your bike for you; self-recovery should always be your last resort, to be used only if the police are unwilling or unable to help you recover your bike and if self-recovery is your only option.

Reporting Suspicious Activity

Whether your bike is stolen or not, there are a few more things that you personally can do about bike theft. First, if you see suspicious activity—for example, a bike lock being cut—report it to the police immediately as a crime in progress. Police might be slower to respond to a bike-theft report after the crime has already been committed, but a crime in progress will always carry a high priority for law enforcement. Don't try to decide if the person is a thief or the owner cutting his own lock—let the police determine that. Second, become familiar with the stolen-bike listings in your town; if you spot a bike matching a stolen-bike report, notify the police and the owner. And third, if you're buying a used bike, and you have reason to suspect that it's stolen—for example, if it matches the description of a stolen bike, or it's registered to somebody other than the seller—notify the police. It may help reunite a bike with its rightful owner. If we all watch out for each other, it will help put a dent in bike theft.

CONCLUSION

*It's clear we are not doing very much. I think if there were a push
from bicyclists to do a better job, I would certainly work toward
making theft more of a priority.*

—*Supervisor Chris Daly, San Francisco Board of Supervisors*[24]

Bicycle theft thrives owing to a confluence of factors. Bike thieves often
have drug addictions to support and thus are in need of fast and easy
cash. Bicycles are ideal targets for thieves because they are valuable
items that are relatively easy to steal. Cyclists often don't take the time
to lock their bikes when they'll be gone "just for a minute"; when they
do lock up, they either use cheap, easy-to-cut locks or use their locks improperly. Bicycles are valuable items, and therefore it's not difficult for a
thief to find ready customers, including pawn shops and other secondhand shops, professional "fences," and people on the street whose sense
of greed overcomes any personal ethical objections to purchasing an obviously stolen bike at a bargain price. There is almost no risk of getting
caught stealing; on the rare occasion when a thief is caught, there is almost no risk of being prosecuted. When there is a prosecution—a very
rare event—the penalty is negligible. In other words, for the bike thief,
there is literally no downside to the crime; it's almost risk-free.

And that must change. As we've seen, cyclists can take measures to
protect their bikes from theft. What's often sadly lacking in the fight
against bike theft is the interest and participation of the criminal justice system. Both police departments and prosecutors have their attention focused on other crimes, and they often consider bike theft to be a
low priority for their limited resources. Even when a bike thief is caught,
proving theft is often impossible: The thief will have a well-practiced
story about buying the bike from "some guy." Even if the police confiscate the stolen bike and return it to its rightful owner, proving theft, absent other convincing evidence—such as witnesses who can identify the
thief—will be impossible.[25] Given all those difficulties, it's easy to understand why prosecution of the crime takes a low priority.

Clearly, law enforcement can do more—much more—to combat bike
theft. Currently, the burden for combating bike theft rests almost entirely on individual cyclists: We're advised to buy locks and register our
bikes. What's often missing are the interest and effort from both law

24　"Chasing My Stolen Bicycle."

25　If there is sufficient evidence to convict—for example, eyewitnesses and your bike in the thief's possession—you can and should request that criminal charges be filed against the thief.

enforcement and the criminal justice system to do their fair share. To that end, cyclists *must* organize within their communities to lobby for increased attention to bike theft from both law enforcement and the criminal justice system. Rather than treating bike theft as an individual, low-priority crime, police officers and prosecutors must begin to understand that bike thieves are typically involved in other criminal enterprises as well, and that arrest and prosecution for bike theft will often lead to evidence of other criminal activity. There are impediments to lobbying for these changes, however. For example, the often hostile adversarial relationship that cyclists have developed with local law-enforcement agencies may make it difficult for cyclists and police officers to work together to solve the problem. This difficulty can be overcome. Thus, while law enforcement and the criminal justice system can and should do more to combat bike theft, cyclists also can and should do more, by developing better relationships with their local law-enforcement agencies.

Both communities and individual cyclists could do more to prevent bike theft. Several innovative proposals to combat the problem have been advanced, and although they are all possible with current technology, such programs are still rare.

One proposed method of deterring theft targets infrastructure rather than individual prevention practices. Specially designed bicycle parking facilities utilizing chain-link fencing, coded entry systems, and security monitors would provide a more secure place to store bikes at workplaces and other sites within a city. However, such systems can be defeated. One trick that has been used, right under the noses of security personnel, is for a thief to ride in on a cheap bike, park next to a target bike, break the lock on the target bike, and ride out on the stolen bike. Presumably, the use of coded entry systems would provide law enforcement with some ability to identify the thief, but when one considers the volume of cyclists coming and going, and the difficulty in pinpointing an exact time of theft, it is easy to see that identification is no simple matter even in these controlled circumstances. Nevertheless, if combined with security patrols of the facility and proper locking techniques, it is a method with the potential to significantly increase bicycle security.

Another method involves the use of "Datatags"—inexpensive miniature electronic transponders with a unique identification code that can be hidden within a bicycle and read by law-enforcement officers with a handheld scanner. Datatag also manufactures the Datadot, an electronic microdot that allows you to electronically mark all of your components with a unique identification code. The weak link in the Datatag system is law enforcement. On the one hand, the system can't work if law enforcement doesn't check for Datatags; on the other hand, law enforcement isn't going to check for Datatags if they aren't in widespread use. Still, it's an interesting method that may catch on if both cyclists and law-enforcement personnel are using the system.

In Canada, police have tried a variation of the Datatag in bike-theft stings by placing a tracking device in the seat tube of decoy bikes, which, after they are stolen, can be tracked to warehouses full of stolen bikes. This strategy has allowed Canadian police to go after the bike-theft rings themselves rather than trying to catch individual bike thieves in action, and it has reportedly led to a significant reduction in bike theft. There is no reason this strategy couldn't be employed by law-enforcement agencies in the United States.

Some have proposed putting serial numbers in a highly visible standard location. Manufacturers would engrave the serial number in a visible and consistent location on the top tube; when you buy a bicycle, you would register the serial number in your name with the manufacturer, who would then send you a certificate of ownership. When you sell the bicycle, the buyer would return the certificate of ownership to the manufacturer and receive a new certificate in her name. This system would be similar to the current motor vehicle registration system, except that it would be privately operated by the manufacturers. If a bicycle was stolen and subsequently recovered by police, the manufacturer would provide the law-enforcement agency with the name and address of the registered owner. If the serial number had been removed, that would be admissible as evidence of theft in a court of law. The weak link in this system is the manufacturer. Unlike your state's Department of Motor Vehicles, manufacturers occasionally go out of business.

A similar proposal has been advanced by the Chicago Police Department. In this system, the serial number issued by the manufacturer would be registered in a nationwide registration database along with the bicycle description and the personal information of the owner. When the police recovered a stolen bicycle, they would check the registration number against the database to locate the registered owner. The advantage of this system is that it doesn't rely on manufacturers to maintain records of ownership.

These schemes are, of course, analogous to automobile registration, which acts as a deterrent to auto theft. In China, bicycles are required to be licensed; if a bicycle is stolen, the license plate provides easy identification of the bike. If the police see a bicycle without a license plate, they stop the cyclist and seize the bike. Some motorists in this country argue that bicyclists should be required to be licensed, registered, and insured if they are to have an equal right to the roads. Cyclists themselves have varying opinions on the subject—some would support such a system to deter theft, while others see mandatory licensing and registration as an infringement of their liberties. While it's true that one is relatively anonymous on a bicycle, it's also true that thieves profit from that anonymity. Ultimately, licensing and registration to combat theft will need the support of cyclists to be enacted into law; until there is widespread and strong support, this solution is likely to remain a proposal.

No licensing and/or registration system will work, however, without the interested participation of law-enforcement agencies and the criminal justice system. Police departments would need to have bike-theft policies in place that require law-enforcement personnel to enter stolen-bike reports into the nationwide database and to check the nationwide database whenever officers recover a stolen bike. If a licensing and registration system is to be put in place, it will have to be enforced. For some cyclists, this would undoubtedly feel like harassment; however, without enforcement, thieves will remain free to openly ride stolen bikes. The criminal justice system must also take bike theft seriously. Without prosecutions, there is no downside to theft for a bicycle thief. Working together, law enforcement and the criminal justice system could make a licensing and registration system work. The only question to be worked out is whether we cyclists actually want one.

Although an individual bicycle theft is a relatively minor crime, cumulatively bicycle theft is a serious matter; the total dollar value of the bikes that thieves steal annually is higher than the total take from bank robbery. And yet it is bank robbery, without a doubt, that garners more law-enforcement attention. There are far too many reports of law-enforcement indifference to bike theft; this is a mystifying response to criminal activity, given the cumulative dollar value of stolen bikes and the close association of bike theft with other forms of criminal activity. It's difficult to believe that an anticyclist bias doesn't lie at the root of this apathy. When a bicycle is stolen, it is, for many cyclists, the equivalent of auto theft; and sometimes a stolen bike is worth as much or more than an automobile. Therefore, law-enforcement agencies and the criminal justice system must treat bike theft as more than a distraction from their "real work." Cyclists have a right to equal treatment under the law, and they deserve no less.

7

Defective Products
Law for Cyclists

by Steven M. Magas

INTRODUCTION

By now, we've seen that every person owes every other person a duty of care. When you're out riding, you owe Joe Schmoe a duty of care whether Joe is walking, riding, or driving a car. And Joe owes a corresponding duty of care to you. If you injure Joe Schmoe, or if Joe Schmoe injures you, the law provides a remedy for redress of that injury.

But what if your injury is caused by Schmoe Incorporated? Can Schmoe escape liability if Schmoe is a corporation instead of a regular Joe? Nope. Since 1886, a corporation has been considered a person under the law, with all of the rights, and all of the duties, of any other person. When Schmoe Inc. injures you, whether through breach of contract or through negligence, an intentional act, or what the law calls "strict liability," you have remedies under the law to redress that injury.

PHOTO 7.1 Defective Bicycle

One source of injury that cyclists potentially face—from the corporate Schmoes, as opposed to the regular Joes—is defective products. Actually, there are two separate types of defective products problems:

1. *Obvious defect:* You buy a product—maybe a bicycle, a helmet, or a tire—and when you get it home, you discover that it's defective.

2. *Hidden defect:* There is a defect in the design, the materials used, or the manufacture—and you are unaware of the problem until after you are injured as a result of the defect.

Although both of these scenarios involve a defect in a product, the law addresses them differently. Obvious defects are usually addressed by contract law, but they may be addressed by tort law in some circumstances. Hidden defects are addressed by both contract law and tort law. Let's take a closer look at both situations and examine what your rights are under the law.

Lemon Laws and Implied Warranties of Merchantability

The so-called Lemon Laws were originally designed to protect consumers who were purchasing automobiles, who may not be able to assess possible defects prior to the purchase—the colloquial term "lemon" refers to a new car with persistent problems. The inability of consumers to obtain fair and prompt redress for persistent and apparently unfixable defects in new cars has prodded the legislatures in about two-thirds of the states to adopt such laws. These laws force manufacturers to provide standardized language in warranties to provide owners with the right to return the car for a refund, repair it, or have it replaced under certain circumstances. Furthermore, Lemon Laws require used car dealers to provide a written minimum guarantee of the used cars they sell for a short period of time.

Now there's a novel idea—requiring that products manufactured and sold actually work! Well, perhaps not so novel: While Lemon Laws have been expanded to cover the sale of everything from puppies to recreational vehicles, the law of warranty comes to the rescue for some bicycle purchasers. Thanks to the broad provisions of the Uniform Commercial Code (UCC) and the federal Magnuson-Moss Warranty Act, the sale of virtually every type of consumer product today—including bicycles—is covered by some kind of warranty. Consumer goods must meet a certain level of quality, and the "implied warranty of merchantability" is the basic warranty of quality. Under the UCC, there is an "implied warranty of merchantability" in every sale of goods, as long as two conditions are met: The seller is one who ordinarily sells such goods, and the warranty has not been validly excluded or modified.

"Implied warranty" means that if a product is manufactured for sale, it is implied that the product "shall be merchantable." "Well, that's interesting," you might say, "but what does *merchantable* mean?" It basically means that the goods are of average, acceptable quality in the trade and fit for their ordinary purposes. But beware, as a seller is generally permitted to exclude or modify these implied warranties of merchantability by the use of appropriate language. However, there are specific requirements that the disclaimer be set forth conspicuously in writing and that it mention the word "merchantability."

Before a consumer can enforce any rights under a warranty, he or she must notify the seller that the warranty has been breached. This must be done within a reasonable time after the consumer discovered or should have discovered the breach. Another time limitation to keep in mind is the "statute of limitations"—the time limit you have for filing a lawsuit— which under the UCC is four years. The time clock begins to run in most warranty actions from the time of delivery, and not from when you discover the defect.

As for remedies available to you for a breach of warranty, if you act fast enough, and if the defect in the product is serious enough to "substantially impair" its value to you, you can return it for a refund. That means that if you find a defect in the bike you just purchased, you should be able to get your money back. In addition, you may be able to obtain an order for "specific performance" or for "replevin." You may even be able to recover "incidental" damages, "consequential" damages, or "general" damages and "punitive" damages, depending on the circumstances.[1]

In addition, depending on whether the manufacturer of your bicycle provided a written warranty, you may opt for relief under the federal law regulating warranties, the Magnuson-Moss Warranty Act. This act applies to written warranties on consumer products and is designed to achieve practical relief for the consumer without clogging federal courts

---

1 An order for *specific performance* means that the court will order the other party to perform his or her end of the contract. An order for *replevin* means that the court orders the return of property to its rightful owner. *Incidental damages* are damages, including "expenses reasonably incurred," incident to the breach of warranty. This means, for example, that if you have to have your bike inspected by a forensic engineer, or it has to be shipped for inspection, you are entitled to recovery of these incidental expenses (note, however, the advice in §7-5 concerning disposition of your defective bicycle product). *Consequential damages* are damages "resulting from general or particular requirements and needs of which the seller at the time of contracting had reason to know." This means that if the product is defective, and as a consequence of that defect you incurred some loss, these damages are available to you. *General damages* are not the actual money damages you suffered—those are called *special damages*—but are intended to compensate you, in addition to your special damages, for the other party's actions. Finally, *punitive damages* are money damages intended to "punish" the behavior of the seller where such punishment is warranted by the facts.

with warranty actions. It complements rather than supersedes state warranty law, and since some states have special consumer warranty statutes that may give the consumer greater protection than the federal warranty act, the Federal Trade Commission has required that all written warranties covered by the Magnuson-Moss Act clearly and conspicuously disclose that you may have more favorable state rights.

Even though there's no Lemon Law specifically designed to protect bicycle consumers, warranties provide comparable safeguards and should sufficiently protect consumers of any goods. If you have purchased a product that is defective, take the following course of action:

→ NOTIFY THE SELLER. *The fact is, no local bike shop can afford to alienate customers by selling defective products; if you notify the seller of the problem, the odds are that your defective-product problem will be addressed to your satisfaction. If your defective-product problem isn't addressed to your satisfaction, you have remedies available under the law.*

→ PRESERVE YOUR EVIDENCE. *Keep your evidence intact. This means you should not take anything apart and put it back together. Do not have anyone look at, examine, or inspect it. Most importantly, do not send any part of the bicycle, helmet, shoes, or components to anyone.*

→ CONSULT WITH AN ATTORNEY. *As with any legal action, there will be time limitations for protecting your rights. In the case of a breach-of-warranty claim, the time limit is four years. Do not wait until your four years are up—it takes time to develop a legal case. Therefore, if you have a defective-product problem that isn't being addressed by the seller, talk with an attorney right away.*

Products Liability Law

Now suppose you've been injured by a defective product. If you are reading this book looking for a "do-it-yourself" guide to handling products liability claims, I have three simple words of advice: *Consult a lawyer.*

Products liability claims are complicated, expensive, and risky. Most lawyers do not even consider looking at them unless the results of the accident are catastrophic. This chapter provides a broad overview of the law of products liability as well as some of the risks and costs. However, if you think you were injured because your bike or some component was defective, then it's absolutely essential that you consult with a good lawyer right away.

PHOTO 7.2 Close-up of Broken Fork

7-1 BACKGROUND ON PRODUCTS LIABILITY LAW

"Products liability" refers to situations where a product is "defective" and the "defect" causes personal injury, property loss, or economic damage. The particular laws vary from state to state, but generally, once it is proven that the product was defective and that the defect led to injuries, the law permits recovery from everyone who is in the "chain of custody" of the defective product. Over the past forty or so years, the concept of what is a "product," what types of things constitute "defects," and numerous other matters have been litigated thousands of times. Products liability cases can also include numerous theories of recovery, including "negligence," "strict liability," "breach of warranty," and "negligent or fraudulent misrepresentation."

THE EARLY YEARS

Before products were mass-produced, the sale of goods usually amounted to an exchange of money for handcrafted items—chairs, tools, buggies, wheels. You knew who made the product and you frequently bought it directly from the manufacturer. You also knew whom to scream at if there was a problem with your purchase. Consumers were charged with the duty of taking care of themselves, inspecting the goods they purchased, and avoiding problem goods. The legal doctrine that ruled disputes was *caveat emptor,* or "let the buyer beware."

Once machines started making products or parts for products, which were sold through a chain of agents, distributors, or large mass-market stores, the legal concepts that were easily applied in the old days no longer seemed to fit. Further, products began to get more and more complex, which made inspection by the purchaser more and more difficult. Whom do you scream at when a component buried inside a complex piece of machinery breaks and causes injury? The guy who made the component, the guy who designed the machine, or the guy who put the machine together? And then there's the guy who bought a bunch of the machines and distributed them to several stores, and the guy who purchased hundreds of them from this distributor and sold one to you.

Formerly, the law required that you show "privity" in order to sue. This meant that you had to have some direct relationship with the person you were suing. Thus, if the consumer never dealt directly with the component manufacturer, she could not sue the component manufacturer. Furthermore, contract law governed these transactions, and trying to fit claims for injuries caused by faulty products into a body of contract law that focused on economic losses was a bit like smashing the proverbial square peg into a round hole.

The law began to change in the early 1900s when courts first recognized that tort law could be used instead of contract law in these "sale of goods" situations. An early case involved the sale of a Buick.[2] In this case, a wheel collapsed, causing the motorist to get hurt, and the motorist sued the entity that had sold the car to the dealer. The claim was unique because there was no "privity," since the motorist had not dealt directly with the person he sued. The court looked at this situation through the lens of tort law, not contract law, and found that there was no requirement of privity in a tort claim.

Subsequent cases expanded the ability of injured consumers to pursue the manufacturers of products. Ultimately, courts held that where a defective product injured a consumer, the consumer did not even have to prove the manufacturer was "negligent"—only that the product was "defective." This "strict-liability" theory was based on the notion that manufacturers are in the best position to prevent defects, inspect their complex machinery for defects, and spread the risk and cost of a few defects out over the thousands or millions of products they sell.

2 *MacPherson v. Buick Motor Co.*, 111 N.E. 1050 (N.Y. 1916).

The Restatement of Torts

One who sells any product in a defective condition unreasonably dangerous to the user or consumer or to his property is subject to liability for physical harm thereby caused to the ultimate user or consumer.

—Restatement (Second) of Torts

The *Restatements* are a series of treatises on specific areas of the law, such as contracts or property, that reflect the consensus opinion of eminent legal scholars. The second *Restatement of Torts* was published in 1965 and contained Section 402A, one of the first codified descriptions of strict legal liability for defective products in the United States. The language of Section 402A became well-known throughout the land as lawyers struggled to figure out how to prove that products were in a "defective condition unreasonably dangerous to the user or consumer." As a result of the *Restatement of Torts*, terminology like "design defect" and "manufacturing defect" entered the legal lexicon.

Section 402A has guided courts and legislatures in all fifty states since it was published in 1965. In the third *Restatement of Torts*, published in 1997, the American Law Institute reviewed forty years of products liability litigation and modified the rules somewhat. Today, three different types of defects are generally recognized—manufacturing defects, design defects, and information defects—and each is associated with a specific type of claim.[3]

7-2 Three Types of Products Liability Claims

Manufacturing defects

The first type of products liability claim occurs when there is some error in the manufacturing process. Perhaps some parts are made incorrectly, or the wrong material is used. Perhaps the parts are put together wrong.

In one bicycle products liability case I handled, for example, a custom bicycle manufacturer actually put the headset together improperly on a $6,000 bicycle. When my client rode the bike off her driveway, the bike came apart, with the wheel/fork assembly separating. Her injuries included a cheekbone fractured into some eleven pieces. In another case, my client's aluminum-frame bicycle fell apart when it struck a curb. Our metallurgist determined that the cause was improper heat-treating of the

3 Restatement (Third) of Torts: Products Liability Section 402A (2004).

frame during the manufacturing process. In each case, we spent *a lot* of money on engineering to reach those conclusions.

DESIGN DEFECTS

In the second type of products liability claim, a lawyer will argue that the design of the entire product was defective. This does not mean that every example of the product is going to fall apart or cause injury; it does mean, however, that the product fails to adequately protect consumers, or that it didn't meet the "state of the art" when it was designed. Thus, even though the product may have functioned without failing, it was still defective. Here's how the Supreme Court of California defined a design defect: "We hold that a trial judge may properly instruct the jury that a product is defective in design (1) if the plaintiff demonstrates that the product failed to perform as safely as an ordinary consumer would expect when used in an intended or reasonably foreseeable manner, or (2) if the plaintiff proves that the product's design proximately caused his injury and the defendant fails to prove, in light of the relevant factors discussed above, that on balance the benefits of the challenged design outweigh the risk of danger inherent in such design."[4]

Thus, in this 1978 case, *Barker v. Lull Engineering Co., Inc.,* the court set forth two of the leading tests for design defect.[5] The first is the "consumer expectation" test. This test is somewhat analogous to the UCC's warranty of fitness and merchantability, which means that the goods must be of average, acceptable quality in the trade and must be fit for their ordinary purposes. The second test is the "risk/benefit" test, in which the jury weighs whether the risk of danger inherent in the design outweighs the benefits of the design.

The third test for design defect is "negligence with imputed knowledge." This test was developed by the Supreme Court of Oregon in *Phillips v. Kimwood Machine Co.* in 1974.[6] The *Phillips* court articulated the test in the following language: "The problem with strict liability of products has been one of limitation. No one wants absolute liability where all the article has to do is to cause injury. To impose liability there has to be something about the article which makes it dangerously defective without regard to whether the manufacturer was or was not at fault for such condition. A test for unreasonable danger is therefore vital. A

4 *Barker v. Lull Engineering Co., Inc.*, 573 P.2d 443 (Cal. 1978).

5 A *test* is a method of analysis that courts devise to determine whether the fact patterns of a particular case meet or do not meet what the law requires.

6 *Phillips v. Kimwood Machine Co.*, 525 P.2d 1033 (Ore. 1974).

dangerously defective article would be one which a reasonable person would not put into the stream of commerce if he had knowledge of its harmful character. The test, therefore, is whether the seller would be negligent if he sold the article knowing of the risk involved. Strict liability imposes what amounts to constructive knowledge of the condition of the product." This decision established that a manufacturer can be held liable in products liability for defective design—even if the manufacturer didn't know about its harmful nature. For instance, if you were injured on a bike that developed serious wobbling problems at high speeds that were later attributed to a flawed frame design, you would have a products liability case against the manufacturer for defective design. The fact that the bike producer did not know about the speed wobble problem is no defense. It is as if the manufacturer did know when the case law "imputes knowledge" upon them.

INFORMATIONAL DEFECTS

The third type of products liability claim relates to the warnings that come along with, and form a part of, the product. This could include the labels on the box and packaging, the language in the flyers or inserts, and the instructions in the owner's manual. All of these are subject to attack if they are insufficient.

7-3 THE CURRENT STATE OF THE LAW: ATTACKS ON YOUR RIGHTS

When the average Joe is injured by corporate negligence, the average Joe has rights for redress under the law—and that costs corporations money. And though corporations don't like paying compensation to consumers when their products injure or kill, some of them don't seem to mind paying to set up "tort-reform" groups that advocate for restricting your rights. "Astroturf groups," as they are commonly called, are special-interest groups that portray themselves as "grassroots" organizations, but in reality they are funded by corporations seeking to limit your rights. Their goal is to point to the so-called explosion of litigation in the products liability field as evidence of what is wrong with the justice system. Lawyers who represent injured people counter this position with the argument that without products liability litigation, all sorts of dangerous products would be out there in the stream of commerce, causing all sorts of injuries to unsuspecting consumers. Companies would have little incentive to test their products or to ensure their safety if they were not held liable for defects.

The American Association for Justice lists several important cases involving "corporate misconduct" that led to positive changes for consumers (see Table 7.1). Some of our most well-known products and biggest corporations have had problems with products and elected to change to a safer design or formula, revised their instructions, or added

TABLE 7.1 Defective Products and Litigation

Defective Product	Problem	Solution through Products Liability Litigation
Bulletproof vests	Vest material was defective, allowing bullets to penetrate vest.	More than 100,000 vests were recalled.
Tires	Tires were known to explode and cause rollovers.	Tires were pulled off the market
Flammable pajamas	Manufacturer was aware that material used was flammable but chose not to treat pajamas with flame retardant.	Punitive damages totaling $1 million forced the product off the market.
Auto transmission	Manufacturer failed to warn of a known problem that caused cars to suddenly move backward.	Transmission was redesigned after $4 million punitive damage award.
Football helmets	Manufacturers were slow to acknowledge problem or defect that caused death and spinal injuries.	Liability claims spurred helmet redesign. For the first time in sixty years, there were no deaths caused by football helmet defects in 1990.
Ford Pinto	Failure to redesign a known problem caused the car to burst into flames upon impact.	Vehicle was redesigned after a $125 million award for punitive damages.

warnings following litigation: Tylenol, Dalkon Shield, Chrysler, Basset Furniture, Eli Lilly, Ford, Johnson & Johnson, asbestos makers, producers of contraceptive devices, manufacturers of farm equipment, makers of tampons (which were found to be a cause of toxic shock syndrome), toy manufacturers, and, of course, manufacturers of bicycles have all faced products liability cases.

Truth be told, there was no "explosion" of products liability cases. Lawyers understand that these cases are complex and expensive. Most clients cannot afford the $50,000 to $100,000 that must be spent on engineering tests and expert testimony, so the lawyer or law firm "fronts" or loans this money to the client with the hope of winning the case and recouping expenses later. Sometimes they do; often they do not.

In 2007, as this book heads to press, the pendulum is in midswing back toward a more restrictive viewpoint on products liability cases. Many conservative state legislatures have grown weary of the expansion of rights in the courts and adopted products liability laws that are more restrictive and conservative than the decisions that have come down in actual cases. These new products liability laws can have the effect of significantly limiting the rights of injured victims to pursue a claim.

Further, Astroturf groups continue to attack both the victims of faulty products and the lawyers who help them seek redress. Those seeking redress for their injuries are portrayed as being in it "for the money," as are their lawyers. Media hype over some cases is used to support a fanatic effort to push through tort-reform laws that would ultimately have widespread effects, reducing the rights of people who have been injured by defective products and possibly leading to less assurance of safety in the products we need to rely upon.[7]

In fact, the truth is borne out by the numbers. Products liability cases make up an incredibly small portion of the litigation docket—far less than 1 percent. In the cases taken to trial, verdicts for the defense are not uncommon. There have been some large verdicts for injured consumers, but in virtually every case involving a large verdict, there is a catastrophically injured person who had to fight for years for the right to go to trial for his or her "day in court."

How does all of this apply to bicycles? The Consumer Products Safety Commission (CPSC) is charged with "protecting the public from unreasonable risks of serious injury or death" from more than 15,000 products, including bicycles, that fall under the agency's jurisdiction. If you go to

---

7 The "McDonald's coffee case" (*Liebeck v. McDonald's Restaurants, P.T.S., Inc.*, 1995 WL 360309 (Bernalillo County, N.M. Dist. Ct., Aug. 18, 1994) is one of the most famous–or infamous–of these personal-injury cases and is deliberately misrepresented by tort-reform groups to convince the public that there is an urgent need for citizens to abandon their rights under the law.

the CPSC website (www.cpsc.gov) and punch "bicycle" into the search engine, you will find hundreds of hits advising you of recalls due to defects in frames, brakes, pedals, seatposts, seats, suspension systems, entire lines of bicycles, forks, chains, bike trailers, bike racks, lights, stems, aerobars, rims, and more. Those companies required to issue recalls have ranged from the various wholesalers that sell millions of mass-produced bikes to the high-end manufacturers of elite bicycles and components.

Bicycle companies and manufacturers have also been forced to pay fines and penalties. In 2004, one company was given a $1.4 million penalty because it "failed, on multiple occasions, to inform the government in a timely manner about a serious defect with their mountain bicycles."[8] Federal law requires manufacturers, distributors, and retailers to immediately report to the CPSC (that is, within twenty-four hours of obtaining information supporting a conclusion) if a product has a defect that could create a substantial risk of injury to the public.

Court cases involving bicycle products liability are actually very rare. My suspicion is that cases of significant injuries and clear liability due to a defective bike or component are quickly and quietly settled for a large sum of money so that no public record is generated. Only the manufacturers and insurers know for sure, and they are not talking. Frequently, "confidentiality" provisions are demanded that ban the lawyer and victim from talking about the claim or revealing the amount of money obtained in settlement.

7-4 CYCLING'S MOST COMMON PRODUCTS LIABILITY CASES

Though they are relatively rare, there have been products liability cases involving bicycles. Quick-release mechanisms have come under fire many times, for example. Some experts have expressed the opinion that quick-release devices are so simple and effective that they can never be defective unless they simply break. Other experts take the view that getting a quick release to operate properly requires an engineer's knowledge of force and torque and a mechanic's touch on the skewer itself! What happens in these cases is simple. A cyclist is riding down the road, and a wheel—usually the front wheel—comes off, leading to catastrophic injuries. Why did the wheel come off? Is there a products liability claim?

One problem with a quick-release mechanism is that it can be overtightened, which can cause the axle itself to crack or break and the wheel

8 "Dynacraft to Pay $1.4 Million Penalty for Failing to Report Hazard with Mountain Bicycles," U.S. Consumer Product Safety Commission Office of Information and Public Affairs Release #05-053, November 19, 2004.

PHOTO 7.3 Defective Helmet

to come off while you are riding. The other problem—undertightening—is probably more prevalent. If the device is not tightened enough or properly, the wheel can disengage when the rider simply shifts his or her weight. A manufacturing defect in the device itself can also cause it to fail.

Frequently, the cyclist was the last person to tighten the device. The rider had his hands on the bike, tightened it to a point of satisfaction, and rode off. How can the manufacturer or seller be liable in such a case? Such a case requires a detailed investigation and analysis of the bike's components and the accident to try to determine what really happened. If "detailed investigation and analysis" sounds expensive to you, then you are correct: Many hours of engineering time may be required to completely analyze the matter. Furthermore, such cases are vigorously defended; the manufacturer often rightly feels that its reputation is on the line. This means that litigation is required—another long, costly experience not to be undertaken lightly.

Other products liability cases have focused on helmets—remember the infamous "Skid Lids"?—frame failure, brakes, and other components. Any part of a bike that "fails" under normal use can lead to a products liability claim.

Defenses to a products liability case often include misuse of the product, a common theme in bike cases. If you ride your bike hard and the frame breaks, you may face a tough battle. The way you use the bike will come under close scrutiny, and the aggressive defense lawyers will magnify every crash you ever had to argue that *you* broke the bike. Often, the only way to combat this defense is through expensive metallurgical testing, which may show that some defect in the construction of the bike led to the frame failure.

In one products liability claim I handled, a physician who owned numerous bikes chose to ride an older aluminum-frame bike in his collection one day. He was run off the road by a little red car and hit a curb. At that point the bike basically fell apart. The top tube and head tube separated. The down tube separated at the bottom bracket and the bike collapsed, causing the physician to strike the pavement face-first.

Our legal team retained experts in metallurgy, bicycle accident reconstruction, bicycle design, and more—as did the defense team. The defense claimed "no defect," but our metallurgist took a look under an electron microscope and showed defects in the frame at the failure points. The defense team claimed that even if the bike was defective, the nature of this crash was such that the rider was going to suffer a head injury even if the bike had not failed. Our accident reconstructionist debunked that theory. The defense team claimed that the physician was *faking* his brain injury. The case drove on toward trial for four years. Our legal team spent over $100,000 on medical and engineering experts, depositions, trial exhibits, and the like. My understanding is that the defense team spent double that! Ultimately the case was resolved the day before trial. My point—the same one I started with—is that these cases are complex, take a long time, and are very expensive.

7-5 WHAT TO DO IF YOU ARE INJURED BY A DEFECTIVE PRODUCT

Can you handle your own products liability case? Short answer: no! Virtually every case requires expert testimony about the nature of the defect. Expensive testing, modeling, or other engineering work is usually also required. Extensive legal research is normally required as well to combat the various legal procedures thrown at you by an experienced and aggressive defense team.

Still, there are two steps you can—and in fact must—take to protect your rights. First, if your bike, or some component on your bike, failed or broke, and you suffered severe injuries as a result of that failure, you *must* preserve your evidence. This is critical: *Preserve all evidence in the exact condition that it was in at the time of injury.* All elements of the crash must be preserved. Do not move or bend anything. Do not take anything apart and put it back together. Do not have anyone look at, examine, or inspect the bike or the component. Most importantly, do not send *any* part of the bicycle, helmet, shoes, or components to anyone.

Second, time is of the essence here. You must talk with an experienced products liability attorney right away. Don't wait and see what happens first, because there are statutory limitations to filing suit. Some people are reluctant to file lawsuits—they think that there's something distasteful about it. The fact is, your right to file a lawsuit is ultimately the only means you have of obtaining justice when you've been injured by another person. This is why corporations litigate all the time—even though corporate interests are behind the call for tort reform—because they're asserting their rights. They're not shy about asserting their rights, so you shouldn't be shy about asserting yours. Nevertheless, if you have some reservations about lawsuits, it may give you some comfort to know that most lawsuits never even get to court—they're settled outside of court. However, in order to preserve your right to a trial, you *must* file suit within the statute of limitations: the time limit for filing suit that the legislature has imposed by statute. If you fail to file suit within the time frame allowed, you lose your right to file suit. These time limits may vary by jurisdiction, so if you have been injured by a defective product, you will need to talk with an experienced products liability lawyer—or maybe several—right away.

8

Liability Waivers: Can You Really Sign Your Rights Away?

INTRODUCTION

When you think of "the law," what comes to mind? How about all those laws the legislature makes? You know that statement "The judge threw the book at him"? Such sayings conjure up an image of a stern judge with a fat statute book and a strong pitching arm. For most of us, the statutes passed by legislative bodies are "the law," so maybe you would be surprised to learn that the statutes are not the only laws. The most familiar judges and lawyers in our society are those often seen on TV shows or in movies, and it's the courtroom scene that is always the climax of the story. But "the law" goes far beyond legislatures, stock characters, and even the courtroom. As a cyclist, you will no doubt encounter an area of law—even though you may not realize it—that receives little attention in the movies or in the media, although it is very much a part of our everyday lives.

In Chapter 1, we looked at your right to use the road from three perspectives: statutory law, which is the law the legislature makes; common law, which is the body of law formed by centuries of judicial decisions that cumulatively provide precedential direction for both trial and appellate courts; and constitutional law, which is the law that establishes governments and defines their powers. But these are not the only types of laws. It may surprise you to learn that every time you enter into a contract, you are creating a private law between yourself and another party.

Virtually everyone has signed a contract at some time or another, whether an apartment lease, a loan agreement, or a major purchase. In fact, you probably enter into contracts every single day without even realizing it. Every single time you buy something, you're entering into a contract. These small, everyday contracts are rarely thought of as contracts by most people, because few people take the time to consider what a contract really is. The general consensus, as expressed in the *Restatement of Contracts,* is that a contract "is a promise or set of promises for breach of which the law gives a remedy, or the performance of which the law in some way recognizes as a duty."[1]

There are three basic elements to every contract:

1. *The offer,* an expression of willingness to enter into a bargain.

2. *The acceptance,* an expression of assent to the offer.

3. *Consideration,* an exchange of the promises and acts that are required to complete the bargain. Often, the consideration will be money, but

---

1 Restatement (Second) of Contracts Section 1 (1981).

consideration can be anything that benefits the person making the offer.

If these three elements are present, a contract has been formed, and it can be enforced by a court.[2] Of course, there's more to contract law than offer, acceptance, and consideration, as we shall see.

Although most cyclists aren't professional athletes, as a cyclist you will nevertheless enter into cycling-related contracts at least occasionally. Consider the following contracts, for example:

- Bicycle or accessories purchase
- Product guarantee
- Bicycle repair agreement
- Insurance policy
- Shipping agreement
- Parking receipt

Whether you're a professional athlete, a weekend warrior, or a daily commuter, you will occasionally enter into cycling-related contracts, and thus you may encounter a cycling-related contract problem. So what do you do when you're the "little guy," and somebody else is using the contract you both entered into to enforce a condition that you don't think is fair? Can you be forced to sign your rights away? In this chapter we will look at some common cycling-related contract problems for an answer to that question, but first, let's go over some concepts common to each problem we'll be discussing.

Contract Basics

8-1 ADHESION CONTRACTS

As we've seen, every contract will have three elements: offer, acceptance, and consideration. Generally, contracts that are mutually bargained for between parties that have equal bargaining power will be upheld. However, most of the contracts that average consumers enter into are on preprinted forms written by the business, with terms that favor the business, and are offered on a "take it or leave it" basis, with

---

2 Every contract must contain these three elements. However, contracts and contract law are a complex subject, and there are many more variables that enter into a contract. Usually, as long as these three elements are present, a contract has been formed; usually, except in certain types of contracts, such as land purchases, it is not even necessary to have a contract in writing. As a practical matter, however, it is almost always advisable to put contracts into writing.

no equality of bargaining power. These types of contracts are called "adhesion contracts," and the courts are far less inclined to uphold unfair clauses in adhesion contracts than they would be if the contract was between parties with equal bargaining power.

8-2 EXCULPATORY CLAUSES

Many courts will allow a waiver of liability—meaning you won't sue the other person—in a contract as long as that waiver does not purport to relieve the other party of gross or willful negligence. The legal term for this waiver of liability is "exculpatory clause." No court will uphold a liability waiver for gross negligence, and many courts will void the entire liability waiver, even though it would have reluctantly upheld a narrower liability waiver that waived liability only for ordinary negligence. Thus, depending on the state, if someone presents you with a contract containing one of these blanket waivers, she overreach at her own peril.

8-3 TORTS

Contracts often contain an exculpatory clause in which you agree to release the other party from liability for negligence. As we saw previously, negligence is a type of civil wrong—a tort—and as we've seen, a tort is any civil wrong, except breach of contract, for which the law provides a remedy—either money damages or a court order. Here's an example: Suppose you enter a race and you win. After the race, Roger Racer, another entrant who has a reputation as a sore loser, approaches you and accuses you of cheating. Although you might be angry about the accusation, Roger Racer probably hasn't done anything for which the law provides a remedy, because things like making you angry or hurting your feelings do not rise to the level of a civil wrong. Now let's suppose that after the race, Roger Racer publishes a fabricated account of your alleged cheating. Now he's done something for which the law does provide a remedy, and you can file a lawsuit for libel.

Although the law differentiates between civil and criminal wrongs, it is possible that the same act can be both a civil wrong and a criminal wrong. Here's an example: After you win the race, Roger Racer approaches and punches you, saying, "You beat me, now I beat you." By punching you, Roger Racer has just committed a crime, and he has also committed a tort. If somebody has engaged in tortious conduct, the injured party can file a lawsuit against the responsible party even if the act is also a crime. Now let's look at some types of torts.

NEGLIGENCE

As we discussed in Chapter 3, negligence is an act or a failure to act that breaches the duty of due care that the defendant owes to every other person. This duty of due care is to behave as a reasonable person would under similar circumstances—a legal standard of conduct to protect others from unreasonable risk of harm. A breach of duty occurs when a person's behavior exposes others to unreasonable risk of harm because this person has either acted or failed to act as a reasonable person would. Those first three elements—an act or failure to act, a duty of due care, and a breach of duty—when combined, form a negligent act. If the negligent act is both the actual and foreseeable cause of the defendant's injuries, the law provides a remedy to right the wrong done to the plaintiff.

GROSS NEGLIGENCE

Gross negligence is more extreme than ordinary negligence but falls short of an intentional act. What separates gross negligence from ordinary negligence is a reckless disregard for the rights or safety of others; this reckless disregard is manifested by a conscious indifference to the consequences of the negligent act. Here's how it works: With ordinary negligence, the negligent conduct breaches a duty of due care that the defendant owes to every other person to behave as a reasonable person would under similar circumstances in order to protect others from unreasonable risk of harm. With gross negligence, that breach of duty is done with conscious indifference to the likely consequences.

INTENTIONAL ACTS

Intentional acts differ from negligence in that the defendant must have acted with the intent to cause the tortious injury to the plaintiff, whereas a negligent act—even gross negligence—does not include the element of intent. Examples of intentional acts include:

→ ASSAULT. *The intentional infliction of an apprehension of harmful or offensive contact.*

→ BATTERY. *The intentional infliction of harmful or offensive contact.*

→ FALSE IMPRISONMENT. *The intentional infliction of unlawful confinement.*

→ INTENTIONAL INFLICTION OF EMOTIONAL DISTRESS. *The intentional infliction, through extreme or outrageous conduct, of severe emotional distress.*

→ TRESPASS TO CHATTELS. *The intentional interference with the use or enjoyment of a person's property. For example, if Roger Racer were to ride your bike in the event without your permission, that would be trespass to chattels.*

→ CONVERSION OF CHATTELS. *The intentional interference with the possession or ownership of a person's property. For example, if Roger Racer were to steal or deliberately damage your bicycle, that would be conversion of chattels.*

In addition to these intentional acts against your person or property, other examples of torts that may contain an element of intent include:

→ DEFAMATION. *A false and defamatory public statement.*

→ INVASION OF PRIVACY. *For example, publicity regarding a person's private life.*

Now that you know the basics of contracts, exculpatory clauses, and tortious conduct, let's look at some typical situations in which cyclists are asked to sign away their rights, and the limitations, if any, that might apply when you sign away your rights.

Pre-Event Releases

Cyclists who participate in events—whether the event is a race, a group ride, or even joining a professional team—are all familiar with the "liability release," which purports to waive liability for negligent acts on the part of the event sponsors or team. These pre-event releases are the price of admission to the event, so everybody signs. But what if something happens at the event and you're injured? Can these liability waivers be upheld? Have you really signed your life away when you sign the release? Possibly, but not necessarily.

First, let's talk about what a pre-event release is. When people get together to organize a cycling event, they have a lot of different tasks to pull together. They must get permission from the responsible public agencies to hold the event. They have to find sponsors. They need to ensure that medical personnel are standing by. They must promote the event and sign up riders. And in order to gain the approval and participation they want, the organizers need to assure everybody involved in assisting with the event that they won't be exposing themselves to lawsuits if they participate. For that reason, the organizers will require riders to sign a pre-event release (technically known as an exculpatory clause) when they register for the event, waiving their right to sue.

Here are two examples of excerpts from real pre-event releases:[3]

In consideration for being permitted to participate in this event, I agree to assume all risks and to release, hold harmless and covenant not to sue the Organizer, any designated beneficiaries, sponsors, officials, participating clubs, communities, organizations, friends of the event, including the event medical sponsor, the Medical Director, and members of the Medical Team, and all other government or public entities including, but not limited to, the Department of Transportation and affiliated organizations and all their respective directors, officers, agents, employees and members (collectively, "the releasees"), for any claim, loss or liability that I may have arising out of my participation in the event, including bodily injury, death or property damage, whether caused by negligence or carelessness of the releasees or otherwise.

For and in consideration of the right to participate in the event, the undersigned does hereby release, absolve and hold harmless the Organizer, their sponsors, heirs, successors, assigns, employees, agents and personnel from any and all actions, cause of action, liability or responsibility whatsoever, or any injury, harm, loss or inconvenience suffered or incurred by the undersigned during or as a result of taking part in the event.

What are these releases really saying? Just by knowing the three elements of a contract, you can begin to see them in a new light. Notice that the first sentences of both releases contain the words "in consideration." This is an interesting choice of language, given that the three basic elements to a contract are offer, acceptance, and consideration. The *offer* being made is the right to participate in the event. The consideration that will be *accepted* for this right is an agreement not to sue the organizer or anybody else associated with organizing the event. The *consideration* offered by the organizer is the rider's actual participation in the event. By agreeing to the terms, the rider has accepted the offer.

Before pinpointing exactly what it is you're signing away with a pre-event release, there's a broader issue that cyclists who participate in organized cycling events must be aware of: the assumption of risk.

---

3 All quotations from pre-event releases are from actual releases supplied to participants by the organizers or sponsors of cycling events.

8-4 ASSUMPTION OF RISK

Under ordinary circumstances, all persons owe all other persons a duty of care. If somebody breaches this duty and the breach causes an injury to another person, we call that negligence. However, when you participate in a sport in which certain inherent risks are involved, you have, under the law, assumed the risk of injury inherent in the "vigorous and active participation" of that sport, even if the injury is the result of another person's negligence. You have, in effect, agreed by your participation to release other persons involved in the event from their duty of care.

Despite this, the risk you have assumed is not limitless. The following rules apply:

1. You are releasing only persons who are involved with the event from their duty of care; your assumption of risk does not relieve persons who are not involved with the event from their duty of care.

2. You have not assumed the risk of injury resulting from reckless or intentional acts.

3. The "inherent risk" you assume will vary from sport to sport, and it includes only the types of risks one might expect to encounter in the sport—even, as we've seen, if that risk arises from another participant's negligence.

In the case of the third point, when you register to ride in a cycling event you assume the risk of crashes with other cyclists. Likewise, football players assume the risk of being tackled by other players. When you "assume the risk" of participation in your sport, you do not assume risks that are not inherent to your sport. For example, a cyclist hasn't assumed the risk of being tackled by another cyclist, and a football player hasn't assumed the risk of a collision with a bicycle.

Assumption of risk is a broader issue than release of liability, because there are actually two different kinds of assumed risk: express assumption of risk and implied assumption of risk. Express assumption of risk is the risk you assume when you sign a pre-event release that expressly states that you assume the risk, whereas implied assumption of risk is the risk that you assume by your conduct—for example, if you play a game of football with some friends, your participation implies acceptance of the risks of the game even if you do not sign a release saying you are accepting the risks of the game. In both situations, you have accepted the risks of the sport.

But if you have accepted the risks of the sport in both situations, why does the law differentiate between express and implied assumptions of risk? The reason is that the type of risk you've assumed—express or implied—will determine whether you can recover compensation for your injuries. An express assumption of risk on your part will completely bar you from any recovery for injuries you incur through another person's negligence.[4] With an implied assumption of risk, you may or may not be able to recover compensation for your injuries, depending on the state.

In some states, implied assumption of risk has been "merged" with comparative negligence. This means that if the assumption of risk was implied, rather than express, your case may be heard at trial, where a jury will consider the other person's negligence, as well as your assumption of the risks, and decide your compensation, if any, accordingly.

In other states, the courts will determine if the implied assumption of risk is a "primary assumption of risk" or a "secondary assumption of risk." Like an express assumption of risk, an implied primary assumption of risk acts as a complete bar to recovery. In determining whether the implied assumption of risk is primary, courts will look into two factors: the risks inherent in the nature of the sport and whether the plaintiff and the defendant were coparticipants in the event. If they were coparticipants, and if the injury was caused by a risk inherent to the sport, the court will determine that the defendant owed no duty to protect the plaintiff from injury, and the assumption of risk will completely bar the plaintiff's recovery of compensation.

But if the defendant is involved in the event as a sponsor or organizer, rather than as a coparticipant, or if the defendant has increased the risks beyond what are inherent in the sport, the court will determine that the defendant owed the plaintiff a duty of care. As a defense to the alleged negligence, the defendant will then assert that there was an implied secondary assumption of risk. This defense will not bar recovery, but it may reduce the recovery, because under comparative negligence principles, the jury will consider both the defendant's negligence and the plaintiff's assumption of risk in apportioning liability for the injury.

Thus, in every state an express assumption of risk will completely bar you from compensation for injuries incurred through another person's negligence, whereas an implied assumption of risk, depending on the state and facts of the case, may allow you to recover compensation for those injuries.

Still, is it possible for you to "sign your life away" with a pre-event release?

4   Although, as we'll see, there are limits to liability releases.

8-5 THE LIMITATIONS ON EXCULPATORY CLAUSES

Despite the assertions of exculpatory clause language that makes it seem like you're signing your rights away, there are in fact limits to exculpatory clauses. Depending on the circumstances and a number of factors involved in the contract, you may not be signing your rights away—at least not to the extent the contract claims.

Let's consider the excerpts from the two actual pre-event releases we're using as examples to see why exculpatory clauses have their limits. First, both of these events are open to minors, so let's look at the contract language about age limits. On the first release, the minimum conditions necessary for participation are as follows: "You must be at least 16 years of age, have medical insurance at the time of the Ride, and agree to the following Agreement and Waiver of Liability." Compare that with similar conditions in the other release: "When no parent or guardian is assigned where indicated below, the entrant specifically warrants and represents that he or she is over the age of 18 (eighteen) and is not suffering under any mental or physical infirmity which might adversely affect his or her judgment or safety."

Unlike the first release, this release requires the signature of a parent or guardian if the entrant is under the age of eighteen. It says: "I am the parent/guardian of the entrant, above, who is under the age of 18 (eighteen). By executing this document, I do consent to the entrant's participation in the event. I do consent to the terms of the Release and I do further agree to be fully bound by the terms of this Release, both individually and as a parent/guardian of the entrant."

Because these events are open to participation by minors, both of these contracts raise issues of *capacity,* which refers to the mental capacity of the person entering into the contract. As a general rule, persons under the age of majority—eighteen in most states—do not have the capacity to enter into contracts, and although they may sign contracts, the contracts are not enforceable against them if they later choose to void them. With that in mind, it should be obvious that the first release, if signed by a minor, could not be enforced against that minor if the minor later chose to void the release.[5]

But what about that second release—the one that requires a parent's signature for entrants who are minors? Can that release be enforced? The answer is no. When a parent signs a release, that signature binds the parent, but it does not bind the minor. If the minor later chooses to void

---

5   However, it may be that the minor would still be held to have impliedly assumed the risk. See *Kabella v. Bouchelle*, 672 P.2d 290 (1983).

the release, it cannot be enforced. Okay, so the release is not enforceable against minors, but it is enforceable against adult riders, right?

Not necessarily. Let's look again at what the pre-event releases say to see who's released from liability. With both releases, you've agreed not to sue persons associated with organizing the event, but you haven't waived your rights to sue coparticipants and other persons for negligent or intentional acts. The only parties who are exempted from liability are the event organizers and other named parties associated with organizing the event. However, as we've seen, even if you haven't expressly assumed the risk of injuries inherent to cycling, you have impliedly assumed the risk, so the other participants may nevertheless be released from liability for negligence, as long as the injury results from a risk inherent to cycling. So you can sue other parties not associated with organizing the event, and you may or may not be able to sue the event coparticipants, but you can't sue parties associated with organizing the event, right?

Not necessarily. The releases appear to release the organizers from liability for intentional acts; that appearance is deceiving, because pre-event releases cannot exempt a party from liability for intentional acts. Thus, with any pre-event release you sign, you are not waiving your right to sue any party for an intentional act; you are only releasing the organizers from liability for their own negligence. Okay, so you can sue the event organizers or anybody else for intentional acts, but you can't sue the event organizers for negligence, right?

Not necessarily. Although the courts will uphold exculpatory clauses, they do so reluctantly. Thus, these clauses are interpreted very narrowly by the courts to exempt defendants from liability for *ordinary negligence* only; where *gross negligence* is alleged, the exculpatory clause will not exempt the defendant from liability. Okay, so minors are not bound by exculpatory clauses, and nobody is immune from liability for intentional or grossly negligent acts, but exculpatory clauses will protect event organizers from liability for ordinary negligence, right?

Not necessarily. Depending on the state you live in, there are additional factors to consider. Let's look at two cases from California, for example. In the first case, *Okura v. United States Cycling Federation,* the plaintiff was a cyclist who was injured during a race sponsored by a local affiliate of the United States Cycling Federation (USCF).[6] The plaintiff, who had signed a pre-event release, fell when his bicycle hit loose debris as he was crossing railroad tracks on the course. The issue before the court of appeals was whether the pre-event release was valid under

6 *Okura v. United States Cycling Federation*, 186 Cal. App.3d 1462 (Cal. App. 2 Dist. 1986).

California law, which provides, in Civil Code Section 1668, that "all contracts which have for their object, directly or indirectly, to exempt anyone from responsibility for his own fraud, or willful injury to the person or property of another, or violation of law, whether willful or negligent, are against the policy of the law."

Following guidelines established by the California Supreme Court for interpreting the validity of pre-event releases, the *Okura* court upheld the pre-event release, largely because, compared with banking, hospitals, escrow companies, and common carriers, a bicycle race is not a "service of great importance to the public." Furthermore, the court held, a bicycle race is "a leisure time activity" and therefore "people are not compelled to enter the event but are merely invited to participate." For these reasons, the court held that the pre-event release did not violate California law.

The second case illustrates the limits of releases, however. In *Bennett v. United States Cycling Federation,* the plaintiff was a cyclist who was injured after colliding with an automobile that a race attendant had allowed onto the closed racecourse.[7] At issue was whether the pre-event release exempted the race organizers from all liability for negligent acts, or exempted them only from liability for foreseeable hazards. The court of appeals held that the pre-event release exempted the race organizers from liability for the reasonably foreseeable hazards of racing, but that a jury must decide whether a car on a closed racecourse was a reasonably foreseeable hazard of racing. The court observed:

> There is little doubt that a subscriber of the bicycle release at issue here must be held to have waived any hazards relating to bicycle racing that are obvious or that might reasonably have been foreseen. As plaintiff points out, these hazards include "collisions with other riders, negligently maintained equipment, bicycles which were unfit for racing but nevertheless passed by organizers, [and] bad road surfaces . . ." On the other hand, accepting plaintiff's declaration that the course was known to be and was in fact closed to automobiles before the race (presumably when he signed the release), it is doubtful whether he or any participant would have realistically appreciated the risk of colliding with a car traveling in any direction along the closed racecourse.[8]

---

7   *Bennett v. United States Cycling Federation*, 193 Cal. App.3d 1485 (Cal. App. 2 Dist. 1987).

8   Ibid.

Because the validity of pre-event releases in California now hinges on "reasonably foreseeable hazards," the bicycle-racing safety standards of the USCF and the Triathlon Federation will likely be an issue in future negligence cases; if the safety standards have been violated and an injury occurs, the pre-event release will probably not exempt the organizers from liability for negligence.

Okura and *Bennett* are the law in just one state, however; other courts in other states may decide the validity of pre-event releases differently. As *Okura* demonstrates, though, state laws may invalidate some exculpatory clauses, and depending on the state court interpreting the release, it is possible that pre-event releases will be invalidated as well.

Even in the absence of a specific statute, courts may still rule against pre-event releases. For example, West Virginia's Supreme Court of Appeals, applying the same test that the California court used in *Okura,* reached the opposite conclusion in *Kyriazis v. University of West Virginia* (1994).[9] In this case, the court held that a sporting event sponsored by a state university is a public service, and that the pre-event release was therefore void because it was against public policy. In *Spencer v. Killington, Ltd.* (1997), the Supreme Court of Vermont also reached the opposite conclusion of the *Okura* court, holding that a pre-event release for an amateur ski race that was open to members of the general public was void because it was against public policy.[10] In Oregon, a federal court held in *Farina v. Mt. Bachelor* (1995) that a pre-event release was against public policy and therefore unenforceable, *even for ordinary negligence,* because it "exculpates [the defendant] from liability for more than ordinary negligence, including gross negligence and wanton or wilful misconduct. This attempt to escape liability for more than ordinary negligence renders the release clause invalid."[11] And in *Hiett v. Lake Barcroft Community Association, Inc.* (1992), the Supreme Court of Virginia held that a pre-event release signed by a triathlete who was rendered a quadriplegic during the swimming event was invalid because exculpatory clauses are "against public policy."[12]

8-6 IF YOU'RE INJURED

As these cases show, pre-event releases that appear to make you "sign your life away" have a number of legal exceptions that make them less

9 *Kyriazis v. University of West Virginia*, 450 S.E.2d 649 (W. Va. 1994).

10 *Spencer v. Killington, Ltd.*, 702 A.2d 35 (Vt. 1997).

11 *Farina v. Mt. Bachelor, Inc.*, 66 F.3d 233 (9th Cir. 1995).

12 *Hiett v. Lake Barcroft Comm. Assoc., Inc.*, 418 S.E.2d 894 (Va. 1992).

binding than they appear to be, and depending on the jurisdiction, they may even be held invalid as against public policy. If you are injured (and remember, an "injury" isn't necessarily a bodily injury) as a result of somebody's tortious conduct, and you have signed a pre-event release that purports to exempt certain parties from liability for tortious conduct, don't assume that you have no recourse. Consult with an experienced attorney to determine the extent, if any, that the release exempts those parties from liability.

Group Ride Liability

Anybody who participates in cycling at a serious level has likely been on, or perhaps even organized, a group ride. Cyclists often ask whether they can be held liable if they organize a group ride—even informally—and somebody is injured. Although the question seems simple enough, it is in fact very difficult to answer with any specificity, because the answer will be highly dependent upon both state case law and the specific facts of the ride. Nevertheless, it's possible to discern some general principles of liability, which will give you some idea of what you need to do to protect yourself from liability when you organize a group ride.

8-7 LIABILITY IN INFORMAL, UNORGANIZED RIDING

Let's start with liability for the most basic riding before proceeding to liability for organized rides. Say you're out for a ride, and other cyclists, as well as motorists, are also out on the road. As you know from Chapter 2, you owe all other persons a duty of care, and all other persons owe you the same duty of care. This means that you can be held liable to others for your breach of that duty—in other words, for your negligent actions—and others can be held liable to you for their breach of that duty. You can also be held liable for your reckless actions, as well as your intentional actions, and others can be held liable to you for their reckless or intentional actions. And, as you know by now, if you're injured by another person, you haven't "assumed the risk" of your injuries—let alone consented to them—just because you got on your bike and went for a ride.

So far, that seems pretty straightforward. Now let's say you're out for a ride, but this time your ride is an organized event. In this scenario, you're in a different world when it comes to liability. But why? What's changed?

8-8 LIABILITY IN ORGANIZED SPORTS

Once your ride has changed from an informal, unorganized ride to an organized ride, a new issue enters the picture: the "assumption of risk." As we saw, when you participate in a sport, you assume the risk of injury inherent in the "vigorous and active participation" of that sport, even if the injury is the result of another person's negligence. You have not, however, assumed risks that are not inherent to the sport, nor have you assumed the risk for injuries caused by a person not associated with the event, or from anybody's reckless or intentional acts. But what if you and the "other athletes" are just weekend warriors on an informal group ride? Is assumption of risk still an issue? Generally, yes. As courts have held in many cases, involving such diverse sports as waterskiing, football, and yes, cycling, amateur athletes participating in informal sports assume the risk inherent to the sport.

When the event is formal, it is likely that the participants will be required to sign a release in which they assume the risks inherent to the sport. This express assumption of risk will release the event organizers from liability for negligence. When the event is informal, the assumption of risk will likely be implied, and a court's treatment of implied assumption of risk will depend on the jurisdiction. In some states, implied assumption of risk has been "merged" into comparative negligence; in others, the courts will conduct an inquiry into the relationship between the plaintiff and the defendant and consider the risks inherent to the sport.

8-9 COPARTICIPANT LIABILITY

Unless an express assumption of risk has been made in regard to coparticipants, an implied assumption of risk will be at issue when an event participant negligently injures a coparticipant. In *Kabella v. Bouschelle* (1983), a case involving an injury incurred during an informal football game between friends, a New Mexico court held that an implied assumption of risk would shield a coparticipant from liability for negligence, but not for reckless or intentional acts:

> Here, the players at the time of Kabella's injury were not involved in any organized athletic activity being played under the supervision of coaches or referees, or a definite set of rules. The participants were playing under a loose set of rules informally agreed upon among themselves. The contact was not intentional, willful

or reckless. Although Kabella alleged the players had agreed to stop play when the ball carrier yelled "I'm down," Kabella does not allege that violating this rule constituted an intent to harm him, or that it amounted to reckless conduct.

Vigorous and active participation in sporting events should not be chilled by the threat of litigation. The players in informal sandlot games do not have the benefit of written rules, coaches, referees or instant replay to evaluate a player's actions. A cause of action for personal injuries between participants must be predicated upon recklessness or intentional conduct, not mere negligence.[13]

Thus, the court was engaging in the two-part implied assumption-of-risk inquiry: whether the risk—in this case, a tackle made in violation of the informal rules agreed upon by the participants—is inherent in the nature of the sport, and whether the plaintiff and defendant are coparticipants in the event. In *Kabella,* the court adopted a standard of reckless or willful conduct for "participants engaged in contact athletic activities." This meant that there was an implied primary assumption of risk barring recovery from coparticipants in contact sports for merely negligent acts: The act would have to be reckless or willful for the coparticipant to be held liable. This is, in fact, the rule in most states.

When we move away from contact sports into so-called cooperative sports, however, the issue of coparticipant liability becomes less clear. In *Novak v. Virene* (1991), a New Hampshire case involving a collision between two skiers, the court allowed a lawsuit in a skiing collision caused by simple negligence to go before a jury, stating: "Other cases have applied an exception to ordinary negligence liability for team sports in which contact was virtually inevitable. As in the individual sports of running and bicycling there is the possibility of collisions in downhill skiing. But by participating one does not voluntarily submit to bodily contact with others, and such contact is not inevitable. Therefore, defendant's conduct should be governed by ordinary negligence standards."[14]

Keep in mind that the "ordinary negligence standard" still requires a showing that the allegedly negligent skier was behaving less prudently than a reasonably prudent skier of similar abilities and experience under similar circumstances. The most common way in which participants act negligently is to get themselves in over their heads, such as when a beginner tries to tackle a difficult "black diamond" ski slope, or when an inexperienced cyclist tries to grimly hang on to a 22 mph pace line.

13 *Kabella v. Bouschelle*, 672 P.2d 290 (N.M. App. 1983).
14 *Novak v. Virene*, 586 N.E.2d 578 (Ill. App. 1991).

Not all states agree with New Hampshire's "if it's a noncontact sport, negligence applies" formula. California, for instance, insists that even if it is a noncontact sport, it is still the inherent nature of the sport that determines whether the risk has been assumed. For example, in *Stimson v. Carlson* (1992), a sailing case involving an injury incurred during a race, Thomas Carlson, the helmsman, was supposed to call out "Jibe ho!" before moving the tiller for a course change to warn the others that the boom would sweep across the boat. During the course of the race, Carlson forgot to call out, and Michael Stimson was hit by the boom. The court said the possibility of getting hit by the boom was an inherent risk of sailing and denied the suit:

> Generally, defendants have no duty to protect plaintiffs against risks inherent in an active sport. A swinging boom is a risk inherent in the sport of sailing. Thus, Carlson owed no legal duty to eliminate or protect Stimson against this inherent risk. When an inherent sports risk is involved, the defendant is liable only if he or she intentionally injures another player or engages in conduct that is so reckless that it is totally outside the range of the ordinary activity involved in an active sport. Failing to call out course changes does not amount to intentional or reckless conduct. Stimson alleged that Carlson was negligent, not that he committed an intentional tort. Carlson's failure to declare a course before executing it was not so reckless as to be totally outside the range of ordinary activity involved in the sport. While his conduct was unexpected, it did not alter the fundamental risk of sailing–the boom and its sheets remained the danger.[15]

A very similar case—*Moser v. Ratinoff* (2003)—dealing with bicycling was heard by the same California court. Both riders were involved in the "Death Valley Double Century," and they were riding in a group of three. Before dawn, distracted by a police car, Joanne Ratinoff drifted to the right and collided with Christian Moser, who went down. The court very plainly stated that "the issue in the instant case is whether an organized, noncompetitive, long-distance bicycle ride is one of those sports activities to which the primary assumption of risk doctrine applies."

The question was both unique and important. Bicycling is, of course, regulated by traffic law. Under normal circumstances, a cyclist riding by herself for transport is governed by traffic law and negligence applies: If she is negligent, as defined by the traffic code, she will be held liable

---

15 *Stimson v. Carlson*, 11 Cal. App. 4th 1201 (1992).

to another for any injury she causes; the inverse will also be true. But a group ride starts to take on some of the characteristics of a sport, so if two riders bump into each other, is it more like two cars colliding at an intersection, or more like a helmsman forgetting to call out a sweeping mainsail boom? Here's what the court said: "It is true that bicycle riding is a means of transportation—as is automobile driving. Normal automobile driving requires skill, can be done for enjoyment, and entails risks of injury. But organized, long distance bicycle rides on public highways with large numbers of riders involve physical exertion and athletic risks not generally associated with automobile or individual bicycle riding on public streets or on bicycle lanes or paths. In view of these considerations, the organized, long-distance group bicycle ride qualifies as a 'sport.'"[16]

The court was careful to point out that its decision affected only non-competitive performance riding, stating, "We express no opinion as to such other forms of recreational bicycle riding." Even for such extreme events as a double century, the holding was limited to coparticipant liability: As the *Moser* court observed in a footnote to its analysis of assumed risk, the "mere riding of a bicycle does not mean the assumption of risk by the rider that he may be hit by a car," so a negligent auto driver could not use the defense that the cyclist "assumed the risk" that a careless motorist would come along.

8-10 ORGANIZER AND COACH LIABILITY

So far, we have talked about implied primary assumption of risk, which involves coparticipant liability in a sport. But what if you are not just riding along? What if you have invited the participants and are "leading"? In this situation, there are two possibilities: You could be considered either a sponsor/organizer or a coach. Either way, you're not a mere coparticipant, and therefore the possibility exists that, absent an express assumption of risk, you could be held liable for negligence.

In determining whether you are an event organizer, the important factor to consider is the control, involvement, knowledge, and direction that you exercise over the event. A second important factor is the lack of knowledge or sophistication that your participants bring. The court will consider both your ability to prevent trouble and the participants' ability—or lack of ability—to stay out of trouble. The fact that some of the participants are minors is not, in and of itself, a significant factor, except

---

16 *Moser v. Ratinoff*, 105 Cal. App. 4th 1211 (2003).

as it relates to the general tendency for younger and less experienced participants to depend on adults for control and guidance during sports.

Also surprising is what is not important: money. Whether you are getting paid or not, and how much, are usually not a factor, except to establish a clear line of authority and responsibility. A good explanation of organizer liability was given in *Vogel v. West Mountain Corporation* (1987), a New York case in which a competitive skier was injured in a badly designed slalom course. The resort settled, and Ellen Vogel, the skier, went after the event's sponsor, Miller Beer. The court decided in Miller Beer's favor. The decision lays out a pretty complete blueprint of what it takes to sue an event organizer for negligence and, though it never uses the word, states what an "organizer" is:

> Mere sponsorship, absent control, does not render Miller legally responsible. It is well established that before a defendant may be found liable for negligence, a duty must exist. The difficulty with this case is that Miller is merely a sponsor of an athletic event. Nonetheless, Vogel urges that as a result of the fact that she was induced to enter the race on the basis of Miller's involvement, coupled with the financial benefits enjoyed by Miller as sponsor, Miller owed a duty to ensure that the event was conducted in a safe manner.
>
> An important criterion is whether the realities of everyday experience demonstrate that the party to be made responsible could have prevented the negligent conduct. Here, Miller was not in a position to supervise West Mountain's running of the race, since they didn't enjoy the necessary expertise. Moreover, the record demonstrates that West Mountain, not Miller, actually designed, supervised, and controlled the event. Under these circumstances, it would be unreasonable to impose a duty on Miller since, very simply, it was not in a position to prevent the negligence.[17]

Likewise, coaches have a duty to exercise reasonable care consistent with their skill, training, experience, and position of responsibility, and they can be liable for negligence if they breach that duty, as a judge explained in *Tan v. Goddard* (1993), a California case: "There are precedents reaching back for most of this century that find an absence of duty in negligence between co-participants, and often, to spectators, but the law is otherwise as applied to coaches and instructors. For them, the general rule is that coaches and instructors owe a duty of care to persons in

17 *Vogel v. West Mountain Corp.*, 97 A.D.2d 46 (N.Y. App. Div. 1983).

their charge. The coach or instructor is not, of course, an insurer, and a student may be held to notice that which is obvious and to ask appropriate questions, but all authorities have recognized the existence of a duty of care."[18]

This duty of care is not limited to competition or competitive activity. The *Tan* case involved a horseback-riding school, and the court concluded that the school "owed Tan a duty to see that the horse assigned was safe under the conditions for a given activity."[19] A few months later, in another 1993 riding-school accident case, *Galardi v. Seahorse Riding School,* the same court made the point even more clearly: "The occasion of plaintiff's fall was not during competition with other riders. Instead, she had placed her training in the hands of defendants, who were employed to instruct and coach her. The defendants certainly had a duty to avoid an unreasonable risk of injury to Galardi and to take care that her jumping array was not beyond the capabilities of horse and rider."[20]

Notice the language: The defendants "were employed to instruct and coach" the plaintiff. The obvious follow-up question is "What does it take to be considered a coach?" Although there are numerous cases involving coparticipants in informal sports, there aren't many cases regarding informal coaching. In fact, I've come across only one case alleging an informal coaching relationship, and unfortunately, that case has no precedential value, so for now it's a question that hasn't been addressed by the courts.

8-11 How to Protect Yourself

If you are merely a coparticipant in an organized ride or event, you cannot be held liable for simple negligence, as long as any injury you cause is an inherent risk of cycling. However, if you recklessly or intentionally injure a coparticipant, you can be held liable for gross negligence or assault and battery. Likewise, if you are a participant who is injured by a coparticipant in an organized ride or event, your coparticipant can't be held liable for negligence, but he or she can be held liable for reckless or intentional conduct.

If you have actually organized the ride, your liability is heavily dependent on detailed facts and the law of your specific state. The more control and direction you exercised over the organization of the ride, the closer you came to acting as a "road captain"; and the more the other

---

18 *Tan v. Goddard*, 17 Cal. Rptr. 2nd 89 (Cal. App. 2 Dist. 1993).

19 Ibid.

20 *Galardi v. Seahorse Riding School*, 20 Cal. Rptr. 2nd 270 (Cal. App. 2 Dist. 1993).

participants looked to you to use your expertise to help them and reduce their risk, the higher your exposure to liability as an organizer or promoter of the event.

Similarly, if you can reasonably be considered a coach or instructor, even an informal coach, you will have a duty of care. To reduce your liability, the ride should be cooperative, not competitive, and you should avoid challenging, testing, or pushing the limits of the riders—that is, engaging in what the courts call "confrontational preparedness." If you offer any advice, confine it to suggestions about general skills. Anything that reduces the expectations of the other riders—in terms of what they are expecting from you—works in your favor. The age of the riders is not an issue, but their lack of experience and knowledge, and the degree to which they look to you for guidance, are relevant. The fact that your ride invitation is in writing is also not an issue—written documents make things easier to prove, but they rarely change any aspect of the underlying law.

As a rough guide, ask yourself this question: "Are these riders placing themselves in my hands?" If the answer is no, then you are probably a mere coparticipant. If the answer is yes, then you are probably a coach or event organizer, and you should have the riders sign a pre-event release and assumption-of-risk form. Keep in mind, however, the hazards of pre-event releases that overreach by purporting to absolve organizers of liability for all tortious acts. If you keep your pre-event release limited to waivers of liability for simple negligence, you'll likely be more protected than if you had overreached.

Shipping Liability Waivers

One common contract that cyclists must occasionally deal with is the shipping contract—that is, the liability waiver that limits the amount of money the shipping company will pay you if the package containing your bike or components is lost or damaged. Before we begin, let's get some potentially confusing terminology out of the way. You, the owner of the goods being shipped, are the "shipper." The company transporting the goods is the "carrier." Retail shops, such as commercial pack-and-ship stores (even most UPS Stores, which are independent franchise locations licensed under the UPS name), are called "freight forwarders" because they broker shipments but do not carry the goods themselves.

8-12 CARRIERS AND THE COMMON LAW

Going all the way back to English common law, certain types of businesses were considered different from other types of businesses because of the amount of control they exercised over their customers; businesses that were assumed to exercise a lot of control included innkeepers, utilities such as water or canal companies, and what were called "common carriers." Because they exercised a lot of control, they were also expected to exercise a lot of care on their customers' behalf. Therefore, as even a recent American court explained in *Barnes v. New Hampshire Karting Association* (1986), these firms, unlike other companies, could not enforce waivers absolving them of liability for negligence: "A defendant seeking to avoid liability must show that the exculpatory agreement does not contravene public policy, i.e. that no special relationship existed between the parties and there was no other disparity in bargaining power. Where the defendant is a common carrier, innkeeper or public utility, or is otherwise charged with a duty of public service, the defendant cannot by contract rid itself of its obligation of reasonable care."[21]

8-13 CARRIERS AND THE CARMACK AMENDMENT

Since 1906, the common-law liability of carriers has been preempted by federal legislation limiting the liability of interstate carriers. Because this federal statute, called the "Carmack Amendment," preempts both the common-law liability and the state-law liability of interstate carriers, it is the only remedy for consumers whose freight has been lost or damaged by interstate carriers. Note that I said "interstate carriers." That's because the Carmack Amendment applies only to freight shipped interstate. For freight shipped entirely within state, either the common law or the state law would apply.[22] Under the Carmack Amendment, the fees that package delivery services may charge have been regulated by the Interstate Commerce Commission. The carrier's liability for lost or damaged shipments is limited if:

- the carrier provides the shipper with a copy of its rates on request; and

- the carrier obtains the shipper's agreement as to his or her choice of liability; and

---

21 *Barnes v. New Hampshire Karting Assoc.*, 509 A.2d 151 (N.H. 1986).

22 Transportation between Alaska and other states, if it passes through Canada, is exempt from the Carmack Amendment.

- the carrier gives the shipper reasonable opportunity to choose between two or more levels of liability as reflected in shipping rates; and

- the carrier issues a receipt or bill of lading prior to movement of the goods that accurately reflects the agreement.

Most Carmack Amendment cases have turned on the definition of "reasonable opportunity to choose." This means that if the shipper—that's you—is given a "reasonable opportunity to choose" between two or more levels of liability, as reflected in the shipping rates, the carrier's liability will be limited to the level that you choose.

8-14 REASONABLE OPPORTUNITY TO CHOOSE

Now let's look at some examples of how the courts have interpreted the requirement to give you a "reasonable opportunity to choose." Suppose you take your bike to a carrier, and the carrier tells you that there's no need to declare the bike's value. In *Jones v. Yellow Freight System, Inc.* (1987), the carrier lost an oriental rug valued between $20,000 and $25,000. The owner, an unsophisticated shipper, told the carrier's employee that the rug was "very valuable." The employee explained the procedure for declared valuation, but he assured the shipper that she did not need to follow these procedures, as the carrier was "very reliable." Consequently, the owner left the declared value column on the bill of lading blank. The employee who told the shipper not to bother with the declared value box was held to have waived his employer's limitation of liability.[23]

Now, suppose that you ask the carrier to fill in the declared value of your bike on the bill of lading, but the carrier makes a mistake and neglects to do so. Or suppose the carrier makes a deliberate error in filling out the bill of lading. In *United Parcel Service v. Smith* (1994), a case from Indiana, the shipper took one of those "sex-machine" jungle-gym things to Bruce and Bob's Auto Parts (no, I am *not* making this up), who had a "pack-and-ship" agreement with UPS, to be boxed and shipped. The employee of Bruce and Bob's, who was not trained, screwed up the bill of lading, and when the machine disappeared, the shipper was entitled only to the minimum claim. The court found that Bruce and Bob's was acting as an agent for UPS, that the carrier therefore had a duty to adequately train the staff to carry out its Carmack Amendment responsibilities, and that when the employee agreed to fill out the paperwork for

---

23 *Jones v. Yellow Freight System, Inc.,* 656 F.Supp. 550 (M.D. Ga. 1987).

the shipper and messed it up, UPS waived its liability limitation under the federal law.[24]

Depending on the jurisdiction, the carrier's liability may turn on whether the bill of lading was signed by you or the store employee. As the New York Superior Court concluded in *Mohertus Trading Company v. United Parcel Service* (1994), the law in that state is "you sign, you lose": "The signature of plaintiff's officer, a sophisticated business executive, provides 'the most satisfactory evidence of the owner's agreement to the statement of released value' conspicuously set out in the shipping receipt."[25]

One more example: Suppose you're given the bill of lading to sign, and the carrier does not explain your choices to you. This time, you'd be out of luck—at least in one jurisdiction. In *Jackson v. Brook Ledge, Inc.* (1997), the owner of a racehorse arranged for its shipment from Florida to Kentucky. The owner, Kenneth Jackson, delegated the job of meeting the truck to his trainer, Gene Daisey, who got the horse safely on the truck. But Daisey followed the carrier's instructions in signing the bill of lading, and he was never told about the declared value box on the form, which limited the carrier's liability to a maximum of $1,000 unless a higher declared value was selected. The court upheld the limitation:

> Jackson and Daisey . . . as his agent, as experienced shippers, are presumed to have constructive knowledge of the liability limitation provision. Even if Daisey, a trainer, was unaware of the law, we question why Jackson chose to absent himself from the stable on this important day without leaving adequate instruction . . . . One who signs a contract in the absence of fraud or deceit cannot avoid it on the grounds that he did not read it or that he took someone else's word. It is not necessary that an employee of the carrier explain the options to the shipper. Rather, the carrier must provide only reasonable notice of the opportunity to declare a higher value.[26]

To recap the "reasonable opportunity to choose" jurisprudence: Under the Carmack Amendment, a carrier may limit its liability only by granting its customers a "fair opportunity" to choose between a higher

---

24 *United Parcel Service v. Smith*, 645 N.E.2d 1 (Ind. App. 2 Dist. 1994).

25 *Mohertus Trading Co. v. United Parcel Service*, 160 Misc.2d 259 (N.Y. App. Div. 1st Dept. 1994).

26 *Jackson v. Brook Ledge, Inc.*, 991 F. Supp. 640 (E.D. Ky 1997). Note, however, that the court based its decision on Jackson's sophistication as both an attorney with experience in commercial law and an experienced racehorse owner. Had Jackson not been a sophisticated party to the contract, the court may well have decided differently.

and a lower liability level, as reflected in a correspondingly greater or lesser shipping charge. A fair opportunity means that the shipper had both reasonable notice of the liability limitation and the opportunity to obtain the information necessary for making a deliberate and well-informed choice. As we've seen, this means that you must be offered the opportunity—even if it's just the choice of two boxes on a bill of lading—to choose a higher or lower level of liability; however, as we saw in *Jackson v. Brook Ledge,* in at least in some jurisdictions this doesn't necessarily mean that the choices must be explained to you.

When you walk into your local carrier's office—for example, UPS or FedEx—and ask to ship a package, the employees are *probably* going to ask you how much it's worth and how much you want to insure it for.[27] The employee will probably either ask you to fill in a "declared value" box or just ask how much you want the shipment insured for. At a minimum, you will be presented with a form that asks you for a declared value. If you leave the declared value box blank, or accept the default "minimum" shipping rate, you will also be accepting the minimum liability from the carrier. If you declare a value in excess of that default value, you will be "insuring" your shipment for the amount of your declared value. This "insurance" is actually a fiction—the carrier is really setting a differential rate schedule based on the value of the cargo. One of the best capsule summaries of the rule was stated in *Husman Construction Co. v. Purolator* (1987), and applied in *Wagman v. Federal Express Corporation* (1994): "Ignoring the clear and valid limitations of liability in the contract he signed, [plaintiff] brought this suit in district court. No relief will be forthcoming. Those using delivery services to transmit bids are in the best position to procure insurance fro their time-sensitive cargo or to otherwise proceed at their own risk. It is unreasonable to subject a carrier to liability for enormous and unforeseeable consequential damages in return for an $11.75 shipment fee."[28]

8-15 HOW TO PROTECT YOURSELF

This one is a no-brainer: If you are shipping a bike or bike parts interstate, and the freight you are shipping is worth more than the default maximum value on the bill of lading, you *must* declare the value of the bike on your bill of lading in order to recover its full value if it is lost

27 However, as we saw in *Jackson v. Brook Ledge*, you may be held to your "choice" for the default rate if you are merely presented with a form, if the carrier doesn't ask about the value of your shipment, and if you neglect to declare a higher value, depending on your experience and level of sophistication.

28 *Wagman v. Federal Express Corp.*, 894 F.Supp. 247 (D. Md. 1994). See also *Husman Construction Co. v. Purolator*, 832 F.2d 459 (8th Cir. 1987).

or damaged. This will often mean that you are paying a slightly higher shipping rate. This won't guarantee safe delivery of your bike, but it will guarantee that you are fully compensated for its value if it is lost or damaged.

The only exceptions to this requirement are if:

- the carrier does not provide the shipper with rates on request; or

- the carrier does not obtain the shipper's agreement as to his or her choice of liability; or

- the carrier does not give the shipper reasonable opportunity to choose between two or more levels of liability as reflected in shipping rates; or

- the carrier does not issue a receipt or bill of lading prior to movement of the goods that accurately reflects the agreement; or

- the carrier is not shipping your freight interstate.

If your bike is lost or damaged by a carrier, and if any of these exceptions apply, or if the loss or damage to your bike was intentional, the carrier's liability may not be limited by the Carmack Amendment. Time limits for filing claims will apply, however, so be absolutely certain that you file your claim within the time limits and in the manner specified in your contract. If the carrier is not resolving your claim satisfactorily, you will need to consult with an attorney to determine to what extent the carrier may be held liable. Because time limits also apply for filing suit, you should consult with an attorney well before your time limit expires.

Airline Liability Waivers

As with other common carriers, airline liability for lost or damaged baggage—we're calling it baggage here, instead of freight—is limited. The laws governing liability, however, will vary depending on whether the flight is domestic or international, so let's look at both scenarios.

8-16 LIABILITY ON DOMESTIC FLIGHTS

For domestic flights, airline liability for lost or damaged baggage is delineated by the federal common law. Under the common law, airlines may not *exempt* their liability for negligence; however, they may *limit* their liability for negligence. But if an airline limits its liability for negligence, it must conspicuously communicate that limitation to the shipper, and the shipper must have the opportunity to choose a higher level of liability coverage by paying a higher rate for shipping. Although airlines may limit their liability for negligence, they cannot limit their liability for gross or willful negligence or for intentional acts. In this sense, the law for airline baggage sounds a lot like the law for common carriers under the Carmack Amendment. In fact, airline liability jurisprudence is an interesting mixture of Carmack Amendment analogues and contracts common law.

Under federal common law, courts will consider three factors when determining the validity of airline liability limitations. First, the carrier must have given adequate notice of the liability limitation to the shipper. This factor is analogous to the requirement under the Carmack Amendment to obtain the shipper's consent. Second, the courts will consider the economic stature and commercial sophistication of the parties to the contract. Here, the courts are considering whether the contract containing the liability limitation is an adhesion contract; this is a departure from the jurisprudence for contracts subject to the Carmack Amendment. As we've seen, contracts that are mutually bargained for between parties that have equal bargaining power will generally be upheld. But courts are far less inclined to uphold unfair clauses—for example, exculpatory clauses—in contracts that are on preprinted forms written by the business, with terms that favor the business and that are offered to the consumer on a "take it or leave it" basis, with no equality of bargaining power. When the average consumer purchases flight tickets and checks a bicycle in as luggage, that consumer is being offered an adhesion contract containing an exculpatory clause, and the courts will not likely uphold the exculpatory clause. The third factor considered by the courts is whether "spot" insurance was available to the shipper. This factor is analogous to the requirement under the Carmack Amendment to give the shipper reasonable opportunity to choose between two or more levels of liability as reflected in shipping rates.

Putting questions of contract validity aside, let's take a look at how these airline liability limitations work.

AIRLINE LIABILITY LIMITATIONS

Typically, airlines will limit their liability to a default amount. As of 2007, airlines are liable for $2,800 per passenger for lost, damaged, or delayed luggage, unless the passenger has declared a total maximum value of about $4,000, even if the actual value of the luggage is more than $2,800. Regardless of the declared value, the passenger must exercise "reasonable effort" to minimize the amount of damage (similar to "reasonable person" standard that determines liability for negligence).

This means you have to pack your bike with the care that a "reasonable person" would use in packing it for transport. Airlines will typically release themselves from any liability for certain valuable or fragile items, including antiques and collector's items. However, airlines will accept liability for bicycles that are properly packed according to airline instructions—with a few qualifications. If you pack your bicycle in a hard-shell bicycle travel case, the airline will accept liability. But if you pack your bicycle in a cardboard bicycle box, following the airline's instructions, the airline will accept your bicycle, but it will not accept liability.

But what if your bike is an antique or collector's item—or even a unique or irreplaceable item, an heirloom, or an "item for sale"—and you pack it according to the airline's instructions? Will the airline be liable for loss or damage? The answer to that question seems unclear. On the one hand, as we've seen, airlines will typically release themselves from liability for loss or damage to antiques or collector's items. On the other hand, the airline does accept bicycles as baggage, it does accept liability if the bicycle is packed properly, and it does charge a higher rate for a declared value in excess of the default value. These factors indicate that the airline will be liable for loss or damage to the bicycle even if it is an antique or collector's bike. Complicating matters is the fact that the airline contract typically does not define what the airline means by "antique" or "collector's item." If a bike is packed according to airline instructions, and the declared value is within the airline's liability limits, can the airline nevertheless unilaterally declare your bike to be a "collector's item" or other item exempt from the airline's liability coverage? I would argue no, because the airline has accepted payment for carriage, and thus has accepted liability. But as I've said, the point is unclear, so if you want to play it safe, you might consider shipping your "collector's item" bike through a common carrier that will accept liability for it.

WHAT TO DO IF YOUR BIKE IS LOST OR DAMAGED

If the worst happens, and your bike is lost or damaged, you *must* observe the mandatory time limits for making a claim, or you won't be allowed to make your claim. These time limits will be found in your contract of carriage and may vary from airline to airline. As an example, let's look at the time limits contained in one contract. If your bike is lost or damaged, it says, you must make a preliminary notification to the airline within four hours after arrival of the flight. You must follow up on this preliminary notification with a written notice within twenty-one days after the arrival of the flight. The airline will then provide you with a claim form that you must return within forty-five days of the flight. Finally, any legal action—in other words, a lawsuit—must be filed within one year of the date of the airline's written denial of your claim.

Of course, these time limits may vary from airline to airline, so you must be familiar with your contract of carriage before you check your bike in for carriage. As always, if the airline won't resolve your claim to your satisfaction, consult with an attorney.

8-17 LIABILITY ON INTERNATIONAL FLIGHTS

For international flights, liability for loss or damage is covered by one of two international treaties, the Warsaw Convention or the Montreal Convention. The convention that applies to your baggage will depend on which treaty has been signed by the countries you are flying between. The Warsaw Convention is the older of the treaties and has been replaced by the Montreal Convention, which is really just an updated version of the Warsaw Convention. If you are flying between two parties to the Warsaw Convention, the Warsaw rules will still apply; if you are flying between two parties to the Montreal Convention, the Montreal rules will apply. But what if you are flying between a party to Montreal and a party to Warsaw? You're probably having a lot of fun—at least until you try to untangle the rules that apply to those flights.

Both conventions limit the liability of carriers; the maximum liability specified in each convention is in something called "Special Drawing Rights," or SDRs. There's no easy way to define what an SDR is; think of it as a kind of "paper gold" that countries use to balance trade surpluses and deficits. The SDR is a mix of several currencies, weighted by the relative importance of the currency in international trade. The mix is set by the International Monetary Fund (IMF) and is adjusted every five years. Currently, the currencies "in the mix" are the U.S. dollar, the euro, the Japanese yen, and the pound sterling. The value of one SDR fluctuates daily, based on the exchange rates of the currencies in "the mix," and can be found on the IMF website (http://www.imf.org/external/np/fin/data/rms_sdrv.aspx).

Under the rules of the Warsaw Convention, the liability of carriers is limited to 17 SDRs per kilogram, which, as I'm writing this, converts to $9.07 per pound of baggage. Imagine being told by the airline that just lost or damaged your 15-pound unobtanium-framed racing bike that they have generously decided to pay you the princely sum of $136. Are you ready to take them up on that offer?

There are only two ways around this liability limit:

1. The liability limit covers only negligence. This means that the carrier will be held liable—without limit—for gross negligence or intentional acts on the part of its employees, if they are acting within the scope of their employment.

2. If you make a "special declaration of interest in delivery at destination" and pay a "supplemental sum"—similar to the higher shipping rate for common carriers when you declare a value—the liability limit will be raised to your declared value.

If the airline can prove that your 45-pound rusting gas-pipe bike was not really worth the $11,000 you declared, it will not be liable for the declared value. And if the airline proves that the damage to your bike was the result of your own negligence—for example, if you packed it improperly—it may be partly or wholly exonerated of liability.

If you do have a liability claim against an airline, you must first heed the time limits, or you won't be allowed to make your claim. Under the Warsaw Convention, if you accept your damaged baggage without complaint, it will be prima facie evidence that the baggage was delivered to you in good condition. If you recall, this means that your acceptance of the baggage will be evidence that it was delivered in good condition unless you introduce contradictory evidence. Second, if your bike has been lost or damaged, you must notify the airline—in writing—within seven days from the date of receipt of your baggage, or you lose your right to file an action for liability. Finally, if you can't resolve the liability issues with the carrier, you must file suit within two years from the date of arrival at the destination, or you lose your right to damages.

Now let's look at the Montreal Convention, which is replacing the Warsaw Convention. Under the Montreal Convention, the liability of carriers for loss or damage to baggage is limited to 1,000 SDRs per passenger, which, as I'm writing this, converts to $1,492.14 per passenger. Compare this new liability limit with the liability limit of 17 SDRs per kilogram under the Warsaw Convention. It's obviously a much better liability limit, and it might actually cover many bikes, but it still won't pay for loss or damage to your unobtanium-framed racing bike.

So what can you do to get around this liability limit? Recall that under the Warsaw Convention, the liability limit covers negligence, but not gross negligence or intentional acts. Under the Montreal Convention, liability is not limited to negligence, so that liability limit applies regardless of how your bike was lost or damaged. This is a bizarre omission in the convention, to say the least, and it's unclear if courts would limit liability for grossly negligent or intentional acts merely because the convention fails to exclude them from the liability limits.

Nevertheless, under the Montreal Convention there's only one obvious way around the liability limit: You must make a "special declaration of interest in delivery at destination" and pay a "supplementary sum" in order to have the liability limit raised to your declared value. Once again, however, if the airline can prove that your toy bicycle was not really worth the $11,000 you declared, it will not be liable for the declared value. Finally, as under the Warsaw Convention, if the airline proves that the damage to your bike was the result of your own negligence (for example, you packed it improperly), the airline may be partly or wholly exonerated of liability.

As with the Warsaw Convention, time limits apply under the Montreal Convention. First, if you accept your damaged baggage without complaint, it will be prima facie evidence that the baggage was delivered to you in good condition. Second, if your bike has been lost or damaged, you must notify the airline—again, in writing—within seven days from the date of receipt of your baggage, or you lose your right to file an action for liability. Finally, if you can't resolve the liability issues with the carrier, you must file suit within two years from the date of arrival at the destination, or you lose your right to damages.

So how do you know which rules apply? Most likely, you'll be flying under Montreal Convention rules. Most European nations are signatories to the Montreal protocol, as are the United States and Canada. Mexico is not a signatory, however. About half of the Central American nations are signatories, as are about half of the South American nations and several Caribbean nations. A handful of Asian nations, including China and Japan, are signatories, as are two-thirds of the nations in the Mideast and half of the African nations. Tonga is the only signatory Pacific nation; New Zealand is a signatory, but Australia is not. For a complete list of the parties to the protocol, you can view the Montreal Convention at http://www.jus.uio.no/lm/air.carriage.unification.convention.montreal.1999/doc.

8-18 PROTECTING YOUR RIGHTS WHEN FLYING WITH YOUR BIKE

1. *Read your contract of carriage.* This document will specify the airline's conditions for carriage of your bike and for making a claim if your bike is lost or damaged. You must follow these conditions for packing your bike, declaring its value, and filing claims.

2. *Pack your bike properly per airline instructions.* Furthermore, even if the airline will allow you to pack your bike in a cardboard box, don't do it. Use a hard-shell bicycle travel case. This is the only means you

have of ensuring that the airline bears full liability for damage to your bike.

3. *Make sure that the liability limits provide adequate coverage for your bike.* If they don't provide adequate coverage, you *must* declare your bike's value and pay an extra fee in order to raise the liability limit. An alternate approach would be to ship your bike separately, through a common carrier, but again, you *must* declare the value of your bike and pay an extra fee in order to raise the liability coverage. Generally, the airline liability limits will be higher and the fees less costly than for a common carrier, so checking your bike in as baggage may be the most cost-effective means of shipping your bike when you're flying.

4. *If your bike is damaged, preserve your evidence.* Although you are your own witness, it will only help your case if you have witnesses who can testify as to what they saw. It's best to have a witness with you, both when you accept your bike from baggage claim and when you inspect your bike. Remember, you packed your bike in a hard-shell travel case, so if you can inspect your bike at baggage claim with a witness present, do it. If your bike is damaged, you *must* retain all damaged property, including the travel case, until it can be inspected by an airline representative. After your evidence has been inspected by the airline, you *must* preserve it for later use as evidence, in case of a lawsuit for damages. Do *not* tamper with your evidence; preserve it *exactly* as you found it.

5. *If something does happen to your bike, you must observe the required time limits.* If your bike has obviously been damaged while in the care of the airline, report it to the airline *immediately*. If you don't, your failure to report it will allow the airline to introduce that failure as prima facie evidence that your bike arrived in good condition. If the damage is concealed, report it to the airline *immediately, in writing,* as soon as you discover it, but *no later* than the time allowed by the airline. For domestic flights, this time limit will be specified in your contract but will usually be within hours of discovering your loss; for international flights, you must report the damage within seven days after taking possession of your bike. And finally, if you can't resolve your claims with the airline, you *must* file an action within the time limitations—within two years of the date of arrival for international flights, or as specified by the jurisdiction for domestic flights—or you lose your rights to damages.

Now let's assume that you've done everything possible to protect yourself, and your bike is lost or damaged. Let's further assume that the airline isn't resolving your claim satisfactorily. For domestic flights, if the liability limitations are contained in an adhesion contract, you should consult with an attorney. You should also consult with an attorney, for both domestic and international flights, if

- the airline has not conspicuously communicated its liability limitation to you; or

- the airline has not offered you the opportunity to choose a higher level of liability coverage by paying a higher rate for shipping; or

- the airline has lost or damaged your bike through a grossly negligent or intentional act; or

- the airline is disputing its liability after you've paid for a higher liability limit.

Bailment Liability Waivers

Suppose you park your bike in a parking garage, and it's stolen or damaged. When you question the garage about it, you're shown a big sign saying "Not responsible for loss or damage." Can they do that? Are you really out your bike? Suppose instead your bike is stolen or damaged while in a building's parking facility. Or you leave it with a bike mechanic, and it's stolen or damaged while in his or her shop. Can the shop escape liability with an exculpatory clause in the repair contract? Let's look at the law of bailments for an answer.

8-19 Bailments

A *bailment* is a type of contract in which you leave your property in the care of another person.[29] When a bailment is created, you—the *bailor*—are the owner of the property, and the *bailee*—the person you leave your property with—is your agent. Common situations involving bailments include leaving your watch for repair at a jeweler's shop, leaving your clothes to be cleaned at a dry cleaners, and leaving your car at a parking lot that charges a fee for parking. When you take your bike to a bike shop to get it fixed, the shop owner is a bailee, and while he or she has it, your bike is a bailment.[30] The bike shop does not own the bike, but the law

---

29 The contract does not need to be an express contract—for example, stating "This is a contract to . . ." The courts have also found "implied contracts" where no express contract existed and one party would be unjustly enriched at the expense of another absent an "implied contract."

30 California and some other states refer to the bike shop as a *depository*, the person leaving off the bike as the *depositor*, and the bike as a *deposit*.

gives it enough ownership power to protect it, carry out the repairs, and return it. These types of bailments are called "voluntary bailments," as distinguished from "involuntary bailments," which include such things as accidentally leaving your keys on the counter at the dry cleaners.

The bailee has two duties. The first of these is the duty of care. The traditional rule under the law is that the bailee has a duty to exercise care for your property while it is in his or her possession; the level of care that must be exercised depends upon who benefits from the bailment. If the bailment is for the sole benefit of the bailee, the bailee must exercise extraordinary care; at the other extreme, if the bailment is for the sole benefit of the bailor, the bailee must exercise at least slight care and can be held liable only for gross negligence. If, however, the bailment benefits both the bailor and the bailee, as is usually the case, the bailee must exercise ordinary care and may be held liable for ordinary negligence. The modern trend recognizes that under almost all circumstances, both parties benefit; thus, the trend has been that the duty of care is the standard of ordinary care under the circumstances. The duty of the bailee is to return the property to you as agreed.

Despite the general rule on the duty of care, bailees may attempt to limit their liability by including a liability waiver in the contract. Most states allow these contractual liability waivers as long as the waiver does not purport to relieve the bailee of gross or willful negligence. So does this mean that you are simply out of luck if your bicycle is stolen from a parking garage that has a sign clearly stating, "Customers park at their own risk"? Or if it's stolen from a repair shop that has included a liability waiver in the repair agreement? Generally no, but as with all liability waivers, it all depends on the circumstances.

8-20 EXCULPATORY CLAUSES AND BLANKET WAIVERS

As noted above, most courts will allow a contractual waiver of liability—what the law calls an "exculpatory clause"—as long as that waiver does not purport to relieve the bailee of gross or willful negligence. I mentioned the judicial limitation on waivers above, and I'm repeating it here, because it's important. If you have a bailment agreement that purports to relieve the bailee of all negligence—even gross or willful negligence—and your bike is stolen or damaged, no court will uphold the liability waiver for gross negligence, and many courts will void the entire liability waiver, even though they would have reluctantly upheld a narrower liability waiver that waived liability only for ordinary negligence. Thus, depending on the state, bailees overreach at their own peril.

8-21 ADHESION CONTRACTS

Now what if the bailment contract waives liability only for ordinary neg-ligence? Will it be upheld? Possibly, although courts will uphold them only under certain conditions. Generally, contracts that are mutually bargained for between parties with equal bargaining power—what the law calls parties who are at "arm's length"—will be upheld. Most con-tracts the average consumer enters into, however, are on preprinted forms written by the business, with terms that favor the business, and are offered on a "take it or leave it" basis, with no equality of bargaining power. As we've seen, these types of contracts are called "adhesion con-tracts," and the courts are far less inclined to uphold unfair clauses in adhesion contracts.

So you're handed a parking receipt that says, "Not responsible for loss or damage." Maybe the bailee even has a prominent sign stating those terms. Or maybe the terms are contained in a repair agreement. Your choice is to accept the terms or not to park your bike. So if you accept the terms, and your bike is stolen or damaged, are you bound by those terms? Probably not. In *Miller's Mutual Fire Insurance Association of Alton, Illi-nois v. Parker* (1951), the Supreme Court of North Carolina held:

> The complexity of today's commercial relations and the constantly increasing number of automobiles render the question of park-ing a matter of public concern which is taxing the ingenuity of our municipal officials. People who work in the business sections of our cities and towns and who rely on automobiles for transporta-tion find it difficult–sometimes impossible–to locate a place on the public streets where daily parking is permitted. They are driven to seek accommodation in some parking lot maintained for the ser-vice of the public. There they are met by predetermined conditions which create a marked disparity of bargaining power and place them in the position where they must either accede to the condi-tions or forego the desired service.
>
> Such was the case here. The defendant was engaged in the busi-ness of accepting automobiles for parking for hire, both on a daily and a monthly basis. He required the owner-bailor to surrender the keys to his automobile so that he or his employee could park it at any place of his choosing and move it from time to time during the day as occasion might require. He had a "pretty good-sized sign," "very prominently displayed" saying "Not responsible for loss by fire or theft." He told Mrs. Jenkins "we would not be responsible

for loss by fire or theft." "I told her if there was any loss from fire or theft, it would be her responsibility. She left the car. She did not make any statement." This same provision was printed on the identification tokens furnished those who parked by the day only. Under these circumstances it is against the public interest to give force and effect to the exculpatory agreement which would relieve defendant from all liability for his own negligence.[31]

Of course, the law may vary by state, but generally, courts take a dim view of exculpatory clauses in adhesion contracts. So why are these exculpatory clauses included if courts are reluctant to enforce them? Simple: If your bike is stolen or damaged, the bailee is hoping that you'll just give up and shut up.

8-22 STATUTORY EXCEPTIONS FOR EXCULPATORY CLAUSES

The courts have tended to say that you can't be bound by exculpatory clauses in an adhesion contract, but what have the legislatures said? Section 1630 of the California Civil Code says that a parking-garage operator cannot waive its liability for loss or damage unless the customer is given a written contract with notice of the waiver in capital letters of 10-point type printed at the top, and with all of the provisions of the contract printed legibly in 8-point or larger type. Additionally, a copy of the contract, printed in large type, in an area at least 17 by 22 inches, must be posted. This statutory language clearly upholds the exculpatory clause in the parking garage's adhesion contract, in effect eviscerating judicial decisions protecting consumers from these types of contracts; several other states have enacted similar legislation. However—and this is the kicker—the statutory language addresses "a printed contract of bailment providing for the parking or storage of a motor vehicle." Did you see that? The motor vehicle language? It means the statute doesn't apply to your bike—at least in California. Again, the situation in your state may be different.

8-23 IS IT A BAILMENT, AND ARE THEY LIABLE?

Now suppose that you park your bicycle in a building's parking facility—maybe it's a building where you work, maybe it's a building where you have business—and your bicycle is stolen or damaged. The building management claims that they're not liable for your loss. Are they right?

---

31 Miller's *Mutual Fire Ins. Assoc. of Alton, Ill. v. Parker*, 65 S.E.2d 341 (N.C. 1951).

As in all legal questions, it all depends on the circumstances. If you've merely left your bike in a parking area, haven't paid a parking fee, and haven't placed your bike in the care of an employee of the building, you haven't created a bailment. Instead, your situation is more analogous to locking up to a bike rack on the sidewalk. But suppose instead that you park your bike in a designated parking area that is controlled by an employee of the building—for example, a security guard or parking attendant. Now you've placed your bike in the care of an employee of the building, and it's starting to look like a bailment. But what if the parking facility is free? Remember, if the bailment is for your sole benefit, the bailee is required only to exercise slight care and can be held liable only for gross negligence. If you haven't paid for parking, wouldn't that mean that even if there is a bailment, it's for your sole benefit, and thus the building can be held liable only for gross negligence?

Well, maybe, maybe not. Remember, in all legal questions, it always depends on the circumstances. In this situation, we can't just assume that consideration is money; consideration could be something else—for example, the benefit the business in the building receives from keeping the area around the building free of bicycles, or the benefit it receives from attracting cyclists to the building. The bottom line is, if you've left your bike in the care of another person, and your bike is stolen, you may have created a bailment even if money wasn't paid for the bailment; under these situations, a bailee can't escape liability by simply denying that it has any liability.

If your bike has been stolen or damaged while it was in the care of a bailee, and you're being told that the bailee has no liability, you don't have to take their word for it. Depending on your state, the common law may not uphold the liability waiver; even in those states that have statutorily validated these waivers, the waivers may be applicable only against motor vehicles. If you haven't paid for parking, and the bailee is arguing that no liability exists, there may still be liability. If your bike has been stolen or damaged, and the bailee refuses to "make you whole"—legalese for putting you back in the same position you were in before your bike was damaged or stolen—consult with an attorney about your rights under the law.

Conclusion

When Evylyn Thomas set out on her Columbia bicycle on the morning of May 30, 1896, the automobile—all of eleven years old, having been invented by Karl Benz in 1885—was just taking its tottering first steps on the roads of America. It had made its debut on American roads a mere six months earlier, in the fall of 1895, but it wouldn't really begin to appear on American roads in any appreciable numbers until after 1908, when Henry Ford cut his production costs—and therefore the price of his Model T—by building on and significantly developing the assembly-line concept pioneered by Ransom Olds.

But on that fateful spring morning in 1896, as Henry Wells's automobile careened toward Evylyn Thomas, and years before the automobile became a common sight on the roads, the right of cyclists to the road was already a well-settled question, having been firmly established nine years before.

That right to the road was no accident.

It was the result of a deliberate campaign to gain legal rights for cyclists—a campaign that was financed by Albert Pope of Columbia Bicycles. Pope had been manufacturing bicycles since 1878;[1] within ten years, the rights of cyclists had been established in the legislature and in the courts. The campaign to gain the legal right to the road was the first civil rights movement for cyclists, and the first statutes and seminal cases were the cyclist's Magna Carta, in which bicycles were declared vehicles and cyclists were recognized to have an equality with the driver of any other vehicle.

---

1 The bicycle as we know it–a two-wheeled human-powered vehicle driven by a crank–had been invented by a Frenchman in 1863, twenty-two years before Karl Benz invented the automobile. This much we know. Exactly which Frenchman invented the bicycle–or as they called it then, the velocipede–is the subject of some dispute; both Pierre Michaux and his employee Pierre Lallement claimed to have been the inventor. Disgruntled with Michaux, Lallement emigrated to America, where he obtained a patent on the bicycle. By 1868, Lallement had returned to Paris, disappointed by his failure to sell his velocipede in America. Albert Pope had first become interested in the bicycle in 1876, and by 1879 he had bought out the Lallement patents.

From that time forward, cyclists have retained their hard-won rights. But they've also been pushed to the margins of the road, and often, to the margins of society. From its first faltering steps a little over a century ago, the automobile has become the dominant vehicle on the roads of America, and motorists have asserted a superior right to the road, both in the design of transportation infrastructure and in their day-to-day mistreatment of cyclists on the road.

The time has come for a second civil rights movement for cyclists.

It's time to build on the work of Albert Pope and the 1880s generation of cyclists. It's time to press for a Cyclists' Bill of Rights. And like the first civil rights movement for cyclists, the second civil rights movement for cyclists must be the result of a deliberate campaign.

But if cyclists already have their Magna Carta—the right to the road—why would they need a Cyclists' Bill of Rights? Simply because the rights of cyclists are not only disregarded but, as we've seen, abused every single day. Can cyclists truly have an equal right to the road when the road itself discriminates against cyclists? Can cyclists truly have an equal right to the road when they don't receive equal treatment under the law? Can cyclists truly have an equal right to the road when motorists freely take it upon themselves to remove them from the road?

I argue they cannot—and that a Cyclists' Bill of Rights is needed to level the playing field. But of course, this raises the question: What would a Cyclists' Bill of Rights look like? Based on the issues facing cyclists today, I believe it should look something like this:

1. *Cyclists have the right to equality of infrastructure.* This means that cyclists must be accorded equal consideration in the design and execution of transportation infrastructure. "Equal consideration" means that cyclists are not treated as an afterthought by transportation planners, but accorded consideration equal to the consideration transportation planners accord to motorists. Their needs must be taken into account. This does not mean that cyclists must be treated exactly as motor vehicles are treated. In some instances—for example, at intersections—cyclists must receive more consideration in the design and execution of infrastructure, because they are especially vulnerable to collisions with automobiles at intersections. It does mean that in some circumstances, where road conditions are suitable, cyclists and motor vehicles will share the road, and in other situations, where sharing the road puts cyclists at a disadvantage, the infrastructure will provide cycling facilities that mitigate that disadvantage.

2. *Cyclists have the right to equal treatment under the law.* This means that cyclists must not receive less consideration than motorists re-

ceive. The criminal justice system must accord cyclists the same consideration that motorists expect and receive. This means that when a cyclist is injured in a collision, for example, the cyclist must not be assumed to be at fault; when a bicycle is stolen, the police should not give that theft less consideration than they give to an equivalent automobile theft or an equivalent bank robbery; when a cyclist is assaulted, the criminal justice system must recognize that the cyclist is the victim of a violent physical attack intended to dissuade the cyclist from exercising and enjoying fundamental rights, and respond accordingly. In addition, legislatures must recognize cyclists as vulnerable users of the road and establish prohibitions against assaulting cyclists that reflect the seriousness of the crime.

3. *Cyclists have the right to equal access to insurance protection.* Automobile ownership must not be a prerequisite for access to insurance protection. Cyclists must have equal access to affordable medical coverage, underinsured motorist and uninsured motorist coverage, and liability protection.

The cyclists of the 1880s were both determined to be accorded equal rights to the road and tenacious in their pursuit of that right. During the 1890s—the Golden Age of Bicycles—there were 1 million cyclists on American roads, and American cyclists represented 1.6 percent of the total U.S. population. By 1897, the bottom dropped out of the bicycle market and the Golden Age of Bicycles was nearly over. The age of the automobile was yet to come.

Today, as global oil supplies decline and global temperatures rise, we may be witnessing the end of the Golden Age of Automobiles. And yet today, at the peak of the automobile's Golden Age, American cyclists represent 19 percent of the total U.S. population. The cyclists of the late nineteenth century, though small in number, won the right to the road through their sheer determination. Over a century later, that right is violated with impunity at every turn. It is up to the cyclists of the early twenty-first century—more numerous and no less determined than our cycling forebears—to take up the torch of liberty and secure that hard-won right.

Glossary

action in replevin *see* replevin.

adhesion contract preprinted, "take-it-or-leave-it" type of contract between consumer and seller, in which the parties have unequal bargaining power and the consumer is given no realistic chance to bargain about the terms.

aiding and abetting helping in or somehow facilitating the commission of a crime.

ambiguity uncertainty of meaning; when two or more meanings are reasonably possible.

annotations explanatory comments on or interpretations of the text of a statute or case.

assault the intentional infliction of an apprehension of harmful or offensive physical contact; threatening to cause harm. An intentional tort.

assumption of risk legally presumed acceptance of the risk of injury or harm inherent in a sport or activity; participation acts as an agreement to release others involved in the event from their duty of care. May be express or implied.

bailee person to whom an owner entrusts property.

bailment a type of contract in which the owner of property delivers that property to or leaves it in the care of another person.

bailor the owner of property who entrusts that property to another.

battery the intentional infliction of harmful or offensive physical contact; an intentional tort.

binding precedent a law or earlier decision that *must* be followed by a court.

***bona fide* purchaser** an unsuspecting, innocent person who buys a stolen item, in good faith and without knowledge of the preceding crime.

breach of duty any violation or omission of a duty; in relation to duty of care, occurs when a person acts or fails to act as a reasonable person would, exposing others to unreasonable risk of harm.

burden of proof standard of evidence and persuasion required to win a dispute; varies between civil suits ("preponderance of the evidence" standard) and criminal cases ("beyond a reasonable doubt" standard).

capacity legal qualification; competency; in particular, the legal and mental ability of a person to enter into a contract.

Carmack Act federal statute that limits the liability of interstate carriers for loss of or damage to goods.

carrier a person or entity that transports goods for a fee.

case law the body of all prior judicial decisions; *see* common law.

caveat emptor "let the buyer beware"; doctrine of purchaser responsibility to inspect for product defects.

certification (to state court) referral of a case from a federal court to a state supreme court, usually for interpretation of a state law.

citation a noncustodial arrest; official document charging commission of an offense and commanding the person cited to appear in court on the day named.

civil rights personal, natural rights guaranteed by the federal Constitution.

civil rights claim lawsuit alleging that two or more persons conspired to deprive, "either directly or indirectly, any person or class of persons of the equal protection of the laws, or of equal privileges and immunities under the laws."

civil rights statutes Sections 1983 and 1985 of the Civil Rights Act of 1871 (42 U.S.C. Sections 1983 and 1985), enacted to implement and enforce constitutional rights. A state may have analogous laws.

code a collection of all the statutes of a state or the federal government; may be published officially or unofficially.

code book a book of related statutes; may be arranged by topic or code section number.

common law body of law created by prior judicial decisions that cumulatively provide precedential direction for courts (both trial and appellate); previous decisions and interpretations of the law in previous cases that act as precedent and guidance in future cases.

comparative negligence damage recovery system in which negligence is allotted by percentages; any damages for the plaintiff are awarded in proportion to the percentage attributable to him or her.

conspiracy concerted action or collaboration of two or more persons for the purpose of committing some (usually unlawful) act.

constitution the fundamental law of a country; "a charter of government deriving its whole authority from the governed."

constitutional law law that establishes governments and defines their rights and organization.

constitutional rights rights guaranteed to the people by a constitution; inviolable by legislative or governmental action.

Consumer Products Safety Commission (CPSC) a federal agency charged with "protecting the public from unreasonable risks of serious injury or death" from a wide range of products.

contract an agreement between two or more persons that creates legal obligations; a "promise or set of promises for breach of which the law gives a remedy, or the performance of which the law in some way recognizes as a duty"; to constitute a contract, an agreement must include the elements of offer, acceptance, and consideration.

contract law law governing private agreements; *see also* Uniform Commercial Code.

contributory negligence affirmative defense and damage recovery system in which an injured person cannot recover if his or her own negligence contributed to the injury in any way.

conversion tort of intentional, unlawful interference with the possession or ownership of a person's property.

crime violation of a penal statute or regulation.

criminal negligence gross negligence that is an element of a crime (punishable as a crime), or so wanton and reckless as to create criminal liability.

custodial arrest arrest in which the arrestee is taken into official confinement or detention.

damages monetary compensation for the injury and/or losses caused by a tort or crime. May be compensatory or punitive (*see* punitive damages); general, special, economic (incidental, consequential), or noneconomic.

defective product product that is in a condition unreasonably dangerous to the user or consumer; the condition may be a manufacturing defect, a design defect, or an information (labeling, warning, or instructional) defect.

disclaimer *see* liability release.

disorderly conduct an act that creates a substantial risk of public inconvenience, annoyance, offense, or alarm that was done for no legitimate purpose.

due process refers to fairness in legal procedures and protection of property from unfair government action.

duties legal, contractual, or moral obligations; *see* duty of (due) care.

duty of (due) care "obligation to conform to legal standard of reasonable conduct in light of apparent risk"; duty not to impose an unreasonable risk of harm upon another person.

equal protection constitutional right to equal and impartial application of the law for similarly situated persons.

evidence proof or probative material.

exculpatory clause contract clause in which one party releases the other party from liability; relinquishment of a legal right to sue.

federalism principle of government under which those powers that are not specifically delegated by the U.S. Constitution to the federal government are reserved either to the states or to the people.

freedom of speech First Amendment constitutional right to express oneself, verbally or by publication, without government restriction; limited by some statutes containing time, place, and manner restrictions and dealing with certain categories of "speech."

freedom of the press First Amendment constitutional right guaranteeing media that their methods and choices in reporting will not be abridged by the government; also, to publish and distribute one's views without government interference or restriction. *See also* freedom of speech.

freight forwarder a business person or entity that brokers shipments but does not carry goods itself.

fresh pursuit common law right to use reasonable force to retake one's own property if the retaking is done immediately after the theft.

gross negligence an act that was so careless or in such reckless disregard for the rights or safety of others that the tortfeasor knew or should have known that injury was a likely consequence, but nevertheless acted in disregard of (with conscious indifference to) that likely consequence, even though the injury was unintended.

harassment action(s) taken with the intent to intimidate, frighten, or harm, that have no legitimate purpose.

hate crime crime committed against one or more persons who are members of a "suspect class"; hate-crime legislation usually requires an intent to intimidate, terrorize, or harm a member of the suspect class and may require proof that the act was done because of the victim's membership (or perceived membership) in the suspect class.

highway the "entire width between the boundary lines of every way publicly maintained when any part thereof is open to the use of the public for purposes of vehicular travel."

implied warranty automatic, unstated guarantee that a product manufactured for sale is merchantable and fit for its intended purpose.

incitement Arousing, provoking, instigating, and/or encouraging another person to commit a crime.

indecent exposure crime of revealing the private parts of the body in a lewd or indecent manner in a public place.

injury any harm, wrong, or damage; not necessarily physical.

intentional tort civil wrong in which an injury was the intended consequence of the act.

jury instructions court-given directions to a jury as to what law to consider when the jury decides, based on the facts and evidence presented at trial, whether the defendant violated his or her legal duties to the plaintiff.

laned roadway a roadway that is divided into at least two clearly marked lanes for vehicular travel.

larceny the unlawful taking of property of another with intent to convert (steal) it.

legal justification defense based on some fact or circumstance that makes an otherwise unlawful act lawful.

"lemon" laws statutes designed to protect consumer-purchasers who buy products (specifically motor vehicles) with persistent but initially nonobvious defects.

liability broad legal term for the condition of being responsible, bound, or obliged.

liability release a waiver of liability for negligent acts by a person (such as an event sponsor or team).

libel intentional or negligent publication of a falsehood (defamation) about a person that injures that person's reputation.

licensing issuance by an administrative agency or other governmental body of a permit for certain ownership or acts.

Magnuson-Moss Warranty Act federal statute regulating warranties; 15 U.S.C. Section 2301 *et seq.*

merchantable of average, acceptable quality in the trade and fit for the ordinary purposes for which the product is used.

misdemeanor non-felony crime; generally punishable by fine, penalty, forfeiture, or jail (rather than prison) time.

mistake of fact defense based on physical circumstances or incorrect belief beyond one's control that led to a violation of a legal duty.

modified comparative negligence damage recovery system in which an injured person cannot recover if his or her negligence (liability) is 50 percent or more.

motor vehicle mechanically powered device for transporting persons and/or goods; exact definition varies according to state law. *See also* vehicle.

necessity defense based on existence of an emergency that made breaking the law necessary to avoid harm to oneself or another person.

negligence an act or failure to act by a person who has a duty of due care and breaches that duty.

negligence *per se* negligence based on proof that a statute was violated.

no-fault insurance system in which an injured person is compensated under his or her own insurance policy, up to certain limits; usually restricted to economic damages.

noneconomic damages compensation for nonmonetary losses and injuries, such as pain and suffering,

normal flow of traffic the mainstream flow of traffic on a roadway.

ordinances laws or rules enacted by a municipality; applicable only locally.

penumbra of rights fundamental liberties and rights implied by the Bill of Rights to the federal Constitution.

person a legal entity; includes human beings and many types of business, corporate, and government groups.

persuasive precedent an earlier decision that is regarded as influential by but is not binding upon the present court.

plea bargain an agreement between an accused and a district attorney in which the defendant agrees to plead guilty to a lesser charge and the D.A. agrees to drop more serious charges.

precedent a decision of a court that acts as an example or authority for other similar cases; principles of law established in prior court cases.

prima facie **evidence** proof that is presumed to be sufficient and conclusive, unless contradictory evidence is available and introduced to rebut the presumption.

privity a direct, mutual relationship; formerly required in some tort actions and in contract law for breach-of-contract suits.

product liability area of law dealing with the legal liability of manufacturers and sellers for injury (personal injury, property loss, or economic damage) caused by defective products.

prosecutorial discretion the ability of a district attorney or other public prosecutor to choose which cases to bring and what charges to file.

public indecency *see* indecent exposure.

punitive damages damages awarded to penalize the person who committed a negligent act and to deter others from acting in a similar manner; usually awarded when the negligent conduct is particularly outrageous.

pure comparative negligence damage recovery system in which each person pays according to his or her percentage of liability.

"rational basis" standard of review standard stating that a court determines whether the government has a constitutionally permissible interest in the activity being regulated and whether the statute at issue is rationally related to that governmental interest.

reasonable care the degree of care that is prudent in a particular set of factual circumstances.

"reasonable person" standard standard of behavior for determining negligence; relies on what a person of ordinary prudence would do (or not do) in a particular set of factual circumstances.

regulations rules made by government agencies (federal or state) rather than a legislative body.

release *see* liability release.

replevin an action or suit for the return of personal property wrongfully taken or detained.

replevin order a court order for return of property to its rightful owner.

respondeat superior doctrine that holds employers liable for the negligence (or other tortious conduct) of employees who are acting within the scope of their employment.

right to travel basic constitutional liberty to move from place to place.

rights power, privileges, or immunities guaranteed under a constitution, statutes, or the common law.

risk hazard; the possibility or danger of a loss or injury.

robbery stealing of property that is in the owner's physical possession (the owner must be present at the time of the taking).

rules of interpretation guidelines and standards used by courts for deciding the meaning of a law.

self-defense right to defend oneself with a force that is proportionate to the threat and that is necessary to end the threatened, imminent, or actual attack.

settlement resolution by the parties of a dispute, lawsuit, or legal claim, without a trial.

shipper the owner of goods being transported ("shipped").

specific performance order a court order requiring a party to perform his or her part of a contract as previously agreed.

standing having sufficient legal interest in a dispute to obtain legal resolution of the controversy.

statute law enacted by a legislature (state or federal); state statutory law is usually applicable statewide.

statute of limitations time limit for filing a lawsuit.

statutory law law made by a legislature (state or federal).

strict liability liability without fault or intent. In products liability law, assignment of responsibility without proof of negligence or wrongdoing; in reference to pet owners, the lack of a requirement that an owner have prior notice of the pet's vicious nature in order to be held liable for its actions.

"strict scrutiny" standard of review standard of judicial review under which the government must have a compelling interest in the issue being regulated, the statute at issue must be narrowly tailored to address the government's interest, and the statute must be the least restrictive means for achieving that governmental interest.

subrogation right of an insurance company to "stand in the shoes" of its insured once it pays money to the insured.

theft stealing of property; larceny.

tort any civil wrong, except breach of contract, for which the law provides a remedy (as opposed to a criminal act).

tort liability system (of insurance) damage recovery system that assigns liability for damages to the negligent tortfeasor.

tortfeasor person that commits a tort.

traffic the subjects of transportation; "pedestrians, ridden or herded animals, vehicles, street cars, and other conveyances" on a highway or other public route.

Uniform Commercial Code a set of model statutes, drafted by the National Conference of Commissioners on Uniform State Laws, covering commercial transactions; has been adopted in whole or part by all 50 states.

Uniform Traffic Laws a set of model statutes governing the movement of vehicles on public roadways.

Uniform Vehicle Code a set of model statutes defining the term *vehicle* and setting forth requirements and prohibitions for the use and movement of vehicles.

vehicle a means of conveyance, transportation, or carriage of persons, goods, or both; depending on state law, may or may not include a human-powered bicycle.

vehicle code set of statutes governing the use, ownership, and movement of vehicles.

victim's rights legislation statutes that permit involvement of victims and afford victims some (limited) rights in disposition of criminal cases.

waiver of liability *see* exculpatory clause.

warranty law statutes and regulations governing assurances and guarantees in commercial transactions.

warranty of merchantability (fitness) basic guarantee of product quality; requires that goods must be of average, acceptable quality in the trade and must be fit for their ordinary purposes.

writ of replevin a court order authorizing the owner's retaking of personal property wrongfully taken or detained.

Index

About the Author

Bob Mionske has loved cycling and bicycle racing since the age of six, when he taught his grandmother to ride a bike. A two-time Olympian, he made the winning break in the 1988 Olympic road race and finished mere inches out of the bronze medal. In 1992, Bob was again selected for the U.S. Olympic road team, this time assisting teammate Lance Armstrong to a fourteenth-place finish.

Following the 1992 Olympics, Bob raced as a pro with the Saturn professional cycling team for one season and then retired to become director of the team before heading off to law school.

After passing the bar exam, Bob set up a cycling-only law practice representing top riders David Zabriskie, Michael Barry, Tom Danielson, and Kevin Livingston, while also defending the legal rights of weekend warriors, commuters, and bicycle messengers. Bob also began offering legal advice to cyclists in *Legally Speaking*, a national column featured on velonews.com. In 2001, Bob authored the legal analysis section in *Bicycle Accident Reconstruction for the Forensic Engineer*. Most recently, Bob has sharpened his focus on protecting the civil rights of all cyclists by establishing the Constitutional Rights for Cyclists Center (CRCC).

Today Bob divides his riding time between his racing bike and his cruiser in Portland, Oregon, where he lives with his daughter, Pepper. He can be reached through his website, www.bicyclelaw.com.

Steven M. Magas is an avid cyclist and Ohio trial attorney who has written articles on legal topics of interest to cyclists for more than 15 years. In his practice, he has handled cases ranging from $50 traffic tickets to multi-million-dollar settlements. Steve sits on the board of the Ohio Bike Federation and regularly travels to Washington D.C. for the National Bike Summit to lobby for a bike-friendly national transportation policy. He can be reached at BikeLawyer@aol.com.